H0792

FIRING ON ALL CYLINDERS

The Service/Quality System for High-Powered Corporate Performance

FIRING ON ALL CYLINDERS

The Service/Quality System for High-Powered Corporate Performance

Jim Clemmer
with Barry Sheehy
and Achieve International/Zenger-Miller Associates

IRWIN
Professional Publishing
Burr Ridge, Illinois
New York, New York

This publication is designed to provide accurate and authoritative information in regard to the subject matter covered. It is sold with the understanding that neither the author nor the publisher is engaged in rendering legal, accounting, or other professional service. If legal advice or other expert assistance is required, the services of a competent professional person should be sought.

From a Declaration of Principles jointly adopted by a Committee of the American Bar Association and a Committee of Publishers.

Sponsoring editor: Jeffrey A. Krames
Project editor: Jean Lou Hess
Production manager: Diane Palmer
Designer: Larry J. Cope
Jacket designer: Image House, Inc.
Art coordinator: Mark Malloy
Compositor: Precision Typographers
Typeface: 10.5/12 Palatino
Printer: R. R. Donnelly & Sons

Library of Congress Cataloging-in-Publication Data

Clemmer, Jim
   Firing on all cylinders : the service/quality system for high-powered corporate performance / Jim Clemmer with Barry Sheehy and Achieve International/Zenger-Miller Associates.
      p.   cm.
   ISBN 1-55623-704-9
   1. Total quality management. 2. Customer service. 3. Executive ability. I. Sheehy, Barry. II. Title.
HD62.15C54 1992
658—dc20   91-44281

Printed in the United States of America
   2 3 4 5 6 7 8 9 0 DOC 9 8 7 6 5 4 3

To Heather, Christopher, Jennifer, and Vanessa
who are teaching me to love, laugh, and live.

Foreword

Many readers of this book, if under the age of 40, will not catch the full message of the metaphor "firing on all cylinders." Unless you have driven a car that barely started and, after starting, vibrated, coughed, and poured out smoke, the emotional message of this book may be lost to you.

Unfortunately, the metaphor is apt: Not many of our cherished institutions are firing on all cylinders. North American businesses face fierce competition from abroad and continue to lose market share. Their productivity is not increasing as rapidly as that of many other nations. Our school systems don't produce graduates with the skills needed to succeed in today's world. Universities face declining enrollments, fail to use modern learning technology, and are beset with severe budget deficits. Governments at the city, county, state, and federal level seem unable to address the pressing problems of crime, homelessness, drugs, and the economy. There is surely a need to learn how to help organizations fire on all their cylinders.

You needn't be a trained mechanic to know when an engine is running on all cylinders. But when it isn't, the diagnostic process is challenging.

Clemmer's book provides that diagnostic process to figure out what's wrong. It is a practical manual on how to get your organization running smoothly. It blends the overarching strategy issues with proven tactics to make them work. It presents a comprehensive, clearly organized strategy for implementing a quality improvement process—by far the best technology available to tune up the organizational engine.

Thought-provoking questions are posed throughout to get readers to analyze what's misfiring in their organizations. Compelling data are presented to help readers understand the importance of these issues. Up-to-the-minute sources are cited, providing the reader with an excellent summary of the latest thinking from some of the best minds addressing these issues.

Firing on All Cylinders is an honest book. In contrast to the stream of "fix-your-organization-in-one-day" books, Clemmer describes how complex and difficult it is to get any organization to peak performance. This view is balanced, however, with a clear description of how to go about it, with compelling examples of the fact that it can be done, and with lots of encouragement to get started.

The content ranges from the movement toward teams and employee involvement to ways to smash the vertical chimneys in every organization that impede the move toward total quality.

Clemmer writes not as an automotive engineer, but as a working mechanic. He has effectively led and managed a rapidly growing business organization. His approach reflects the practitioner's practicality and provides a linear, step-by-step process to make any organization run better.

Finally, the author has directed the message to the correct target—the executives. For many, the message is painful. Quality is their responsibility. It demands their personal commitment, but they cannot make it happen. They must provide the fuel and the lubrication, but the people of the organization make it happen. That often requires the executives to get out of the way.

Thousands will read this book. Most will move on to the next popular book, searching for some magic to cure their organization's ills. A few will take this book and use it as their road map to high performance. They should know that it contains all the necessary directions and information. Those few will resist looking for "what's new" and will be content to stay with "what's good." For them, these powerful ideas will be sufficient. Because implementation is neither quick nor easy, their organization will be differentiated from the rest.

For the executive or manager who wants to bring about a major leap forward in performance, *Firing on All Cylinders* is an ideal manual. It helps us see the end from the beginning. It provides a practical checklist to see what needs to be done and gives guidance to make it happen. It provides reasonable timetables and helps us see the benefits of getting to the "bleeding edge," where organizations are doing new things for the first time.

It is rare to see such a combination of solid theory, practical examples, and guidance on how to make changes happen. For everyone, it will be an enjoyable read (thanks in part to the great quotes that Clemmer has been collecting all his life). But, for the few who elect to apply the discipline to have their organization fire on all its cylinders, this book will be a priceless treasure. These ideas have never been tried and found wanting—they've just been tried and found difficult. That difficulty comes from the unswerving dedication and consistency required to make them happen, along with the discomfort of tossing out old ways of doing things and replacing them with something new.

John H. Zenger
Chairman and CEO, Zenger-Miller, Inc.

Acknowledgments

"If I have been able to see further than others, it is because I have stood on the shoulders of giants."

Sir Isaac Newton,
English philosopher and mathematician

The service/quality improvement system described in this book is the result of more than a decade of evolution and collective learning within The Achieve Group and Zenger-Miller in conjunction with our Clients. From that cast of hundreds, the following people deserve special recognition for their contributions and pioneering efforts:

Original system developers—Jim Clemmer, Barry Sheehy, Paul Levesque, Mark Henderson, Art McNeil, Peter Strickland, and Rob Ell.

Pioneering Achievers—Kay Marie Wallace, Vic Bergman, Gerry Conger, Judy Dick, Walter Nymark, Owen Griffiths, Dave Carson, Gisèle La Rocque, Danielle Dagenais, and Merle Dulmadge.

Achieve International associates—Mike Yates, Ron Sepielli, Andy Parisien, Bob Beggs, Tony Hampson, Jerry Hogeveen, David Hutton, Frances Horibe, David Williams, Margaret Strus, Andrew Vujnovich, Tom McNulty, Anne Bloomer, and Judy Stipancic.

Clients—Alberta Blue Cross, Alling and Cory, American Express, Becton Dickinson Canada Inc., Bell Cellular, Black & Decker, Canadian Airlines International, Canadian Tire Corporation Limited, Crouse Hinds, Ecolab Ltd., Finning Ltd., Freeport Hospital, Heartland Health System, Health and Welfare Canada, IBM Canada, International Multifoods, Le Groupe Permacon, Matsushita Electric of Canada Limited, North American Life Assurance Co., Ontario Hydro, Technologies Industrielles SNC Ltée, Texaco—Bakersfield Division, Timeplex Field Services, Inc., the Keg Restaurants, the Stroh Brewery Company, University of Alberta Hospitals, Victoria General Hospital (Halifax), Wesley-Jessen (a division of Schering-Plough), and Xerox Canada.

Zenger-Miller—Jack Zenger, Ed Musselwhite, Dick Wilson, Jan Latham, Donna Jenkins, Pamela Fischer, Craig Perrin, Kathleen Hurson,

Amy Klausner, Elaine Pershing, Katherine Youngblood, Jackie Ramirez, Sheila Billingsley, Birdy Ellsmore, and Nancy Winship.

Other partners and contributors—consultant and Baldrige Examiner Roland Dumas, Macmillan of Canada's Bob Dees and Denise Schon, and Jeff Krames of Business One Irwin.

J.C.

Contents

Introduction

"Quality is never an accident; it is always the result of intelligent effort."
John Ruskin
English art critic and historian

Any attempt to improve, it's been said, can be compared to a parade. Essentially, three groups of people are involved: (1) the small number of people in the parade, (2) the larger group of people watching the parade, (3) and the mass of humanity left saying, "Huh? What parade?"

When it comes to attempts to improve service/quality, any North American executive unaware of the parade either has been living in a cave for the past decade or just doesn't care about his or her organization's future. For those leading the parade, improvements in service/quality have contributed to growth, cost containment, and profitability at almost obscene levels. And for the rapidly growing mob watching, learning, and waiting to join the parade, service/quality improvements are clearly the way to survive in a radically changing world.

Throughout this book, the term *service/quality* is used. We coined the term to convey the dual focus—service and quality—of effective efforts to improve performance. If you're familiar with the broad and growing field of customer service, our approach to "service" improvement will no doubt fit well. The improvement system outlined in this book is founded on the basic premise that your customers' perception of value is the beginning (and end measuring point) of *everything* your organization does. *The only reason your organization exists is to satisfy your customers.* Excellence, or high performance, comes from moving beyond customer satisfaction to customer delight.

Our focus on "quality" will be familiar to you if you have been part of or have been watching the quality improvement parade of the past few years. Most often called total quality management (TQM) or continuous quality improvement (CQI), this movement is relentlessly shattering many of the traditional models of organizational effectiveness that we have evolved since the turn of this century. Pioneers in total quality management have shown that by improving the way products or services are produced and supported, costs drop, efficiency and productivity rise, and customer as well as employee satisfaction (or delight) soars.

The third organizational field brought together in the improvement system described in these pages is that of human resource and organization development. For years, Zenger-Miller has been researching the role of human resource and organization development on service/quality improvement. This research, along with other similar studies now emerging, shows that many organizations are "hitting the wall" of their organizational culture and having difficulty breaking through. Many never do. So, customer-focused approaches and highly effective quality improvement tools and techniques "crash and burn," only to build more cynical and change-resistant people throughout the organization.

If you are familiar with the basics of good human resource and organization development, you'll recognize many of the fundamental principles tightly interwoven in the system described here. We don't have a magic formula for transforming an organization's culture and building broad-based leadership skills at all levels. But through our work with thousands of organizations on this critical issue, we have developed a broad experience base pointing the way toward what does and doesn't work. You'll find much of that experience distilled and distributed throughout the pages ahead.

Achieve's experience in service/quality improvement began with the outstanding leadership-training work done by our consulting associates of over a decade now, California-based Zenger-Miller Inc. Zenger-Miller has led the field in the research and development of employee, supervisor, manager, and executive nontechnical performance-skills training. The effectiveness of its programs is best measured by one of the truest tests of enduring quality—a highly competitive marketplace.

In 1982, Zenger-Miller developed a team leadership skills program called "groupAction." This series of sessions helped quality circle leaders develop the group process and problem-solving skills so vital to getting people to work together effectively. While the program has worked very well through the years (it is still being used), it gave us our first look at the formidable cultural obstacles that quality improvement faces (such as why so many quality circles failed in North America). We also began to learn about the power of effective teams—and the key elements in developing them. The research and development of skill-building systems to build effective teams has been especially intense in the past few years.

In 1983, Zenger-Miller and Achieve worked with Tom Peters (co-author of *In Search of Excellence, A Passion for Excellence,* and *Thriving on*

Chaos) to develop a process to bring an organization closer to "excellence." Called "Toward Excellence," this process added extensively to our understanding of the critical steps needed for long-term customer service and quality improvement. Over a six-year period, we learned much from the hundreds of North American organizations that used the process to move toward higher levels of performance.

However, a number of organizations tried to but never did implement the "excellence" principles. Performance didn't change, and the attempt became a source of cynical internal laughter and derision ("Well, we've all been 'excellenced'; what's next?").

Our experience with Toward Excellence taught us a great deal about the vital role that vision and values play in building a leadership base for cultural change. We also came to understand the effect that employee commitment has on service/quality improvement. (While quality *might* be driven higher solely by technomanagement—management systems and technology—service goes *nowhere* unless employees decide to improve it.) Most importantly, we gained deeper insights into what is needed to change an organization's culture and to foster a commitment to continuous improvement.

The Service/Quality System outlined in this book is based on the process of the same name developed by The Achieve Group and now offered throughout North America, the Pacific Rim, and Europe through the partnership of Achieve International and Zenger-Miller. It is built on our varied and broad experiences, as well as continuing research and study of the common elements shared by the highest service/quality providers.

Throughout this book, I have attempted to weave together our service/quality improvement models and experiences with recent research, the teachings of Japanese and American service/quality gurus, plenty of short examples, pitfalls and traps to avoid, along with numerous tips and suggestions. To provide a cornucopia of perspectives, examples, tips, and so on, point form lists are used to get right to the point without a lot of introductory verbiage and editorial comment. My goal was to give you a densely packed "one-stop" source of rich ideas, insights, and practical advice across the broad scope of our improvement system. You will find that I have cited a number of outstanding books and publications that shed some light on this emerging new management field. I leaned especially heavily on material from *Fortune, Harvard Business Review*, and the American Society for Quality Control. These organizations are doing an excellent job of helping to wake up North American managers and showing what the best managers are doing to effectively lead the service/quality improvement parade.

You will also find a number of quotations heading up many sections or topic areas. Some of these are meant to provide a lighter side to the topic at hand. Others are especially pithy observations of current executives and improvement experts or just ordinary "folks" with a particularly relevant observation to contribute. Many are classical quotations that go back centuries. Whenever I come across a relevant classical quotation from the past, I am always struck by the timelessness of the human issues that we've struggled with since the dawn of civilization. Nothing really is new under the sun. Since service/quality improvement is largely about people serving people (both inside and outside the organization), I have tried to select a few great thoughts from some of history's greatest poets, philosophers, writers, and other thinkers that illustrate the ageless humanness of today's improvement efforts.

May this book provide some guidance to you and your organization as you travel the road to higher performance.

Jim Clemmer

Chapter One

The Service/Quality Revolution

"There is one thing stronger than all the armies in the world, and that is an idea whose time has come."

Victor-Marie Hugo,
French poet and novelist

Whether we are living in the worst of times or the best of times depends on your perspective. However, it is clear we are living in radically changing times. Around the globe, whole societies are in the midst of dramatic transformation as our world order is fundamentally restructured. In his latest book, *Powershift*, futurist Alvin Toffler calls our current period of upheaval and major change a "hinge of history." According to Toffler, we are in one of only three periods throughout civilization when society undergoes such a major break with the immediate past that it leaps to an entirely new era. He adds, "What is emerging is a radical new economic system running at far faster speeds than any in history."[1]

The world of management is also in the midst of a revolution. The principles of mass production deeply ingrained throughout the Western world are now recognized as a major contributor to lack of competitiveness and the poor economic performance of many corporations and public institutions. Nowhere has the change in management thinking been more drastic than in North America. Having defined and achieved economic leadership through management practices developed in America at the turn of this century, leading U.S. executives and academics are now reconstructing management practices for a rapidly changing world.

"The pressures on American businesses have reached an intensity unparalleled since the 'modern' industrial society began to evolve at the end of the 19th century," concludes the American Society for Quality Control in a series of reports on our revolution in management practices.[2] A major reason for this sudden growing level of unprecedented pressure has been North America's prosperity. We have had little reason to question our management methods because for most of this century we have been the world's economic leaders. However, one of the failures of success is the complacency, arrogance, and certainty that sets in all too easily and naturally when "everything is going our way." It is easy to believe we have found the magic formula for everlasting success. We just assume the natural universal order is our permanent position as number one because we are obviously smarter, faster, stronger, and better in so many ways.

But growth, expansion, and "good times" can mask a number of problems. When revenues are growing, a host of problems can be papered over. Unhappy employees can be bought off with higher wages or replaced; poor quality products can be repaired or replaced; customers can be bought with expensive sales and marketing efforts or replaced. In a world of plenty, there's "always more where that came from." In the midst of this prosperity, good times easily become mistaken for good management, especially if the competition is no better, or is even worse, than we are. T. J. Rodgers, founder and Chief Executive Officer of Cypress Semiconductor Corporation wrote:

> The seeds of business failure are sown in good times, not bad . . . during times of prosperity danger lurks everywhere. Growth masks waste, extravagance, and inefficiency. The moment growth slows, the accumulated sins of the past are revealed all the way to the bottom line.[3]

THE EMERGENCE OF TOTAL QUALITY MANAGEMENT

"We are in a new economic age. Western management must awaken to the challenge, must learn their responsibilities, and take on leadership for change."

W. Edwards Deming[4]

In the early 1980s, the complacency and certainty of North American manufacturers were shattered. Suddenly, demand for products and revenues stopped growing. While the North American economy had experienced fits and starts in its decades of continual growth, the severe recession of the early 80s was a shock. Even worse was the appearance of strong, international competitors to challenge the dominance of North American manufacturers. And these competitors—particularly the Japanese—were not playing by the established rules. Japanese companies were landing higher quality products on our shores than we were making and at substantially lower prices. Frantic investigations revealed these powerful new Japanese manufacturers were boldly defying a management law thought to be as certain as the law of gravity; they were improving productivity and quality simultaneously.

This intense competition began a period of equally intense re-education among manufacturing management. As we will explore in depth in Chapter Three, "quality" was redefined and broadened. Its new definition brought productivity, cost reduction, customer service, and product quality together in a new and powerful combination much greater than the sum of its individual parts. The new management approach has a variety of names. The two most widely used are "total quality management" (TQM) and "continuous quality improvement" (CQI).

A growing number of major corporations are pointing to their use of total quality management methods as their salvation in dealing with a fast-changing, fiercely competitive world. Harvard Business School's David Garvin has been studying management practices in the United States and Japan. He finds that a dramatic shift in perspective is under way in Western management practices.

> For the first time, top managers, at the level of presidents and chief executive officers, have expressed an interest in quality. They have linked it with profitability, defined it from the customer's point of view, and required its inclusion in the strategic planning process. And in the most radical departure of all, many have insisted that quality be viewed as an aggressive competitive weapon.[5]

John Pepper, president of Procter & Gamble, exemplifies the strategic role being given to service/quality in leading organizations:

> Total quality has been responsible for creating the most lasting change in our culture and our approach to business that I've seen in 27 years with Procter & Gamble. But even I underestimated the impact it could have. Quality is seen by 98 percent of our people as absolutely essential to our success.[6]

General Electric has long been a pioneer in developing more effective management methods. Jack Welch Jr., CEO and leader of GE's worldwide transformation, sees service/quality improvement as central to his company's future success: "Quality is our best assurance of customer allegiance, our strongest defense against foreign competition, and the only path to sustained growth and earnings."[7] James Houghton, chairman of Corning Glass Works, has become a well-known leader of the service/quality revolution. Reflecting on his company's remarkable success in beating back international competition, he says: "Without quality, we cannot be a world-class competitor. It's as simple as that."[8]

THE JAPANESE MIRACLE: MADE IN THE USA

"When written in Chinese, the word crisis *is composed of two characters—one represents danger and the other represents opportunity."*

John F. Kennedy, *U.S. president*

The economic success story of our time has been the dizzying rise of Japan from the defeat of World War II to a position of global leadership in just a few short decades. With only 0.3 percent of the world's land surface and 2.7 percent of its population, Japan's gross national product (GNP) was over 11 percent of the world's total GNP by the early 1980s. Long associated with Matsushita, a leading Japanese corporation, Hajime Karatsu is one of Japan's best-known quality experts. He is a Deming Prize winner and has received many other honors and academic positions. In his book *TQC Wisdom of Japan: Managing for Total Quality Control*, he writes:

> There are many reasons for this success, and quality control has definitely been a key factor. The Industrial Revolution was sparked by the development of the steam engine; a second revolution grew out of Henry Ford's assembly line production; now, Japan is showing the world the way to a third industrial revolution—through the effective use of quality control.[9]

The greatest challenge to U.S. economic strength is coming from Japan, but the total quality management/control methods now proved so successfully by the Japanese were made in the USA. To add to the irony, the most prestigious quality prizes awarded in Japan to individuals and companies are named after an American, W. Edwards Deming.

During World War II, America used a number of statistical control techniques to maintain quality levels among a large and diverse group of armament and military equipment suppliers. The techniques also helped to control quality on wartime production lines while keeping volume and productivity high. Based on the ground-breaking work in the 1920s and 1930s of Walter Shewhart and a group of researchers at Bell Telephone Laboratories and its manufacturing arm, Western Electric, the emerging field of statistical quality control contributed mightily to the war effort.

However, once the war was over, an unprecedented economic boom began in North America. With expanding domestic economies, no international competition, and worldwide reconstruction under way, North American managers quickly became more concerned about quantity than quality. Eager consumers snapped up goods and services in increasing volumes, especially as marketers learned how to drive demand even higher. With an abundance of natural resources, plenty of working capital, a strong, well-educated work force, and the Disposable Society driving consumer demand, North American managers were on top of the world. And many came to believe it was and would always be so—a natural birthright.

In Japan, the picture was quite different. Struggling with heavy costs from the war effort, weak demand, lack of natural resources, an international reputation for low-quality products, and poor access to any major market, Japanese businesses, especially manufacturers, were wide open to more effective management methods. In 1950, W. Edwards Deming, an American statistician, gave a series of lectures to the Union of Japanese Scientists and Engineers (JUSE) on the statistical quality control techniques he had learned under Walter Shewhart and applied so successfully during the U.S. war effort. The new manufacturing methods taught by Deming set off a national management re-education effort throughout Japan. To encourage and recognize the fledgling attempts to improve quality, JUSE created the Deming Prize for individuals making significant contributions to the new field of management and the Deming Application Prize for corporations that best demonstrate use of the new quality management techniques.

In 1954, Joseph Juran, an engineer who had been a member of Shewhart's Quality Assurance Department at Bell Laboratories, was invited by JUSE to conduct seminars in Japan for top and middle managers on their role in managing the quality improvement process. One of the pioneers in this growing quality movement was Kaoru Ishikawa. His academic research, practical models and methods, best-selling books, and numerous other contributions to quality control (QC) in Japan have been recognized through his receipt of the Deming Prize and other honors and awards in Japan and the United States. Looking back at Juran's first seminar series, Ishikawa concludes: "Dr. Juran's visit marked a transition in Japan's quality control activities from dealing primarily with technology based in factories to an overall concern for the entire management." He goes on to explain, "The Juran visit created an atmosphere in which QC was to be regarded as a tool of management, thus creating an opening for the establishment of total quality control as we know it today."[10]

After a number of subsequent visits to Japan, Juran saw firsthand the deep, encompassing changes under way in Japanese management methods. In 1966, he boldly declared to the Conference of the European Organization for Quality Control in Stockholm, "The Japanese are headed for world quality leadership and will attain it in the next two decades because no one else is moving there at the same pace."[11]

THE NEW SERVICE BATTLEGROUND

"Business is a lot like tennis; those who don't serve well end up losing."

In a world awash in good products, service is quickly becoming the competitive battleground. In studying this emerging trend, Bro Uttal wrote in *Fortune* magazine:

As global competition intensifies and companies around the world invade each other's markets, cost [from improved productivity] and quality differences among all sorts of goods and services are shrinking. The company that coddles customers best has a competitive edge.[12]

The expectations of North American consumers are also changing. In a cover story, *Time* magazine reported:

Disgruntlement with services runs almost counter to the prevailing attitude about products. Consumers show a reasonable level of satisfaction with the merchandise they buy, thanks largely to technological advances. But the harsh world of the service economy intrudes once again on their contentment when a modern product suffers a breakdown.[13]

Extensive research conducted within major industries throughout North America by the Strategic Planning Institute in Cambridge, Massachusetts, found that we all tie service and product quality together. SPI, a nonprofit organization dedicated to the advancement of management strategy, has more than 200 member companies in the United States, Canada, Australia, Western Europe, and other countries. The authoritative PIMS (Profit Impact of Market Strategy) data base, from the Strategic Planning Institute, contains the good and bad experiences of more than 2,000 business units (division, product line, or profit center) tracked since 1972. SPI found that "customers value good repair work, delivery, and sales assistance almost as much as they value the quality of the product itself. Those who get top-notch service often think more highly of the product they have purchased."[14]

The combination of competitive forces and changing consumer expectations has made service *the* management issue of the 90s. A number of surveys now confirm that improving service is the highest priority of executives across North America and Europe. A Gallup poll commissioned by the American Society for Quality Control found service quality to be the single most important business issue faced by more than 615 U.S. CEOs in both the manufacturing and the service sectors.[15] A study by INSTEAD's Strategic Marketing Institute found that of the 128 concerns of leaders of European corporations, the top three were: (1) "coping with the increasing importance of product quality and greater service content," (2) "assessing changing customer characteristics," and (3) "creating a marketing culture throughout the corporation." Reporting on the study, international consultant and author John Humble observes, "Service is not a management trend that is going to die in one or two years, or a case of leaders and followers. It is a simple case of survivors and casualties."[16]

THE SERVICE/QUALITY REVOLUTION: THE RESULTS ARE OVERWHELMING

"Quality control which cannot show results is not quality control. Let us engage in QC which makes so much money for the company that we do not know what to do with it!"
Kaoru Ishikawa, *What is Total Quality Control: The Japanese Way*[17]

Throughout this book, and in Achieve International's process, the term *service/quality* is used to bring equal weight to both sides of this powerful equation. Chapter Two not only will define this in greater detail, but also will add the third crucial ingredient—organization development.

Management consultant and author Richard Schonberger has studied and written extensively on world-class manufacturing in both Japan and North America. His research and international consulting experience have led him to conclude: "We have learned more about the right way to run a business in the 1980s than in the preceding half century. In a nutshell, we've learned this: that world-class performance is *dedicated to serving the customer*" (his italics).[18]

As organizations in every industry and sector move to improve service/quality and adapt the new management approaches, the results are so overwhelming as to be unbelievable. The next few pages are a *small sample* of the dramatic and far-reaching results now pouring in from a diverse number of North American organizations.

Revenue Growth

The PIMS (Profit Impact of Market Strategy) data base from the Strategic Planning Institute (SPI) shows that high service/quality providers have average annual sales growth rates more than double that of the low service/quality providers. The research shows the low performers have been increasing their sales at an average rate of 8 percent per year.

Considering inflation since the data were first collected in 1972, that is not very impressive. High performers, on the other hand, have been increasing their sales at a rate of 17 *percent* a year.

Some companies implementing a comprehensive service/quality improvement process report the following sales results:

- Houston-based Wallace Co., Inc., is a small (280 "associates") distributor of petroleum and chemical pipes and fittings. Begun in 1985, its highly successful implementation of a service/quality improvement process was rewarded in 1990 with a Malcolm Baldrige National Quality Award. From 1987 to 1990, sales grew a hefty 69 percent! CEO John Wallace says: "These results reflect the cumulative impact of quality improvements undertaken in literally every phase of operations. There is not a single process in the company that hasn't been changed."[19]

- CalComp, a Lockheed company, manufactures computer plotters, digitizers, and graphic display terminals. Over a 24-month period in the late 1980s, revenues in the Plotter Products Division increased 70 percent "as a result of the continuous improvement philosophy."[20]

- Mary Anne Rasmussen of American Express Travel Related Services reports implementation of its worldwide service/quality improvement effort has "added hundreds of millions of dollars to the bottom line." Within two years of focusing on card member application processing, the time required dropped by 37 percent. "This single improvement has added up to $70 million in increased revenues over the past 10 years."[21]

Price

The Strategic Planning Institute concludes, "With the PIMS data base, we can test and quantify (the) relationship between price and performance. The data clearly show that, on average, better products command higher prices." In fact, PIMS shows that price index relative to competition puts those companies with low perceived service/quality at 98 percent compared to high-service companies at 107 percent. In other words, high-service/quality companies can charge *almost 10 percent more* for their goods and services.[22]

Management consultant Milind Lele and Jagdish Sheth, Brooker Professor of Research at the School of Business of the University of Southern California, spent two years studying customer satisfaction and service levels of 15 firms in 13 diverse industries. They conclude, "In industry after industry, happy customers are willing to pay extra for the additional satisfaction they derive."[23]

Having studied the relationship between service/quality and price, the Strategic Planning Institute concluded:

> Beating competitors in a race for a relative quality advantage is a more certain route than trying to win a price war. To improve the customer-perceived quality of your products and services relative to those of your competitors—and thereby gain the ability to increase prices—is the less perilous route to renewed competitive advantage.[24]

Customer Satisfaction and Retention

North American business has developed an insane imbalance between customer acquisition and customer retention. Many companies will invest millions in sales and marketing costs to bring customers in the door and then throw a few thousand dollars at trying to keep them. The proportion is way out of whack. The obsession with customer acquisition rather than retention is a holdover from our North American "fat, lazy, and stupid days" of plenty. There were always more customers to be found to replace those ingrates who didn't realize what great service/quality we were giving them. Obviously, we just weren't selling or marketing hard enough. After all, "a good salesperson can sell freezers to Eskimos"—and we had a load of product to get rid of to keep our mass production factories and offices running.

Leading service/quality providers are now showing the incredible payoffs that come from building a growing base of loyal customers. A number of studies have found that it costs from four to seven times more to attract a new customer than to retain an existing one. Writing in the *Harvard Business Review*, Christopher Hart, James Heskett, and W. Earl Sasser, Jr., report on their study of this critical issue:

> Managers often underestimate the profits lost when a customer departs unhappy, and therefore they undermanage ways to avoid such losses. They concentrate on attracting new customers that may actually represent unprofitable business and neglect to take steps to retain more valuable existing customers.[25]

In his study of the automotive industry for *Fortune*, Thomas Moore found, "the leverage in satisfying customers is enormous. Satisfied customers are twice as likely to stick with their old make and three times as likely to return to the dealer who sold them the car."[26] A large food processor found in a series of studies conducted by A.C. Nielsen Co. that 34 percent of its unhappy customers quietly switched brands without a complaint to the company. Another 4 percent stopped buying *any* of the company's brands.[27]

A well-implemented service/quality improvement effort increases customer satisfaction on an array of minor and major issues. As we'll explore in depth in Chapter Eighteen, these are measured in a variety of ways. Here is a sample of the possible results:

- U.S. West Cellular's customer "save rate" has increased 150 percent and monthly attrition has dropped by one third. The company estimates its service/quality improvement effort has added $8 million to the bottom-line in its early stages.[28]

- Xerox Canada's customer satisfaction index has increased from 90 to 96 percent since it began focusing on customer service in its "Leadership through Quality" improvement process.

- Wesley-Jessen, a division of Schering-Plough Corporation, is a Chicago-based contact lens manufacturer that has embarked on one of the fastest and most intense service/quality improvement efforts we have ever seen. From August 1990 to April 1991, it cut customer complaints by almost two thirds. Research clearly shows Wesley-Jessen's customers have noticed a significant turnaround in the company's service levels.

- Through its intensive service/quality improvement effort, University of Alberta Hospitals in Edmonton has reduced abandoned weekend phone calls to the switchboard by 80 percent through revising staff scheduling.

Stew Leonard and his thriving dairy store in Norwalk, Connecticut, have become famous through videos such as *In Search of Excellence*. He operates his store with an unparalleled obsessive focus on customer service. His sales per square foot set records unimagined in the U.S. grocery business. *The Service Edge* newsletter reports that Leonard likes to talk about a conversation with the chairman of one of America's largest supermarket chains. He asked this executive about the average wait his company's customers experience at the checkout counters. The chairman had no idea and basically didn't see the need for someone at his level to be concerned with such operating details. Yet when we go into a grocery store, the major beef we all have is the wait at the counters. We couldn't care less about inventory turns, capitalization, or whatever else the chairman and his boardroom buddies are sweating over. The king of grocery sales, Stew Leonard, puts it in perspective: "What could be more important than customer satisfaction?'' He goes on to outline a way of looking at his business that we find is common among that tiny group of top service/quality providers: ''Our average customer spends $100 a week; that's $5,200 per year or $52,000 every 10 years. When I see a dissatisfied customer, I see a potential loss of $52,000.''[29]

Market Share

Your company's market share is a direct reflection of the value customers place on it. Quite simply, when enough customers believe your products or services provide the highest value for their dollars, you will beat your competitors and gain a higher share of available customers. The PIMS data clearly show that high-service/quality providers are gaining the market share given up by low-service/quality providers. The difference was a loss of 2 percent per year for low performers versus gains of 6 percent per year for the high performers. The rich truly are getting richer. Those companies perceived by their customers to produce and deliver high service/quality are moving ahead of their lesser competitors at a rate of *8 percent a year!*[30] You don't have to be a marketing genius to realize that at that rate it doesn't take long for top companies to move into commanding positions in their markets. And the weak performers' position continues to weaken—victims of the service/quality revolution.

A major determinant of market share is a company's image in its marketplace. In the past decade, word of mouth and its more formal manifestation found in many consumer and industry protection movements have been playing a much bigger part in broadcasting what kind of service/quality a company is consistently delivering as perceived by its customers. Technical Assistance Research Program (TARP) is a Washington, D.C.-based nonprofit organization that has made a specialty of researching consumer complaints. Like the Strategic Planning Institute, it has amassed a large, solid research base that can shed light on a key area of service/quality. For years, it has studied customer complaints and the multiplying consequences for the offending organization.

TARP finds that while only a small percent of your unhappy customers bother to tell you about their dissatisfaction, they are eager to tell lots of your potential customers about the problems they have had dealing with you. TARP has studied the ripple effects of dissatisfied customers and word-of-mouth testimonials. The results will rock anyone concerned about sales and marketing. It found that each dissatisfied customer will tell *9 to 10* other people about his or her negative experience. For products and services in excess of $100, those disgruntled rumor-mongers will tell *16* others about their unhappy experience. On the other hand, happy customers tell only half as many people about the delightful experience they may have had with you.[31]

Based on TARP's findings, let's look at the cumulative effect of one unhappy customer who "lost" over $100 and didn't bother to complain:

The original customer who won't return	1
Potential customers not gained because the original customer didn't tell them how satisfied he or she was	8
Potential customers lost because the original customer told them how *dis*satisfied he or she was	16
Total customers lost from *one* unhappy customer	25

Now here's the $64,000 (for many companies, $64 million) question: What does it cost your company to get 25 new customers?

If those numbers make you sick, it gets worse. Writing in *Harvard Business Review*, marketing guru Regis McKenna (author of *The Regis Touch*), said: "With so much choice backed by service, customers can afford to be fickle. As a result, references have become vital to product marketing. And the more complex the product, the more complex the supporting references."[32] For marketers who ignore the impact of service/quality word of mouth, here's a marketing study to chew on: General Electric found that it (word of mouth) can be an even more influential factor than mass media advertising. . . . Only 29 percent of those surveyed found manufacturer's advertising "useful" during the prepurchase period. On the other hand, *61 percent* felt that the "opinions of friends" were "useful."[33]

Here are some of the changes in market share experienced by a few of the travelers on the road to higher service/quality:

- Wallace Co., Inc., saw its market share grow from just 10 percent in 1987 to 18 percent in 1990.[34]
- When Corning Glass Works began losing large chunks of its picture-tube business to Japanese manufacturers, it decided to battle back through improving product quality. The result, says James Houghton, chairman and CEO, is "the Japanese tube makers now tell us, 'We don't believe your numbers—they're too good.' Demand for our products is growing so rapidly we've launched a major expansion."[35]

- Motorola's relentless focus on six sigma quality levels (3.4 defects per million) has won it both a Malcolm Baldrige Quality Award and a rising share of Japan's highly competitive and very demanding telecommunications market.[36]

Cost Reduction

As we'll explore in depth in Chapter Three, successful service/quality improvement doesn't just contain costs; it also drives them in a continual downward spiral. During much of the 1950s, 60s, and 70s, North American managers believed higher quality cost more. Today's broader definition of quality includes productivity improvement and cost reduction.

Service/quality improvement leads to cost reductions in many ways. Chief among them are reduction of inventory levels and the lessening of accounts receivables outstanding with the heavy carrying costs that both bring. Reductions in administrative and service delivery error rates and product defects are prime examples of how service/quality improvement often both reduces costs and improves customer satisfaction (as well as employee morale). The same can be said for cycle-time reduction, which is now emerging as a major competitive weapon.

Since the 1950s, Toyota has been a Japanese leader in the application of total quality control techniques such as quality circles, just-in-time, and statistical methods in many parts of its operations. United Kingdom-based consultant Philip Atkinson reports on a conversation he had with the senior management team after touring the Toyoda plant in Toyoda City, Japan: "We have moved from quality philosophy to measuring defects on an acceptable quality level basis to reducing our defect rate to below 5 to 6 parts per billion. Our last product recall was 1969 when we first started introducing what you know as total quality management."[37]

In the International Motor Vehicle Program, the Massachusetts Institute of Technology (MIT) sent 53 researchers through 90 assembly plants in 17 countries to compare the results from what they came to call "mass production" and "lean production" (total quality management) management methods. The researchers found that Toyota epitomized lean production. Toyota spends the same amount of worker hours (19) building its new luxury car as its major European competitor spends fixing its mistakes. Toyota cars also have half the number of defects and one tenth the in-process inventories in manufacturing. It builds its cars with half the worker hours and half the factory space as the mass producers do. And Toyota's new-car development cycle is 46 months and falling versus the industry average of 60 months.[38]

These dramatic cost reductions coupled with rising customer satisfaction is why the company is becoming known as "the Bank of Toyota." In his *Fortune* article titled "Why Toyota Keeps Getting Better and Better and Better," Alex Taylor III reported, "Toyota sits on $22 billion in cash—enough to buy Ford and Chrysler at current stock prices, with nearly $5 billion to spare."[39]

Here are further examples of the sharp fall in costs coming from service/quality improvement efforts:

- Wesley-Jessen's distribution errors fell 425 percent in a nine-month period, while back orders dropped by a factor of 5 in a corresponding six-month period.
- By 1987, Hewlett-Packard failure rates were declining at a rate of 20 percent per year. Inventory levels were more than $200 million lower than they would have been without the service/quality effort. And application of the process to selected administrative functions resulted in savings of over $100 million.[40]
- During a 12-month period, University of Alberta Hospitals reduced its costs for total hip replacements by 21 percent. Patient care was not compromised and hospital staff were satisfied with the process used.
- By its sixth year of effort, Xerox had reduced its average manufacturing costs over 20 percent, despite inflation. New-product development time was reduced by 60 percent.[41]
- CalComp reduced cycle time from nine weeks to three days, took 14 percent from overhead costs, reduced space by 45 percent, increased inventory turns to 5.5 from 1.7, saw cash flow rise 21 points, and raised field reliability 22 percent.[42]
- Canadian Airlines International cut the processing time for a new frequent flyer application from six weeks to two minutes. The cycle time to overhaul a B727 jet engine was reduced from 120 days to 40. On-time performance was increased by 30 percent and customer complaints decreased by the same amount.
- Milliken Textiles reduced the turnaround time for its commercial carpet tile from 12 weeks to seven days.[43]

Productivity

Given the increases in volumes and revenues and the decreases in costs outlined in the previous examples, it is easy to understand why quality and productivity improvement go hand in hand. Lester Thurow, dean of the MIT Sloan School of Management, reports:

In Japanese, when you say the word *productivity*, it's not clear whether you are talking about higher quality per unit of output or more units of output for less cost. Productivity means both of those things. In the U.S., we have made a distinction between quality and productivity.[44]

In *TQC Wisdom of Japan*, Hajime Karatsu explains the quality-productivity relationship: "Increasing productivity actually means the opposite of longer work hours: Make a job easier and complete it sooner—only then does productivity rise."[45] The term *qualitivity* is increasingly being used to show the inseparable relationship between the two.

Here are some of the productivity increases documented through the service/quality improvement process:

- Globe Metallurgical Inc., another Baldrige winner, increased its productivity 360 percent over two years. Vice President Ken Leach said: "We can document $10.3 million in savings. We have saved nearly 10 percent of our gross revenue by implementing TQM."[46]
- In the early 80s, Japan's Bridgestone Corporation bought a Firestone plant in LaVergne, Tennessee. Retaining the original unionized work force, from 1983 to 1987, Bridgestone increased plant output 200 percent, reduced defect and scrap rates by 60 percent, and achieved a safety record of 2.2 incidence rate for injuries compared to 14.0 for the industry.[47]
- Photography and illustration staff members at University of Alberta Hospitals were able to prepare 57 percent more artwork without any increase in staff or budget.

Profits

It doesn't take a financial genius to figure out that higher market share, higher prices and sales, higher productivity, and lower costs all add up to higher profitability. What is astounding is just how much more profitable top service/quality providers are. On this key measure of performance, executives of lower-service/quality firms might be tempted to dismiss the PIMS data because the profit levels seem like fantasy. But the research is too extensive, broad-based, and solid to do that. According to the Strategic Planning Institute, low service/quality companies have a return on sales averaging just 1 percent. High-service/quality companies have a return on sales averaging 12 *percent*. High service/quality providers have a profitability more than 10 *times higher* than their lesser counterparts![48]

To corroborate the PIMS data, John Groocock, retired vice president for quality at TRW, applied the same analysis to that $6 billion, highly diversified conglomerate. Using the customers' evaluations of quality, he measured 148 product lines in 47 TRW business units and compared them with 560 competitors' product lines. He found that the top third of TRW's quality providers (as measured by their customers) had returns on assets three times higher than those of the bottom third of quality providers. Groocock made a penetrating comment based on this discovery: "The PIMS results are so impressive that it is surprising that they have had so little effect on management."[49]

Safety

Just as poor quality work processes lead to increased cost and higher levels of both customer and employee frustration, low quality levels also create an unsafe workplace. Paul O'Neill, CEO of Aluminum Co. of America, explains, "You can't get safety unless you really understand your processes."[50] Safety consultants Thomas Krause and John Hidley came to the same conclusion as they worked with clients who were implementing total quality management practices and compared the success of their safety programs with those clients who were not using TQM approaches: "Process approaches to quality and safety are so complementary that when they are both at work in a facility, they tend to reinforce each other, the safety effort gaining strength from the quality effort, and vice versa."[51]

Paul Vita of Wallace Co., Inc., reports his company found that "quality and safety go hand in hand." He explains, "Before we began our quality program, our accident rate had been climbing steadily, yet going unnoticed." Eventually, Wallace became such a high risk that insurance companies would no longer cover the company.

> We had to be insured by the state of Texas, which meant our premiums increased five or six times—to $600,000 to $700,000 annually. That was a big hit for a small company facing hard times. Today we have a world-class safety program. Insurance companies took us back—two years earlier than required—and are using us as a model for others.

CEO John Wallace adds, "In my mind that program alone paid for the quality movement. It saved us half a million dollars."[52]

Milliken's highly successful service/quality improvement effort also correlates with an equally strong safety improvement record. In 1985, Milliken had a 0.36 disabling incidence rate per 200,000 hours worked. By 1988, that rate had been cut to 0.18. This improvement occurred while the textile industry's safety rate moved from 0.46 in 1985 to 0.52 in 1988 and general industry's slipped from 1.98 to 2.17.[53]

Employee Morale

You don't have to be an organizational psychologist to figure out that if customers are more satisfied, management is seeing costs drop and productivity rise, safety is improving, cycle time is reduced and responsiveness increased, and the company is financially healthy and clearly on a winning streak, chances are morale and satisfaction throughout the organization are higher. Later chapters will explore further the cause-and-effect relationships between employee morale and organizational effectiveness.

Here are some of the indicators of increased employee satisfaction coming from service/quality improvement efforts:

- University of Alberta Hospitals tracked a sharp reduction in grievances as a result of management's obsessive focus on the core values of partnerships, respect, and continuous improvement. Costs for grievance arbitration dropped from a high of $220,000 in one year to $50,000.

- From 1987 to 1989, Wallace's "key indicators of associate well-being and morale" show that absenteeism fell from 1.7 percent to 0.7 percent—less than half the industry average. Turnover dropped from 7 percent to below 3 percent.[54]

- Since Dow Chemical U.S.A.'s aspirin facility in Midland, Michigan, began its quality improvement process, attendance has improved 50 percent.[55]

- One of our Clients in the insurance business conducted an attitude survey during the first year of its service/quality implementation. The change in employee morale and satisfaction was so dramatic from two years earlier that the survey company launched a special investigation. It had never seen any organization development process produce such a sharp and deep change.

AMERICA FOCUSES ON SERVICE/QUALITY

"If you think you've lived in a competitive environment in the last half century, you haven't seen anything yet."

Lestor Thurow, *dean of the MIT Sloan School of Management*[56]

Based on his years of extensive research of Japanese and American management practices, David Garvin concluded in 1987:

One of the most distinctive features of the Japanese quality movement has been its national focus. New ideas have diffused rapidly throughout the country. Success stories have been quickly publicized; the latest techniques have been translated almost immediately into training programs; and the same philosophy and approaches have emerged in industries as diverse as electronics and steel. The overwhelming impression is one of unity and purpose, with the entire nation moving en masse toward the goal of improved quality.[57]

Through the early to mid-80s, it became clear to business and political leaders that America was in a crisis of international competitiveness. It also became clear that when the quality management techniques exported from the United States to Japan (where they were greatly refined and improved) were brought into American companies, the increase in competitive performance was dramatic. High-profile companies such as Xerox and Motorola took back huge chunks of market share and turned their companies around. Xerox CEO David Kearns said:

> We implemented Quality to survive. By the late 70s, the Japanese nearly put us out of business. They were able to produce and deliver reliable products at prices that were below our cost to manufacture. We turned to Total Quality as a vehicle to regain our market share, our competitiveness, and our viability as a company.[58]

In 1987, the U.S. Congress passed, and President Reagan signed, the Malcolm Baldrige National Quality Improvement Act. Named after the late Secretary of Commerce Malcolm Baldrige (who was killed in a rodeo accident in 1987), the award was intended to provide the same national focus on quality as the Deming Prizes have done since 1950 in Japan. The award is administered by the American Society for Quality Control under the management of the National Institute of Standards and Technology. Its objectives are: (1) awareness of quality as an increasingly important element in competitiveness; (2) understanding of the requirements for quality excellence; and (3) sharing of information on successful quality strategies and on the benefits derived from implementation of these strategies.[59]

The award's application and extensive on-site examination process addresses about 90 areas within seven categories: (1) leadership, (2) information and analysis, (3) strategic quality planning, (4) human resources implementation, (5) quality assurance of products and services, (6) quality results, and (7) customer satisfaction. Each year, the categories and weighting are reviewed to ensure they accurately reflect changes in knowledge and application of the fast-moving field of total quality management.

By the early 1990s, the award had galvanized national attention on service/quality improvement. Award winners received overwhelming national attention. And because all the publicity of being a quality leader doesn't hurt sales, a number of companies set out to "bag a Baldrige." One of the negative results has been a backlash of criticism against the application and examination process and the cynical drive by some companies (hyped up and aided by "instant Baldrige expert" consultants) to get the trophy at almost any cost—except by actually transforming their organization through service/quality improvement. But those are the exceptions.

By 1990, 180,000 applications had been sent to American companies. By mid-1991, the rate of application requests was up more than 200 percent from 1990. Most of these companies are using the detailed application guidelines as a guidebook on their journey to dramatically higher levels of service/quality. Corning Glass CEO James Houghton said, "The guidelines are outstanding. We have passed out the guidelines for divisions and just said, ' If you want to know what quality is all about, take a look at this.' "[60]

Having foreseen the rise of Japan in the 60s, Joseph Juran, one of the fathers of total quality management, concludes:

> In three short years, (the Baldrige Award) has grown in stature and influence to a degree unprecedented in my 66 years of experience in this field. A large number of U.S. companies are already using the Baldrige Award as a basis for self-audit. It is quite likely that the Baldrige will become a major rallying point for a renaissance in quality in U.S. industry. I have become optimistic for the first time since the quality crisis descended on the United States . . . during the 90s the United States will make great strides toward making 'Made in the USA' a symbol of world-class quality.[61]

THE REVOLUTION CAN DRAMATICALLY IMPROVE OUR WORLD

"Rarely in human history has any institution emerged as quickly as management or had as great an impact so fast. In less than 150 years, management has transformed the social and economic fabric of the world's developed countries. It has created a global economy and set new rules for countries that would participate in that economy as equals. And it has itself been transformed."

Peter Drucker, *management professor and prolific author*[62]

If you have never been part of an organization that has successfully undergone a service/quality revolution, the results probably seem farfetched. Yet countless studies and numerous examples show that the results are substantial and real. Our experience and a growing mountain of evidence clearly say you can count on these four facts: (1) your customers expect sharply higher levels of service/quality; (2) your competitors are already working flat out (or getting ready to) to entice your customers with higher perceived value than you have been offering; (3) to the victor will go the spoils; (4) no matter where you currently sit in your industry, if your organization doesn't have an aggressive plan to dramatically improve your service/quality levels, you are already behind and in serious trouble. You may be well on your way to becoming victims of the service/quality revolution as you cling to the old management order.

But improving service/quality has much bigger implications than just your own organization. Quality guru W. Edwards Deming wrote:

> The wealth of a nation depends on its people, management, and government, more than on natural resources. The problem is where to find good management. If Japan be an example, then it is possible that any country with enough people and with good management . . . need not be poor.

Assessing the state of American management in 1981, Deming went on to state: "It would be a mistake to export American management to a friendly country."[63]

And moving beyond national borders, the one issue that may unite our many diverse nations more than any other is working together to deal with the damage our modern lifestyle is doing to our environment. Of course, that is a major issue beyond the scope of service/quality improvement. However, just as the last management revolution that moved us to mass production at the turn of this century dramatically altered society, the service/quality revolution will also create major societal change. And one effect promises to be a reduction in waste, energy use, and pollution. More companies are finding numerous ways to link service/quality improvement with their successful efforts to reduce, reuse, and recycle.

Do we want to pass on to our children a nation poorer than we inherited from our forebears? Do we have the right to use more resources than we need because of our sloppy management habits? While improving your organization is critical, there is an even bigger reason for you to participate in the service/quality revolution; it's the right thing to do.

Chapter Two

What Is "Service/ Quality"?

"*The organization must learn to think of itself not as producing goods and services but as buying customers, as doing those things that will make people want to do business with it.*"

Ted Levitt,
*professor, Harvard Business School
and author of* The Marketing Imagination

W e complain that it is disappearing. We all want more of it. When asked to define "it," we say, "I'll know it when I see it."

Organizations want to be known for delivering high levels of "it." Many understand that "it" will increasingly determine their success. Employees would like to be known for delivering high levels of "it" to their internal and external customers. And they would like to be appreciated and rewarded for providing "it."

But when we write about "it," and you agree your organization needs more of "it," are we talking about the same thing? Even more importantly, when you talk to your people about improving "it," are they seeing "it" the same way you are? Or is everyone signing up for "it," then heading off in opposite directions toward their own vision of "it"?

"It"—service/quality—is fast becoming the most talked about and least understood concept in organizations today. "Quality is an unusually slippery concept," suggests David Garvin. "It's easy to visualize and yet exasperatingly difficult to define. It remains a source of great confusion to managers."[1] According to Joseph Juran, the confusion is caused by the "hidden obstacles arising from differences in premises, concepts, and even in the meanings of key words." He finds that many people do not even realize the differences exist.

Some of the managers are thinking that a "higher quality" deluxe hotel costs more than a "lower quality" budget hotel. Other managers are thinking that product from a "higher quality" process with yields of 98 percent will cost less than product from a "lower quality" process with yields of 80 percent. All managers are drawing logical conclusions from their respective premises. However, they are not aware that their premises differ and that is traceable to the meaning of a word—that the same word *quality*, pronounced and spelled identically, has more than one meaning.[2]

Many definitions of "service/quality" depend on the mind-set of the employees and especially on the atmosphere of the organization. In some organizations, just showing up for work every day, never mind in how snarly a mood, is considered a heroic feat. A receptionist under siege on the switchboard might consider connecting the caller to the right department, regardless of how long the person has been on hold, as good service/quality.

So what's the point of all this? *Your organization needs a clear and consistent understanding of what service/quality means and how to deliver it.* If your organization cannot consistently define service/quality, how can you measure it? And if you can't measure it, how can you achieve it? Most managers and employees want to improve service/quality, but they are not all reading the same road map. In fact, they are not even all heading to the same place.

USING THE CUSTOMER'S YARDSTICK

"What concerns me is not the way things are, but rather the way people think things are."

Epictetus, *Greek philosopher*

Service/quality, like beauty, is in the eye of the beholder. The answer to the question, "What is high (or low) service/quality?" is "Whatever the customer says it is." To define service/quality in your organization you must look to the customers your organization serves. *Your customers' perceptions of the value they are receiving must become the common yardstick against which all activities throughout your entire organization are measured.* Defining service/quality through the eyes of your customers is such a fundamental starting point to improving service/quality that the Malcolm Baldrige National Quality Award weights 30 percent of the total possible score to the category of customer satisfaction. Point number one in the award's "examination criteria" states: "Quality is defined by the customer."

One of the drivers of the rapid success of the Four Seasons international hotel chain has been its definition of service/quality through the eyes of the customers served. Executive Vice President of Operations

John Sharpe explains the fundamental philosophy that underlies a standard of service/quality at the Four Seasons that has led to constant rankings as one of the top five hotel chains in the world:

> Customers don't buy a product, they buy what the product does for them. Quality in product or service is not what *we* think it is. It's what our customers perceive it is—and what they need and want. If we don't give customers what they expect, they'll perceive our service as poor. If we give them what they expect, they'll perceive it as good. If we give them more than they expect, they'll perceive it as excellent.[3]

Sharpe makes another point that is critical in developing a customer-focused definition of service/quality: "Perception is largely a matter of expectation." Duke University Associate Professor Valarie Zeithaml and Professors A. Parasuraman and Leonard Berry of Texas A&M University have been doing exploratory research on service quality since 1983 under the auspices of the Marketing Sciences Institute. In their book, *Delivering Quality Service*, they conclude:

> It was clear to us that judgments of high and low service quality depend on how customers perceive the actual service performance in the context of what they expected. Therefore, service quality, as perceived by customers, can be defined as *the extent of discrepancy between customers' expectations or desires and their perceptions* (their italics).[4]

Building an organization capable of continually narrowing the gap between customer expectations and customer perceptions of service/quality being delivered is the overarching goal of Achieve's Service/Quality System™ and this book. Not only will we be continuously returning to this theme, but also a number of chapters are built around this basic premise.

Too often the features, attributes, or service/quality expectations of the customer are out of sync with what the organization considers to be important and is focused on delivering. As customers, we have all dealt with organizations that have done an outstanding job delivering a service or product feature we could care less about. So as the salesperson prattles on about that "wonderful" feature, or the company heavily promotes some "unique" service, we are being driven crazy by the lack of attention to some other feature or service the company obviously considers trivial or much less important.

Customer and organization perceptions of value may be out of sync because customer expectations are changing so quickly today. Organizations that are not tuned into their customers often miss these shifts—until someone else bursts onto the scene with more customer-responsive products or services. In her *Fortune* article titled "How to Deal with Tougher Customers," Faye Rice illustrates just how fast customer expectations are changing by citing a Yankelovich Clancy Shulman poll taken in the spring of 1990:

> Americans rank quality's components in this order: reliability, durability, easy maintenance, ease of use, a known or trusted brand name, and *finally*, a low price. In a Gallup poll conducted five years ago, consumers thought a well-known brand name connoted quality with price coming in third, right after workmanship.[5]

Service/Quality From the Outside In

"The single most important thing to remember about any enterprise is that results exist only on the outside. The result of a business is a satisfied customer. The result of a hospital is a healed patient. The result of a school is a student who has learned something and puts it to work 10 years later. Inside an enterprise there are only costs."

Peter Drucker[6]

Art Burnham, vice president of quality and regulatory affairs for the medical technology products company, Medtronic Inc., puts his finger on a rampant North American disease: "We tended to design products and services based on *our* needs, on what we could do based on the technologies we had, then introduce them to the marketplace." Identifying the source of this widespread affliction, *Total Quality* newsletter observed, "That strategy worked in the high growth 1980s, but the 1990s present a vastly different business environment."[7]

The difference between an organization producing a consistent level of customer-defined high service/quality and one with low performance ratings can most clearly be seen in the perspective from which they view the world. The common, and less-effective, approach is to narrowly see the world through the glasses of one's own discipline, function, or experience base—to look from the inside out. Zeithaml, Parasuraman, and Berry found: "When this happens, companies provide services that do not match customers' expectations; important features are left out and the levels of performance on features that are provided are inadequate."[8] Measures, priorities, and resource allocations with a narrow, internal perspective are at the base of the large gaps between what customers expect and what they perceive is delivered.

High service/quality can be delivered only by finding a multitude of ways to keep everyone in your organization looking at what they do from the outside in. Kaoru Ishikawa declares Japanese companies have found this is where quality begins: "The basis of quality control is *market in*. The company must produce something that the consumer needs and then sell it. To sell merchandise is called *product out*."[9] This means *everyone* in your organization must be able to define, plan, implement, and measure their job around external customer expectations. However, because many people in your organization are not dealing with your external customers directly every day, they need to define their contributions on the basis of how well they are serving their internal customers so that external customers can be better served.

This "service/quality chain" of customer-supplier relationships is a vital concept that we will return to many times in the chapters ahead. George Fisher, CEO of Baldrige Award winner Motorola, said:

> Successful companies are going to integrate the entire production and delivery chain—not necessarily around a factory but around a customer need. We have to change the conventional ways we think about who really develops products and who bundles services. There's a team that satisfies a customer need. That team may even include the customer.[10]

THE THREE RINGS OF PERCEIVED VALUE

> *"Quality is not the absence of defects as defined by management, but the presence of value as defined by customers."*
>
> Sign in a Milliken plant[11]

In the early stages of developing Achieve's approach, we focused on "service quality," which was pursuing primarily the improvement of customer service. To that end, Ted Levitt's model of the total product provided an inspiration for looking at service quality from the customer's broad, outside-in perspective. Renowned as the Harvard Business School's "guru of marketing," Levitt, in his classic book *The Marketing Imagination*, outlined a four concentric ring model building on the organization's "generic product" to differentiate it in the marketplace and increase customers' perception of value as far outward as possible.

In a later book, *Thinking About Management*, Levitt explains:

> A product is not just its defined or descriptive core, but everything that is done with respect to it, including how it is packaged, sold, distributed, delivered, promoted, installed, repaired, field-supported, and upgraded, how users are trained in its use, and much more.

He asserts that if the whole cluster does not meet the customer's "wants and wishes" then the product or service will not do well in the marketplace. And when management sees its products or services only as their defined core, differentiation becomes next to impossible—and commodity thinking sets in. But Levitt argues:

> There is no such thing as a commodity, only people who act and think like commodities. Everything can be differentiated . . . historically, companies that have taken and stayed resolutely on the commodity path, even when they have driven their costs deeply down, have become extinct.[12]

Levitt's view of an ever expanding product leading to clear differentiation in customers' perception provided a stimulus for our development of the "three rings of perceived value" model. The concentric rings show that as higher levels of customer-defined support and service are added to a high-quality product or service, the customer's perception of value increases. In high-service/quality organizations, all three rings are strong and growing. Perceived value is high.

We originally used the three rings model to show that adding value through third-ring, enhanced service was the key to increasing customer-perceived value. However, as we helped clients apply this approach, we ran into two problems: (1) the customer-perceived quality of the organization's core product or service and the quality of the support processes often subverted attempts to enhance third-ring service, and (2) our narrower focus on service was not harnessing the power of the techniques within the emerging quality improvement movement, particularly process management.

Our search for a way to incorporate quality into our approaches revealed nearly as many definitions of service, quality, and total quality management as there are gurus, experts, consultants, and organizations striving to improve "it." As we worked with various—sometimes conflicting—definitions, we looked for a way to find the common ground among them. We were searching for a simple way to bring many of the service/quality improvement approaches into a common framework that allowed them to work together. Our goal was much like the movement within the computer industry: to develop a common operating language—as "user friendly" as possible—to allow various service, quality, and total quality management definitions and improvement systems to communicate with each other and work together.

In the late 1980s, this developmental effort led to expanding our system to bring together service, quality, and our long experience in the field of organization and skill development. The balance of this chapter, and the next one, will immerse you in the broad service/quality definition that emerged from our research and conceptual development. The sys-

Three Rings Model

Three Rings of Perceived Value

BASIC PRODUCT OR SERVICE

SUPPORT

ENHANCED SERVICE

tem described here is proving to be a useful framework for dozens of major international corporations, health-care institutions, and public agencies in their progress toward higher service/quality.

The Inner Ring: The Basic Product

"A composition for cheapness and not excellence of workmanship is the most frequent and certain cause of the rapid decay and destruction of arts and manufacturers."

Josiah Wedgwood, *English potter*

The inner product ring is the basic, bare product, service, or core offering. This could be a widget, financial service, government program, hotel room, or complex technical system. Internally, it can also be an answered phone, information for the manager in plant number 3, training and development, or technical support. The size of this ring depends on the level of quality the customer believes he or she is getting. The customer appeal of that product or service depends on the extent to which it meets minimum requirements.

If an organization, department, or individual contributor's basic product doesn't meet basic standards or specifications, then the rest of the rings don't matter. In their book, *Total Customer Service*, William Davidow and Bro Uttal underline the importance of a strong inner ring:

> It is possible to put the cart before the horse, trying to capitalize on customer service when your core product or service is grossly inferior in design, performance, or cost . . . the current drive by airlines to please customers will backfire unless the airlines can reliably produce their core service—getting passengers from point A to point B on time and with their luggage.[13]

Today, the minimum standard considered acceptable in product manufacturing is much higher than it was just a few years ago. Similarly, the standards of basic service requirements such as ease of access, flexibility, and suitability of the service for the need are also rising. Just to get into the game today, you must have a good, functional basic product. There is simply no market for products and services that do not work. However, in a world with an unprecedented supply of good products and services, minimum standards of acceptable quality are increasing exponentially. Just keeping your product or service up to swift-changing minimum standards of more demanding customers is an increasingly tough job.

Those whose basic products or services are primarily for internal consumption also feel this pressure to improve. Changing requirements of external customers, coupled with growing pressures on every organization to do more with less, are radically shifting internal customers' base requirements. Internal support groups need to keep their basic product strong and evolving just to keep up with the fast-moving needs of the organization they serve.

One of the biggest challenges to expanding the inner ring is getting the technical experts who design and build the basic product or service to look beyond their specialty, industry standards, tradition ("we've always done it this way"), competition, or their own "I know best because I am the expert" tendencies and understand what problem the customer is trying to solve or what need the customer is trying to fill. The customer's glasses need to be used to determine what kind of product or service features to offer, and then the customer's yardstick must be used to measure the product or service's quality level. This calls for a much closer relationship with customers to get behind the product or service itself and see "where the customer is coming from." Along these lines, a growing number of organizations are moving out of the traditional "product (or service) push" approach that involves selling "things" and moving to "customer pull" that involves finding solutions. That involves a very high degree of customer listening.

The Second Ring: Support

Stopping the service/quality improvement effort once the customer's basic requirements are met is the road to an undifferentiated commodity. When times get tough, another alternative comes along (perhaps a similar basic product or service at a lower price) or customers decide to do it themselves, commodity businesses or departments may find themselves out of business.

Increasingly today, customers are looking beyond the core product or service to how well it is supported. The support ring includes a huge array of services and factors. It includes anything an organization does to make the basic product more reliable, accessible, usable, enjoyable, convenient, dependable, accurate, or useful. This may consist of training, electronic data interchange, parts, repair service, warranties, emergency assistance, information, status updates, user hot lines, instructions or manuals, recipes, partnerships, and so on.

With the huge growth in the number and quality of inner ring products available today, customer expectations (and relentless competitive pressures) are dramatically expanding the amount, type, and quality of support services and activities required to just keep customer perceptions of the second ring static, let alone push it outward. In "Beyond Products:

Services-Based Strategy,'' James Brian Quinn, Thomas Doorley, and
Penny Paquette write in *Harvard Business Review*:

> Overall, services account for over three-fourths of all costs in most U.S.
> industries . . . not long ago, most of a product's value added came
> from the production processes that converted raw materials into useful
> forms. Now, however, value added is increasingly likely to come from
> technological improvements, styling features, product image, and
> other attributes that only services can create. More and more compa-
> nies are beginning to look like those in the personal computer industry,
> where producing the actual ''box'' is a low-margin activity, and soft-
> ware and service support activities create most of a product's value to
> customers.[14]

Software company WordPerfect Corporation provides a good example of the growing importance of the support ring. At WordPerfect, 750
operators—almost a third of the company's total staff—take more than
16,000 calls a day to help users of the company's software programs.
This free service is provided on toll-free lines to support the 7 million
users of the popular software. Says President and co-founder Alan Ashton, ''We want to encourage people to call and get help rather than
hesitate and become frustrated if they are having a problem.''[15] Like
many automobile manufacturers, financial services companies, hospitals, and a growing list of organizations, WordPerfect Corporation is well
aware of customers' tendency to rate the basic product as low or high
quality depending on how easy they find it is to use. That depends on
how well it is designed and supported.

Numerous examples are emerging of companies whose weak support
rings undermined investments in building strong basic products. James
Koontz, a director of the National Machine Tool Builders Association,
says failure to deliver on time was a major contributor to the U.S. machine tool industry's loss of half the domestic market to Japanese suppliers. ''It killed us,'' he says. ''This lack of service was the single most
important contributor to the Japanese success.''[16] *The Service Edge* newsletter reports that Cray Research, the world's leading supplier of super-
computers, attributes lack of service to the loss of a $60 million sale to
Japanese archrival NEC Corp. ''According to John Rollwagen, Cray's
CEO, the customer's decision wasn't based on product capabilities. It
reflected service—or the lack of it.''[17]

As you look at your organization's basic products and services in the
inner ring and then assess what makes up your organization's support
ring, you will probably have trouble deciding what the minimum requirements are and what second-ring expectations would lead to satisfied customers. If you took that discussion to your management team,

conflicting opinions would further confuse things. One way of clarifying what belongs where would be to ask those employees on the serving lines who hear what customers are asking for and commenting on. Their opinions and weighting of customer expectations have been shown to be more valid than those of management.

But the obvious people to ask are your customers. And there's the power and simplicity of the three rings model. Ask your customers what their minimum standards are and have them rate how you have been doing. Then do the same to find out what support they expect and how you have been doing at satisfying those expectations. Get each employee team to do the same for the external or internal customers they serve and to communicate the results to everyone. Do that, and you have just taken a giant step toward developing a consistent definition of service/ quality in your organization. You will be building a base. But it is just the beginning.

A Broader Definition of Quality

US West Cellular discovered that when company representatives periodically called customers, "those customers perceived improvements in their cellular telephone service—such as fewer dropped calls and less static—whether there were or not."[18] This growing trend to merge the basic product and support ring is explained by marketing guru Regis McKenna: "The line between products and services is fast eroding. What once appeared to be a rigid polarity now has become a hybrid: the servicization of products and the productization of services."[19]

Many companies that once viewed quality in a narrow product or technical definition are expanding their focus to include both the inner and second ring. Kaoru Ishikawa writes:

Broadly interpreted, quality means quality of work, quality of service, quality of information, quality of process, quality of division, quality of people, including workers, engineers, managers, and executives, quality of system, quality of company, quality of objectives, etc. To control quality in its every manifestation is our basic approach.[20]

Particularly vital to the quality of the second ring are organization and management systems, processes, practices, and structure. Sitting in the middle ring between the basic products and the enhanced service ring, these vital components determine what comes outside in to strengthen the basic products and the cost and effectiveness of all support and enhanced service activities that move inside out along the service/quality chain to external customers.

The Third Ring: Enhanced Service

"We can no longer afford to merely satisfy the customer. To win today, you have to delight and astound your customers—with products and services that far exceed their expectations."

Tom Peters

The first two rings deal with things—technology, products, services, systems, processes, structures, and so on. Broadly speaking, we could say this is the high-tech component of service/quality. The third ring deals with people—in futurist John Naisbitt's words, the "high touch" side of service/quality. To push our customer's sense of perceived value well beyond price objections or any competition, we need a healthy balance of service/quality high tech and high touch.

The third ring moves beyond customer satisfaction to *customer delight*. It exceeds expectations. At Stew Leonard's incredibly successful dairy, it is the "wow" factor. As Leonard constantly drills into his people, "We want our customers saying 'wow' at every corner." And those "wowed" customers keep coming back for more—and tell their friends to do the same. W. Edwards Deming wrote: "It will not suffice to have customers that are merely satisfied . . . profit in business comes from repeat customers, customers that boast about your product and service, and that bring friends with them."[21]

The third ring is where your large investments in basic products (first ring) and supporting services (second ring) can multiply your payoff. Third-ring enhancements are usually small investments with huge payoffs. The third ring is where the human touch is added. It is those intangible signs of personal care and commitment that say, "We're pleased to serve you. We want to do whatever we can to make your relationship with us as delightful as possible." In the first two rings, you can objectively point to specifications, selection criteria, equipment, facilities, support systems, and the like to give clear, rational reasons why an organization did or did not live up to your requirements and expectations. The third ring is much more intuitive and irrational. At its best, the third ring is a series of tiny gestures and insignificant signals that make dealing with an organization a rare delight. It is a sense of warmth and attention that makes for true user-friendliness.

The American Society for Quality Control (ASQC) warns: "Unless a customer is completely satisfied—to the point of being positively delighted and willing to brag about the product or service received—there exists great potential for market damage and future trouble for the company." ASQC goes on to report the following study showing reasons companies lose customers:[22]

Die	1%
Moved away	3
Influenced by friends	5
Lured away by the competition	9
Dissatisfied with product	14
Turned away by an attitude of indifference on the part of a company employee	68

Third-ring high touch service is a key to retaining customers and increasing perceived value.

The third ring is made up of thousands of little things that either add up to a high "wow index" or that bit by bit drive customers nuts. Jan Carlzon, president of Scandinavian Airline Systems (SAS), popularized a simple, powerful concept in his turnaround of that company in the early 80s. His key concept, which he calls the "moment of truth," is that any time a customer makes contact with the organization, whether by phone, fax, letter, or in person, some kind of impression is formed. In an organization of a few hundred employees or more, there are thousands of moments of truth daily. Each one is so minor it is almost insignificant. So what if the phone rings a few extra times? And does one little typo really make that much difference?

On its own, each moment of truth is small stuff. The organization is not going to sink or soar on the basis of that one tiny event. But each moment of truth is like a grain of sand placed on the scales of justice. Either that minute, almost weightless grain of sand goes on the side of mediocrity ("So what else is new? You just can't get decent service these days") or it is placed on the side of outstanding performance ("Incredible! What unbelievable service. They are a delight to deal with!"). Over time, the scale will start to tip in one direction or the other. Thus are apathetic, antagonistic, or enthusiastic customers created. And from such tiny beginnings are reputations made.

American Express has become famous for its countless examples of delightful, unexpected third-ring service. These are honored in Travel Related Services' Great Performer Awards. These service feats have included:

- Improvising a travel office in the middle of a downtown street for travelers caught in Mexico City's earthquake.
- Helping hundreds of tourists who were caught in a civil war to find safety by communicating with the outside world despite local curfews and travel prohibitions.
- Housing a group of stranded tourists whose belongings had been stolen while on holiday.

- Working day and night to reissue lost travel documents to a traveler and reunite him with his tour group.[23]

Richard Garfein, director of worldwide market research for American Express's Travel Related Services, says one of the most sensitive issues people have to deal with is how to tell a cardholder who has been called to the phone in an establishment that the credit card purchase cannot be authorized. Garfein reports that customer research shows, "The manner in which the situation is handled actually has a greater effect on satisfaction than whether the customer is approved or declined for the charge."[24]

Who makes your organization's first- and second-ring decisions? Who decides what products, services, and support your organization will offer? Who establishes the organization's systems, processes, practices, and structure? In virtually every organization, the answer is management. Those are big dollar or overhead decisions. The bigger the decisions, the higher up they are made.

What about your moments of truth? Who decides whether to bend a rule to help out a customer? Who decides whether to answer that phone on the second ring? Who spots the error in the invoice and pulls it out for correction? The answer, 9 out of 10 times, is that employees make those third-ring decisions. If you studied a thousand moments of truth in a given day, you probably would find that 900 of them were managed by an employee with no supervisor or manager in sight. Employees live in, control, and get their job satisfaction (or hatred) from the third ring. This is their territory. They own it.

John Sharpe of Four Seasons summarizes the distinctive challenges of the third ring:

> The trouble with service delivery is that it can't be checked in advance, like a piece of crystal, or a luxury car. We can't sample it, package it, systemize it or automate service, though Lord knows a lot of managers try. It's only produced at the moment of consumption, our win-or-lose moment. That service delivery is often performed by the most junior of our employees, often the lowest paid and presumably least motivated.[25]

IT'S A TOTAL EXPERIENCE: CUSTOMERS SEE ONE BIG RING

How likely, or typical, is this scenario in your organization? A customer calls with a question, and the harried receptionist (generally overworked, undertrained, and underpaid) tries to get Joe. His phone rings

Defining the Three Rings of Perceived Value

	First Ring	Second Ring	Third Ring
Focus	Core products and services	Administration and field support	Moments of truth
Objectives	Requirements	Satisfaction	Delight
Customer Concern	Does it do the job?	Are all my needs satisfied?	Are they delightful to do business with?
Key Elements	Technical expertise (high tech)	Systems, processes, practices, and structure (high tech)	People (high touch)
Control	Management and professionals	Management and professionals	Frontline performers
Costs	Large and visible	Huge and hidden	Small and seemingly insignificant

and rings, but no one answers. The call comes back to the switchboard (or the customer calls back), and the receptionist tries Sue. Sue reluctantly listens to the customer and passes the call to Brenda, because that is her area of expertise. Brenda is in a meeting. The customer leaves a message. When Brenda finally does call back (she's extremely busy because so many people rely on her strong abilities), she tells the customer that the organization can't do anything to help him.

Sound familiar? Everyone did his or her job. But the customer was made to dance to that old familiar tune, "The Bureaucratic Shuffle." That is because the organization was organized for its own convenience rather than for the customer's. Looking from the inside out, everyone did his or her job. Looking from the outside in, the customer was greeted with a confusing mishmash of departments and busy people. Service consultant and author Karl Albrecht wrote:

> Sometimes the customer is the only one who sees the big picture (his emphasis) . . . each specialist has his or her arms around one leg of the elephant; only the customer sees the whole elephant. And some parts of the elephant—or the cycle of service—are left largely to chance.[26]

Your customers often experience the three rings exactly opposite to the way those inside your organization look at them. Customers start on the outside and move into your basic product from the third ring. If your third ring is large, their first impressions will be very positive. That gives you great momentum as customers move into your inner rings. Even the odd failure in one of the inner rings will be forgiven if everyone is delighting your customers in the outer ring of enhanced service. Extensive customer research by Toyota Motor Sales USA showed, "Those customers who have a positive sales experience are more likely also to have a positive service experience." Toyota's research showed that when customers rated their sales experience as positive, 84 percent went on to rate their service experience as positive. But of those who had a negative sales experience, only 43 percent rated their subsequent service experience as positive.

Toyota's customer research also illustrates how product, support, and enhanced service all blur together for customers into one total experience—good, bad, or otherwise. When a Toyota customer had a good sales and service experience, the intention to repurchase from that dealer was 85 percent. However, if those same customers have both a bad sales and service experience, their likelihood of repurchasing from that dealer is just 1 percent!! Robert Schrandt, vice president of customer relations, explains how Toyota's research proves that the outer rings profoundly influence the inner product ring:

> The quality of the sales and service experience not only determines where customers will purchase their next vehicle, but whether they'll purchase a Toyota at all. Customers having a good sales and service experience have an intent to repurchase Toyotas of 83 percent versus only 38 percent if those experiences are bad.[27]

A critical part of the journey to higher customer perceived value—as well as cost reduction—is breaking down the "vertical chimneys" between departments and looking at customer, production, and support processes from the inside out as they flow across functional and departmental boundaries. We will turn our attention to this essential service/quality improvement issue during the journey ahead.

SERVICE, QUALITY, AND ORGANIZATION DEVELOPMENT

"The despotism of custom is everywhere the standing hinderance to human achievement."
John Stuart Mill

Even the best tools, techniques, and methods are useless in unskilled hands or the wrong environment. A rapidly growing number of organizations, worshiping at the feet of service or quality gurus, are having trouble implementing their commonsense bromides. Points such as "break down barriers between departments," "drive out fear," "improve your moments of truth," "make your entire organization customer-focused," or "gain management commitment" are right on track. The problem is *how* do you make this happen. Knowing, for example, that the best way to get rich is to make a lot of money points you in the right general direction, but it doesn't leave you too much further ahead.

In the late 1980s Zenger-Miller conducted a major study involving over 800 North American organizations two years or more into the implementation of a service/quality improvement effort. The research showed that some efforts were very successful, some had died, and a large number were stuck or stalling. A number of reasons were uncovered for the majority of ineffective implementations. The bulk of the problems revolved around leadership, skills, strategy, and people issues. In other words, the tactical service/quality methods, tools, and techniques were often strong, but the "how-to's" of long-term cultural change were weak.

We call this spreading problem "hitting the wall." This is the increasingly common phenomenon of heavy investments in customer service inspiration, training, or slogans dying as they crash against the wall of daily reality defining "the way we do things around here." Or it is process improvement techniques that are embraced enthusiastically at first, met with exciting short-term success only to be crushed against the wall of traditional management systems, measurements, and rewards (such as top-down management by objectives or individually focused performance appraisal practices) that contradict the new approaches.

Cultural change is easy to talk about but enormously difficult to achieve. It involves issues not well addressed in most service/quality improvement efforts—pride, trust, change, innovation, and the like. How effectively the improvement effort is managed depends a great deal on the technical, quality improvement, interpersonal, and leadership skills throughout the organization. Developing these skills within the context of the organization's vision and values is one of the key barriers or boosters to implementing the powerful service/quality improvement tools. Those rare organizations that significantly boost their performance are doing so with a balanced approach bringing together the three fields of customer service, quality improvement, and organization development.

Chapter Three

Ricochets, Recoveries, and Bridges

"For want of a nail the shoe was lost; for want of a shoe the horse was lost; and for want of a horse the rider was lost; being overtaken and slain by the enemy, all for the want of care about a horseshoe nail."

Benjamin Franklin,
Poor Richard's Almanac

L ittle errors. A few mistakes here and there. What's the big deal? After all, everybody makes mistakes. It's not a perfect world, right? Doing it right 98, 95, or even 90 percent of the time is the best we can hope for, isn't it? Besides, how much can a 2, 5, or even 10 percent error rate really hurt—especially if we catch the problem before it hits the customer, or at least make a good recovery?

Every organization is full of many different types of errors with varying degrees of severity. Some of the more glaring, like products that break down or services that clearly miss the mark, are easy to spot and so get attention. Consultant and professional speaker Joel Weldon declares, "Elephants don't bite. It's usually the little things—like mosquitos or blackflies—that get you." And so it is with errors; it is the seemingly innocent, common "everyday variety" that does the biggest long-term damage to most organizations. It is not just the error on its own that is so dangerous. It is the insidious tendency of most errors to multiply and spread unnoticed like cancer throughout the organization. And even worse, like some mysterious malignancy, the symptoms of these errors are often misleading or appear innocent even while the often undiagnosed disease is slowly robbing the organization of its vitality and effectiveness.

We call these errors, defects, mistakes, or failures "ricochets" because of the way they rebound throughout the organization like stray bullets. Ricochets come from breakdowns in the processes that produce the team, department, or organization's inner products or services or from the second-ring support efforts. Often the ricochets are caused by a combination of process problems in both rings. Once a ricochet is fired, it is either caught (ideally with a minimum of damage) or it hits somebody inside or outside your organization.

If you are frustrated with internal or external customer service levels being delivered by individual contributors in your organization, start tracking the daily ricochets these people have to deal with. William Davidow and Bro Uttal found that system and process breakdowns were often at the heart of service delivery problems:

> The gurus of customer focus seem to look exclusively at human behavior and to assume that producing customer service means having the right mind-set. Yet in dozens of cases, employees with the "right" mind-set can't deliver good service because they lack training, or have to handle unreliable products, or can't count on getting spare parts quickly. . . . We also see that basically unhealthy companies destroy themselves when they mount service offensives while ignoring underlying breakdowns in operations.[1]

When a ricochet hits a customer, the resulting reduction in that customer's perception of value will be in proportion to the frequency and degree of the ricochet (or the continuing series it is part of) and the tolerance level of the customer. It doesn't take an advanced marketing degree to figure out that preventing ricochets from hitting customers or helping wounded customers recover quickly will reduce dissatisfaction and shrinkage of perceived value.

RECOVERIES

"The surest way to own a small business is to buy a big business and pay only lip service to service/quality."

We have boiled down the many recovery actions into two major categories both named from the customer's point of view: pre- and postimpact.

Post-Impact Recovery

A post-impact recovery is any action an organization takes to do it right the second time; that is, acting on customer complaints and dissatisfaction to reverse the customer's shrinking perception of value. As we saw in Chapter One, the penalties of not doing this are huge. For one thing, dissatisfied customers start looking for alternatives. TARP's research shows that 81 percent of consumers with minor unresolved complaints ($5 or less) will not buy again. TARP also found that more than 54 percent of consumers with major (over $100) unresolved complaints will not buy again.[2] In "The Profitable Art of Service Recovery," Christopher Hart, James Heskett, and W. Earl Sasser, Jr., report: "Considering how much it costs to lose a customer, few recovery efforts are too extreme. At Club Med, one lost customer costs the company at least $2,400 . . . it also has to replace that customer through expensive marketing efforts."[3] And dissatisfied customers turn off 10 to 16 of your potential or existing customers as well. So quick ricochet recovery is vital to balancing your customer acquisition and retention strategies.

The good news is that handling complaints effectively can build customer loyalty. TARP says, "Complaining consumers give business a chance to rectify their problems. Responsive companies are rewarded by the greatest degree of continued brand loyalty."[4] In fact, research shows that when complaints are resolved quickly, *up to 95 percent* of customers will return and buy again. Clearly, then, recovery after your product or service fails is a critical factor in holding your customers. As much as companies are pushing themselves to deliver top service/ quality the first time, customers will be very forgiving if they believe the organization wants to make things right after a service/quality breakdown.

To stem any loss of existing customers and prevent bad word of mouth from spreading, most top service/quality performers have highly responsive complaint resolution systems. A top priority of these organizations is to increase the number of complaints they receive. Given that only a small percent of unhappy customers complain, top-performing organizations work hard to get complaints out in the open where they can quickly be resolved. For example:

- Toyota Motor Sales, U.S.A.'s Customer Assistance Center handles about 1,200 contacts per day on its national toll-free 800 phone number. Complaints are assigned to the dealer by the center's customer relations representative through a direct computer link. The customer is told the dealership customer service representative will call within two working days. The dealership has 15 days to resolve the complaint. Through this system, Toyota's complaint resolution time has fallen from 27 days to 6.[5]

In addition to a formal, systemized process for drawing out and resolving customer complaints, top service/quality also empowers frontline service providers to resolve many customer problems on the spot. At Canada's Red Lobster and Olive Gardens restaurants, food servers are authorized to give customers an instant cash payment for dry cleaning if something should be spilled on the customer's clothing. President Bill Dover explains:

> We used to require customers to mail or bring back a dry cleaning receipt for payment. But how many customers are going to "profit" from the situation by leaving their clothes stained and pocketing the money? Cash payments for the occasional spill not only make the customer feel better, but it empowers the embarrassed food server to take some immediate action to correct the problem.

This degree of empowerment to recover immediately from ricochets caused by the frontline server or from elsewhere in the organization is very rare. Hart, Heskett, and Sasser report:

> Studies we've done show that more than half of all efforts to respond to customer complaints actually reinforce negative reactions to service. The surest way to recover from service mishaps is for workers on the front line to identify and solve the customer's problem. Doing so requires decision making and rule breaking—exactly what employees have been conditioned against . . . even if they'd like to help the customer, they are frustrated by the fact that they are not allowed to do it. Worse yet, they don't know how.[6]

Pre-impact Recovery

A pre-impact recovery is any action the organization takes to prevent a ricochet from hitting customers. As effective as a good post-impact recovery strategy can be in retaining customers, pre-impact recoveries that reduce the number of ricochets getting through to customers are even more effective. Dinah Nemeroff, corporate director of customer affairs at Citicorp/Citibank, explains how research confirmed the importance of catching ricochets: "Even with first-rate customer service, customers do not 'fully recover' from service problems. Citibank research shows that customers who've had problems resolved to their satisfaction are, nevertheless, on average 20 percent less satisfied than problem-free customers." Zeithaml, Parasuraman, and Berry's study of this issue supports the importance of not letting ricochets hit customers: "The most important thing a service company can do is *be reliable* (their emphasis)—that is, to perform the service dependably and accurately . . . do it right the first time."[7] From the research at Citicorp/Citibank, Nemeroff concludes, "Every business should aim to close its customer complaint department! Problem prevention, not problem resolution, is a superordinate service-quality objective."[8]

While pre-impact ricochet recovery is more effective than post-impact recovery, it comes at a *very high* cost to the organization. Those costs are both in fairly tangible and measurable dollars as well as intangible wear and tear on individual contributors and frontline performance teams. Frequently, pre- or post-impact recoveries are heroic. That is, they require extra, sometimes superordinary, efforts to catch or make up to customers for problems created by ricochets. A steady routine of heroic recoveries is a prescription for stress and burnout. And constant first- and second-ring ricochet-catching by frontline performers reduces the time and energy available for third-ring enhanced service.

It is about here that we see the customer service and quality roads either diverge or converge. Traditional service-focused approaches as found in the retail or hospitality industry concentrate on pre- and post-recovery strategies. The focus is on developing systems and motivating frontline service deliverers to catch ricochets or recover quickly from them.

While recoveries are vital, customer satisfaction, cost-effectiveness, productivity, and employee morale need a strategy that goes much further. Rather than ricochet recovery, top service/quality performers put much more attention on ricochet prevention. This is where the quality field has a great deal to contribute. Curt Reimann, associate director of the National Institute of Standards and Technology and director of the Baldrige program, writes:

> The excellent companies use all avenues to put together services that minimize the cost of a product and are not merely intended to do a customer good when you've done him bad. Many companies need to put a major emphasis on monitoring services in such a way that they go to the root causes of problems in order to eliminate customer dissatisfaction.[9]

THE COST OF QUALITY

"When the foundation of a pyramid erodes, the top can be supported on nothing but money."

Laurence J. Peter, *author of* The Peter Principle

What percentage of your revenues are wasted as a result of less than perfect service/quality? Is it 5, 10, 15, maybe 20 percent? In a 1987 Gallup poll commissioned by the American Society for Quality Control, more than 70 percent of executives responding believed their cost of poor quality was less than 10 percent. Twenty-seven percent admitted they had no idea what those costs were.

With such misguided notions circulating, it is no wonder service/ quality is so bad in so many organizations. From the viewpoint of a company that has a good handle on its costs of low service/quality, David Kearns, chairman of Xerox Corporation, comments, "The (ASQC) survey shows that many people still do not understand the connection between cost and quality. You will not change the culture with that kind of data or those kinds of perceptions."[10]

An estimate of low service/quality costing organizations 10 percent of their revenues is far too low! The American Society for Quality Control has been studying these costs for years. It consistently finds that the cost of quality (COQ) for North American organizations can run as high as *40 percent* of revenues.[11]

Bad Costs + Good Costs = Total Cost of Quality

"It costs a lot to build bad products (or deliver bad service)."

Norman R. Augustine,
author of Augustine's Laws *and CEO of Martin Marietta*

Many definitions have been used for the costs of providing high enough service/quality to internal or external customers to keep a team, department, or entire organization in the game. The American Society for Quality Control breaks total cost of quality into four categories: (1) prevention—money spent to make sure things are done right; (2) appraisal—money spent on inspection and checking to detect things that were done wrong; (3) internal failure—money spent correcting errors or redoing activities that were not done right the first time; (4) external failure—money lost because customers were dissatisfied with the service (or product) they received.[12] Except for some argument about where "appraisal" belongs, the above four quality costs can simply be classified as good or bad. You may hear words like *compliance* and *conformance* used to describe good COQ and *noncompliance* or *nonconformance* used to describe bad COQ.

Of the two types of costs of quality, many service/quality experts estimate bad COQ is about two thirds of total COQ in a typical North American organization. Joseph Juran writes:

> We define cost of poor quality (bad COQ) as those costs that would disappear if our products and processes were perfect. Those costs are huge. As of the 1980s, about a third of the work in the United States economy consisted of redoing prior work because products and processes were not perfect.[13]

Retired Westinghouse executive Don Povejsil reflects on his work to improve service/quality: "The things that take the most time are the

Examples of Good and Bad Cost of Quality

Bad COQ	Good COQ
Rework	Inspection and testing (could also be
Redesign	bad COQ)
Scrap	Training
Warranty costs	Market research
Back orders	Standardizing procedures
Absenteeism	Preventive maintenance
Staff turnover	Quality and process audits
Safety and health costs	Clarifying customer expectations
Excess receivables	Supplier management programs
Excess inventory	Reward and recognition programs
Excess overtime	System and process redesign
Excess managerial and professional	Hiring and orienting programs
staff	Competitive and key process
Excess marketing costs	benchmarking
Excess services or product features	Strategic quality planning
Heroic recoveries	Measurement and feedback systems
Lawsuits	
Lost customers and market share	

things that go wrong. By eliminating the things that go wrong, you can vastly shrink the time it takes to order, produce, and deliver."[14]

David Blumenthal, M.D., is a senior vice president of Boston's Brigham and Women's Hospital and Glenn Laffel, M.D., is the hospital's director of quality assurance planning. Both participated in the National Demonstration Project on Quality Improvement in Health Care hosted by the Harvard Community Health Plan to see if "industrial" service/ quality concepts applied to medicine. The results were so encouraging the project has contributed to a North American-wide service/quality revolution in health care. Writing in the *Journal of the American Medical Association,* Blumenthal and Laffel report:

> We repeat tests because they are not performed correctly the first time. We rewrite requisitions because they are lost or filled out incorrectly. We look for lost charts and reschedule appointments. Because the time required for such activities reduces that available for direct patient care, there is a strong rationale to improve the execution of such processes.[15]

Here are examples of the costs of poor quality, or bad COQ:

- Doug Pierce, president of the insurance company Colonial Penn, asked a team member, who happened to mention the company issued many duplicate policies, how many she thought were issued. When the response was "a lot," Pierce asked for analysis of the problem. In *Deming Management at Work*, Mary Walton reports: "A lot turned out to be a very, very big number, something like 16,500 copies a year at about $10 apiece."[16]

- The Technical Assistance Research Program (TARP) worked with a number of American gas utilities to determine the actual dollar costs of low service/quality. In 1981 dollars, TARP found it cost utilities from $20 to $300 *each time* a customer complained to an officer, asked for an investigation of a high bill, requested a meter check or a reread of a meter, or delayed payment because of a complaint. TARP concluded, "Poor service results in substantial extra explicit costs. . . . These result in extra head count. . . . Many service calls are preventable." TARP found that one utility handled 2,000 calls a month from customers trying to read their confusing bill format. These calls alone cost $72,000 per year. In another gas company, 50 percent of all supervisors' time was spent talking to customers whom the representative couldn't satisfy.[17]

- David Garvin reports that General Electric found "error costs rise by an order of magnitude each time a product or component moves a step further along the production chain. An error that costs $.003 if found at the supplier level costs $300—100,000 times more—if left undiscovered until the product is in the field."[18]

Downsizing and Cost Reduction

"Nothing is so useless as doing efficiently that which should not be done at all."

Peter Drucker

Many downsizing efforts are not only necessary but also long overdue. If they are handled properly, the organization emerges leaner, smarter, and faster. But all too often, downsizing is handled with all the finesse of a butcher wielding a chain saw. When that happens, the effect can be devastating. Ill-conceived across-the-board cuts (such as reducing the work force by 10 percent) can severely damage service/quality levels. They reduce service levels by crushing the spirit of the frontline employees whose voluntary efforts are the *only* means by which high service is delivered to customers. After all, management is not out there providing the lion's share of customer service.

Those who advocate traditional cost-containment efforts also rarely question the current methods used to produce and deliver products or services. Instead, they whip employees to speed up the inefficient processes and then tie their hands by reducing the resources available to support their efforts. Of course, these managers are then very puzzled when employees not only don't appreciate the heroic efforts being made but also are even bitter about them. This bitterness leads to a widening of the we/they gap between management and employees—and efficiency plummets further.

"Cost control and quality control are two sides of the same coin," contends Kaoru Ishikawa. "To engage in effective cost control, effective quality control must be implemented."[19] A major study of this burning issue, conducted by *Fortune* reporter Ron Henkoff, came to the same conclusion when looking at how America's most effective companies kept their costs under control:

> Clearly, a new approach is needed. Downsizing has become an opiate for many companies. Administered in repeated doses, it can hurt quality, alienate customers, and actually cut productivity growth . . . learning from their mistakes, managers at some companies have begun to adopt a new approach to downsizing for the 90s—cut the workload, not just the work force.

Henkoff quotes William Fowble, general manager of photographic products at Kodak: "Costs exist for a reason. If you don't take the reasons away, the costs will return." The challenge to continuous quality improvement and cost reduction is permanently changing what and how work is done in your organization. Adds Gary Ames, CEO of US West Communications: "At some point in your dieting process you come to the realization that if you really are going to keep the weight off you have to change your habits."[20]

Investing in the Good to Drive Out the Bad

"The more bureaucratic an organization becomes the more useless work displaces useful work."

The law of bureaucratic displacement

Low levels of service/quality often lead companies into a negative downward spiral. Many crash. The fatal spin is set in motion by three powerful and destructive forces. These are the dark side of the same forces that work so effectively to boost high-service/quality performers out of sight financially. First, poor-service/quality companies must spend ever greater amounts to replace the customers who are charging out the back door vowing never to return. These sales and marketing activities must also counter the negative word-of-mouth advertising that spreads the horror stories of just how bad (or mediocre) the experience of dealing with that company really is.

Second, low-service/quality providers have higher costs because they are not doing it right the first time. Their production and support processes are out of control. This situation exists despite the illusion of tight management by bottom-line slash-and-burn managers who have boldly "trimmed the fat," "tightened their belts," and otherwise brutalized the organization to cut operating costs. In his classic study of the room air-conditioner manufacturing industry, David Garvin found, "When quality declined, total quality costs rose." He went on to document that the total quality control methods used by the Japanese manufacturers resulted in

> defect and field failure rates between 17 and 67 times lower than their U.S. competitors . . . averaged total costs of quality that were 1.3 percent of sales. The best American plants averaged rework, scrap, and warranty costs that alone were 2.8 percent of sales. At the U.S. plants with the poorest quality, these costs exceeded 5.8 percent of sales.[21]

Third, low-service/quality providers must lower their prices to attract business, especially if the company has failed to carve out a market niche and is competing in a commodity market with "me-too" look-alike products or services.

So as we can see, these companies suffer the worst of all worlds. Their sales and marketing costs are high; they are inefficient with low productivity levels; their prices are low and revenues are dropping. They are well on their way to decline and death. It is just a question of how long and how agonizing the process will be.

But there is hope. A growing number of companies are finding that by investing heavily in well-planned, good COQ efforts, bad COQ can be reduced dramatically. The result is a sharp reduction in total cost of quality and an increase in customer satisfaction and employee morale. For example, Solid State Circuits dropped its total COQ from 37 percent to 17 percent by increasing its investment in good COQ to drive out the bad COQ.[22]

Investing in good COQ to reduce bad COQ is much like investments in proven new technology that moves organizations to new levels of effectiveness. Joseph Juran gives an example of the economics found in quality improvement. To reduce by one third over five years a total COQ of $300 million (on sales of $1 billion), a company would typically invest about $15 million. He observes, "In contrast, if the company set out to accomplish an equivalent improvement in profit by growth in sales, the investment needed would be over 10 times as high . . . the return on investment in quality improvement is among the highest available to managers."[23]

The bad news is quality is not free, it requires *huge* investments— particularly of everyone's time. But the good news is that the returns on those investments are routinely measured in three and four digits.

BRIDGES: FIXING PROCESSES, NOT PROBLEMS

"At some point in the life cycle of virtually every organization, its ability to succeed in spite of itself runs out."

Richard Brien

A bridge is a systematic investigation into the root cause of a ricochet to determine how processes or systems can be improved to prevent future ricochets. This often leads to confronting the lack of standardization of many work processes. We consistently find that most root causes of ricochets are because no standard exists or it is not being followed. The lack of consistency in passing work from one group to another or not following the same production, support, or delivery methods leads to variation. These variations create haphazard conditions that inevitably produce ricochets.

Consultants Harold Sirkin and George Stalk, Jr., wrote a *Harvard Business Review* article called "Fix the Process, Not the Problem" that presented a useful sequence of steps to building a series of ever more effective bridges. Sirkin and Stalk's model outlines a four-stage approach to service/quality improvement: (1) fix-as-fail—problem arises and is fixed; (2) prevention—solution leads to preventive action; (3) root causes—fewer problems create time to find underlying causes; (4) anticipation—systems changes create time to find improvements. Like a play within a play, the authors outline another type of bridge that is needed to progress up their process improvement process, "developing learning loops to feed information rapidly from the point where problems can be discovered to the people who can keep them from recurring." According to Sirkin and Stalk, an organization that has made it to the root-cause and anticipation levels "will typically spend 80 percent of its time on root-cause and anticipatory problem-solving loops. In contrast, a lesser performer is likely to spend 90 percent of its effort in the fix-as-fail loop."[24] That, as we have seen, is extremely expensive and time-consuming.

CONTINUOUS IMPROVEMENT: THE ENDLESS JOURNEY

Red Queen said, "It will take all the running you can do to stay in place. If you want to go somewhere else, you will have to run twice as fast."

Through the Looking Glass

The three rings are dynamic. Expectations gravitate inwardly quite rapidly. What was once an unexpected delight soon becomes a second-ring expectation. What was once a support to the basic product or service, soon becomes a minimum requirement. And those inner-ring minimum standards and requirements keep rising. John Sharpe of Four Seasons explains, "Standards are moving targets. Quality never stands still. The new high-tech service offered to business travelers today will be taken for granted tomorrow."[25] Walter Raab, chairman of AMP Incorporated, agrees: "Our products are more complex, and customer expectations are higher than ever before. In this environment, you can't survive by staying in place. You've got to get better."[26] Kaoru Ishikawa tells us that because basic product or service standards are never perfect, and customer support requirements change, "Standards that were adequate when they were first established, quickly become obsolete." He believes this state of constant change is healthy and to be expected in a vital, growing organization. "If standards and regulations are not revised in six months, it is proof that no one is seriously using them."[27]

Standards often trap organizations because they are too low. A major lesson emerging from the service/quality revolution is that the only standard is zero defects. Any measure, acceptable quality level, or error rate less than 100 percent is planning for mistakes. Physicians David Blumenthal and Glenn Laffel write: "The approach implicitly assumes that some rate of poor outcomes is acceptable . . . should standards be set too low, quality assurance programs may breed complacency and thus contribute to poor quality."[28]

The flip side of setting standards of perfection is that they can be so high they are uneconomical to reach. And not having unlimited resources, companies shooting for 100 percent on one standard will divert resources from improving in other areas. We can't do it all at once. This further underscores the need for understanding and continually tracking changing customer requirements and support expectations so well that resources can be leveraged to gain maximum customer-perceived value. And that requires careful preparation and planning. You do not have enough time or resources to wander down every side street and side road you come to. You need to map out and stick to the route that will take you ever closer to your destination.

The problem with many standards is they are based on using yesterday's inefficient practices. Shooting for 100 percent conformance to a standard or expectation is prohibitively expensive if you are using a defective process or system. Throwing more money or resources into this kind of situation will drive quality down and costs up. This realization has led many top service/quality providers to adopt a philosophy of continual improvement. One of Deming's 14 points for organizational transformation is "Improve constantly and forever the system of production and service, to improve quality and productivity, and thus constantly decrease costs."[29]

Centuries ago, the Greek poet Hesiod said, "If you add a little to a little and do this often, soon it will become great." North American managers readily embrace sweeping innovation as a strategy for dealing with change and making our organizations more effective. Many managers will "swing for the fences" in an attempt to develop a "home run" product, deal, organizational structure, or new technology. We have a lot more difficulty maintaining interest and momentum in tedious, unglamorous, little daily improvements.

Yet the evidence shows overwhelmingly that Hesiod's observation is still as relevant today as it was in the eighth century b.c. Ted Levitt writes:

> Trying routinely to get better one step at a time is a far better way to get better than shooting constantly for the moon . . . sustained success is largely a matter of focusing regularly on the right things and making a lot of uncelebrated little improvements every day. Getting better and better one step at a time adds up.[30]

In his cover story titled "Why Toyota Keeps Getting Better and Better and Better," *Fortune* writer Alex Taylor III concludes "rapid inch-up" was at the root of Toyota's service/quality success: "While many other companies strive for dramatic breakthroughs, Toyota keeps doing lots of little things better and better."[31]

Embracing and living a philosophy of continuous improvement is a major change for many North American managers raised on an almost sacred belief in the quick fix. *Continual improvement only comes from continually learning organizations*. Richard Schonberger's study of service/quality approaches used around the world puts the issue into a bigger perspective:

> We may think of the world-class company as progressing through phases; in the 1970s, alarm, and in the 1980s, discovery, learning, and here-and-there flurries of action. Discoveries continue, and the learning never ends, since one of the key discoveries is the power of continuous learning.[32]

Michael Beer, Russell Eisenstat, and Bert Spector, organizational behavior and management professors, concur, "Create an asset that did not exist before—a learning organization capable of adapting to a changing competitive environment. The organization has to know how to continually monitor its behavior—in effect, to learn how to learn."[33]

The greatest enemy of continuous improvement is the complacency and arrogance bred by success and being at the top of the heap. History is rife with examples of nations and institutions that succumbed to this disease. Harvard Business School's Len Schlesinger applied the same criteria to the same companies in 1991 as Tom Peters and Bob Waterman used in their landmark book *In Search of Excellence*. He found that only 10 of the original 43 could still be called "excellent" today.[34] Here are perspectives on continuous improvement from service/quality award winners:

> *"The further you go into the quality improvement process, the more you realize you'll never get there. If you think you've arrived, you're going downhill."*
>
> Roger Milliken[35]

> *"One thing our company is not is a company that believes it has achieved superior quality in its products and services."*
>
> David Kearns, CEO, Xerox[36]

> *"You have to have continuous improvement. If you stand still, no matter how good you are today, you'll still get run over by the crowd that once was behind you but is doing better."*
>
> Paul Vita, Wallace Co, Inc.[37]

> *"Extensive interviews with Toyota executives in the U.S. and Japan demonstrate the company's dedication to continuous improvement. What is often mistaken for excessive modesty is, in fact, an expression of permanent dissatisfaction—even with exemplary performance."*
>
> Alex Taylor III, Fortune[38]

> *"Through quality, we are developing the attitude: 'If it ain't broke, fix it anyway.'"*
>
> Lloyd Smith, *division manager, Texaco Bakersfield Producing Division*

Continuous learning is an issue we will return to a number of times in the pages ahead. Service/quality improvement will not happen without massive learning, feedback, readjustment, relearning, and continuous improvement and change. And you must take it personally. Peter Senge, director of the Systems Thinking and Organizational Learning Program at MIT's Sloan School of Management, says, "Organizations learn only through individuals who learn. Individual learning does not guarantee organizational learning. But without it no organizational learning occurs."[39] Continuous learning is contagious. Are you a carrier?

Chapter Four

Dysfunctional Assumptions

"When all is said and done, a lot more is said than done."

Lou Holtz,
Notre Dame football coach

In another of *Fortune*'s growing series of service/quality wake-up calls to managers, writer Joel Dreyfuss reports, "Reading about the principles of quality and hiring an expert to explain them is easy. The hard part is making them work."[1] Although the payoffs for service quality improvement are immense and the basic concepts and goals are simple, turning well-intentioned rhetoric into reality is proving to be very difficult.

- According to one study, 70 percent of all total quality management initiatives fail.[2]

- The Strategic Planning Institute has found "attaining better service quality is difficult: only 1/10th of PIMS businesses beginning with equivalent or worse service quality were able to improve to the point where their service quality was perceived as better than the competition."[3]

- A 1990 Gallup survey sponsored by the American Society for Quality Control cited "a lack of participation in quality programs and serious disillusionment with the rate of improvement."[4]

- Zeithaml, Parasuraman, and Berry write: "Clearly many companies are still struggling to get out of first gear on the service quality journey. The case for improving service is strong, yet outstanding service quality is more the exception than the rule."[5]

- *Total Quality* newsletter states: "Often, after years of trying, after years of 'proclaiming, professing, and publicizing' their commitment to total quality management, many companies still fail."[6]

VALUES AND BELIEFS

Edgar Schein of MIT defines organizational culture in three layers. The surface layer is "artifacts"—the visible rites and rituals of daily organizational activities and events. Artifacts are based on the second layer of values—how the organization explains or decides what is good or bad about the visible artifact activities; that is, which of the activities at the artifact level the organization does, and does not, value. The third level provides the foundation for the organization's values and artifacts. This very deep, often unspoken and invisible base is made up of the underlying assumptions. "These are the views that most companies haven't attempted to examine, mostly because they're so ingrained and so much a part of everyday organizational life as to defy objective analysis," according to *Total Quality* newsletter's report on faulty business assumptions.[7]

In most of the small number of successful and sustained service/quality improvement efforts, senior executives spent considerable time defining the kind of culture they wanted to build, clarifying their shared values, and examining their deep, usually unconscious underlying assumptions, thus eliminating what motivational speaker Zig Ziglar calls "stinkin' thinkin'." This effort often helps an executive team get at the deeper issues underlying the common failure of executives, managers, and supervisors to "walk the talk." All too often, executives talk quality while rewarding volume; talk service while personally avoiding customer contact; talk teamwork while behaving like Lone Rangers; talk about "people, our most important asset," and then kick them around or kick them out; talk about the importance of improved communications and then retreat to their offices and boardrooms; or talk about the need for human resource development and then cut the training budget. The deeper reasons for these visible discrepancies are to be found in a series of dysfunctional—and deadly—assumptions.

"QUALITY HOSTILE" ASSUMPTIONS

"To be ignorant of one's ignorance is the malady of the ignorant."
                              Amos Bronson Alcott, *American teacher and philosopher*

Behavioral scientist David Nadler and his colleagues at the New York-based Delta Consulting Group have guided numerous Fortune 500 companies along the continuous service/quality improvement journey. Nadler contends many companies try to alter behavior at the artifacts and values level, but they don't examine and change their basic assumptions. As a result, their service/quality achievements are cosmetic at best, and often short-lived. He finds that many of those basic assumptions are "quality hostile" and clash directly with the assumptions underlying total quality management. "In fact, they may be mutually exclusive," Nadler says.

David Nadler identified 15 of the most common "quality-hostile" assumptions that unwittingly doom service/quality improvement efforts. As you read through his list and the items we have added, complete each one by asking yourself: "Would my management team, employees, or customers say I acted as if I held this erroneous assumption?" But don't guess—ask. Start your personal journey of continuous improvement by getting feedback on what values seem to be reflected in your actions, then trace these back to your underlying assumptions. Muster your leadership courage, swallow your managerial pride, and *go ask them*.

1. We're smarter than our customers—we know what they need.

2. Quality is not a major factor in customer decisions—they usually can't tell the difference.

3. Our primary and overriding purpose is to make money—to produce near-term shareholder return.

4. Our key audience is the financial markets—especially analysts.

5. The primary way to influence performance is through portfolio management and creative accounting.

6. It costs more to provide a high-quality product or service, and we won't recover the added cost.

7. We will never be able to manufacture competitively at the low end.

8. Managers are paid to make the decisions—workers are paid *to do*, not think.

9. Strategic success results from companies making large onetime innovative leaps, rather than from continuous improvement.

10. Senior management's job is strategy, not implementation.

11. The key disciplines from which to draw senior management are finance and marketing.

12. To err is human—perfection is not an attainable or realistic goal.

13. Quality improvement can be delegated—it is something the top can tell the middle to do to the bottom.

14. There is not much to learn from dwelling on mistakes, so celebrate successes and shun failure.

15. If it ain't broke, don't fix it.[8]

In our executive retreats, academies, and workshops, we often explore with participants how management's unconscious, deadly assumptions are at the root of the high failure (or stunted growth) rate of most service/quality improvement efforts. Those discussions have uncovered a number of additional assumptions that, often unknowingly, shape management's values base and create contradictory service/quality activities and behaviors:

- Price is more important than quality in buying decisions.
- Standardized processes inhibit individuality and creativity.
- Heroic recoveries are exciting—but fixing processes so recoveries aren't necessary is boring, mundane work.
- Investments in employees, such as training, will have little impact on corporate performance.
- Employees don't care about the organization.
- There must be "one right formula" for improvement. We must adopt a single guru and reject the others.
- An organization can succeed without the commitment and support of employees.

CORE DYSFUNCTIONAL ASSUMPTIONS

Many of the dysfunctional assumptions listed can be traced back to, or are variations of, the following four:

1. Service/quality improvement can be delegated.

The president of a rapidly growing high-tech company asked us to help fine-tune its service delivery. He was quite convincing when he explained his was truly a customer-oriented company. "After all," he said, "we're in the service industry." He thought customer service was well ingrained throughout his operation. But he agreed to "indulge" us as we studied the organization to see if that was true.

What we found was unfortunately typical of those executives who assume service/quality can be ordered up like breakfast at the Four Seasons. The company featured service in its marketing with convincing, clever ads. It had set up a customer service department and provided extensive technical and "customer handling" training. When we checked the operational systems and processes we found that a customer orientation was conspicuous in the planning and budgeting, hiring, promoting, compensation, and performance evaluation. But it was conspicuous by its absence. It was nowhere to be found.

Who's Responsible For Your Organization's Service/ Quality?

The service/quality revolution has ushered in a major shift from quality inspection and quality assurance to quality management. North American managers in a number of industries such as manufacturing and health care realize quality can't be inspected in. Rather, customer-focused quality must be designed in from the beginning and refined with each step in the production or delivery process. This approach means many organizations have moved responsibility for quality from the "quality Gestapo" (inspectors) to the work teams and managers who are producing, delivering, or supporting the organization's basic products and services. A total quality management specialist, Professor Shoji Shiba, captures the new philosophy found in many of these organizations: "Quality improvement must be the job of every person; it is not the job of a quality specialist."[9]

While a growing number of companies, at their operational level, are now moving their inner-ring technical quality from quality inspection to quality management, a large number of organizations have yet to do so in their support systems and processes. Too often, responsibility for the quality of human resource management rests with the human resource department; the usefulness of the information system belongs to the information systems department; accounting is responsible for the relevance of that system; and customer satisfaction is the purview of sales, marketing, or customer service. This is not to say these departments shouldn't continue to contain the expertise in these areas and provide leadership and guidance to the organization. However, these support functions can't inspect in or add on quality to these systems and practices any more than quality inspectors can in the production or delivery of the basic product. The ultimate quality of many support systems and processes must be designed in from the beginning and refined with each step in the support process.

Customer service departments are a good example of how many organizations have tried to delegate service/quality improvement. A customer service department, like a quality control department, may serve a useful purpose. But it is *not responsible* for the organization's service/quality levels. In *Service America!*, Karl Albrecht and Ron Zemke pose a critical question: "If you have a customer service department, what's the rest of the organization doing?"[10] In a later book, *The Service Advantage*, Karl Albrecht and Lawrence Bradford go even further:

> When you have a customer service department it may not be a good sign . . . a mixed message can go out through the company that if there are any problems with customers, send them on to the customer service department. That effectively relieves everyone but the customer service representatives of any responsibility for managing moments of truth and, ultimately, the quality of service.[11]

A similar argument can be made for managers' tendency to delegate human resource problems (that their own systems and practices created) to the human resource department.

Your organization exists only to provide products or services to customers. Period. And your customers' satisfaction as well as your organization's cost-effectiveness and financial performance depend on the quality of your production and support operations. So *everything* that goes on in your organization must be a subset of this overarching strategy. If it is not—and a huge number of activities aren't—then those activities are not adding value to the organization. So service/quality improvement and management can't be separated. They are one and the same thing. This puts continual service/quality improvement at the top of every executive and manager's priority list.

What Are Your Actions Signaling?

"If senior managers are to assume the mantle of service leadership, they best be prepared to work at it. Senior managers cannot delegate responsibility for service-quality improvement; they themselves must lead the charge or nothing will happen."

Valarie A. Zeithaml, A. Parasuraman, and
Leonard L. Berry, *Delivering Quality Service*

There is no stronger message managers can send about their true priorities than their daily actions. When executives play the service/quality tune but dance to something else, their behavior drowns out the music. In *The Service Edge*, Ron Zemke and Dick Schaaf paint an all-too-familiar scene:

> American boardrooms are full of senior managers who are all for signing service proclamations and making bold speeches reminding "those people down in the trenches" how important customers are,

but can't seem to find the time to actually "work" the problem of improving service.[12]

Where are senior executives spending their time? Are they busy putting out fires because things weren't done right the first time? Are they cost cutting the organization's pathway to long-term profitability? Are they manipulating assets to increase book value? Are they restructuring the organization? Are they looking for ways to increase market share and grow revenues?

If you are a senior executive or manager spending most of your time in those areas, then you do not believe in service/quality, despite what you may say to the contrary. As we saw in Chapters One and Three, there is no better way to cut costs and increase revenues than through service/quality improvement. If you truly believe in service/quality improvement, it would be your top priority. And you would then make it the top priority of your management team. As Bro Uttal writes in *Fortune*: "The most important factor in outstanding customer service sits in the corner office. When the CEO eats, sleeps, and breathes service, the rest of the troops catch the spirit pretty quick."[13] What would your "troops" say you eat, sleep, and breathe? Would your actions leave no room for doubt that you truly do assume service/quality improvement and management are the same thing and can't be delegated?

2. We know what our customers need.

"We did not always listen to what the customer had to say before telling him what he wanted."

John F. McDonnell, *chairman and CEO, McDonnell Douglas*[14]

No executive would ever stand up and say, "We know what our customers need." Instead, executives confidently mouth variations of "find out what your customers want and give it to them." But behavior often conveys an underlying contempt for customers. The *words* say, "We believe in uncovering our customers' requirements or support expectations and meeting or exceeding those." The *actions* say, "I've been in this business for 35 years; I know our customers' needs better than they do." Ron Zemke's extensive service consulting experience has put him face to face with the continual evidence of this deadly assumption. He and Dick Schaaf write:

One of the greatest temptations is to believe that, because of years of experience in "the business" . . . we know what the customer wants and needs even better than the customer does. Time and again, we find this is just not the case. Our logic is not necessarily the customers' logic, nor our perceptions of quality and value the same as theirs.[15]

Karl Albrecht and Lawrence Bradford add, "One of the lessons to be learned about service is that the longer a business has been in existence, the more likely it is that it has lost sight of what is important to customers."[16]

The gap separating mediocre and outstanding service/quality performers is often widest in the amount and frequency of customer listening. From his broad vantage point in directing the Baldrige program, Curt Reimann reports, "The best companies are close to their customers. The weaker companies are not using all their listening posts well. They have a limited sense of specific features that are important to customers and a limited sense of the weights of those features."[17] Lacking an outside-in definition of service/quality, most companies build products or deliver services according to industry standards, competitive "me-too" standards, "this is our edge and we'll bring customers around by hard marketing or selling," "if I were a customer, this is what I would want," the organization has heavy investments in a particular product or service process, "we don't know how to do anything else," or "we have always done it this way." Using anything other than customer-perceived value to define service/quality can lead to highly efficient services or productive products that miss the mark—efficient ineffectiveness. W. Edwards Deming warns:

> It is possible and in fact fairly easy for an organization to go downhill and out of business making the wrong product or offering the wrong type of service, even though everyone in the organization performs with devotion, employing statistical methods and every other aid that can boost efficiency.[18]

One of the consequences of not truly listening to customers' needs is inconsistent levels of service/quality across the organization. All employees, service/quality teams, and managers provide the kind of performance they think their internal or external customer needs (assuming the care and commitment to do so is there, another dangerous assumption). So when customer concerns or problems arise, the response depends on how seriously that individual or team views the problem, *from its own perspective*. Because the customer's true needs are not understood or appreciated, they are often minimized.

One sure sign of an organization that is not listening to its customers is the "vertical chimneys" separating functions, departments, and groups. This typifies an organization that is structured from the inside out. The service/quality chain pulling customer needs across the organization is weak or nonexistent. Instead, departments throw what they think their internal or the external customers need down that group's "chimney." Richard Schonberger writes:

Companies get sidetracked by their own functions and factions. The functions problem refers to maintaining a functional work life well away from the customer: the chefs staying in the kitchen and avoiding contact with patrons, buyers shut in the purchasing department and not visiting users or supplier companies, managers hiding out in their offices and not out looking for ways to help press shop supervisors who do not want to see a press pulled out and moved into a cell, and so forth.[19]

In a "we're the experts" environment, customer perceptions are often discounted or ignored. When trying to refocus people on customers, Xerox found that marketing's reports to engineering on the frequency of paper jams were not taken seriously. The engineering department argued the customers were wrong. The engineer who originally designed that particular photocopy machine defended the machine's maintenance rating "as good as or better than all the competition out there, and I can't help it if the customer doesn't like it."[20]

Serving the Servers

A major contributor to the poor internal and external customer listening, and the resulting "functional chimneys," is management's failure to listen to the needs of work teams and individual contributors. "If you don't listen well, you can't involve people," says Newt Hardie, Milliken's vice president of quality. "Involvement means winning the hearts and minds of your associates. If you don't listen, they know you think they're unimportant."[21] Personnel consultants at the Hay Group found that of the million workers they have surveyed, only 34 percent say their organization listens to their complaints.[22] How can a team member eagerly seek to understand the needs of his or her internal or external customer if that team member's own needs are not looked after? In *Managing to Keep the Customer*, Robert Desatnick, former McDonald's vice president of human resources, writes, "If management solves employee problems, employees solve customers' problems."[23]

One litmus test of how well management is listening to, and serving, employees is the user-friendliness of the organization's technology and administrative systems. In far too many cases, *management-driven* systems and technology hinder more than help the delivery of high service/quality. It is often a wonder that performance isn't worse when you consider the defective tools and interference many employees have to work with. Service/quality is delivered in spite of, not because of, systems and technology. The president of a major aircraft manufacturer puts the problem into perspective: "In a lot of ways, management has handcuffed and shackled our people, then told them to hop out there and build better products or deliver improved service. And then we beat them up when they fail to overcome the restraints we've put on them.''

Far too often, the organization's technology and especially its administrative systems are designed either for management's convenience or because in all management's benevolent wisdom, it knows what the front line needs. In fact, top managers are mind readers—they don't even have to ask their employees! So, if employees think the systems or technology are hindering service/quality improvement, then they obviously have an attitude or motivational problem or they don't know how to use the stuff properly. So let's give them a good stiff dose of training or motivation injections so they will use *management's* systems and technology!

Examine your *actions*. How well do you listen to your internal and external customers?

3. Our work force creates most of our service/quality problems.

''The supposition is prevalent the world over that there would be no problems in production or in service if only our production workers would do their jobs in the way they were taught. Pleasant dreams. The workers are handicapped by the system, and the system belongs to management.''

W. Edwards Deming, *Out of the Crisis*[24]

How reasonable would it be to hold a shipping-dock worker responsible for the quality of the goods in the boxes he or she is shipping? Not only would that be unfair, it also would be bad management. A good manager would argue, quite rightly, that the manufacturing process should be traced to find the ultimate source of the defects.

Then how reasonable is it to hold the final deliverer responsible for the quality of the products or services he or she is delivering? The person on the front serving line is a symptom carrier, not the source of the problem. While he or she may be contributing to low service delivery, blaming him or her is also not only unfair but unproductive. Karl Albrecht contends, ''Systems are often the enemies of service.'' He explains, ''Many of the problems of poor or mediocre service originate in systems, procedures, policies, rules and regulations, and organizational craziness.''[25] Even if the ricochet did originate with the service deliverer, who hires, trains, rewards, coaches, and measures that person? If the same pattern of ricochets shows up across a number of deliverers, is it really because of ''declining work ethic'' or because ''you just can't get good help these days''? How is it that high-performing organizations don't have the same ricochet pattern from these same kinds of people?

Safety consultants Thomas Krause and John Hidley consistently find that when an accident occurs, everyone tends to blame the individual for unsafe work practices rather than looking at the bigger picture. "In 80 percent to 95 percent of all accidents, employee behavior provides the last link and common pathway for an accident to happen. However, the unsafe behavior at issue is a part of the management system, implicitly encouraged or condoned by management. Therefore, to blame employees is counter-productive."[26]

The 85/15 Rule

In his decades of international quality improvement consulting, Joseph Juran concludes management tends to blame workers for service/quality problems because of "biases in the flow of information." The basic problem is that people are visible, but the systems and organization culture by which group and individual behavior is shaped are not easily seen. So when something goes wrong, it is easy to trace the ricochet back to whoever touched it last and lay the blame there. But, Juran points out, that is far too superficial and will not get at the root cause of the problem: "Objective researches have regularly shown that about 80 to 90 percent of the damage done by poor quality is traceable to managerial actions."[27] Deming takes it even further. He believes 94 percent of "most troubles and most possibilities for improvement" belong to the system, which is controlled by management.[28]

Like so much about service/quality improvement, it really is common sense; *if you put a good person into a bad system, the system will win most of the time.* This obvious observation has been proved so many times it has become a truism in the quality field called the "85/15 rule." The 85/15 rule shows that if you trace ricochets back to the root cause, about 85 percent of the time the fault rests in the system, processes, structure, or practices of the organization. Only about 15 percent of the ricochets can be traced to someone who didn't care or wasn't conscientious enough. But the last person to touch the process, pass the product, or deliver the service may have been burned out by ceaseless ricochet catching; overwhelmed with the volume of work or problems; turned off by a "snoopervising" manager; out of touch with who his or her team's customers are and what they value; unrewarded and unrecognized for efforts to improve things; poorly trained; given shoddy materials, tools, or information to work with; not given feedback on when and how products or services went wrong; measured (and rewarded or punished) by management for results conflicting with his or her immediate customer's needs; unsure of how to resolve issues and jointly fix a process with other functions; trying to protect himself or herself or the team from searches for the guilty; unaware of where to go for help. All this lies within the system, processes, structure, or practices of the organization.

Many of the manifestations of the "our work force is to blame" assumption stem from the common, but badly misguided, inclination to begin error "seek-and-destroy missions" by asking "who" rather than "what" went wrong. Symptom carriers of the organization's system and process problems are hunted down and hung by the neck on lamp-posts. The result is a culture of fixing the blame rather than the problem, a culture of fear, cover your backside, and finger pointing.

Physician Don Berwick was the principal investigator for the National Demonstration Project on Quality Improvement in Health Care and is a Baldrige Award judge. Writing in the *New England Journal of Medicine*, he traces many of North America's quality and cost problems to what he calls the "theory of bad apples." In the medical profession, the response to "a search for deficient people" automatically creates three types of defensive responses, according to Berwick: "Kill the messenger; distort the data or change the measurements; and if all else fails, turn somebody else in . . . we are wasting our time with the theory of bad apples and our defensive response to it in health care today, and we can best begin by freeing ourselves from the fear, accusation, defensiveness, and naiveté of an empty search for improvement through inspection and discipline." Berwick concludes:

> When fear does not control the atmosphere (and thus the data), when learning is guided by accurate information and sound rules of inference, when suppliers of services remain in dialogue with those who depend on them, and when the hearts and talents of all workers are enlisted in the pursuit of better ways, the potential for improvement in quality is nearly boundless.[29]

The "errors come from shoddy work" assumption is widely shared and deeply rooted. The belief that workers are the source of errors shows up in a host of ways. Here are a few of the places to begin tracing some of your common management activities back to their underlying assumption.

Customer Service Training

Customer service training can be a potent corporate weapon, but without proper work force training, well-intended service strategies quickly run aground. Unfortunately, many companies confuse customer service improvements with quick tune-ups of frontline employee attitudes. But frontline workers don't create service quality, they deliver it. A key to effective training is a holistic approach spearheaded by management to create a companywide spirit committed to outservicing the competition.[30]

Bob Grimm, director of training and development at Hecht's retail stores, came to those conclusions after an extensive study of customer service training practices.

"Fix our customer-contact people" is a natural outgrowth of the assumption that frontline service delivery people have sole responsibility for the quality of service they are delivering. *The quality of external customer relationships is a direct reflection of the quality of internal customer-supplier relationships.* Just as a chain is no stronger than its weakest link, an organization's service/quality is usually no stronger than its weakest internal customer-supplier relationship. The service deliverer is but the last link in the chain. Granted, he or she may be the weak link, but usually he or she is no worse than the many who provide the myriad of production and support services backing up that person. Zeithaml, Parasuraman, and Berry's years of extensive research on the factors involved in delivering high service/quality led them to conclude:

> First-line service providers are often considered the root cause of America's service malaise. We disagree . . . the success or failure of first-line service providers is influenced greatly by the quality of service leadership they receive. When managers lead, service excellence is within reach. When managers do not, excellent service is a pipe dream.[31]

In fact, many frontline servers provide delightful third-ring service *in spite of*, not because of, the organizational support and systems. Given the many obstacles, it is a minor miracle that service is being provided at all by some exceptionally caring employees!

Karl Albrecht paints a typical picture of the sentiment (and underlying assumptions) behind far too much customer service training:

> When the stack of complaint letters on the president's desk gets too high, he pounds his fist and calls for action. Characteristically, whichever executive is charged with solving these kinds of problems will direct that there will be customer service training. They round up the usual suspects—the contact-level employees—and put them all through "smile training" courses.[32]

There's no question that basic courtesy skills are sadly lacking in too many organizations. Rude, gruff, or indifferent treatment can quickly make moments of truth negative experiences. But the painted-on smiles will be quickly wiped off trainees' faces by poor organizational support, lack of teamwork, or an abrasive supervisor. This kind of training can also send the wrong signals to participants about how bright management thinks they are. Many smile-training packages or one-day-wonder seminars are insulting to employees with their simple-minded approach and "you're the problem" messages.

Motivation and Exhortation

It is amazing how many managers still treat their people like rechargeable batteries. They are consistently searching for bigger, better, and longer-lasting ways to "keep our people motivated" or "get them charged up." "If we could just get them turned on to the need for improvement, we'd be all set." Toward that end, audiotapes, videos, motivational speakers, workshops, seminars, and executive speeches are used. W. Edwards Deming not only considers what he calls "exhortations" useless, but he also finds they actually demotivate. "Such exhortations only create adversarial relationships, as the bulk of the causes of low quality and low productivity belong to the system and thus lie beyond the power of the work force."[33] Decades of experience applying Deming's philosophy in Japanese companies has led Kaoru Ishikawa to conclude:

> In quality control one cannot simply present a goal and shout "work hard, work hard." One must understand the meaning of process control, take hold of the process, which is a collection of cause factors, and build within that process ways of making better products, establishing better goals, and achieving effects.[34]

A study by the American Society for Quality Control found that the common exhortation to "do it right the first time" is, in fact, demotivating. ASQC says this "slogan . . . will backfire in America" because it implies workers don't do it right now.[35] Telling workers "to do it right the first time" is too often just another manifestation of the underlying assumption that the reason they don't is lack of conscientiousness, care, or concern. The 85/15 rule gives management a nice big mirror to use in its search for the guilty.

There is no question that the more excited and energized employees are about improvement, the higher service/quality levels will go. But the real question is, why aren't they motivated? The answer is to be found in the day-to-day environment, not in short-term bursts of hype. While inspirational sessions can help kick off or revive a service/quality improvement drive, this approach has little lasting power on its own. All the best intentions and resolutions to do better will have only minor effects if skills, strategies, processes, structures, practices, and systems are weak.

"Sloganeering" and Internal Marketing

Many organizations have fallen into internal marketing traps. They have developed slick internal campaigns with snappy slogans on buttons, posters, hats, T-shirts, coffee mugs, and so on. These have often been combined with convincing executive speeches, videos, kickoff rallies, newsletters, and the like, all aimed at urging, prodding, or inspiring frontline performers to improve.

There is nothing wrong with solid internal marketing. In fact, the best service/quality providers are masters at it. There is a big problem, however, when marketing is too far ahead of real change in the culture or it constitutes the majority of the improvement effort. Richard Davis, senior vice president for Security Pacific National Bank, warns:

> Don't play games with service quality. Don't create a program out of it, because that in itself is implicitly short term. Create a focus, but don't even talk about it until you're ready to do something. The worst thing that can happen is to let it fall on deaf ears or to announce you're going to have a focus on the customer. "The Year of the Customer!" That's ludicrous! What's next year going to be?[36]

The problem is you've boldly declared "the dawn of a new age" before. The "flavor of the month" syndrome is probably well entrenched as a sacred management rite. "So what's the flavor this month? Service/ quality, you say? Well, just sit it out and they'll be on to productivity, cost cutting, innovation, or God knows what soon. This too shall pass." Lynn Shostack, chairman and president of Joyce International, says, "I don't think anyone is resistant to the *idea* that service/quality is important. But many are legitimately cynical about all the talk, 'touchy-feely' programs, and motivational claptrap they've been forced to participate in that has had no demonstrable results."[37]

Deming considers slogans to be just another form of exhortation, and just as deadly. Both come from the same deep-rooted assumption that the work force creates most of the organization's service/quality problems.

> What is wrong with posters and exhortations (is that) they are directed at the wrong people. They arise from management's supposition that

the production workers could, by putting their backs into their job, accomplish zero defects, improve quality, improve productivity, and all else that is desirable . . . in fact most of the trouble comes from the system.[38]

Performance Management

"How long have you been working here?" "Ever since I heard you coming down the hall, sir."

Executives seem to have a strong, almost primeval, need for accountability. Someone must be in charge of and responsible for each process, system, and work activity in use throughout the organization. Boundaries, roles, and responsibilities need to be clear. Customers, work teams, managers, supervisors, and executives need to know who to turn to for help or guidance in producing particular products, delivering services, or making improvements to either. The buck must stop somewhere. And leadership must start somewhere.

But accountability cuts both ways—it can help slash through the bureaucratic bramble bushes, or it can cut deep into the organization's muscle. The dark and dangerous side of senior management's search for accountability is a frequently unrecognized offshoot of the theory of bad apples, or "hang the guilty," the side of accountability that aims to "pin this problem (error or ricochet) on someone." This is the executive tendency to form a search party to scour the hills for the service/quality villain.

Performance appraisal systems are an outgrowth of the dark side of accountability, ignorance of the 85/15 rule, and "we know what our customers need." Management consultant Peter Scholtes has extensively studied performance appraisals and their effects on service/quality performance. He warns, "Using performance appraisal of any kind as a basis for reward of any kind is a flat-out catastrophic mistake. It is a sure road to demoralizing your work force . . . just don't do it."[38] Deming heaps some of his greatest scorn for North American management practices on performance appraisals:

> "The manager under the review system, like the people he manages, works as an individual for his own advancement, not for the company . . ." Deming reports that a seminar participant told him, "One gets a good rating for fighting a fire . . . . If you do it right the first time, you are invisible . . . . Mess it up, and correct it later, you become a hero."[39]

4. We exist to produce profits

"So, short-term thinker, repeat this a hundred times every morning while shaving or putting on your makeup: Profit is a result. Profit is a result. Profit is a result."
Richard Schonberger, *Building a Chain of Customers*[40]

Many executives have enormous difficultly getting their heads around the service/quality-profit paradox. As a result, they mislead their organizations by putting profit ahead of service/quality. That inevitably leads to less profit, which is generally responded to by desperate "slash and burn" short-term cost cutting that further reduces service/quality and actually increases costs. This drops profit even more. Eventually, this organizational tailspin leads to a "crash and burn," takeover, or occasionally, as in the case of Xerox and Motorola, a turnaround by putting service/quality and profits back into a priority set that enhances both.

As we saw in Chapter One, high-service/quality companies have the profits to match. But the profit paradox is that these companies did not become so profitable by establishing profit as their primary objective. Kaoru Ishikawa explains:

> Management that stresses "quality first" can gain customer confidence step by step, and the company's sales will increase gradually. In the long-run, profits will be substantial . . . if a company follows the principle of "profit first" it may obtain a quick profit, but cannot sustain competitiveness for a long period of time.[41]

But, paradoxically, companies without healthy profit margins can't sustain high levels of service/quality either.

The two main reasons setting service/quality as your top priority is so much more effective over the long term have to do with rallying your key stakeholders and focusing on the principle factors and processes that contribute to profitability. It is tough to get people to rally around a dollar sign. If you do succeed, you build a shallow culture more concerned with "what's in it for me" than one where service and quality are not only points of pride, but also often idealistic goals for the deeper values they represent. That is a critical consideration as North Americans turn their backs on the greed and excess of the 1980s and search for an organization, a team, a family, a set of spiritual values, or a cause we can believe in and be part of. In addition to rallying management and employees around your organization's cause, you also need to bring unions, governments, suppliers, customers, and other partners on board. Even if the goal of making your shareholders and executives rich galvanized your own people into action, rallying your other stakeholders around that cause is next to impossible.

An *effective* process of continual service/quality improvement will bring your organization huge and sustained profits. But they come as a *result* of superbly serving customers with high-quality product and services using top-quality support processes and systems that continually drive up productivity. "Profit is a yardstick for measuring the extent of a company's contribution to society," according to Konosuke Matsushita, founder of the highly successful international electrical and electronics giant Matsushita. In 1932, he established the "basic business principle" to provide a philosophical foundation for the fledgling, young firm. "A decrease in justified profit is a sign that our company is not contributing as it should," Matsushita writes. He established his company's mission as: "create new products from raw materials, thus contributing to a more desirable and richer life for all." Turning his attention to quality issues, he says:

> Management that is constantly cost-conscious can provide useful and valuable products and services at the lowest possible prices. This will allow more people to take advantage of our products, for which we, in turn, will be justifiably rewarded . . . we devote ourselves to the continuous improvement of our company.[42]

The other problem with the "resulted-oriented" approach so many managers proudly claim they use is that it doesn't produce very good results over the long term. Sure, squeezing costs, pushing the sales force, aggressive marketing, or driving production numbers up will produce profits—often lots of it—*in the short term.* Deming calls this approach "running the company on visible figures alone." But this method does not produce growing customer perceptions of value and an organization on the road to continuous improvement. Using the bottom line as the prime management measurement and guiding focus does not light the way to the most effective processes, structures, systems, or practices that will build revenues and drive out your bad cost of quality, which is running between 20 and 30 percent of your revenues. In fact, a "profit first" approach will ultimately lead to lower customer satisfaction, more apathetic employees and managers, and alienated suppliers, governments, unions, and other partners. After five decades of international consulting, Deming has very little patience for such shortsighted and fatalistic management: "He that would run his company on visible figures alone will in time have neither company nor figures."[43]

Here's how a number of business leaders view the profit paradox:

> *"If a man goes into business with only the idea of making money, chances are he won't. But if he puts service and quality first, the money will take care of itself."*
>
> Joyce C. Hall, *founder of Hallmark Cards, Inc.*[44]

> *"You're really not in business to make a profit, but you're in business to render a service that is so good people are willing to pay a profit in recognition of what you're doing for them."*
>
> Stanley Marcus, *chairman emeritus, Neiman-Marcus*[45]

> *"If we provide the best product and service, the bottom line takes care of itself."*
>
> Alan Ashton, *cofounder and CEO, WordPerfect Corporation*[46]

TAKE A LONG LOOK IN THE MIRROR

"To be conscious that you are ignorant is a great step to knowledge."

Benjamin Disraeli, *English statesman*

If you are honest with yourself, you have recognized a lot of you and your management team's behaviors and values in this chapter. But how about the underlying assumptions? Can you be even more honest with yourself and trace those behaviors and values back to their core assumptions? Facing up to and changing your underlying assumptions can be a real challenge. As George Bernard Shaw once observed, "No question is so difficult to answer as that to which the answer is obvious." What are your assumptions?

Sometimes the best way you and your management team can exorcise your dysfunctional assumptions is to get them out into the light of day for further examination. Talk about them. Explore which assumptions you hold nearest and dearest. Most of the rest of this book will provide you with a continuous improvement framework built on a very different set of assumptions than we have looked at in this chapter.

The next time you catch yourself pointing fingers at your customers, your frontline employees, managers, supervisors, or support staff, take a look at the end of your arm. There are three times as many finger pointing back at the real culprit. Roger Milliken found three barriers to overcome in turning around his textile company and making it a very profitable Baldrige winner in a mature industry besieged with cheap imports: "Top management, middle management, and first-line management."[47]

Chapter Five

A New Organizational Paradigm

"I have been in this business 36 years. I've learned a lot—and most of it doesn't apply anymore."

Charles Exley,
CEO, NCR Corp.

The word *paradigm* comes from the Greek for "pattern." We use patterns everyday to make sense of the world around us. Our traffic paradigm helps discern the pattern of cars buzzing around on our streets and enables us to reach our destination safely. Our gravity paradigm keeps us from stepping off tall buildings. Established paradigms keep us from having to constantly test and make up new guidelines everyday for a variety of routine activities. But paradigms also limit our thinking and often trap us into old patterns that no longer fit the new circumstances. Information system consultant Michael Hammer writes:

> Every business is replete with implicit rules left over from earlier decades. "Customers don't repair their own equipment." "Local warehouses are necessary for good service." "Merchandising decisions are made at headquarters." These rules of work design are based on assumptions about technology, people, and organizational goals that no longer hold.[1]

Chapter Four looked at the dysfunctional assumptions that created most of our service/quality problems. This chapter is designed to give you an overview of the emerging new organizational paradigm or model being used by high-service/quality performers. In a *Fortune* article titled, "A New Age for Business?" Frank Rose reports, "The new paradigm puts people—customers and employees—at the center of the universe and replaces the rigid hierarchies of the industrial age with a network structure that emphasizes interconnectedness."[2]

In this chapter, you will see how the new service/quality organizational paradigm is designed to nurture frontline contributors' "voluntarism" through involving, empowering, and enabling them to continually improve the organization's processes and systems. We will then look at the team-based organization that is proving to be the most effective method of employee involvement. As well, we will see the "upside-down organization" needed to make a team-based organization serve its customers with the highest quality products and services available. You will find that the new organizational paradigm is also designed to smash the old "vertical chimneys" and flatten our tall, stifling hierarchies. And we will see the new skills needed to make the team-based organization effective. The rest of this book is devoted to showing you how to make the transition from the old to the new organizational paradigm.

VOLUNTARISM: EXTERNAL SERVICE/QUALITY EQUALS INTERNAL SERVICE/QUALITY

Complaint department manager to customer: "If it's any consolation to you, we treat our employees worse than we treat our customers."

It is a "blinding flash of the obvious" that obviously isn't so obvious or it would be practiced more often; delivering delightful service, being involved in the improvement process, and contributing to a team's effectiveness is a voluntary effort. No amount of prodding, pushing, or punishing will produce continuous improvement. "Firings will continue until morale improves" may snap people into toeing the line, but it will not nurture the creative spirit so vital to the improvement process. Putting people together in groups and locking them away until they emerge with bright ideas for improvement may force some immediate change, but it will not establish the cooperation and teamwork needed to sustain continuous improvement. According to Kaoru Ishikawa:

> One can force subordinates to implement work by giving a command, but that will never go over smoothly. Conditions change constantly, and the commands given by superiors can never catch up with changing conditions. I stress voluntarism in quality control for this very reason."[3]

Voluntarism is especially important in improving customer service, particularly third-ring enhanced service that "delights and astounds." As we discussed in the last chapter, service/quality is a reflection of the system, more than the individual. The title of an article on customer service in *The Wall Street Journal* said it all: "Poorly Served Employees Serve Customers Just as Poorly." In the article, Robert Kelley explains the phenomenon this way: "Service providers treat customers similar to the way they as employees are treated by management. In many organizations, management treats employees as unvalued and unintelligent. The employees in turn convey the identical message to the customer."[4] Tom Peters agrees wholeheartedly: "I can think of no company that has found a way to look after external customers while abusing internal customers. The process of meeting customer needs begins internally."

It is really just common sense. Beat up your people and they will beat up your customers. Research provides documented evidence of this phenomenon. Zemke and Schaaf report in *The Service Edge* that Benjamin Schneider, a management professor from the University of Maryland, compared the levels of satisfaction employees felt in the levels of service they received from the organization with levels of customer satisfaction. He found that when employees feel well treated, when they have the right tools available to do the job, and when they have management's strong support for delivering high service, customers see higher levels of service being delivered.[5] Professor David Bowen of the University of Southern California found the same thing in his study of 51 branch banks. He concluded: (1) there was a strong correlation between customers' and employees' views of service/quality and the internal service climate; (2) favorable views of human-resource policies by employees are reflected in favorable views of service/quality by customers; and (3) a positive work climate directly improved service/quality levels.[6]

The internal or external service delivered by an individual or team tends to be no better or worse than that they receive from the organization. The American Society for Quality Control says simply, "The frontline providers of service treat customers in much the same way that they, as employees, are treated by their employers."[7] Charlie Stroupe, president of Wesley-Jessen, said: "It has been proven time and time again that the manner in which we treat each other is the manner in which we will treat our customers." This cause-and-effect relationship is why Embassy Suites puts a general manager's interpersonal skills at the top of their criteria for hiring and promoting. President Hervey Feldman said, "Where you win or lose the ball game is with the way the general managers treat employees. If they treat 'em well, then the employees treat the customers well, and the rest is merely scorekeeping."[8]

EMPLOYEE INVOLVEMENT

"The magic of employee involvement is that it allows individuals to discover their own potential—and to put that potential to work in creative ways. . . . People develop in themselves pride in workmanship, self-respect, self-reliance, and a heightened sense of responsibility."

Philip Caldwell, *retired CEO, Ford Motor Company*[9]

Leading organizations are finding that a key way to nurture frontline voluntarism is through employee involvement—getting those using the work processes and systems everyday involved in making them more effective. Of course, it is just common sense; we all feel a much higher degree of ownership and commitment to ideas and approaches that we help develop. In fact, *a large majority of service/quality improvement efforts owe much of their success to effective employee involvement*. In a review of published case histories and articles as well as interviews with managers and change agents involved in over 1,000 cases of attempted service/quality improvement, Zenger-Miller concluded, "During the past 20 years, it has been rare for U.S. organizations to achieve and sustain major gains in quality or productivity *without* a major increase in employee involvement."[10] Studies by the Work in America Institute have led to similar conclusions: "The participative model is the emerging new form of organization . . . (it) signals an institutional change of major proportions."[11]

An involved work force not only implements changes more effectively, but also, if properly guided and trained, the work force makes better improvement decisions. The employees are closer to the process and know from intimate personal experience—not some theory or model—what will work and what won't. The separation of decision makers from those who will make the decision work is a major shortcoming of the traditional organizational approach. Author and management consultant Bob Waterman said: "Carrying out a decision doesn't start after the decision; it starts with the decision. Figuring out how to get something done is just as important as deciding what to do." So why aren't employees more involved in decision making? Waterman points to one of the reasons: "We are so busy grandstanding with 'crisp decisions' that we don't take the time to involve those who have to make the decisions work." In the 1940s, Allan "Mogie" Morgensen found in his consulting work with General Electric and other large companies that it was possible to increase the work force's output by as much as *50 percent* by involving employees. One of the basic principles underlying his successful consulting work was "the person doing the job knows far better than anyone else the best way of doing that job and therefore is the best person fitted to improve it."[12]

Employee involvement works so well in improving service/quality because of *relevance* and *ownership*. With their experience and training, managers and staff professionals can be a valuable resource to frontline teams. But improvements made by those who are using the process or system everyday are far more likely to be practical and relevant. And when they have been involved in making the improvement decisions, employees have a much higher degree of ownership for the service/ quality standards they have helped to set. This then moves managers out of their traditional "policing" role.

INVOLVED AND EMPOWERED THROUGH TEAMS

Teams are rapidly emerging as an effective way to structure and focus employees to improve service/quality. Zenger-Miller executives, authors, and training specialists Jack Zenger, Ed Musselwhite, Kathleen Hurson, and Craig Perrin explain the wide variety of teams now appearing:

> Depending on organizational needs, teams may be ongoing or temporary; functional or cross-functional; synonymous with, or auxiliary to, the natural work group; conventionally supervised or to various degrees self-managed. Typical designations include the functional team, task force, problem-solving council, project team, business unit team, process improvement team, and self-directed team.[13]

The new organization uses such a large and diverse number of teams that we have come to call it the team-based organization.

A small but growing number of organizations are moving all the way to self-directed work teams. Based on their extensive research of employee involvement practices in America, Zenger-Miller defines a self-directed work team as "a highly trained group of employees, from 6 to 18, on average, fully responsible for turning out a well-defined segment of finished work." In their book *Self-Directed Work Teams: The New American Challenge*, Jack Zenger, Ed Musselwhite, Linda Moran, and Jack Orsburn explain that self-directed teams

> represent the conceptual opposite of the assembly line where each worker assumes responsibility for a narrow technical function. . . . Work teams plan, set priorities, organize, coordinate with others, measure, and take corrective action—all once considered the exclusive province of supervisors and managers. They solve problems, schedule and assign work, and in many cases handle personnel issues like absenteeism or even team member selection and evaluation."[14]

Having seen the power and results of self-directed work teams, a number of service/quality improvement experts believe they will be a prominent feature in the effective organization of the 1990s. For years, Procter & Gamble considered its remarkable success with self-directed work teams to be such a competitive edge it did not disclose details. In the past few years, in the spirit of North America's service/quality revolution, P&G has been actively sharing its experiences. David Hanna, P&G's manager of organization development, reflects:

> I have worked with and observed the results of work teams in many P&G plants, and I have observed them in other companies and industries . . . the same outcomes always show up. Better results. More satisfied customers. More committed people. Innovative and flexible responses to changes from outside. Breakthrough improvements initiated at all levels. In short, high performance.''[15]

In his book, *Thriving on Chaos: Handbook for a Management Revolution*, Tom Peters writes, ''*The self-managing team should become the basic organizational building block*'' (his emphasis).[16] And Joseph Juran gives us this forecast: ''If I may be permitted another look into my fallible crystal ball, I suggest that self-supervising teams will become the dominant successor to the Taylor (traditional departmentalized 'command and control' management) system.''[17]

Your organization may not be ready to move all the way to self-directed work teams. Some of the process and system improvements needed to improve your service/quality may not lend themselves to this type of approach. But to break down barriers between departments, manage processes across functions, get people pulling together, make your standards and practices more relevant, and increase ownership for the many improvements and changes needed, you require a number of different teams and lots of teamwork. *You will not see significant improvement in your organization's service/quality performance without a heavy use of intact (daily or departmental work group), cross-functional, special project, and coordinating teams.* In other words, you need to replace your traditional top-down, segmented organization with a team-based organization that harnesses the voluntarism of everyone who can make contributions to the improvement process.

TURNING YOUR ORGANIZATION UPSIDE DOWN

''Leaders who do not learn to serve produce organizations that do not learn to serve.''
Charles Garfield, *''peak performance'' researcher and management author*

You have heard it said that no one can serve two masters. In a traditional organization with its top-down hierarchy, that means frontline teams are too often focused on serving the boss as their master. High-performing service/quality organizations turn their organization chart upside down to keep everyone focused on the only master who counts—the customer who pays the bills. James E. Burke, chairman and CEO of top-performing Johnson and Johnson, said, "The energy in this business comes from the bottom up. Not the top down. They (the employees) run us (the management), not we them."[18] Adds Motorola CEO George Fisher,

> We want to put the salesperson at the top of the organization . . . members of our sales force are surrogates for our customers. They should be able to reach back into Motorola and pull out the technologists and other people they need to solve problems and anticipate customer needs.[19]

Embedded in this upside-down view of the organization is another variation of the 85/15 rule; service/quality is produced by the organization and delivered by the frontline. *Everyone* beneath the frontline servers needs to understand and, even more importantly, *act* to serve and support those further up the line. "In fact," asserts Karl Albrecht, "we can argue that the entire purpose of the organization, indeed its *only* purpose, is to support the efforts of the frontline people to do their service jobs" (his emphasis).[20]

Until frontline individual contributors and their teams feel served and supported, they cannot serve customers consistently well. In every study of retail service/quality, Nordstrom Department Stores always gets top marks. In *The Service Edge* newsletter, management consultant and author Ken Blanchard relates a conversation he had with an employee there who thought her boss was "a little weird": "Three or four times a day, he asks if there is anything he can do to help me. He acts like he works for me."[21] Exactly.

Who is serving whom in your organization? If you are not happy with your organization's level of service/quality, get out that mirror again. The performance level people on the front line deliver is less their fault than yours. Their performance is a reflection of the organizational paradigm you and your management team are using.

SMASHING CHIMNEYS AND FLATTENING HIERARCHIES

"Show most executives a defective part or broken machine on the factory floor, and they know what to do about it. Show them an obsolete, broken-down knowledge system, and they don't know what you are talking about."

Alvin Toffler, *Powershift*[22]

The new organizational paradigm not only reverses the up and down focus of the traditional organization, but it also manages much more effectively the cross-functional flow of work processes, information, and customer contact. Joseph Juran explains why this is critical to continuous improvement:

> There is an inherent conflict between the functional organization and multifunctional processes. Functional organization consists of vertical hierarchies. However, things get done through the horizontal multifunctional processes. Those processes extend beyond the boundaries of the company—they include customers and suppliers.[23]

In our traditional management system, each department, intact team, and individual keeps its head down and does the job assigned. Within the thick, high walls of each function's "chimney," individual contributors, teams, and management staff work to optimize the efficiency of their own unit. Performance appraisals, merit rating systems, and compensation are all designed to reinforce this narrow view. In this system, senior and middle managers use their "command and control" hierarchy to plan, direct, staff, coordinate, and control the functional units. Deep inside their dark chimneys, with little or no contact with their internal or external customers or suppliers, workers and their supervisors look up the chimney to management and their support staff for direction and feedback.

We now know this system is obsolete. It is too slow; plans and changes are not relevant because the planners and "experts" aren't close enough to the real job; those who need to implement improvements don't own or care about the changes; deficient supplies or incomplete information get thrown sporadically down the chimney; and improvements are often not focused on customer needs. In simpler times, this system worked. In today's much more complex and fast-moving world, this approach is about as useful as buggy whips and Morse code. Those organizations still clinging to this vertical structure are collapsing, like planned communist economies, under the weight and cost of their lumbering, unresponsive bureaucracy.

Connecting teams to their internal and external suppliers and customers and helping them to cooperatively manage processes as they flow across functions will flatten hierarchies as well as smash chimneys. Layers of management and support staff are removed as work teams take over more of their own planning and coordinating activities. Error rates, redundancy, and "bureaucratic busy work" plummet as work teams manage a customer service, production, delivery, or support process right across the organization. When managed effectively, these changes re-energize workers, increase customer satisfaction, and dramatically reduce costs. In *The New Realities*, Peter Drucker writes:

> The typical large organization, such as a large business or a government agency, 20 years hence will have no more than half the levels of management of its counterpart today, and no more than a third the number of "managers." In its structure, and in its management problems and concerns, it will bear little resemblance to the typical manufacturing company, circa 1950, which our textbooks still consider the norm.[24]

But as in gardening, keeping the bureaucratic brambles under control never stops. Tradition, hierarchy, internal focus, and segmentation continually keep trying to regrow. If left unchecked, they can choke the leaner service/quality organization. This recognition drives the highly effective Toyota organization to continuously work at compressing its hierarchy. *Fortune*'s Alex Taylor III reports that in 1990, President Shoichiro Toyoda "ripped out two layers of middle management (and) stripped 1,000 executives of their staffs. . . . 'We felt we suffered from large-corporation disease. . . . We have a saying: A large man has difficulty exercising his wits fully. We wanted to recertify that customer satisfaction is our first priority.' "[25]

THE NEW ORGANIZATIONAL PARADIGM

An organization that nurtures voluntarism by team-based employee involvement, is turned upside down to serve the servers or producers, smashes its vertical chimneys, and flattens its management layers obviously looks different from those we have grown up with during the past few decades. Here is a look at the traditional organizational paradigm and the new one needed to sustain continuous service/quality improvement:

Traditional Paradigm	New Paradigm
Management is the brains, employees are the hands.	The expert in a job is (or must become) the person doing the job.
Management directs, plans, and controls daily operations.	Management supports frontline teams that run daily operations.
Management's job is to solve operational problems.	Management ensures teams have the skills, tools, information, and support to solve operational problems.

Organizational performance is the cumulative effect of individual peformance.	Organizational performance depends on its systems, processes, and structure.
Errors are caught and corrected by specialists during or after production or delivery.	Errors are prevented by everyone during each step of the entire internal and external customer-supplier chain.
Crisp decision making is the mark of a good leader.	Building team ownership slows decision making but dramatically improves implementation.
Objectives, standards, measurements, and appraisals start at the top and cascade down the organization.	Starting from the outside in, customers set the priorities and measure effectiveness.
Accountability rests with "the chain of command" within each separate functional group.	Roles and responsibilities for managing cross-functional processes are established.

The new organization makes heavy use of numerous teams working together across and up the organization to continuously improve service/quality. This team-based approach has profound and far-reaching implications for management roles.

RESHAPING MANAGEMENT ROLES

"Even top managers who sense they need to 'let go' or loosen the reins, in order to free up the energies of their people, drastically underestimate how far they will have to go to break the grip of bureaucracy."

Alvin Toffler, *Powershift*[26]

Nurturing voluntarism by changing a hierarchical, vertical organization to a team-based organization calls for *drastic* changes in the traditional roles and practices of supervisors, managers, and executives. A study on employee involvement practices by Work in America Institute led President Jerome Rosow to conclude, "Teams are emerging as energy-producing subsystems that depend upon a new breed of manager, perceived as a teacher and a source of support rather than a disciplinarian."[27] This is reinforced by a separate Work in America study titled "New Roles for Managers":

Ground has been broken by trailblazer individuals and companies who have discovered the meaning and value of recasting supervision and management to achieve continuous improvement. . . . A manager is evolving who governs with the consent of the governed, in an open system that accepts dissonance and dissent and that engenders and sustains trust between manager and worker.[28]

Let's look at the changing roles of each management level.

Supervisors

A team-based organization dramatically alters the supervisor role, particularly when work teams move closer to being self-directed. The success of an organization's evolution to higher levels of employee involvement through teams depends very heavily on supervisors. The challenge, as Tom Peters puts it, is to transform supervisors from "cops to coaches."

Supervisors are in a hands-on, direct leadership role with intact teams or members of cross-functional teams. His or her ability to guide and support the team, coach individuals, and let go of the hierarchical authority will make or break the effort. But as Zenger, Musselwhite, Moran, and Orsburn point out, "Supervisors can feel as if they're officiating at their own funerals—as indeed they are, in the sense that these changes will lay to rest old ways of working." In those organizations going all the way to self-directed work teams, the authors report that supervisors become technical consultants to the team, members of the team, facilitators to a number of teams, move to the next level of management, or leave.[29]

The smoothness of the supervisory group's transition to any number of new roles in a team-based organization largely depends on how the group is coached and developed by middle management.

Middle Managers

While supervisors can make or break team effectiveness (especially intact teams) on the front line, middle managers play a pivotal support role to the supervisors. Managers also play a key part in the success of cross-functional and project teams. Valarie Zeithaml, A. Parasuraman, and Len Berry's research led them to conclude, "Middle management are in the center of everything and can either put fuel or sand in the gas tank."[30]

The changing role of middle management continues to be highly studied and much written about. Managers' traditional job to plan, coordinate, staff, control, and organize remains in a team-based organization, but it is hard to recognize those old tasks at the base of the radically different leadership skills used by effective managers in today's high-performance organization. Gone are the days of "Yes, sir!! How many bags full, sir?''—position power. In its place, we see coaching, team building, and guiding—persuasion power.

But in many organizations, middle managers are not operating in these new roles. They may say the words and understand the concepts, but they are not practicing the new skills. As a result, teams flounder, supervisors stumble, and change is painfully slow. These increasingly common experiences have caused a number of executives to become very frustrated, feeling that "you can't live with them (middle managers), and you can't live without them." Some CEOs have even begun decrying the "middle-management mush" they believe is sinking their organization transformation efforts.

But pointing fingers at managers is just as deadly and counterproductive as blaming the work force for service/quality problems. J. Willard (Bill) Marriott, CEO of Marriott Corporation, shows where the executive's fingers should be aimed: "A lot of middle managers are in a state of confusion about what's expected of them . . . most of them don't get enough training. . . . I also think they need leaders to watch and learn from. It's important that top managers lead by example and show them what's expected."[31]

Executives

The role of the executive is so critical to the service/quality improvement effort that Chapter Seven is devoted to this vital topic. *Responsibility for "middle-management mush" rests at the feet of executives.* Executives lead the middle managers and provide the example. Too often, coaching and team leadership are what the top orders the middle to do for the bottom. *If middle managers aren't providing the support for a customer-focused, team-based environment, the root causes can often be traced to the coaching and team leadership they receive.*

Managers' involvement in preparing themselves and the rest of the organization for the improvement journey often reveals what kind of leadership models they are being given to follow. The employee involvement study done by Work in America Institute found, "Companies that make employee involvement a key competitive strategy must extend the same involvement to managers and supervisors . . . management involvement is not nearly as widespread as it should be." The report concludes executives "should extend toward management the same principles of participation, teamwork, and quality of work life that have proved successful for employees."[32] We will be examining how to introduce and involve everyone throughout the organization in the chapters ahead.

NEW SKILLS FOR NEW ROLES

"Many are anxious to improve their circumstances, but are unwilling to improve themselves; they therefore remain bound."

James Allen, *American novelist*

New organization structures and new management roles obviously call for new leadership skills. In a number of upcoming chapters, we will look deeply into the range, mix, and best development methods of the skills all organizational players need to navigate successfully the road to higher service/quality.

As one of North America's largest developers of leadership skill-building modules, Zenger-Miller since 1978 has worked with thousands of major corporations, institutions, and governments to train hundreds of thousands of their supervisors, managers, and executives. Z-M has supplemented this with extensive research on the evolving skill needs of organizations using team-based improvement processes. From this work

three critical layers in the skill makeup of the team manager appear in the following chart: (a) an inner core of traditional management skills, still useful from time to time, (b) a middle layer of skills now widely required in organizations with growing employee involvement, and

Skills of the Team Manager

A	B	C
When Used Alone, Suited Only to Traditional Workplace	*Required in a More Participative Workplace*	*Required in a High-Performance Team Environment*
Direct people	Involve people	Develop self-motivating people
Get groups to understand ideas	Get groups to generate ideas	Get diverse groups to carry out their own ideas
Manage one on one	Encourage teamwork	Build teams that manage more of their own work
Maximize the performance of the department	Build relationships with other departments	Champion cross-functional work-process improvements
Implement change	Initiate change	Sponsor innovation to meet customer needs

(c) an outer layer of team leadership skills that supervisors and managers will increasingly have to master.[33]

According to Zenger-Miller's research:

Competent traditional managers, who apply only the traditional skills from column A, are likely casualties of the trend toward teams. Some of these managers may choose alternative careers within the organization—as team members, for example, or technical advisors; others may seek out organizations more suited to their abilities. Managers who practice both column A and B skills may survive an organizational shift toward teams, but rarely do they play a central role in the transition. True team managers, who through training and perseverance have mastered the skills in all three columns, not only ride the crest toward a team environment, but often play an active part in reshaping systems, roles, and procedures to sustain the transition.[34]

How advanced are your team and coaching skills? What examples are you setting in your meetings, relationships, use of power, focus, improvement activities, or coordinating efforts? Even more importantly—*HOW DO YOU KNOW*? When was the last time you received solid, representative feedback on your leadership strengths and weaknesses from the management staff, teams, and individuals you support? How regularly do you get this feedback? How frequently do you attend skill-building sessions to keep your leadership edge sharp? What's your cost of poor skills?

MOVING TO THE NEW PARADIGM

The transition to a high-service/quality, team-based organization will encounter internal resistance. Most of that resistance will come from supervisors, managers, and executives threatened with the loss of their traditional position power. Karl Albrecht writes: "When I think about the management jobs I've held . . . I realize that much of what I considered management involved serving my own needs to feel in charge. Some of my ideas about direction, visibility, and control were really part of what I have come to call the neuroses of management."[35] In fact, some of your most difficult times on the road to higher performance will be dealing with management and support staff who wouldn't exchange their traditional position power for the ultimately more powerful role of coach, enabler, and team leader. You will have some difficult decisions to make about how long you explain, persuade, coach, nudge, . . . wait, and finally demand more than lip service from a few of your key people. If the new culture does not make this small minority uncomfortable enough to get on board or leave, you may have to "help them find career opportunities elsewhere."

But make sure you have looked hard at your service/quality improvement process itself. For about 10 to 20 percent of your management staff (level doesn't seem to matter), the new paradigm won't fit. But the number can be much higher than that if you don't have a strong team-based service/quality improvement process. Your organization's values must be evident in executive signaling; listening to external and internal customers; education and awareness; and your hiring, orienting, and promotion practices. Massive training is needed in personal, coaching, and team skills throughout your entire organization. Your systems, rewards and recognition, team improvement activities, measurements and standards, as well as marketing strategies, must be aligned with customer expectations and the needs of the frontline producers and deliverers. And the deployment of the whole improvement effort relies on a strong infrastructure, extensive planning and regular reporting, and clear roles and responsibilities. (The rest of this book is devoted to each one of these critical areas that will help you build the new team-based organization.)

So before you declare "middle-management mush," organize a number of teams, or push for higher service/quality, take a long look at your organization's management systems and practices. You won't last long on the endless improvement journey if you are not prepared . . . or don't have a clear idea of which road you want to head down.

Chapter Six

At the Service/Quality Crossroads

"Two roads diverged in a wood, and I —
I took the one less traveled by,
And that has made all the difference."

Robert Frost,
"The Road Not Taken"

If you have decided you want to take your organization to higher levels of service/quality, you are now standing at a critical crossroad. You must decide which road will take you to that higher ground. You have two choices: service/quality programs or a long-term cultural change process. Be careful as you look down the two roads. First appearances are deceiving.

The service/quality programs road looks smooth and inviting. It is broad and well maintained. There is plenty of company, and the road appears to be going uphill in the direction you are heading. But around the first bend, conditions change. The road gets bumpier. As you continue, it gradually becomes apparent that this road will not take you where you want to go. The road winds its way downhill and you advance with little effort. But soon the pavement turns into a dirt track that gets soft and muddy. Before you know it, the road has emptied into a bog. With a sinking feeling, you watch a few organizations struggling up the cultural change road far above. You realize your organization is now firmly stuck and will have a difficult time getting back on track.

On the other hand, the cultural change road is not nearly as appealing at first glance. The grade is very steep; it will clearly require more effort. For the first while, this road runs parallel to the service/quality programs route. In a number of places, they almost merge. You notice that some organizations appear confused and begin following the programs route without realizing it. But as the journey continues, the terrain gets tougher. Many traveling companions fall behind, drop out, or cut across to the much easier program route. As you stay on this course, it gets very bumpy and narrow. In places, it is all you can do to stay on the thin ledge high above the canyon floor. You notice you are almost alone. And the journey seems to be endless. But when you pause to look around, you find yourself in the company of high performers. You have never felt so strong. And then you begin to enjoy the fruits of your efforts.

WHICH ROAD WILL YOU CHOOSE?

"No amount of travel on the wrong road will bring you to the right destination."
                                                                            Ben Gaye III

Service/quality improvement programs, if they are well implemented, will give you some payoffs. Chances are, if you are careful, you won't get stuck in the bog. But a string of programs, no matter how good they are, will not give you the substantial revenue growth and cost reductions that top service/quality performers enjoy. At best, you will see a few improvements here and there.

Venture capitalist Arthur Rock said, ''You can walk up to people on the street and ask them if they want to be rich, and 99 percent will tell you, 'Sure I want to be rich.' But are they willing to do what's necessary to be successful? Not many are.''[1] The same is true of executives who want to improve service/quality. Many declare this to be their strategy, but few are willing to pay the price to make the long and very difficult journey toward higher service/quality. A huge majority of organizations are interested in improving their service/quality. A number have even put those good intentions into mission statements, strategic plans, training, and advertising. But only a tiny minority of organizations are truly committed to taking the necessary steps toward improving service/quality. And an almost minuscule number of organizations are prepared to stay on the course for the time needed to make permanent changes in their culture.

TOO MANY PROGRAMS, TOO MANY "BOHICAS"

"Faddism is as American as the tail fin and the Hula Hoop . . . but quality doesn't work when it's the panacea-of-the-month: Witness the quality circle, which enjoyed its 15 minutes of fame a decade ago before becoming the Nehru jacket of management techniques."
                                Frank Rose, *"Now Quality Means Service Too," Fortune*[2]

As we meet with prospective Clients or help a senior team assess readiness for the service/quality journey during an executive retreat, it is clear that many executives think service/quality improvement is just another business objective, a goal to be set, a program to be established. Theirs is the antiquated, narrow view of technical service/quality—something to be delegated, a project to be worked on, some training to be thrown at those producing or supporting the organization's basic products, or sales and marketing to "position" the organization. In the meantime, so the thinking goes, executives can turn back to other equally, or even more pressing, issues like cost control, productivity improvement, political positioning, or increasing short-term profitability.

As with a joke or work of art, some executives "just don't get it." They don't understand that *service/quality is the only reason any organization exists. Period. EVERY activity in the organization is to support the delivery of ever higher levels of perceived value to the organization's customers with ever lower costs.* If you are not convinced of this yet, reread the last four chapters. If this basic premise is not one you agree with, the rest of this book won't make much sense—or do you much good. And just as we suggest in an executive retreat or initial meeting with a prospective client when this narrow perception is clearly held, there is no use trying to go any further together—we are not even on the same road.

Trying to "improve" service/quality through a series of training programs, slogans, improvement projects, marketing campaigns, motivational programs, educational seminars, and the like produces "BOHICA." This is the all too common "bend over, here it comes again" response. Employees, supervisors, managers, and even other executives have seen these programs come and go. The wise old sages in the organization calmly advise their less experienced colleagues to "lay low long enough, and they'll soon be onto another flavor of the month. This too shall pass." Joseph Juran writes:

> In most companies not a year goes by without a drive of some sort—a drive to improve productivity, human relations, costs. These drives are launched with advocacy and ceremony. The upper managers make the principal speeches at the launching . . . (but) the drive does not persist—it shrivels up and is swept off center stage by the next drive . . . in such companies it is quite logical . . . to draw the cynical conclusion, "Here comes another one."[3]

Adds Karl Albrecht:

> The people in the organization, especially middle managers, have been so overprogrammed that it becomes necessary to trick them into seeing the new one as unique and special. "This is not a program," they (executives) intone solemnly. "This goes far beyond any program we

have ever done before. This is a new way of life." The employees and most of their managers just yawn and go back to work.[4]

In addressing the very common program approach to service/quality improvement, one of the conclusions to emerge from the second Xerox Quality Forum held in Leesburg, Virginia, in 1990 was, "There is a danger in teaching the 'bits and pieces' of quality. What is needed is an integrated approach."[5] That only happens when service/quality is the overarching goal supported by all other organizational activities. From studying numerous American and Japanese improvement efforts, David Garvin reports, "Tools and techniques have dominated with short-term improvement projects often pursued at the expense of long-term quality planning . . . many companies . . . have failed to emphasize quality's connection with basic business objectives."[6] And that happens when quality improvement is mandatory and mandated from the CEO. "The introduction of mandated quality is probably the most beneficial single change that a company can make regarding quality," asserts Joseph Juran. "It also probably has a greater impact on the cultural pattern of the managerial hierarchy than any other change."[7]

THE CULTURAL CHANGE ROAD

"It is a rough road that leads to the heights of greatness."

Seneca, *Roman statesman and philosopher*

Cultural change happens only when service/quality improvement becomes *the* strategic issue for the organization. In the past decade, few cultural changes have been as large, sweeping, and successful as the one led by Xerox CEO David Kearns. He reflects on the long difficult journey:

I became personally convinced that in order to enlist the support of our entire organization in quality improvement, we had to radically change our entire corporate culture—everything from the way we manage and work, the way we reward people, our communications . . . a corporate revolution.[8]

Xerox identified six main thrusts in its "quality intensification" effort: (1) The customer defines our business; (2) Success depends on involvement and empowerment of trained and highly motivated Xerox people; (3) Quality is managed by the line; (4) Management develops and deploys clear objectives; (5) Strategic quality challenges need to be identified by top management with the vital few challenges addressed early in the process; and (6) Business is managed by facts using the quality tools.[9]

Here are a number of perspectives and experiences on the road to higher service/quality through cultural change:

> *"We had quality programs. But the real difference comes when you decide it's no longer a program, it's a business strategy. If I had the last 10 years to live over . . . ."*
>
> Stephen Schwartz, *senior vice president, market-driven quality, IBM*[10]

> *" . . . a radical change in how we think, not a fine-tuning of the existing systems, but a new way of life . . . . We have re-examined our approach to be sure that total quality is the driving force in planning and performance."*
>
> Douglas Danforth, *chairman, Westinghouse Electric Corporation*[11]

> *"The excellent companies have built the concept of total quality into the whole corporate culture. Management has set up total quality processes in all activities, not just in products and services."*
>
> Curt Reimann, *director, Malcolm Baldrige National Quality Award*[12]

> *"Quality problems arise from the nature of the company itself and are inseparable from the company as a whole . . . management is the same thing as quality control . . . the entire company must strive for quality."*
>
> Hajime Karatsu[13]

> *"Quality is a long-term commitment. It means rethinking the way you do business; it may also mean restructuring your operations."*
>
> American Society for Quality Control[14]

> *"Service quality improvement does not happen by accident. It requires and demands professional management and measurement systems. It requires that business decisions be continuously assessed in terms of their impact on quality. It requires a special and deeply ingrained commitment, sustainable over the years."*
>
> Strategic Planning Institute, *"The Strategic Management of Service Quality"*

MAPPING THE TERRAIN

> *"If you don't know where you are going,"* the Scarecrow said to Dorothy, *"it doesn't matter which road you take."*
>
> The Wizard of Oz

If cultural change truly is the road you want to follow, you must have a clear idea of how this route differs from the service/quality programs road:

Significant Components	Service/Quality Programs	Cultural Change
Process delivery	Programs are given by various internal/external experts and specialists	Cultural change is driven by line managers
Building employee commitment	Inspirational messages, seminars, and slogans exhort improvement	An environment of "voluntarism" is nurtured through management's leadership and support of intact, cross-functional, and process improvement teams
Technology and systems	Making better use of what exists	What exists is re-engineered
Managing people	Training "fixes" front-line employees and supervisors	All hiring, promoting, performance management, measurement, and rewards are re-aligned
Senior management involvement	Executives give their "blessing" and make guest appearances	Executives *visibly* lead the continuous improvement process
Roles and responsibilities	Improvement responsibilities are given to a few selected people	Cultural change determines all strategies, structures, skills, and accountabilities
Customer expectations	Management tells employees what customers expect	Teams uncover their customers' expectations and work to exceed them
Planning	Fragments of training, inspiration, project improvements, education, etc. are separate from strategic planning	Strategic planning, budgeting, and service/quality improvement planning are woven into one master plan managed by line managers

BUILDING A HIGH SERVICE/QUALITY CULTURE

"There are hundreds of issues that need to be addressed to improve an organization," says Nate Moore, manager of corporate quality programs at Westinghouse. "No one 'answer' will get a company there. It's a combination of the right approaches, tools, and techniques consistently applied over a period of years.''[15] Indeed, the Baldrige Award criteria cover about 100 interconnected components affecting service/quality levels throughout the organization.

As we pull out the map to get an overview of the territory to be covered, let's look at what we now know needs to be done if your organization is going to be in the minority that actually achieve and *sustain* ever higher levels of service/quality:

- Your organization must continuously monitor its changing external customers' needs and use those rank-ordered priorities to establish the service/quality objectives and indicators for each customer-supplier group in the entire service/quality chain extending right into your external suppliers.

- Senior executives must *visibly and actively* lead the cultural change process and continuous improvement journey from the front of the traveling column. This starts with the senior team being able to answer these questions *in unison*: (1) What business are we in (our strategic niche)? (2) What do we believe in (the values that will guide everyone's behavior)? (3) Where are we going (the vision of our *preferred* future)?

- *All* management and staff support groups at all levels need to begin serving the frontline producers, deliverers, and supporters of the organization's basic products and services. In turning your organization upside down, management and staff groups need to establish a system of continual data collection and feedback for the service they are providing. This needs to be tied to their compensation.

- *Everyone* in the organization needs a thorough introduction to why service/quality is critical; how to define "service/quality" for the organization and the team; how service, quality, productivity and cost relate; the 85/15 rule and its deep implications; what the organization, teams, and team members personally need to do and in what order; the tools, techniques, and skills they and others will be developing and why; senior management's strategic focus, values, and vision; and the infrastructure, roles, responsibilities and plans to implement the improvement process. These messages need to be constantly repeated and reinforced.

- Continuous learning must become entrenched at all organizational levels.

- Your hiring, orientation, and promotion practices must reflect service/quality principles and your organization's values.

- Extensive, massive, and wide-scale continuous skill building will need to be given to everyone involved in, supporting, and leading the improvement process.
- All organizational systems (such as financial, human resource, planning, and so on) and structures must be aligned to serve customer and frontline team needs ahead of serving management.
- Team and individual reward and recognition processes and practices need to be aligned to reinforce service/quality principles and organizational values.
- *Everyone at all levels* throughout the organization needs to be active and contributing members of his or her intact team and process improvement and/or project teams. Executive ownership and operational responsibility for product development, marketing, administrative, and other key processes must be established. These are then best managed by the work teams closest to the action.
- Your measurements and standards must start from the outside and move into the organization along the customer-supplier chain of service/quality. Measurements, standards, and corrective actions need to be owned and managed by work teams with management's support and guidance.
- Your sales, marketing, or public relations strategies need to be aligned continually to move your organization closer to its strategic niche and maintain an open two-way communication channel with external customers and your other external stakeholders.

Clearly, an enormous amount of ground must be covered on the cultural change road. As Achieve began working with Clients to help move from their current state to the desired future state, we saw a clear need for a map to show the lay of the land. Our implementation architecture does just that. This is the key framework or blueprint at the heart of Achieve's Service/Quality System™. Its genesis was with a "12-cylinder" model brought to us by consultant Rob Ell when he joined our organization in Vancouver, British Columbia. Rob used the analogy of a 12-cylinder engine to show the areas that had to be covered to get an organization firing on all cylinders. And so an implementation model (and a book title) was born.

Just like our original three rings model, our implementation architecture has been continuously improved as we have worked with dozens of major organizations over the years. The "12 cylinders" found in the "Values," "Skills," and "Alignment" columns continue to broaden and expand as new service/quality improvement tools and techniques

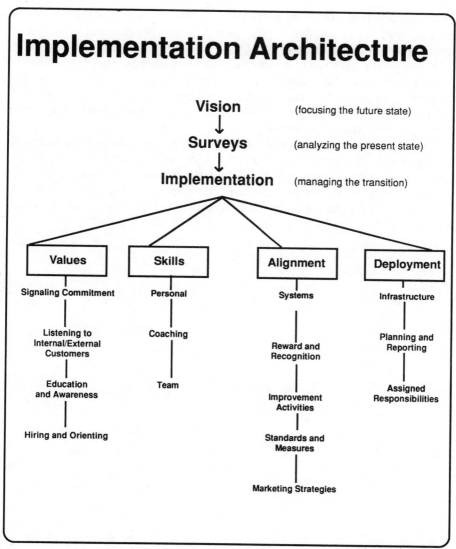

Implementation Architecture

Vision   (focusing the future state)

↓

Surveys   (analyzing the present state)

↓

Implementation   (managing the transition)

Values	Skills	Alignment	Deployment
Signaling Commitment	Personal	Systems	Infrastructure
Listening to Internal/External Customers	Coaching	Reward and Recognition	Planning and Reporting
Education and Awareness	Team	Improvement Activities	Assigned Responsibilities
Hiring and Orienting		Standards and Measures	
		Marketing Strategies	

© Achieve International

(such as process management, quality function deployment, and bench-marking) prove to be useful additions to the field.

The 12 cylinders in the first three columns are the ''what'' that needs to be covered in the continuous improvement journey. Over the next 13 chapters, we will explore the territory each covers in a basic introduction. Many of these areas are so broad, and expanding so rapidly, entire books and complete fields of study are being devoted to them. But the overview here should show you what you need to do to get started, or take the next steps in each cylinder.

A few years after we began using the 12-cylinders model, we broadened it to include the "deployment" section. We found this was necessary to better clarify *how* the improvement process worked. Deployment is where we work on the process to improve the service/quality improvement process (the 12 cylinders).

As you look at the amount of effort required to travel the cultural change road, you may find yourself asking, is this what it really takes to be a top performer? You bet! All that and a whole lot more. The high road to continuous service/quality improvement is not an easy one. It isn't for the halfhearted or the half-committed. That's why it is the road less traveled.

Chapter Seven

Cylinder One: Signaling Commitment

*"Examples lead us, and we will likely see
Such as the prince is, will his people be."*

Robert Herrick,
English poet

There is no one cylinder in the entire service/quality improvement process more critical than this one. *The signals senior management sends with its daily behavior will determine whether service/quality improvement will be just another program or a true cultural shift.* We have constantly found that the intensity and effectiveness of an organization's service/quality improvment effort can *always* be traced to senior management. In over five decades of consulting, observation, and study, in hundreds of organizations, virtually every improvement expert has arrived at the same conclusion:

"Having observed a great many companies in action, I am unable to point to a single instance in which stunning results were achieved without the active and personal leadership of upper managers. . . . In a revolutionary change—a change in culture—leadership is not delegable. Top managers who missed that lesson spent much of the 1980s on a road leading nowhere. In the minds of many of their subordinates, the top managers were not leading, they were only cheerleading."

Joseph Juran[1]

"If there is no leadership from the top, stop promoting total quality control."

Kaoru Ishikawa, *What is Total Quality Control: The Japanese Way*

"The transformation must be led by top management."

W. Edwards Deming[2]

"We have yet to find a company that can provide superior service without top managers who are fanatically committed to service. . . .

Taking care of customers is so much work that it gets done only if the people at the top lead the charge."

William H. Davidow and Bro Uttal, *Total Customer Service: The Ultimate Weapon*[3]

Developing strong commitment to service/quality improvement requires two steps. The first critical one is getting the management team to agree wholeheartedly that service/quality improvement is *the* strategic issue for the organization. The team members then must be prepared to devote substantial resources and personal time for at least *three to five years* of intensive effort to get the improvement journey *started*. But that is not the focus of this cylinder.

Once it is clear that senior management is prepared to stay the course for the long, tough journey, the second step is to build this commitment within the rest of the organization. This cylinder deals with those visible *actions* effective senior managers take to signal their strong, unmistakable commitment to service/quality improvement and to personally lead the journey.

THEY SEE YOU LOUD AND CLEAR

"We judge ourselves by what we feel capable of doing, but others judge us by what we have already done."

Henry Wadsworth Longfellow, *American poet and scholar*

An industrial magnate once told Mark Twain that he would like to climb Mount Sinai and read aloud the Ten Commandments. Twain is reported to have responded by saying, "Why don't you just stay home and live them."

Many corporate sermons given by senior managers are preaching the virtues of improving service/quality and better managing "people—our most important resource." In turn, executives are causing their managers to place their left hands over their hearts, raise their right hands, and pledge allegiance to teamwork, service/quality, continuous improvement, innovation, employee involvement, skill development, and the like.

THE RHETORIC/REALITY GAP

"Example is not the main thing in influencing others. It is the only thing."

Albert Schweitzer, *German theologian, physician, and musician*

Despite the rhetoric, little changes. The people on the front lines actually selling, making, delivering, or supporting the products or services grow ever more wary and cynical about the rising din of words—and inconsistent actions. In a 1990 Gallup survey commissioned by the American Society for Quality Control, 55 percent of employees reported their companies say that showing customers their commitment to quality is extremely important (10 on a 10-point scale). As well, 53 percent indicated their companies say that making quality everyone's top priority is extremely important. But when asked to rate their companies' follow-through on these issues, only 36 percent and 35 percent, respectively, rated their company a 10. The survey results point to executive behavior as one of the reasons for the poor company follow-through. Less than 39 percent of these same employees gave top executives an A or B in trying to improve the quality of U.S. products or services.[4] *Total Quality* newsletter reports that a study by the consulting firm of Brooks International concluded, "Two out of three workers say that quality of work done in their work group is not a measure of performance." Organizational members at all levels were also asked, "Is top management committed to achieving and maintaining the highest quality levels possible?" Seventy-eight percent of top managers answered yes, compared to 54 percent of middle managers, 46 percent of supervisors, and 43 percent of workers.[5]

The perks and special privileges reserved for those "who have made it" contribute to the "we/they" gap between executives and the rest of the organization. Bill Marriott, Jr., identifies one of the key factors in building a culture of teamwork and customer focus at the Marriott Corporation:

> We don't have any big shots around here. Guys come in who want to be big wheels, but they don't last long; they don't get far in the company so they leave. We don't have any executive dining rooms or private elevators; I just don't believe in that stuff. It just isn't part of our culture.[6]

You cannot build an upside-down organization that has management serving frontline teams that serve customers if senior management constantly sets itself apart with special parking, cavernous and luxurious offices, big limos, and a "country club" atmosphere among executives. All your talk about togetherness, reducing non-value-added expenses, and management serving teams just won't wash when it comes from a privileged and pampered mahogany row. Is this stuff really worth the millions of dollars it costs your organization in lower service/quality? It adds a heavy and useless excess weight to your journey. Jettison it—immediately.

"In better than half of the companies that have applied for the award, it's not clear that the leaders walk the talk," says Baldrige director Curt

Reimann. "There are only a few cases of really dynamic leadership, and still many instances of delegated leadership, in which a leader identifies that quality is important and passes the message on but doesn't really lead day to day."[7] At a Xerox Quality Forum, Analog Devices Chairman and President Ray Stata commented on the sad state of leadership, "In 99 percent of the cases, top management is the greatest barrier to effective total quality management implementation in the United States."[8]

THEY *ARE* GETTING YOUR MESSAGE

"Children are natural mimics; they act like their parents despite attempts to teach them good manners."

In the hundreds of executive retreats we have conducted, a common issue, and often source of frustration, emerges—how do you get people to be more concerned about service, quality, innovation, teamwork, partnerships, continuous improvement, or whatever values the executive team has determined it wants to instill. The frustration comes from a sense that managers, supervisors, and frontline performers are not getting the message. They need to be "smartened up."

Values are a contagious affliction that spreads from senior management. The key question is are yours worth catching? Customer surveys, cultural climate audits, and work with others throughout the organization reveal that everyone marches to roughly the same beat as the executives. The values *are* being followed and lived by the majority of the organization; that is, the values *as exemplified by senior management actions*. Too often, senior managers don't recognize their own values being reflected back to them. Their *intended values* are out of step with their *lived values*.

Leading by Visible *Example*

"All the bountiful sentiments in the world weigh less than a single lovely action."

James Russell Lowell, *American poet and critic*

Senior executives live in an organizational fishbowl. Every word and action is analyzed and studied for its deeper meaning about what's really important. These stories and examples are discussed throughout the organization and become part of the folklore from which organizational members define priorities, meaning, and culture. Comments penciled on the margins of a memo, a casual aside at a meeting, what's first on meeting agendas, who is invited, what seems to be uppermost on the senior executive's mind according to the questions he or she asks—these all become grist for discussion and interpretation of what senior management values most.

It's not enough for senior executive team members to be "committed" to service/quality improvement; they must be *visibly seen* to be *obsessed* with this as their top priority. Since we all know that actions speak much louder than words, senior managers need to work hard on *visibly signaling their commitment* so strongly and *consistently* that there can be no room for doubt about how critical service/quality is to the organization's future. Globe Metallurgical Vice President Ken Leach sees this as one of the major challenges facing North American organizations: "Probably the most common problem within the country today is lack of visible commitment from upper management."[9] Eliminating this problem always goes a long way to eliminating "middle-management mush."

In their *Harvard Business Review* article, "Why Change Programs Don't Produce Change," Michael Beer, Russell Eisenstat, and Bert Spector warn, "If the CEO and his or her management team do not ultimately apply to themselves what they have been encouraging their general managers to do, the whole process can break down."[10] *Executives can only lead the improvement journey from the front.* There can be no delegating or merely cheerleading. That means the executive team's daily management style and practices become a pivotal part of setting the tone, pace, style, and example for the whole improvement effort.

Let's look at just three of the many key areas where *active and visible* executive leadership and signaling is needed.

Teamwork

Far too many executive teams are quick to sing the praises of teamwork—for the rest of the organization. A growing number of executives are setting their sights on building a team-based organization. However, their own personal behavior with each other and with their managers is still within the "rugged individualism" mold. Because many come from the segmented, "command and control" era of vertical chimneys, individualistic "fix the problem or person, not the process" is what got them to the executive suite. It may be all they know. As a result, they may be one of the many "Lone Ranger" executives who either act independently of other divisions or departments or swoop in to save the day and help "the poor, hapless townfolk" by solving their problems for them.

In over a decade of working with thousands of organizations, we have concluded *the way an organization behaves as a whole (its culture) is nothing more than a big reflection of the way the executive team behaves.* We often see that the executive group is just that—a *group* of high-powered individualists. They are not a team. Executives take potshots and snipe at each other or other departments. Executives fail to "sing off the same sheet of music" by emphasizing the same areas and delivering consistent messages throughout the organization. The result is always an organization full of thick vertical chimneys, search for the guilty, cover your backside, suboptimization at the expense of the whole process or organization, disharmony, and everyone out for themselves.

As we have discussed in previous chapters, significant and lasting service/quality improvement is not possible without extensive management and employee involvement through a wide variety of teams. But team development has to start at the top. So get out that mirror again and look at your team. Do you deserve that name, or are you really just a group of individuals who meet occasionally?

Continual Learning: Executive Skill Building

"It is not enough that top management commit themselves for life to quality and productivity. They must know what it is that they are committed to—that is, what they must do. These obligations cannot be delegated. Support is not enough: action is required."

W. Edwards Deming[11]

If you are going to lead the journey from the front and apply the service/quality improvement tools and techniques in your own processes and practices, then you have a lot of learning to do. Total quality control has become so widespread in Japan because senior executives are humble students. Deming Prize winner Hajime Karatsu writes:

Quality control is not *nembutsu*, that is, repeating prayers to obtain salvation. Quality control has its own special methodology, and if workers are expected to practice it, management must be prepared to show them how it's done. . . . Top managers must be the first to *practice* (his emphasis) quality control, to nurture a *shafu* (way of doing things) that respects quality. . . . Wherever quality control has been successful, the essential ingredient has been active participation by top management. . . . When we look for examples of successful quality control in Japan, we discover only those companies led by presidents who acknowledge the importance of quality control and implement it throughout the organization.[12]

You cannot build a continuously learning and improving organization if you and your management team are not out in front showing everyone the way. But before you and your team can lead and develop others, you need to personally learn and practice the new team-based skills and service/ quality improvement techniques.

The executive leadership role in building a foundation of continual learning for an organization of continuous improvement is a key theme we will return to many times in the journey ahead.

Management by Wandering Around

"In Endymion, I leaped headlong into the sea, and thereby have become better acquainted with the surroundings, the quick sand, and the rocks, than if I had stayed upon the green shore and piped a silly pipe, and took tea and comfortable advice."

John Keats, *English poet*

In their runaway best-seller *In Search of Excellence*, Tom Peters and Bob Waterman first popularized the notion that effective leaders spend huge amounts of their time out with their customers, suppliers, and employees. A decade after the publication of the landmark management classic, Tom Peters is as adamant as ever about an executive's use of his or her calendar as a key signaling tool:

Attention is all there is. You are what you spend your time on. You're as focused or unfocused as your calendar says you are. Interested in launching, and then sustaining, a program of quality improvement through the empowerment of frontline people? If so, that theme had better be reflected unmistakably on your calendar, hour to hour, day to day, year to year.[13]

Executives in highly effective service/quality organizations spend much more time "managing by wandering around" with employees and customers than traditional "technomanagers" do. This marked difference inspired management consultants Donald Clifford and Richard Cavanagh to identify the CEOs in the high-growth companies they studied, and reported on in *The Winning Performance*, as the "chief evangelical officers."[14] That label is both accurate and misleading. It captures the emotional, even spiritual, dimension that a powerful vision and set of core values tap to release energy for organizational renewal. Bill Marriott, Jr., says, "There needs to be an element of executive evangelism in operation; not only the chief executive but the other senior managers must preach, teach, and reinforce the gospel of service quality."[15] However, that label implies a fire-and-brimstone charisma that galvanizes people into action. While some executives do epitomize that approach, many highly effective ones are very low-key and soft-spoken.

Too many managers deal in a world of paper, not people. In one of his scathing *Fortune* columns on this widespread problem, Walter Kiechl

III asks a good question: "If the top dogs are going to be paid so much, why can't the rest of the kennel reasonably expect a little more of them by way of guts? Guts enough, for starters, to go out and talk to their people face to face, if that's what it takes to make the company work."[16]

Executives who are chained to their desks passing paper from their in-baskets to their out-baskets, issuing orders by memo or phone, or holding court with those wily or privileged enough to make it past the guards (executive assistants) create a legion of managers who aspire to do the same. And so the moat separating management and the riffraff grows wider and deeper.

But even worse, executives grow out of touch with reality. Kay Whitmore, president of Eastman Kodak, insists, "Active involvement in quality . . . can't be done from your desk. Management must get out, walk around, and see personally what's happening in the quality arena."[17] The American Society for Quality Control's extensive studies of best leadership practices for service/quality improvement have led to the conclusion:

> The innovative company is further distinguished by management that is on its feet. . . . Most ideas don't appear all neat and tidy in a memo on someone's desk. Ideas come from discussions with customers (maybe even in the form of a complaint), from problem-solving sessions with suppliers, from talking to workers who've identified a difficulty or proposed a better method, from listening to the sales force.[18]

Many senior executives are locked in their offices dealing with operational details, crisis management, or approving guidelines from staff people to catch errors. Analyzing and fixing problems at their root cause along with operations belongs to empowered teams if the organization is going to develop relevant improvements that are owned by those who must make them work. Executives must get out of their offices and "manage the organization's context." That means, for example, constantly repeating the "stump speech" the executive team has developed on what business the organization is in, where the organization is going, and what the organization believes in. Not only will that help focus and guide the organization, but it also will force executives to push operations down to where it belongs and take them out of the burdensome and destructive "upward delegation" loop.

SIGNALING OPPORTUNITIES

You can signal your unshakable vision/commitment to service/quality in hundreds of ways. Here are just a few:

- Hold regular meetings with employees in groups and individually to discuss your progress toward higher service/quality.
- Make sure service/quality issues have the most prominent place in your meeting agendas and are never bumped.
- Bring customers, customer advocates (salespeople are excellent ones), and frontline service deliverers to key planning and operational sessions.
- Be sure you and your management team spend the bulk of your time out of your comfortable offices. Keep your paper-management and people-leadership activities in the right proportion. Spend that time with suppliers, customers, or those people who are actually producing, delivering, and supporting your products and services.
- Put on an apron or pick up the phone and serve customers without being introduced as the brass. You will send important signals— and might even learn something.
- Get in the habit of reading, circulating, and responding to feedback solicited from customers. You will be amazed at how quickly your people will show a new concern for what your customers are saying. This paperwork will do more for your organization's long term health than "bean counting." Haven't you hired good people to do that?
- Take a hard look at how innovators are treated. Are they quietly kneecapped or hailed as heroes. Don't let your bureaucrats grind them down. The organization is full of little wastebaskets between you and the frontline team members who are full of outstanding service/quality improvement ideas. Give them a process to take what action they can on their own or get the support they need from the organization.
- Serve your producers and servers. *Continually* ask them what management can do to help them provide higher levels of service/quality. Hold your managers accountable for serving the organization.
- Set and *live by* this *ironclad rule—all promises to customers are kept.* Period. Overtime and other expenses are secondary to your organization being known for keeping its word. This rule also puts pressure on everyone to be careful about the promises he or she makes.
- Celebrate, honor, cheer, applaud, reinforce, laud, praise, extol, and otherwise reinforce *all* service/quality achievements. Do this often and consistently enough and your people will start to believe that service/quality is not a "BOHICA" that will go away as soon as the next fad hits.

- Visit other top service/quality providers that your organization can use to benchmark key processes or catch a glimpse of what lies ahead on the improvement journey.

- Put you and your management team first in line for the extensive skill-development sessions your organization will be going through. Then use the skills in all your own meetings, management coaching activities, and team decision making and planning. Deliver these sessions to your next level of management. They will quickly view the training with a whole new sense of priority.

- Search out and destroy all executive status symbols, perks, or privileges that contribute to the we/they gap. Find new ways to compensate executives or let those who need these symbols take their elitist insecurities to some other organization that is not trying to become team based.

- Appoint a senior coordinator reporting to the CEO, establish a steering committee, and develop a three-year, detailed strategic service/quality plan tied to your business plan (we will look at this further later). Whenever any initiative is given significant amounts of scarce resources, it becomes very real very fast to middle managers.

UNCONSCIOUS INCOMPETENCE

"The louder he talked of his honour, the faster we counted our spoons."

Ralph Waldo Emerson, *American philosopher, essayist, and poet*

Most executives, like most frontline employees, don't set out to do a bad job. Seldom will an executive declare a value or behavioral goal and then deliberately contradict that value with his or her actions. Acts of executive hypocrisy are often committed innocently. Many executives simply have no idea their actions are widely perceived to be out of step with their words. And as their personal credibility gulf widens, their declarations of new directions, strategies, or values register an ever higher "snicker factor" throughout the organization.

Many executive behaviors are sadly inconsistent with their loud declarations because of ignorance. The executives are not getting direct feedback on how their actions are perceived. Ironically, those very executives who are the brashest violators of their own fine rhetoric are the ones least likely to hear about it. No one wants to tell the emperor he or she is naked and being snickered at. So the fantasyland surrounding the inconsistent executive rises ever higher. And executive frustration also rises because managers, supervisors, and frontline people aren't grabbing hold of the new values. The we/they gap continues to widen.

While the two broad steps to help you and your management team live your values are easy to describe, they are very tough to do, particularly for insecure power brokers. Step one is to open as many new channels for feedback to the executive team as possible. Numerous informal and formal methods can solicit feedback on your behavior from people in your organization as well as outside suppliers and customers. The second step is to treat the messengers, especially internal ones, with kid gloves. If it looks like they got shot in the process, feedback will instantly revert to "gee boss, you're doing a great job." Only those people with a career death wish will then participate.

EXAMPLES OF SIGNALING COMMITMENT

"True examples of companies where leadership entails more than merely cheerleading for the cause are not so easy to find."

Total Quality newsletter[19]

A few examples of strong service/quality signaling follow:

- At Wesley-Jessen, President Charlie Stroupe begins each bimonthly executive team meeting with a report from each executive on what he or she has personally done to advance the service/quality improvement effort in the past two weeks. This includes such activities as senior vice presidents leading W-J's major process improvement initiatives, president's lunches for top performers, each executive calling at least three customers a week who have experienced a ricochet, and executives kicking off every one of the dozens of service/quality introductory education and awareness sessions running throughout the company.

- One executive team determined the "humorous" barbs vice presidents were throwing at each other had become a thinly disguised form of sniping that rippled through the organization with departments taking shots at each other as well. To give the sniper feedback and help form more constructive team patterns, executives now clang a pen on their water glasses or coffee cups whenever one executive snipes at another team member.

- CEOs of top service/quality companies do a great deal of "managing by wandering around." Bill Dover, president of Canada's Red Lobster and Olive Garden restaurant chains, works in a restaurant two to three days a week as do all his senior executives. In a typical year, Bill Marriott, Jr., visited 100 of his company's hotels, 50 restaurants, and 30 In-Flite kitchens. "I believe in going out into the organization and meeting as many people as I can and personally encouraging them," he says.[20]

- A number of companies, such as IBM, Xerox, Digital, and others, assign a few key accounts to each executive to keep him or her in touch with customers and the sales force. Executives become the corporate contact for the salesperson or customer if special head-office attention to a service/quality issue is needed.

- To dramatize the importance of clean bus depot restrooms, John Munro, president of Greyhound Lines of Canada, warned his managers he would drop into any depot on an hour's notice and dine in the washroom. Within weeks he was getting photos of managers dining in spotless washrooms—and ridership continues to grow.[21]

- Luciano Benetton, head of the Italian textile and retail giant that bears his name, spends six months of the year out of his office. "I must get out into the world where I can sense the preferences of people, see what they like . . . I can talk to people who teach me about their markets."[22]

- In *Deming Management at Work*, Mary Walton reports that part of Bridgestone's turnaround of the old Firestone plant in LaVergne, Tennessee, involved taking away executive parking spaces, getting rid of ties (except for computer consultants and purchasing agents), moving engineers' offices to the factory floor, ripping down office walls among support staff, and locating meeting areas throughout the facility. Statistical quality control supervisor Barry Hill says: "It brings us closer together so we can have mutual respect for each other. I'm not the boss in the office anymore."[23]

- A fine-paper manufacturer, a large hospital, a producer of medical devices, and a federal government department demonstrated their clear commitment to service/quality by making the budgets for these efforts "sacred and off limits" during painful budget cuts.

- In a growing number of organizations, senior executives are the instructors for efforts to develop coaching and team leadership skills that equip every manager and supervisor to live the new culture.

- Corning Glass Works' State College plant was running at capacity making television bulbs. Some bulbs went slightly off spec, yet the desperate customer said he would take them anyway. But the plant manager refused to ship a product that was not up to standard.

Comments Chairman James R. Houghton, "It took about five seconds for the people in the plant to understand that he was serious about quality. Those are the things that have to happen because people are always asking, 'What do you want? Quality or profit?' The answer is 'both.' "[24]

- Executives at Paul Revere Insurance Group developed their own unique approach to "management by wandering around" and signaling called PEET—Program to Ensure that Everybody's Thanked. Each of the 15 executives receives a monthly PEET sheet, which lists the names and leader of three quality teams they are to visit to discuss service/quality. After the visit, the executive notes the visit's highlights and sends the PEET sheet to quality team central. A monthly summary of highlights and trends is compiled and circulated to the executive team.[25]

- Levi Strauss executives spend one Saturday a month on the sales floor of major retail outlets selling jeans. "It's quite an eye-opener to sell our own (brand) and watch people decide to buy other people's jeans," says one senior manager.[26]

COMMON PITFALLS AND TRAPS TO SIGNALING COMMITMENT

"Customers who consider our waitresses uncivil should see the manager."

Sign in a restaurant

Big Talk, Little Action

Three keys to long-term service/quality improvement are: (1) follow through, (2) follow through, (3) follow through. You and your managers cannot set bold new directions and then delegate their implementation. Your time and attention need to stay focused on service/quality improvement. You can't get wrapped up in all the details, but you must stay the course.

Managing by Muddling Around

If you are out to "snoopervise," swoop in and "solve" problems, or do bed checks, you'd do better to stay in your office. Many executives with weak coaching or team leadership skills inadvertently reduce openness and trust by their ineffective interpersonal skills. They are usually the same ones who are too busy to build their own skills but send their overworked supervisors and managers to be "fixed."

Ivory Tower Visions

There is a delicate balance between senior management getting its vision, values, and plans together and building consensus and commitment through broad input. Visions and plans should not be developed in back rooms without the involvement of those people who will make it all work. An even greater danger is low customer input. Many an organization has squandered precious resources providing top-notch products or services nobody wanted.

Month-End Myopia

If you have developed a service/quality objectives statement that boldly proclaims "zero defects," "delighted customers," or "quality is our highest priority," watch yourself when the heat is on. This is one of your managerial moments of truth. What standards will you *really* accept? If you knowingly ship marginal-quality products or deliver poor service, you have just set a new service/quality standard.

Catch as Catch Can

A disciplined, regular process for communicating senior management commitment is essential. Service/quality coordinators can help executives stage-manage their time to get maximum visibility and involvement in key service/quality improvement events.

On a Wing and a Prayer

You have to be aggressive when you go after service/quality improvement. All your best intentions to signal vision and commitment will have little impact if you don't have plans, structures, and processes in place to take you through the long haul. People just won't get on board if you announce a million-dollar destination and then pull up in a patched-up old bus with two miles of life left.

Chapter Eight

Cylinder Two: Listening to Internal/External Customers

> *"Listening, really listening, is tough and grinding work, often humbling, sometimes distasteful. It's a fairly sure bet that you won't like the lion's share of what you hear."*
>
> Bob Waterman,
> *The Renewal Factor*

How can it get any simpler? What could be more obvious? Find out what your customer wants across all three rings of perceived value and establish a continually improving organization working to exceed those expectations. But talk about common sense rarely being put into common practice! As with good nutrition and exercise, we know what needs to be done. It's actually making a disciplined habit of *doing* it that is so tough. David Garvin found in his studies of service/quality practices that "competitively useful quality information is surprisingly scarce. Many companies *think* they know what quality means in their industry; few appear to have taken the time to back their hunches with careful research" (his emphasis).[1]

As discussed in Chapter Two, service/quality can be defined only through the eyes of your customers. You need to develop your priorities, measurements, resource allocations, and the like from the outside in. Richard Schonberger writes:

> The customer is *in* the world-class organization, not outside of it. . . . If left outside, the customer gets treated with indifference—at best—and offers the same in return. That spells temporary relationships: Customers are poised to fly, like a nervous flock of geese in a grain field.[2]

115

Developing a highly customer-focused organization with high customer satisfaction and loyalty demands a heavy amount of listening. You know you *should* be regularly listening to your customers, but are you?

And how are your customers' perceptions treated? Are they seen as facts or as misguided, uninformed opinions? Your customers' perceptions *are* facts—whether or not they match your own view. When dealing with the subjective areas of quality and service, the *only* perceptions that matter are your customers'. According to Jack Welch, chairman and CEO of General Electric and chief architect of the company's revitalization, "The customer either rates us better or worse than somebody else. It's not very scientific, but it's disastrous if you score low."[3]

LISTENING SHARPENS YOUR EDGE

Why do so many executives do so much talking about the importance of good customer listening, then do so little of it? Mainly because they assume "we know what our customers need." The Strategic Planning Institute's research shows just how deadly that management assumption can be:

- Managers don't always know customers' purchasing criteria. "Even when the criteria are correctly identified, management may misjudge the relative importance of individual criteria . . . *sometimes by a factor of 3:1.*"

- Managers often misjudge how their customers perceive the organization's service/quality. "Those differences in perceptions of performance may exist for the most basic of criteria."

- Managers can fail to see how their customers' needs have changed and evolved because of "competitive product developments, technological advances, market or environmental influences."

- "Rather than focusing on customer preferences, management tends to evaluate the quality of products from an *internal* perspective."[4]

If you are determined to increase your organization's performance through higher service/quality, you have no choice but to get very close to your customers. Your organization needs to become hypersensitive to your customers' needs and expectations. Lele and Sheth's study of high-service/quality providers found "the winning companies spend enormous amounts of energy and money to find out what the customer wants . . . we found that 'when one of their customers sneezes, the firm catches pneumonia.' "[5] And as Du Pont Chairman Richard E. Heckert points out, you need to pick up the pace: "As the world becomes more and more competitive, you have to sharpen all your tools. Knowing what's on the customer's mind is the most important."[6]

Top service/quality providers make every attempt to understand their customers' world and speak their language. Intensive listening keeps them in touch and in tune with their customers. And that pushes them to become more user-friendly. We all know organizations that aren't. Their customers are expected to speak the organization's language. They have their own secret code of acronyms and buzzwords that sounds like some foreign tongue. And to the customer it is.

Effective customer listening helps you use your resources better. You can probably think of two or three organizations you have done business with that expend enormous time, energy, and money to provide you with services you don't want. That's one of the key reasons high service/quality providers have lower costs. Leonard Berry, David Bennet, and Carter Brown provide a good insight to this in their book, *Service Quality*:

> When management fails to understand customer desires for the service, a chain reaction of mistakes is likely to follow. The wrong service standards. The wrong training. The wrong types of performance measurements. The wrong advertising. And so forth. It is tough enough to satisfy customer desires without the added burden of not really knowing what desires to satisfy.[7]

An increasingly important strategic issue today is innovation. And team-based customer listening is at the heart of highly innovative organizations. Brian Quinn, a management professor and author who has extensively studied the topic, found:

> Many experienced big companies are relying less on early research and more on interactions with lead customers. Hewlett-Packard, 3M, Sony, and Raychem frequently introduce radically new products through small teams that work closely with lead customers. These teams learn from their customers' needs and innovations and rapidly modify designs and entry strategies based on this information.[8]

EXTERNAL CUSTOMER LISTENING

"Nature has given to us one tongue, but two ears, that we may hear from others twice as much as we speak."

Epictetus, *Greek philosopher*

There are a multitude of ways to listen naively, continually, and systematically to your customers. And you need to use them all as extensively and frequently as possible if you are going to keep up with the dizzying pace of change among your customers. "Every research methodology has weaknesses and limitations," advise market researchers Valarie Zeithaml, A. Pasasuraman, and Len Berry. "It is wise to use multiple methods to transcend the weaknesses of any one approach and to provide richer, more comprehensive insight."[9] Marketing guru Regis Mc-Kenna agrees: "Sensitivity comes from having a variety of modes and channels through which companies can read the environment."[10]

Top service/quality performers use the following methods in dozens of variations. *How many are you using?*

Close up and personal. The simplest way to listen to your customers is to meet them face to face and ask them what they look for in your type of product or service. There really is nothing like getting out on the front serving lines and hearing the candid comments from customers. (Of course, if you would rather just *talk* about how "our customers sign our paychecks" instead of *acting* as though you truly believed it, why bother to listen to "ungrateful customers who just bellyache and complain"?)

Done frequently and broadly enough, face-to-face discussions can help clarify inner-ring standards and expectations you have gathered from other listening sources. In *The Service Edge*, Ron Zemke and Dick Schaaf explain:

> The customer who says your company is "lousy at communication" may have in mind one unpleasant phone call, periodic frustration with a poorly written manual, years of puzzling over incomprehensible bills, or any combination of a dozen other things. You only know what they mean when you ask the right questions.[11]

Market research. This tends to be a fairly rigorous and in-depth method. It can help you get a handle on emerging markets you may want to identify and serve or stay abreast of the markets you are currently serving. Focus groups, surveys, and studies of demographic and psychographic trends are the techniques most commonly used. Your industry probably has data available to help you identify patterns and changes in your markets.

Focus groups and advisory panels. These come in all sizes and varieties. They may be combined with market research, service/quality team visits, surveys, and face-to-face listening. Retailers, electronic manufacturers, and consumer product companies are among a growing list of organizations using this very effective listening approach. Customer focus groups can provide invaluable feedback and guidance on designs, standards, typical expectations, pricing, styles, trends, and more.

Tom Peters urges that

> informal "focus groups" of a few customers ought to be called in every operation—manufacturing, distribution, accounting, not just marketing—on a biweekly or monthly basis. Debriefings with key accounts (annually or semiannually) must include formal survey questions and open-ended discussions with all levels and functions in key account operations.[12]

Customer surveys.   This method is becoming as popular as dieting programs, and too often as effective. Many customer surveys are poorly designed and give back biased or useless information. "A sure way to get misleading, useless results is to call a staff meeting, brainstorm a list of service attributes, make them into a questionnaire, administer the questionnaire to hundreds of customers, and precisely tabulate the answers," warn William Davidow and Bro Uttal in *Total Customer Service*. "The result is a very persuasive argument for adopting a service strategy that perpetuates both the vices and virtues of the existing strategy"[13]— typical inside-out "listening" and measurement.

Effective customer surveys are used in conjunction with focus groups or interviews that help start the effort with a blank sheet of paper. Customers tell you which attributes are important and the relative importance of each for every product, service, and market segment. After this qualitative phase, you can quantify responses to establish rigorous measurement systems, deploy key resources, align organizational systems, guide improvement teams, establish internal service/quality indicators, and engage in a multitude of other strategic activities we will discuss in detail in this and the chapters ahead. Karl Albrecht and Lawrence Bradford explain how a customer-focused organization is built: "Only when you know what factors are on your customers' report cards can you begin to build a business that puts the customer at the center and is truly customer-driven."[14]

Customer hot lines.   *The Service Edge* newsletter calls the toll-free 800 telephone number "one of the most frequently used and most effective methods for staying in touch with customers." Getting executives to listen regularly to calls is also an excellent way to help them keep both feet on the ground. Numerous companies study their calls for trends and ideas for new products and services.

Customer complaints. Considering that less than 5 percent of your unhappy customers complain, your first goal is to dramatically increase your complaints, to get your unhappy customers telling you rather than 10 to 16 of your current or potential customers. But according to David Berliner of Consumers Union, "The number one problem is that people just don't know how to complain and when to complain. They have something wrong . . . they're frustrated, they're angry, they want satisfaction . . . they want to get the thing resolved and they don't know where to turn."[15]

As discussed in Chapter Three, effective recovery from service/quality problems can go a long way toward winning back customers. But fixing problems, rather than preventing them by improving the production, delivery, or support process, is very expensive. Complaint tracking and analysis often is a key analytical tool to focus team attention on those processes with the highest customer satisfaction or delight potential. But knowing the relative value customers give to your organization's product and service attributes becomes critical in sorting out the "vital few" complaints from the "trivial many."

Team visits. Increasingly, intact teams are visiting their customers and seeing how their products or services are used. This approach is especially effective for production teams and the many administrative support teams that work below the external customer's line of visibility. It is easy for these people to lose sight of who will ultimately use what they are producing or "why we all come to work every day." During those visits, teams get a better understanding of where their work fits into the overall service/quality chain. Motorola CEO George Fisher says, "We've established a massive program of increasing customer visits at all levels of the organization. We want everyone in Motorola, from top to bottom, to get out and see customers—to talk with them directly and understand their business better."[16]

But, you may be thinking, it costs a lot of money and downtime to send these people out there. You are right. And what is the cost of not sharpening your axes? But, you may be tempted to respond, we're no different from anybody else. Exactly.

User groups and conferences. This method of staying close to customers is used extensively in the computer business. Groups of customers meet to share ideas and experiences about the use of particular systems. Meetings may be initiated by the company for its customers or by the users themselves.

A growing number of companies are sponsoring customer conferences and educational events as a way not only to provide enhanced service but also to listen to customers.

QUALITY FUNCTION DEPLOYMENT

"The obscure we eventually see. The completely obvious, it seems, takes longer."

Edward R. Murrow, *American broadcaster*

Quality function deployment is another of the many improvements the Japanese have made to the process of continuous service/quality improvement. This highly disciplined process for product development and design builds a detailed, outside-in service/quality chain around the weighted key customer attributes uncovered through a number of listening methods. The goal of quality function deployment is to deploy "the voice of the customer" through a product's entire technical specifications and resource requirements. Detailed matrices listing the customer's rank-ordered "what" expectations are tracked across "how" each will be met and which teams will be responsible for each component. When competitors are also tracked, the data-filled matrix takes the shape of a house, so it is often called "the house of quality."

Some researchers credit quality function deployment as one of the main reasons Japanese automakers gained so much ground on their U.S. competitors in the early 1980s. Ford successfully applied the concepts in developing its highly successful Taurus and Probe models. Procter & Gamble is another one of the growing number of North American companies embracing this approach. Earl Conway, corporate quality director, says it "changes the way you look at the data market research generates . . . it brings clarity out of complexity. Used in the right way, you pick the right means and methods and supporting systems to design a product that meets the most important requirements of your customers."[17]

INTERNAL CUSTOMER LISTENING

"It's hard to see the picture when you are inside the frame."

A team-based upside-down organization that has broad involvement in continuous improvement is built on voluntarism. Management's job is to serve those who are actually doing the work. The teams and their members are the internal customers of management and staff support groups. But this commonsense view is seldom common practice. In *Delivering Quality Service*, Zeithaml, Pasasuraman, and Berry write, "Often overlooked in service research is the importance of employee research. This is a serious oversight as employee research is just as critical as customer research because employees are customers too."[18]

Four Season's John Sharpe makes another important point about internal customer listening: "Listening attentively is perhaps the highest form of respect one person can pay another. It tells our employees we value their opinion—and we do."[19] *Fortune* writer Faye Rice reports, "Fewer than half the employees polled in a 1990 study by Towers Perrin believe management is aware of the problems they face. And in the Hay Group's research covering 1 million employees in over 2,000 organizations, only 34 percent responded favorably to questions about how well their company listens to them."[20] If you really believe "people are our most precious resource," how long, hard, and frequently do you actively listen to your people? If management doesn't show a genuine interest in helping them, why should they be interested in helping the organization improve service/quality?

Most of the listening methods outlined for external customers also apply internally. Focus groups and advisory panels, face-to-face contacts (MBWA), surveys, opening complaint channels and analyzing them, hot lines, and internal team visits are highly effective ways for management to tune in to frontline teams and better focus management's support for the improvement effort and assess organizational readiness for the cultural changes ahead. These also form the basis for the skill needs analysis that helps determine where best to start building the foundation for the improvement effort. However, the frequency of such things as surveys or focus groups needs to be greater than with external customers. Many top organizations run employee surveys every three to six months and have their executives and managers meet frequently with teams to nurture an ongoing two-way information flow.

If you're going to listen, *be prepared to act on what you hear.* Because asking the questions raises expectations that something will be done. Listening and not *visibly* and fairly quickly responding is worse than not listening. If you run a survey, for example, let everyone who completed it know what the results were and what action is being taken. Or better yet, get frontline teams involved in interpreting and prioritizing the data and developing action plans. Empty, token listening is all too often the game played by "concerned" managers.

If you're competing in the marketplace for customers, one group of frontline performers is an especially rich source of customer information. Their contributions are usually overlooked. These are your salespeople. Are your salespeople key strategists in plotting how you can move ahead through higher service/quality? Or are your salespeople treated as "necessary evils who would give away the store if we let them"? At Chaparral Steel, not only are the salespeople treated as key players in improving performance, but also everyone is directed to behave more like salespeople—to listen to customers. President Gordon Forward says:

> We made everyone in the company a member of the sales department. That means people in security, secretaries, everyone. If we have bent bars coming off our production line that are causing a problem for our customers, we might send a superintendent over with the salesperson or the person who did the bundling or somebody from production or metallurgy. It's everyone's job. We mix crews. . . . We want them (employees) to see Chaparral the way our customers do, we also want them to talk to each other.[21]

LOOKING IN ON GOOD CUSTOMER LISTENING

"Know how to listen and you will profit even from those who talk badly."

Plutarch, *Greek moralist and biographer*

There are hundreds, if not thousands, of ways to listen to your customers. No one or two ways are best. The key is to use as many as you can to get the broadest view possible of your customers' needs and expectations. Good listening is also combined with strong feedback and measurement systems (the topic of Chapter Eighteen).

The following examples will give you and your management team ideas on some of the ways others listen to their customers.

• A growing number of companies in retailing, financial services, and the hospitality industry hire "mystery shoppers." Posing as regular customers, these trained professionals provide detailed reports on the service/quality levels encountered. Mystery vacationers at Carnival Cruise Lines ask travel agents to suggest a vacation. If the agent suggests a cruise, he or she is rewarded with $10. If they recommend a Carnival Cruise, they are rewarded with $1,000 on the spot. "The program provides us with hands-on research," says Bob Dickinson, senior vice president of sales and marketing, at Carnival Cruise Lines. "We know what agents are selling and how they're selling."[22]

- An architect built a cluster of office buildings in a large green area. He waited to construct the sidewalks until people started wearing traffic patterns in the grass between the buildings. The sidewalks were then laid to follow the efficient, smoothly curved pathways established by the buildings' customers.

- When Ron Contino became commissioner of New York City's Sanitation Department, he discovered over 50 percent of the fleet was off the road because of breakdowns. To get the operators and mechanics committed to service/quality improvement, Contino solicited suggestions. He quickly provided lunchroom facilities and other requested changes in working conditions and went on to act on the suggestions for improving vehicle maintenance, such as a robotic paint system. The percentage of vehicles on the road jumped to 97 percent, and the department began contracting in maintenance work from other fleets.

- Baldrige winner Federal Express has refined a number of internal listening processes since Fred Smith founded the company in 1973. The survey feedback action is an annual process that starts with every team member in the company completing an anonymous survey expressing his or her feelings about the company, managers, FedEx's service levels, pay, and benefits. Overall results are tabulated and passed to each manager, who must meet with his or her work team to develop action plans for resolving problems. All scores are compiled for a corporatewide leadership ranking tied to incentive compensation for management and professionals. If scores are not as high as the year before, no one in management receives a bonus.[23]

- In starting its improvement journey, contact lens manufacturer Wesley-Jessen hired Minneapolis-based Lakewood Research to conduct extensive focus groups, interviews, and customer surveys. This was done using the three rings of perceived value model to collect customer expectations within each one of the rings. Jim Moritz, director, Total Quality Management, explains:

  > The key here was the research helped the Corporate Steering Committee determine which projects and processes W-J undertook and with what priority. Projects that affected third-ring employees (those in contact with customers) or external customers came first. Then second ring and on to the first ring. If our qualitative feedback didn't specify areas for improvement we aren't working on it.

- To better listen and respond to employee issues, Canadian Red Lobster and Olive Garden restaurants have a bilingual 800 telephone number to call. Every restaurant also has CEO Bill Dover's and other executives' home phone numbers posted on the kitchen bulletin board.

Head office support staff members regularly take their turns as "Johnny Appleseeds" by spending a few days in restaurants hosting, waiting on tables, preparing food, clearing tables, and so on. This keeps them in touch with customers and helps identify employee issues needing attention.

- At Stew Leonard's grocery, service teams scout out their competitors, looking for better ways to "wow" customers back into their own store. Focus groups are also used every week to give management feedback on the store's pricing, displays, selection, specials, and so on.
- Canadian Airlines hired researchers to fly with customers, who were paid an honorarium for participating. The researcher met the customer before departure, and they traveled together to the airport. Customer and researcher went through check-in procedures, flight, and arrival procedures together, and the researcher asked for the customer's perceptions of the service provided during each step of the process. This helped form the basis for further quantitative research.
- Connecting production teams to the customers they served was an important step in implementing the improvement process that saved the ailing Tennessee-based Kingsport Foundry & Manufacturing Corporation. Teams visited their customers' production plant and saw how their products were used. President Bill Ring says, "You'd be totally amazed at . . . the ripple effect throughout the entire work force of 'Hey, here's what we really do for this company up there.' Not only did this help everyone focus on how to better meet customer needs, but it contributed to a much higher level of pride."[24]
- Radio consultant Lee Abrams increases ratings for clients 92 percent of the time. Among his unorthodox methods are surveys he takes while hitchhiking. When he sees drivers punching radio stations on their car radios, he asks why they are changing. Abrams advises, "Don't worry about being scientific. Just be creative. If you're dealing with computers, go hang around a Computerland."
- One step in an intense new focus on customers (which led to a 50 percent increase in profits over two years) had Avco Financial Services Canadian executives contact 10 customers by phone every time they visited a branch. They asked about the service and quality, requested suggestions for improvement, and thanked customers for their business. "They were quite surprised by the little things that could turn a customer off," reflected past President Will Barrett. "And they became extremely concerned about the customers' perception of the relationship."
- B.C. Tel holds regular "defective tool days" to improve internal service/quality. Teams of telephone installers and repairers are invited to bring in the cables, switches, testing equipment, or procedures they

have the most trouble using. Internal and external suppliers listen as a senior executive leads the meeting. Suppliers are told to "shut up and listen. No excuses. No rationalization. Just take notes and ask questions only for clarity." At the end of the session, the chairperson records the dates by which the supplier will have the problem fixed or will report on progress.

• Three disgruntled customers were brought in to talk to a large group of mechanical contractors at their association conference. The customers outlined in detail the frustrations they felt with the group and the consequences resulting from shoddy service/quality. The consequences include secret blacklists, legal entanglements, financial holdbacks, or refusal to settle accounts. Many contractors were surprised to discover that dissatisfaction stemmed more from a series of little things (lateness, not returning phone calls, untidy work sites, not providing good information/updates, disorganization) than from technical incompetence or equipment failure.

COMMON LISTENING PITFALLS AND TRAPS

"We can easily forgive a child who is afraid of the dark; the real tragedy of life is when men are afraid of the light."

Plato, *Greek philosopher*

Among Friends

Don't just listen to your satisfied or friendly customers. Be sure you get a balance of unhappy and dissatisfied ones as well. No reports or memos can capture the impact of being taken to task by a customer who has just had a run-in with your system. You expect your people to take the flak. Quit hiding in your office and experience it yourself. It will bring service/ quality into perspective.

"Yeah, But" Listening

Too often, when managers do bother to listen to their internal or external customers, they do the "yeah, but" kind of listening. They aren't really listening at all; they are rationalizing, explaining, excusing, or defending. "But our customers don't understand our business," or "If only it were that simple. You see, we have some unique problems. . . ."

If one of your colleagues didn't stop defending, rationalizing, or explaining long enough for you to give him feedback on a problem he is creating, would you consider him a good listener? Would you feel he heard you? Do you think the problem would be corrected? And how likely would you be to believe his sincerity if he told you he values your feedback? So how are you coming across to your internal and external customers?

Few and Far Between

Don't become overly reliant on just a few listening channels. You may be getting an incomplete picture. Many organizations rely primarily on complaints and maybe a few simple surveys. "The problem with such methods is they measure only the extremes," says Christopher Hart, an assistant professor at Harvard Business School who studies service industries. According to Hart, "You hear from Mr. Grumpy and Mr. Smiley, but not from Mr. Average."[25]

Introverted Innovation

While organizations can successfully "spring" new products and services on their customers, the deck is severely stacked against winning this game. Evidence clearly shows that successful innovations happen "out there" in the real world with real customers. Paper studies and intuitive hunches that result in products or services being developed in back rooms rarely work. Your customers may have no idea of what product or service you could create, but they do know the problem they need solved or the opportunity they want to seize. Remember this marketing truism: we don't really buy the drill, we buy the hole it will give us. Get close to your customers and work together to find solutions to their problems. Help them see how you can give them the holes they need—or even develop alternatives together that don't need holes.

Hard of Doing

It should go without saying, but it has to be said: *Act* on what your customers tell you. If you don't, you will miss golden opportunities, and your customers and your people will stop talking to you. The legendary industrialist Andrew Carnegie once said, "As I grow older, I pay less attention to what people say. I just watch what they do."

Chapter Nine

Cylinder Three: Education and Awareness

"Learn as though you would never be able to master it; hold it as though you would be in fear of losing it."

Confucius,
Chinese philosopher and teacher

S ay that after listening to and working with your external customers, you develop an exciting product or service that promises to take your customers by storm. Now you want to get the word out to your customers and either attract new ones or expand the perception of value among existing customers.

You photocopy some leaflets, throw together a press release, ask a couple of harried executives to give a few hurried interviews, and just as you get the campaign under way, your executive team gets bored and wants to move on to something new and different. How successful would your campaign be? What impressions would your customers be left with? What kind of return on investment do you think this approach would give you?

Ridiculous? Absolutely. But take a look at your *internal* education and awareness. It is amazing how many organizations will spend megabucks and megahours planning and executing powerful, slick campaigns aimed at their external customers. Many will then turn around and spend 10 bucks and two hours bringing the people on board who ultimately decide whether those external advertising messages are fact or fiction. A few thousand blown moments of truth (and that's likely just a couple of days' worth in your organization) can quickly scuttle hundreds of thousands of dollars' worth of external marketing and public relations. A few piercing ricochets from your product or support rings will deflate your customers' perception of value much faster than your customer service, marketing, sales, or public relations department can expensively pump it up again.

SEEING THE BIG PICTURE

"It is fine to aim high if we have developed the ability to accomplish our aims, but there is no use aiming unless our gun is loaded."

William Ross

It's been said, "If you don't know where you're going, any road will take you there." The same is true for organizations. *You cannot transform your culture into a team-based, continually improving, customer-focused organization if most of the people who are going to make it happen don't see, understand, and embrace this picture.* Strong and lasting commitment at the top of the organization is vital. But it's only the beginning. Executives can't propel the organization toward higher service/quality by sheer force of will. They need a majority of managers, supervisors, and team members enthusiastically moving the process along.

Joseph Miraglia, senior corporate vice president at Motorola, calls "CEO commitment as THE KEY to corporate renewal" a myth. "We had as much commitment as possible—the renewal was launched by the CEO," Miraglia says. "But, we found that his commitment was not enough to stimulate and coordinate the many thousands of changes that would have to be made if an organization of 75,000 people was going to renew itself."[1] Fred Smith, CEO of Federal Express, agrees:

> We in management are probably totally convinced that our companies must provide 100 percent customer satisfaction. But the real trick is communicating that goal to our employees. And the catch is we can communicate that goal all we want, but if our employees don't buy into it—if our employees don't support the commitment by making it *their* commitment—then nothing will happen.[2]

This cylinder is aimed at providing everyone throughout your organization with the knowledge of where the service/quality journey is headed, why, and what the route will look like. The cylinder is also full of activities to continuously supply the information and inspiration to sustain momentum through the peaks and valleys of the difficult and endless trip. But education and awareness don't include the skill building that will actually outfit everyone with the tools and techniques to initiate and sustain continuous service/quality improvement. Our implementation architecture (see page 99) distinguishes between three sets of skills within a few skill categories. We do this because of the widespread misunderstanding and confusion many executives, as well as improvement and development professionals, continually have among service/quality improvement inspiration, knowledge, and skill building. Four upcoming chapters should help you sort through this.

Developing Understanding

"The mind is slow in unlearning what it has been long in learning."

Seneca, *Roman statesman and philosopher*

Every study of high-service/quality providers shows that training plays a huge role in the improvement process. Training consists of understanding what is to be done and why (education and awareness) and then developing the ability to make the targeted changes happen (skills). Both are needed. But the process starts with education and awareness. Everyone needs to know what is expected. Dairy Queen International found that one of the biggest reasons employees quit was because they were frustrated by this lack of understanding.[3]

Often the greatest education and awareness challenge on the road to higher service/quality is getting people to let go of their old paradigms. When the Greek philosopher Antisthenes was asked what learning was most necessary in life he replied, "To unlearn what is not." But our mass production, hierarchical, inward-focused paradigm built over the past century is not easily cast aside and replaced. "Most of quality, in fact, is not teaching new things, it's teaching to forget—you have to unteach—teach people to forget ideas that they've known since childhood," reports Myron Tribus, formerly a Xerox vice president and now director of the MIT Center for Advanced Engineering Study.[4]

Introduction to Service/Quality

You can't just fire off a memo, issue an edict, put together a video, or put on a videoconference to launch your improvement effort. Your people need help grasping the basic service/quality concepts and understanding your organization's vision, values, improvement strategies and plans. They also need a chance to discuss their role, next steps, concerns, and the like. This takes some planning to ensure everyone gets the message you and your management team want to send. Karl Albrecht has found:

What we have learned about organizational life is that, if executives want to mobilize the people of the organization to a new philosophy of excellence, they must find a way to make that direction meaningful and exciting to the people and communicate it to them in such a way that they fully grasp, at a personal level, the value of embracing it.[5]

Your introduction to service/quality should contain the following elements. These are the same messages that every member of your executive team needs to be consistently delivering in formal and informal stump speeches.

Why improve service/quality?   This is where the urgency or appeal of improving service/quality needs to be plainly communicated. If most supervisors, managers, or team members don't get fired up about the need for, or appeal of, attaining continually higher levels of service/quality, the effort won't go far. Service/quality needs to be seen to be alleviating pain or producing significant gain. And as one executive puts it, "Employees have increasingly sophisticated bull (dropping) detectors. They can see when we're giving them a snow job or when we're really serious."

What is service/quality?   As was argued in Chapter Two, your organization needs a common definition of service, quality, total quality, continuous improvement, or whatever you are calling your drive for higher performance. *You all need to be speaking the same language.* Your definition has to start with external customers' perceptions and work back through the service/quality chain to external suppliers. That means everyone must understand they either serve external customers directly or serve internal customers. This will be a new and strange idea to some of your people. They will need to be helped to define who their customers are. Basically, a customer is anyone who benefits from or uses a product or service from another individual or group.

The three rings model is often useful in helping everyone understand the multilayered expectations of their customers. A discussion of ricochets and recoveries shows the impact of little errors on service, quality, costs, workloads, safety, frustration levels, and so on. Cost of quality is an important part of this discussion. Bridges help everyone understand the payoffs of continuous improvement of processes, not just fixing problems.

What are our old assumptions and new paradigms?   Uprooting and discussing dysfunctional assumptions can go a long way toward exorcising them. This is an especially important discussion for all your management staff because they are operating on, and perpetuating, an outdated organizational model. They need to gain a deeper appreciation of that fact and how this outmoded thinking is now hurting your organization. Employee involvement through a team-based organization is another necessary critical management discussion.

Be careful about how far you take the discussion about management's deadly assumptions with your frontline people in the beginning. You may raise their expectations beyond the organization's ability to fulfill them fast enough. On the other hand, some upward pressure on management to let go of the reins can be healthy—as long as you don't make the classic mistake of bypassing management and trying to go straight to the frontline. If you do, management's resentment and passive resistance will haunt you later.

Helping everyone understand the new organizational paradigm will give a clearer picture of the changes that lie ahead. Senior, middle, and perhaps even lower managers should be invited to participate in building the new paradigm. But don't be surprised if they show reluctance or lack of enthusiasm in the beginning. Some will feel like you are asking them to pick out their own casket and describe their preferred method of death. Or they may be skeptical that this is real or lasting. And a great number of managers will need to be re-skilled and see their reward, recognition, measurement, and support systems realigned before they jump into the new paradigm.

What's our reason for being, vision, and values?   Why do we exist? Where are we going? What do we believe in? If you are going to pull together and focus everyone in your organization, then the answers to these questions need to be *clear and compelling*. Get to the heart of the matter. If you and your executive team can't express your reason for being in a short phrase, state your core values in three words or short statements, and describe your vision in a few brief paragraphs, then you are not yet ready to take this out to the organization.

Simplicity makes these critical strategic issues more compelling, especially if they are delivered with emotion and feeling by a credible executive who has his or her audio and video synchronized. Simplicity also makes it much easier to retain and internalize these guidelines, focus, and direction in the flurry of day-to-day activities. But most importantly, boiling these weighty and vital strategic issues down to a few simple statements forces an executive team to chuck all the rhetoric and "we're going to be everything to everybody" and go straight to the heart of things—defining the bare essence of the organization's existence, direction, and beliefs. Again you may want to involve managers, supervisors, and potentially even frontline teams in refining your organization's reason for being, vision, and values. Also, you may want to invite each group, division, or team to interpret or refine these statements for application in their part of the organization.

What's the territory to be covered?   Everyone needs to have a sense of just how big this transformation process is. They need to understand that all of your organization's systems, processes, structures, practices, skills, tools, and techniques will be part of the cultural change and improvement process. For them to see the big picture, you will need to show everyone the planning framework your executive team is using. This may be the implementation architecture, Baldrige criteria, Deming application prize checklist, or some other framework.

How will this be deployed? As we'll discuss in the last few chapters of this book, with so much to do, so many people to involve, and a business to run while you are making all these changes, everyone needs to have a clear sense of the plans, supporting infrastructure, reporting and tracking processes, roles, and responsibilities of this entire change and improvement process. This is also where you can begin to paint each individual contributor, team, supervisor, and manager into the big picture so everyone can see where they fit.

Here is where it will also be apparent whether your service/quality journey is destined to really go somewhere or just turn out to be a lot of executive armchair traveling. If your people, especially your middle managers, see a substantial commitment of resources and executive time, detailed implementation plans, tracking and measurement processes, internal and external customer data, and the like, this effort will begin to look very real. And the more real this looks, the faster supporters of and resisters to the effort will stand out.

What are the next steps? Concrete short-term action plans such as schedules for skill-building sessions; announcements of, or calls for, volunteers on process improvement or project teams; or systems or procedures to be realigned should be announced here. This shows that all these discussions have not just been to exhort everyone to do better; rather, they have been the introduction to a concrete change and improvement process that is gathering momentum. You might seek input to what the next steps should be at this point.

Getting Started

"If you think education is expensive, what's the price of ignorance?"

Usually, the above steps introducing service/quality in an organization are conducted through a workshop. This allows an organization to get managers, supervisors, and work teams together (in functional or mixed groups) to focus collectively on the why, who, what, where, when, and how of the cultural change and improvement process. Introductory workshops also allow you to plan and structure your messages and their delivery so that everyone hears the same thing in the same way. This helps establish the common language and mind-set that is vital to a well-coordinated implementation process. Also, introductory workshops provide an excellent opportunity to leverage senior executive time so that at least one member of the executive team can be involved in presenting all or key portions of the session.

The time needed to adequately cover the introductory workshop agenda varies according to how much and how well some of these topics have already been discussed with those attending the session. A frontline group that has not heard many of these messages before generally needs a one-day workshop to understand what is about to happen and ask questions of the senior executive. If group members have heard many of these messages, half a day may be enough to establish the common language and understanding they will need before their skill training and further involvement begins. Managers and supervisors generally need two days to more extensively understand the magnitude of the change, the implementation plan, and their role in leading the process. If they are going to be involved in the planning or vision and value refining process, more time will be needed, usually in follow-up sessions.

Introducing service/quality needs to start with management. And it *should not proceed further until supervisors and managers are not only educated and aware, but also have developed the coaching and team leadership skills outlined in Chapters 13 and 14.* This is for two important reasons. First, the success of frontline teams depends almost exclusively on the coaching, support, and leadership they receive from their immediate supervisors and managers. No matter how motivated, empowered, and skilled senior managers or staff professionals may try to make frontline teams, if the teams aren't working in a daily nurturing and supportive climate, the vulnerable new tools and techniques will not take root.

Second, supervisors and managers need to be part of the introductory process. No matter how effective the structured, organizationwide introductory sessions may have been, an individual's immediate supervisor is "management." Everyone else further down (in the upside-down organization) the management support layers is a distant figure. So supervisors and management need to help individuals come to grips with "what's in it for me"—to understand and get excited by the personal benefits they can expect to flow from the improvement process. Supervisors and managers also need to focus their teams on service/

quality, to help them understand and get excited by the benefits that will flow from better intact and cross-functional teamwork.

Effective *and credible* organizationwide introductions to service/quality improvement combined with *strong local follow-through and support from supervisors and managers* always produce extremely turned on and receptive frontline teams. In fact, this approach can be so powerful that everyone's awareness and expectations can get way ahead of the organization's ability to deliver, so take care in how far and how fast you begin the whole process. We will return to this important implementation issue in depth in the deployment chapters.

When most people in your organization are tuned in and turned on to service/quality improvement, you can start making the changes needed to build an outside-in, upside-down, team-based culture. In their article, "Why Change Programs Don't Produce Change," Michael Beer, Russell Eisenstat, and Bert Spector write, "Once employees have bought into a vision of what's necessary and have some understanding of what the new organization requires, they can accept the necessity of replacing or moving people who don't make the transition to the new way of working."[6] Now the challenge is to maintain the enthusiasm and "top of mind" for the long, tough journey.

INTERNAL MARKETING AND COMMUNICATIONS

"Only those who have the patience to do simple things perfectly will acquire the skill to do difficult things easily."

Johann Schiller, *German poet and dramatist*

Getting your improvement process off to a strong start is very important. And once the effort is under way, skill training and involvement in well-led improvement activities will keep things rolling. But everyone still needs to be regularly brought back to the big picture and re-energized. The effort to keep everyone informed of, and sold on, where this is all leading and the progress being made is essential.

A multitude of ways are available to keep the process fresh and alive. No one method should be used exclusively. Just like an external marketing campaign, an internal marketing strategy begins with a clear focus on the central message to be communicated and the people to whom it is being directed. Next comes a marketing plan that combines as many media as possible to make the key message "top of mind" with the target audience. Repetition, impact, and consistency are keys to successful persuasion.

But it can't all be one way—a monologue—if you're going to engage the hearts and minds of your people. Two-way communications—a dialogue— is needed to expand everyone's understanding and awareness as well as to increase ownership for the process. In a *Fortune* article titled, "Champions of Communication," Faye Rice reports, "Internal communications— talk back and forth within the organization, up and down the hierarchy— may well be more important to a company's success than external communications."[7] Robert Desatnick explains one of the many links between internal communications and external customer satisfaction:

> If everyone knows what is happening throughout the organization, any chance encounter with a customer, even by a non-customer-service employee, turns out to be a benefit. The well-informed employee never says (and is never permitted to say), "I don't know" or "It's not my job." If in fact the employee does not know, that person quickly finds out or puts the customer immediately in touch with someone who can help.[8]

And, of course, effective communication happens only when everyone involved is speaking the same language and seeing things from a similar perspective.

Following are some of the internal marketing and communications vehicles used to keep everyone educated and inspired to continue the service/quality improvement process and aware of what is happening inside the organization.

Service/quality days and team fairs. This may be a special day set aside for sitewide or, even by teleconference, organizationwide celebration, education, or information sharing on service/quality progress. Teams might show off results they have achieved, or competitions for most improved team, customer and supplier visits, or internal team visits might be featured.

Recognition or celebration events. The recognition may entail a special gala "Academy Award" event or a supervisor bringing doughnuts to a team to recognize the passing of some milestone or achievement. In Chapter 16, we will talk a lot more about the *vital* area of reward and recognition.

Annual service/quality report. An annual report is an often overlooked vehicle to communicate progress across the organization and refocus the planning effort for the next phase. Annual service/quality reports never fail to surprise and energize management and teams alike.

When everyone sees the accumulated improvement projects, process changes, and small steps taking the organization toward higher service/quality, it's always gratifying and informative.

Internal newsletters.   There are some outstanding newsletters, and there are many poor ones. When used effectively, newsletters can be an excellent way to inform, inspire, recognize, reinforce, and market the improvement effort. Here are a few newsletter tips:

1. Do keep the style lively and readable.
2. Don't trivialize the issues or talk down to readers.
3. Do provide a balance. Combine recognition, people-oriented stories, and meaty strategic updates with hard business information and "how-to" tips.
4. Don't let it go out looking like a third-rate production.
5. Do give it as much thought, planning, and resources as you would a customer newsletter.
6. Don't let it become a social register or gossip rag.
7. Do have it produced by, or representative of, its readers.

Visitors and visits.   Many service/quality initiatives are begun after key executives or managers see the impact of the process in another organization. James Womack, Daniel Jones, and Daniel Roos, the three MIT researchers who headed the massive international study of automakers, report:

> We found again and again that middle management and rank-and-file workers in a mass-production company begin to change only when they see a concrete example nearby. The ability for outsiders to see the system in action, understand its logic, and verify its performance is critical to Western acceptance.[9]

A constant stream of outside examples brought to your organization through presentations, videos, or team visits is powerful. Sending teams to visit organizations that are further along the improvement journey can be even more effective. And as we will discuss in Chapter 18, benchmarking your key processes against the best performers of that process, and then studying their methods, also smashes old "it can't be done" paradigms and gets everyone seeing new possibilities. Tracking, publicizing, and encouraging team visits around internal "best practices" can also help to spread learning, broaden experience, and motivate both the visiting and the visited teams.

Visits to and from external customers and suppliers are also a key way to increase awareness and understanding. This can also improve listening and partnerships.

Video and video/teleconferences. Like newsletter quality, the quality of your videos will signal how important senior management believes the whole effort to be. An effective video can highlight your organization's vision, values, reason for being, as well as plans and processes for achieving higher service/quality. It can be used as an internal awareness tool and as an external sales, marketing, and public-relations vehicle. Showing everyone video clips from customer focus groups is also a very powerful way to bring the voice and face of the customer deep into the organization.

However, videos can also backfire. Some organizations suffer from the it's-all-a-marketing-game syndrome. This deadly assumption leads them to produce slick, expensive videos that employees know are a whitewash or just pipe dreams. Like many other internal marketing tools, video can breed better cynics in your organization if it isn't supporting a much larger, fully integrated improvement effort with real substance and planning. If employees are left wondering, "Is that all there is?" videos may do more harm than good.

With the same caveats as videotapes, video or teleconferences can be another way to spread the word to large, dispersed groups. A growing number of large corporations are establishing videoconference networks. As Robert Horton, CEO of British Petroleum, says, "Videoconferencing is very efficient for business meetings, and it helps save the health of executives because it cuts down on travel."[10] While a videotape or videoconference allows everyone to hear it from the horse's mouth, it is still just a monologue.

CONTINUOUS LEARNING

"Improvement of quality and productivity, to be successful in any company, must be a learning process, year by year, top management leading the whole company."

W. Edwards Deming[11]

Nowhere is the evidence that we live in a fast-moving world as compelling as in the field of service/quality improvement. The number and types of tools, techniques, and skills evolve as rapidly as customers' needs and competitive pressures change. The new organizational paradigm is clearly emerging, but it hasn't taken its completed form yet.

We still have a lot to learn about what does and does not move our organizations toward higher service/quality. Futurists John Naisbitt, Alvin Toffler, and others predict the blurring velocity of change and learning will not likely stop—or even slow down much—in our lifetimes. We are in an era where the only thing permanent and unchangeable is a relentless pace of rapid change and evolution. Johnsville Foods CEO Ralph Stayer writes: "Learning is change, and I keep learning and relearning that change is and needs to be continuous . . . change *is* the real job of every effective business leader because change is about the present and the future, not about the past. There is no end to change."[12]

On top of all this rapid evolution and change "out there" you have to learn what works "in here." In other words, given that your organization is unique and has its own idiosyncrasies, you have to discover your own best route to higher service/quality for your own unique culture. In *Managing Quality*, David Garvin says, "Conscious experimentation may well be required to distinguish effective from ineffective practice. Such efforts are likely to be costly and time consuming, but they are essential if real progress is to be achieved."[13]

All this leads to an obvious conclusion (and recurring theme): *if you want to build a continually improving organization, you need to build a continually learning organization.* As Deming says, "What an organization needs is not just good people; it needs people that are improving with education." So one of his famous 14 points is "encourage education and self-improvement for everyone."[14] In the information age or knowledge-based society in which we are now living, future performance potential is largely being carried between the collective ears of everybody in your organization. That is one reason the Strategic Planning Institute suggests a key strategic initiative should be to "promote learning as a way of business life for all employees."[15]

What investments are you making or steps are you taking to make sure knowledge is your organization's fastest appreciating asset? Ralph Stayer believes education is one of the biggest reasons for the phenomenal success his team-based organization has seen in the past few years:

> Today more than 65 percent of all the people at Johnsville are involved in some type of formal education. The end state we all now envision for Johnsville is a company that never stops learning . . . learning, striving people are happy people and good workers. They have initiative and imagination, and the companies they work for are rarely caught napping.[16]

Make sure you and your executive team aren't caught napping. You need a steady stream of continuous service/quality learning to help you navigate the many obstacles, pitfalls, traps, and dead ends. Books, videos, magazine articles, conferences, experience exchange and problem-solving networks, visits and visitors, benchmarking, experiments and pilots, listening and feedback, and consultants should all be used liberally to help you and your organization stay abreast of this fast-changing new management paradigm.

Make sure you use a strategic improvement process that is evolving as rapidly as the field of service/quality improvement. You don't want to lock your organization into a rigid process that purports to have everything you need in one handy tool kit. You need an open system that encourages you to incorporate best practices, new tools, techniques, or skills as your organization's broad learning net catches them. If you're working with an outside consulting firm, you will want to ensure the firm is using an open system that is evolving and adapting—continuously improving.

EXECUTIVE SIGNALING

"He first practices what he preaches and then preaches according to his practice."
Confucius, *Chinese philosopher and teacher*

In their book *The Winning Performance: How America's High-Growth Midsize Companies Succeed*, Donald Clifford and Richard Cavanaugh write:

The winning performers understand that their actions speak louder than words—but they also understand that the words may have to be repeated endlessly . . . so they never stop communicating. The leaders spend prodigious hours writing, speaking, visiting the troops in outposts, doing whatever's necessary to get the essential messages across.[17]

It can't be said too often: *The message repeatedly given by senior management actions is the single most powerful channel for communicating the values, priorities, and strategies of your organization.* But rather than leaving those opportunities to chance, careful planning should determine where and how members of the senior management team should invest their time in communicating and reinforcing service/quality improvement.

EXAMPLES OF EDUCATION AND AWARENESS

"Readiness for opportunity makes for success. Opportunity often comes by accident; readiness never does."

Samuel Rayburn, *American politician*

Following is a brief sampling of the multitude of education and awareness activities under way in many organizations:

• Since 1984, B.C. Tel has taken a number of steps to transform its culture. A continual stream of education and awareness activities provides very strong executive signaling.

Early in the process, executives met quarterly to review progress on the multitude of "mundane action plans" they or their managers had initiated. These sessions were video-taped, and the highlights were used to kick off similar meetings that ultimately included all 2,500 managers and supervisors. This approach not only signaled the degree of commitment, but it also pressured the executives and managers to keep the momentum going and excitement high.

Vice presidents and area general managers travel throughout their entire region (it is a big province) meeting with supervisory and frontline performers to discuss direction and celebrate contributions. These "Infonet" sessions have become an important forum for discussions. In one year, one executive talked to more than 4,000 people in his region in groups of 50 or fewer.

When a new training program was introduced, most executives elected to attend the sessions personally rather than just give the same message by videotape. For some executives, that meant appearing before more than a hundred groups each year.

At least one frontline team is invited to every executive review session to report on the success of its improvement efforts.

• Texaco's Bakersfield Producing Division introduced its quality plan as part of the 1991 "state of the division" presentation. The agenda, presented in three shifts to cover all employees, was:

• Why quality?

• What is quality?

• Our values, mission, and operating philosophy.

• Our strategic approach to continuous improvement.

• Team and individual roles in the process.

• Our 1990 and 1991 business performance.

• Capital and operating plans.

• Vision 2001.

• At American Express' Travel Related Services Company, a number of education and awareness activities are used in the drive for ever higher service/quality:

Employee teams are periodically interviewed on topics such as "what quality means to me." These are videotaped and distributed throughout those divisions.

Extensive printed and audiovisual materials are regularly used in an ongoing series of worldwide employee orientations and education activities. In one campaign, called "Quality—I take it personally," each employee received a "ticket to quality" with a message from the chairman. Videos were developed explaining the organization's service standards, what was expected of each employee, and how those performance expectations—measured against the standards—would be part of each performance appraisal.

Management explained cost of quality to the frontline teams and showed how reducing "nonrevenue generating input" or rework increased productivity, customer satisfaction, and revenue.[18]

• Wesley-Jessen put all of its employees through a two-day "Introducing Service/Quality" program similar to the outline described on pages 131–33. W-J's key service/quality indicators are posted on lighted service quality center bulletin boards, sent by letter to customers, featured in periodic "Service Quality Flash" reports, other bulletin boards, and "newsgrams." Director, Total Quality Management, Jim Moritz says:

> Although our key processes are just in the midst of being analyzed and improved, we feel the reason W-J has experienced more than a two-thirds drop in customer complaints in our first six months was attributable to our third-ring employees (those in contact with customers) understanding the importance of not "ricocheting" (letting errors get through) our customers.

• As GTE began its service/quality improvement journey it "became clear to senior management that managers did not understand how to manage the quality improvement process and to take actions that effectively reinforced the words they used to describe their commitment." In response, a course called "Quality: The Competitive Edge" was developed and delivered by GTE's Management Development Center. Nancy Burzon, director of quality education, says this recognized that "education and training became the new strategic weapon for GTE's quality efforts." The program was different from any others offered before. Burzon explains, "It was mandated for all executive management teams and the business unit teams attended together, along with two to four other teams."

The program gave a historical perspective on the quality movement in the United States, showed how quality was a performance-enhancing strategic tool, outlined the necessary strategic quality planning, and explained how the quality improvement process applied throughout all business processes, the human dimension of quality improvement, the individual and team roles of senior management, getting the work force on board, and how management practice can be established. This last component encouraged executives to study other companies' quality improvement efforts.

Based on the success of this introductory phase, and the need to bring the rest of the organization on board, GTE developed a field version of the educational program. Most of the content was the same as the first version. Burzon explains the key differences: "The instructors were the business unit presidents and staff members. The program objective was to obtain support of the employees in implementing the quality plan."[19]

- To publicize its quality effort and develop new paradigms around what was possible, Eastman Kodak acted on an employee suggestion and established a "No-Error Week." Employees ran a number of dry runs and "minimedia events to pique everyone's interest." After No-Error Week, the results showed "13,000 orders and 50,000 line items shipped; 8,000 customer calls; 199,000 parts received and put away; 5,200,000 computer keystrokes; and 20,000 different parts prepacked during the interval, with 10 reported mistakes."[20]

- When executives of US West Communications Group met for their planning retreat, featured speakers were business and residential customers explaining how they define service/quality.[21]

- As Xerox struggled in the early 1980s to become more customer-focused, it encountered numerous examples of engineers and designers looking at the world from the inside out. Kerney Ladey, vice president of national service, explains what was often uncovered: "They were enamored with, how complex does it make it? How could you make it have so many wheels that they all turn around at the same time? versus Is it going to be pertinent to the customer, or will it take an engineer to fix it?" To re-educate and refocus engineers and designers, Xerox showed them a series of videotapes of customer focus groups complaining about the product, brought in field service engineers, and took engineers and designers out to meet customers. Their urgency for dramatically improving product quality to be more customer-focused vastly increased.[22]

- "Just keep pounding away on all communication fronts," says John West, manager and assistant to the Chief Operating Officer of quality at Federal Express. "We realized that communication is the key to any total quality success. We need to publish successes, acquaint people with new tools, and provide constant refreshers so employees remember how to do things." A weekly memo containing quality news is sent to all managers; videos are regularly produced; and a closed-circuit video program, "Fed Ex Overnight," has daily five-minute features on quality that are recorded automatically on VCRs across the company. "The goal," says West, "is to make sure there's not much chance people can miss the quality message."[23]

COMMON PITFALLS AND TRAPS TO EDUCATION AND AWARENESS

"If you have always done it that way it is probably wrong."
              Charles F. Kettering, *automotive inventor and pioneer*

Mixed Messages

Internal and external marketing must be tied together. Your staff needs to hear the same message your customers are hearing. Too often employees are the last to hear about the wonderful service/quality they are being committed to provide.

Not Walking Your Talk

You and your management team must *behave* in a manner consistent with the messages being broadcast to your people. You do the strongest internal marketing (or blocking) of the true value and priority of service/quality with your tiny, seemingly insignificant *daily actions*. Nothing else will convince (or turn off) employees as effectively as senior management behavior.

Stale and Stalling

Executives involved in building a high-service/quality culture are always shocked by how long it takes to get the message through to those who will make it happen. Often, just as executives are getting tired of repeating the same old vision, values, strategies, or rationale, people on the front line are beginning to think, "Just maybe, quite possibly, they might be serious this time." If at about that time senior management gets bored and moves on to greener pastures, momentum is lost, and employees add yet another protective layer against your future "flavor of the month" campaigns. The watchwords are consistency and repetition, repetition, repetition. . . .

Bits and Pieces

Internal marketing and communications must be given the same planning and follow-through as external marketing. The stakes are just as high. If you don't believe that, you're on the wrong journey. If you do believe that, then carefully think through your internal marketing campaign as any good marketer would. What position are you trying to achieve? To whom are you targeting what messages? How can you ensure continuity and repetition of key themes? What are the best methods to use?

Educated but Unskilled

You can give people plenty of education, information, inspiration, and awareness, but if they don't have the skills to improve service/quality, they will become frustrated and demotivated. Awareness and empowerment are useless without enablement. Team members and leaders need to know *how to* make improvements.

Bypassing Management

You can get your frontline teams excited and committed to improving service/quality but their enthusiasm will be short-lived if their supervisors and managers aren't first brought on board and given the skills to introduce, support, coach, and lead the team's efforts. Remember the 85/15 rule; very few ricochets come from lack of motivation or "not being more careful." Most of them are a result of the system, process, structure, or practices. These are controlled by management.

Once (or Maybe Twice) Is Enough

It needs repeating; *you can't repeat your core service/quality messages too often or in too many ways*. J. Stark Thompson, CEO of Life Technologies, says: "I've learned that just because you think it, write it, or say it doesn't mean employees hear it or believe it."[24] Heed the experience of Edward Mertz, Buick's general manager and corporate vice president: "I vastly underestimated the job. On the first go-round, all I got were glassy-eyed stares, open mouths, and sometimes passionate disagreement . . . establishing our new (car) image took a year, and even then it was not a lasting vaccination. It required booster shots."[25] Just like continuous improvement, education and awareness are never finished.

Chapter Ten

Cylinder Four: Hiring and Orienting

"Get the brightest people and train them well."

Charles Merrill,
founder, Merrill Lynch

This cylinder involves yet more common sense that is not common practice. Stack the deck by hiring the best people, those most likely to uphold your service/quality values, and get them off to a strong start with solid training and orientation. Add careful attention to the signals you send through your decisions to promote or dismiss certain people. Use these practices to focus and direct full attention to service/quality improvement, and you are well on your way to transforming your organization's culture. It's that simple. But judging by the anemic hiring and orientation processes in most organizations, it's not that easy.

When it comes to motivating frontline service providers, Four Seasons "cheats a little because we hire people who are already motivated." John Sharpe explains the company's hiring approach: "We select for attitude and a willingness to serve customers. We believe that technical skills can be taught to motivated people much more successfully than attitude can be taught to people who possess only experience." Sharpe illustrates:

> Our concierge at the Four Seasons Washington was approached by a guest who ran up to his desk wearing a tuxedo and unlaced formal shoes. "Where can I get a pair of shoelaces right away?" the guest asked. The concierge didn't hesitate. He pulled out his own laces and handed them to the guest. That wasn't something we taught the concierge. He was that kind of person when we hired him.[1]

Ron Zemke and Dick Schaaf studied "101 companies that profit from customer care." They identified hiring and orienting, particularly training, as among the most significant reasons these companies are on top. Reporting on their research in their book *The Service Edge*, they write:

"As we have explored company after company, we constantly have been struck by the slow, careful, calculated way they approach the hiring process for even the lowest-paying positions. The 'get somebody, anybody, on those phones' mentality was nowhere in evidence."[2]

Founded in 1982 in San Jose, California, Cypress Semiconductor Corporation by 1990 had grown to 1,400 people and established a solid profit and performance record. Founder and President T. J. Rodgers writes, "The day we founded Cypress we understood that our greatest proprietary advantage would be to do a better job of hiring than the big companies against which we would compete."[3]

ONLY THE FINEST INGREDIENTS

In far too many organizations, the hiring and selection process is done half-well, at best. Sometimes the candidate's knowledge, relevant experience, job skills, career aspirations, stability, motivation, and work ethic are screened, tested, and checked. But rarely is the candidate's fit with the organization's values scrutinized.

Slipshod hiring practices send clear messages about your values: "Ignore whatever we tell you about service/quality; it's not a top priority." Weak hiring and selection processes also sharply downgrade the new recruit's perception of the job's value and importance: "Looks to me like they will hire anybody for this job," or "If the job were worth anything, it wouldn't be so easy to get." We place the highest value on those things that are hardest to get, whether it is a house, a relationship, or a job. When we really have to work to get something, we cherish it. How do your new people feel? Are they just doing a job or do they consider themselves important links in your organization's service/quality chain?

One easy explanation for why so many organizations do such an abysmal job of hiring and orienting around their service/quality vision and values is that they don't have any. Too many organizations have a sort of warmed-over pabulum culture that doesn't smell, feel, or taste like anything. It just is.

Highly effective organizations have a *strong* and *visible* culture. Potential candidates are either excited by and drawn to that organization's way of life, vision, and priorities or repelled and turned away by them. Even if the candidate is perfect in every other way, top-performing organizations want those who are turned off by their culture to look elsewhere. Although Walt Disney World recruits employees in Orlando, Florida, where there is a labor shortage, the organization refuses to lower the standards that eliminate 30 percent of applicants before the interview stage. Top organizations know that every recruit will eventually integrate with and reinforce the organization's vision and values or will detract from them. When it comes to service/quality improvement, everyone must head in the same direction.

All signs point to a tightening of many job markets in the coming years. Good people are going to become harder to find. And the competition for the best people will continue to intensify. Service/quality improvement will significantly enhance your image as a preferred employer.

HIRING RIGHT THE FIRST TIME

"A company is known by the people it keeps."

Harry Klinger, *industrialist*

Top-performing organizations invest a level of time and energy in the hiring and selection process that astounds most managers. They may put their candidates through 10 or more interviews with the managers and team the person would work with if hired. Fairfield Inn puts a potential new recruit through an average of 14 interviews.[4]

Intensive interviewing of this sort serves two purposes. First, it gives the organization a broad look at the candidate's suitability, especially his or her "fit" within the culture. (That is one of the reasons for colleagues being involved in the process.) Second, such interviewing gives candidates plenty of time to eliminate themselves if they realize the organization is not the kind they want to be part of. Richard Pascale, consultant and author of *The Art of Japanese Management*, studied the characteristics of top-performing organizations and how they maintain their strong and distinct cultures. He concludes hiring and selection are their key tools: "The company subjects candidates for employment to a selection process so rigorous that it often seems designed to discourage individuals rather than encourage them to take the job."[5]

The costs (mainly time) of rigorously screening are high. But like bad cost of quality, hiring the wrong people can be costly too. Consider just the costs of turnover. How much does it cost you to rehire and retrain because a new employee stayed only a few months or years? How much management time is lost rehiring and retraining? What is the impact on your service/quality levels if new employees aren't suitable for, or don't care about, providing third-ring service or contributing to team efforts to reduce causes of ricochets? What does it cost you to have positions sit vacant because the last person in that job didn't work out? Harvard Business School's Len Schlesinger poses the question, "Do you want to hire one person 17 times (through constantly refilling the position) or interview 17 people to hire the right one?"[6] As T. J. Rodgers warns, "Hiring the wrong people is a very expensive mistake."[7]

Turnover is just one of the many bad costs of quality associated with not hiring right the first time. "Curmudgeons may complain that turnover is inevitable among low-skill, first-time workers," admit William Davidow and Bro Uttal. But their extensive study of dozens of high-service providers led them to conclude, "The evidence suggests the fault is management's. Careful hiring, intensive and never-ending training, and a cornucopia of inexpensive incentive and motivational programs almost always slash turnover drastically."[8]

Starting with the right raw materials is a critical element in building a high-service/quality culture. Often overlooked and delegated to personnel or human resources departments, hiring is an essential strategic area for executives and managers in top organizations. Cypress Semiconductor uses no executive recruiters, and its human resources department suggests candidates but does not evaluate them. T. J. Rodgers advises, "Use the big guns. If you want job prospects to know that you are serious, high-ranking executives should take the time to get involved in the interview process."[9] That is also an unmistakable signal to everyone just how important you consider the hiring process. Tom Peters adds:

> The task of transforming raw recruits into committed stars, able to cope with the pace of change that is becoming normal, begins with the recruiting process per se. The best follow three tenets, unfortunately ignored by most: (1) spend time, lots of it; (2) insist that line people dominate the process; and (3) don't waffle about the qualities you are looking for in candidates.[10]

OFF TO A STRONG START

"Well begun is half done."

Horace, *Roman poet*

So you have hired well. You have chosen the best-qualified candidates who not only have the right skills and personal characteristics, but they also embody your service/quality values. It took a while to get to this point, but they are now ready, willing, and eager to contribute. You and your managers, as well as the new recruits' team members, are excited about the people you chose after such an exhaustive process. Given these circumstances, you would likely think an extensive training and orientation program would be well worth the investment.

That's how hiring and orientation go hand in hand. If you are just hiring warm bodies, it's not worth spending a lot of time orienting and training them, especially because they probably won't be around long anyway. The irony is they won't be around for long because you weren't selective in hiring them and didn't do much to get them off to a good start.

A strong orientation program not only ensures that your new people are given a better chance to be successful, but it also applies additional pressure to hire the right people in the first place. Although turnover is much more expensive than an in-depth training and orientation program, the investments of time, salaries, and other costs are much more visible in the latter. Therefore, managers will be more careful about who they select as candidates for these substantial investments.

Orientation Starts with the First Interview

"The phrase 'people are our most important resource' has been a management slogan for at least 80 years. But too few executives really look at this resource."

Peter Drucker

Many managers don't consider the hiring and selection process as part of orientation. Yet that's where candidates gather their first impressions about the values and priorities of the organization. Former McDonald's Vice President Robert Desatnick explains how that organization begins orientation during the hiring process:

> During the interview process itself, the organization's values are emphasized. The importance of customer service is made clear. After the open-ended questions are asked by the interviewer, the candidate is told what behaviors are rewarded and what behaviors are unacceptable. This is where the teaching process begins.[11]

An extensive selection process that focuses on values as the final and largest hurdle (experience, skill or education, and personal characteristics being the first) sends these clear signals to the job candidates and to everyone else in your organization:

- We don't hire just anybody. You are one of a select few.
- Our values aren't just pretty words on the wall.
- This is an important job. You are an important person.
- The quality of your work will be every bit as important as "making the numbers."

- We're planning on a long-term relationship.
- We're careful about who we hire because we work hard to invest in and support your success.

Would you like your people to feel this way?

Characteristics of Effective Orientation Programs

"What turns over fastest in many organizations is not inventory but people."

Solid orientation programs have many elements, but two basics stand out in the best organizations: the quality of the program and the involvement of line management. *The Service Edge* newsletter reports that industrial psychologists Kenneth Wexley of Michigan State University and Gary Latham of G. P. Latham found it's critical to do orientation right the first time: "Poor orientation programs can be financially draining to the organization because they can reduce effectiveness for the employee's first few weeks on the job and this can contribute to dissatisfaction and turnover."

In an experiment at Texas Instruments, several groups of new employees went through an orientation program while similar groups didn't. A year later, those employees who were well oriented had learned their jobs faster and had higher productivity and lower absence and lateness than those employees who weren't formally oriented. Robert Desatnick reports on why McDonald's finds orientation so vital to higher service/quality:

> The successful orientation process will result in fewer mistakes, improved customer service, higher levels of productivity, and more harmonious employee relations. It welcomes the employee to a warm, friendly, caring environment . . . (which) adds up to one thing, a message to the employee: "You are important and we treat you with respect.". . . The employee who feels welcomed and important will make the customer feel welcome and important.[12]

Wexley and Latham also found that "orientation training should be the joint responsibility of training staff and the line supervisor."[13] Because the orientation process is such an excellent opportunity to reinforce the organization's vision and values, executives for top-service/quality performers are often involved in the process as well. Training and orienting new recruits is far too critical to be glossed over or delegated away. It is a prime strategic opportunity to instill your values and priorities.

PROMOTION, DEMOTION, AND DISMISSAL

"Humility decreases with every promotion, and disappears completely at the vice president level."

John N. Petroff, *Why Things Go Wrong*

Although promotion, demotion, and dismissal are covered in the systems cylinder (Chapter Fifteen), they are strongly linked to hiring and orienting. Your systems and practices in these areas send strong signals of your true values. Ben Schneider, professor in business management and psychology at the University of Maryland, has been studying corporate culture and its effects on service/quality for over 20 years. According to *The Service Edge* newsletter:

> His research shows the more people in an organization believe they get promoted on who they know, not what they know, the poorer the customers of those organizations describe the service they receive. . . . Schneider says an organization's transitions—entry, promotion, mergers, mentoring, retirement, and termination—give organizations their best opportunity to make a statement about what they value, what gods they worship.[14]

Take a hard look at who's getting promoted in your organization and why. If you're promoting the supervisor or employee who beats up on internal and external customers, then service/quality is *not* a key value in your organization. It may be a goal or even an ideal, but it is not a real living value. In the early 1980s, Terrence Deal and Allan Kennedy first expressed the emerging awareness that every organization has unique patterns of "the way we do things around here." In their book *Corporate Cultures: The Rites and Rituals of Corporate Life*, they make this critical point: "Too many companies are promoting the wrong people and sending conflicting signals through the corporate culture. . . . (An organization) must promote people who embody key values of the business if it is to be successful."[15]

Dismissals and demotions are management's fault. They are usually the result of poor selection, ineffective orientation and training, and weak management coaching. To a manager concerned with the cultural signals his or her actions send, "a firing is a catastrophe. It should never happen . . . if the employee fits with the culture," Deal and Kennedy say.[16] Or as Peter Drucker puts it, "To blame the failed promotion on the promoted person—as is usually done—is no more rational than to blame a capital investment that has gone sour on the money that was put in."[17]

The negative ripple effect of a firing or demotion can be enormously costly. Yet not making changes when someone is not able to handle the job sends the wrong signals about what kind of behavior or performance is acceptable. The whole sorry mess is yet another example of bad cost of quality found in poor hiring and orienting—of not doing it right the first time.

The key question is what are people dismissed or demoted for? The answer defines your organization's values. Deal and Kennedy say: "When a firing is necessary, it should not be the end result of poor performance, but of violations of cultural norms. Moreover, when such an event occurs, it demands the personal attention of the symbolic manager to make sure the cultural message of the firing is fully understood."[18]

HIRING AND ORIENTING IN ACTION

"The secret of success lies not in doing your own work, but in recognizing the right person to do it."

Andrew Carnegie

• Xerox's promotion system is based on five mandatory requirements for management positions that anyone being considered for a higher level management position must meet. Called "role model management," a role model manager "serves as a 'standard of excellence' worthy of imitation." The five assessment areas are:

Business results—continually increases customer satisfaction, return-on-assets, and market share through continuous improvement methods and process simplification.

Leadership through quality—"leads, teaches, and coaches others to continuously improve" through the use of such "quality tools" as a quality plan using basic and advanced quality skills and practices; "manages by fact" with quantified data; establishes challenging continuous improvement goals based on customer requirements, world-class benchmarks, competitive outlook, and process capability of the operation; personally models teamwork, employee participation, and personal growth; constantly enables individual and team learning; continually monitors team and individual performance and provides guidance for improvement.

Human resources management—"hires talented people," develops them, acts decisively and fairly on employee problems, maintains an environment of openness and trust, and actively coaches and supports his or her teams and team members.

Teamwork—is cooperative and supportive within the "family group" and across functions, makes short-term sacrifices for the company, supports other organization's team goals by assigning resources, and implements direction once decisions are made.

Corporate values—supports corporate objectives and directions, openly states own view but fully supports the decision that's made, is open minded, conducts risk assessments and identifies management issues before the fact, establishes environment for his or her organization based on sound business practices.

A key source of rating managers on the above criteria comes through Xerox's reversed performance appraisal process. Those reporting to an individual supervisor or manager complete a questionnaire providing feedback across the five management dimensions.

• When Bridgestone Corporation built a new tire plant in Warren County, Tennessee, plant manager Bob Walsh decided to use self-directed work teams after touring a number of the company's Japanese plants and seeing their level of employee involvement and the results achieved. He determined that a few of the key factors were "the way they do their selection process, and 10 times more training."

The new plant established an assessment center to look at the one in five job applicants that made it through a four-hour general aptitude test administered by the state of Tennessee. The assessment began with a four-hour panel interview with three team leaders followed by a technical test. Only half the candidates made it through this step. The remaining candidates then went through seven and a half hours of simulated group problem solving where they were assessed on participation, leadership skills, and mediation skills. Only 3 of every 100 applicants made it through the entire process and were hired.[19]

• In response to employee surveys that showed confusion and a belief that the promotion process was based on favoritism, the Texaco Bakersfield Producing Division developed an internal job-posting procedure. Central to the assessment of interested candidates is his or her demonstrated history of involvement in the service/quality improvement effort.

• William Davidow and Bro Uttal report that the main reason Network Equipment Technologies (NET) has taken over one quarter of the market for large switches to run private communications networks—and has ballooning profit margins—is "its outstanding service factory, or infrastructure . . . (that) can keep its switches working more than 99 percent of the time." In hiring the field service engineers who are central to NET's successful service record, the company looks for experienced candidates with "the classic personality of Mr. Fixit—pride in getting things to work, a penchant for tinkering, and an affection for gadgets." Every candidate is interviewed by half a dozen NET employees, anyone of whom can reject the candidate even if it's just because of a gut feeling. NET follows up its rigorous hiring process by investing $30,000 in the training of each new recruit in his or her first year, and $15,000 each year after that. Turnover is 5 percent compared to the industry average of 15 percent.[20]

- The first rule of hiring for managers at Flintstones Bedrock City theme park in British Columbia is: Don't hire grouchy people.

- The branch manager of a large water-treatment company found it challenging to fill direct-sales positions while maintaining high standards when few candidates were applying. The successful process he used to build a top sales force started with an initial screening to determine whether to proceed further. Next came a strong sell on the job, which included a video and meetings (and often sales calls) with satisfied employees. Once the candidates were clearly hooked, the tables were turned and the candidates were put through a rigorous multistage screening. The branch not only got the best possible candidates by this method, but also the manager signaled to new (and existing) salespeople that they were not hired just because he was desperate.

- The founder and president of a national clothing retail chain believes it's vital that new head-office employees—management and clerical—understand their role. During their orientation, he takes them to the window and asks: "Do you see any customers bringing money into this building to us?"

"Ah, no, we don't," they reply.

"Well, don't ever forget that! Customers don't pay us for what we do here. They pay for what happens in the stores. That's where the action is. *All of us* at head office are here to serve and support the stores."

- Holland America consistently holds the cruise ship industry's coveted five-star service ranking. A key reason for its success is its hiring and orientation process. Candidates are chosen only from the hospitality industry (usually top Asian hotels or airlines). They are put through a dozen or more interviews and tests with numerous cruise ship professionals and managers. Successful candidates are then sent to the cruise line's hospitality school for a few weeks. Next, they spend months under the supervision of a senior employee on the line's flagship. Only after the recruits have been through this extensive process are they considered ready to come into solo contact with customers on their assigned ship.

- Merck, the pharmaceutical giant, is constantly rated number one among the pharmacists and doctors it serves in the fiercely competitive drug industry. Aspiring salespeople must study basic medical subjects for 10 weeks and score 90 percent or better on a weekly test to stay in the program. Then they spend three weeks learning how to present Merck's products. The recruits next go on trial for six months in the field making calls with their district managers. This stage is followed by three weeks at headquarters polishing presentation and selling skills. All salespeople must attend periodic medical classes as constant refreshers. Says Vice President Jerry Keller, "Training is our obsession. People who come to us from other companies can't believe we have this kind of program."[21]

COMMON PITFALLS AND TRAPS TO HIRING AND ORIENTING

"If we don't change our direction we're likely to end up where we're headed."

Abdicating Responsibility

Don't turn hiring over to human resources or personnel professionals. Their expertise can be very useful, but line managers must manage— not delegate—it. They must "own" the hiring process and the new employees it produces.

"Cap in Hand" Recruiting

Avoid appearing grateful or desperate when there are few qualified candidates or you know you want a particular one. T. J. Rodgers advises, "Make interviews tough and technically demanding—even for people you know you want."[22] If need be, sell the candidate on the job (assuming the fit is right), then turn the tables and encourage the candidate to sell himself or herself.

"Lone Ranger" Recruiting

You must get broad and extensive input from other managers and the candidate's future colleagues. "Fit" is hard to define; it takes a couple of assessments from many people on the team. Also, this process sends a clear signal to a candidate about the value of the job he or she is getting and the need for being a team player. It also builds commitment of other team members to helping "our" newly hired candidate succeed.

Inconsistent Promotions

Make an individual's service/quality contributions and results a key promotion criterion. If managers can get ahead on technical skills while abusing or ignoring internal or external customers, the message of how important service/quality really is to the organization becomes crystal clear.

Chapter Eleven

Developing the Skills to Go the Distance

"You cannot fly like an eagle with the wings of a wren."
William Henry Hudson,
naturalist

A s we explored in Chapter 3, the amount of "quality waste" in your organization is between 20 and 30 percent of your revenue. This is your bad cost of quality. You can't afford to keep carrying that excessive weight. Our top-heavy "command and control" hierarchies with their vertical chimneys not only reduce service and quality levels, but they also add a horrendous overhead burden. Richard Schonberger writes: "We tried it for 70 years. It has been an outright failure. Today, the highest costs are in plants and offices that cling to that system."[1]

In Chapter 3, we also looked at driving out bad COQ with investments in good COQ. This is the only way to permanently reduce the multiplying ricochets that keep driving up your bad COQ. As the service/quality pioneers have shown, there is a *sharp* difference between the good COQ investments they make in training their people and those made by the average organization. And as Chapter 1 showed, the difference in results is just as sharp. Mediocre or poor service/quality providers don't save anything by not training extensively. But because bad COQ is usually not tracked and is out of sight, while good COQ is very visible and its costs look high, a short-term manager often tightens the belt and trims these costs. The result, according to Zeithaml, Parasuraman, and Berry's research, is: "The status of training in many firms is bleak—too little too late."[2]

For all the talk about culture and organizational change, an organization is made up of individuals. As Jack Zenger points out, "Organizations don't change unless and until the people inside them change." As obvious as that seems, too many attempts at organizational transformation are based on a view of the organization as a single large elephant that has to be "taught how to dance." Zenger says:

> If only it were that simple. Transforming a single organization is much more like teaching a thousand smaller elephants to dance: Each employee (including the CEO) must dance in close order with 999 others if the organization as a whole is to meet the needs of the customer. And dance not only the fox trot, but the waltz, the cha-cha, and if the music calls for it, even the limbo.[3]

The next three cylinders (Chapters Twelve to Fourteen) outline the critical skills needed to build the customer-focused, team-based organization that continually expands your customers' perceptions of value while driving down costs. You will get an overview of the skills each person in your organization needs to develop to shift your entire organization to the new, high-performance paradigm. And as you will see, *the success of your improvement effort will be in direct proportion to your investments in skill development*. This chapter looks at how deep that investment is, what kinds of skills are needed, who should be involved in the development effort, and how the most effective training is delivered.

THE TRAINING INVESTMENT IS HUGE

"If you build castles in the air, your work need not be lost. That is where they should be built. Now put foundations under them."

Henry David Thoreau, *American naturalist, poet, and essayist*

Training is the heaviest good COQ investment that drives out your bad COQ. The costs of buying the training systems and materials and the time of taking everyone off the job to be trained are substantial. But when it's done right, the return on investment is routinely measured in three and four digits! U.S. Navy Colonel Jerald Gartman led a service/ quality revolution at Cherry Point Aviation Depot in North Carolina that saved millions of dollars. Extensive training was central to the effort. Colonel Gartman says the payback on training proved to be $14 to $1. He concludes, "So you show me the cost of the training. . . . Training is very, very expensive and ignorance costs more than you can imagine."[4]

Tom Peters sees training and development as critical to the survival of North American companies. For years, he has been urging executives to increase dramatically their training and development investments. He warns, "The Japanese, Germans, and others outspend us wildly on training, especially in-company skill refurbishment and upgrading. In short, our track record is pathetic.''[5] Manufacturing expert Richard Schonberger agrees. In his book, *World Class Manufacturing: The Lessons of Simplicity Applied*, he titled a chapter "Training: The Catalyst." He writes, "Western industry must match the prodigious sums the world-class manufacturing companies in Japan and Germany invest in it.''[6] This is further supported by Japanese consultant Masaaki Imai, who says, "There is a Japanese axiom: 'Quality control starts with training and ends in training.' ''[7]

Following is a brief look at some of the investments in, and observations made of, training in the highest service/quality providers. As you read through the examples, you may want to compare the investment made to the results achieved by these leaders (many are in Chapter One). Then look at your own commitment to training. How does it compare? If you're not at these investment levels, then you may be on the right road, but your effort is destined to sputter and stall because your people won't be able to keep it moving.

• Xerox, a Baldrige Award winner, gives each new employee nine and a half days of training and education within the first 90 days. Every manager gets at least 40 hours of skill training every year. Training is benchmarked against Fuji, Xerox (a Deming Application Prize winner), and other leading U.S. and international firms considered training leaders. Training budgets are set at 2 percent of payroll.[8]

• Federal Express, a Baldrige Award winner, gives its call center agents six weeks of training before they take a call. Every six months, couriers, service agents, and customer service agents must participate in a job knowledge testing program. Each person receives a "prescription" that targets areas needing more work along with suggestions of the resources, such as interactive video and training sessions, to get back up to speed. If anyone fails to pass, he or she is relieved of his or her duties immediately, given remedial training, and then retested.[9]

• Wallace Co., Inc., a Baldrige Award winner, invested more than $700,000 on training its 280 employees (an average of $2,500 per employee). John Wallace says:

> For a change to take place in an organization, there has to be a revolution. That kind of money was a major commitment, especially during the times we were experiencing. In fact, it staggers me sometimes, but it was the only way we could survive. Training is one of the most vital parts of the organization . . . it's amazing to see the transition that takes place once you give people the tools and confidence to unleash their potential.[10]

• Motorola, another Baldrige winner, invests 2.9 percent of payroll (excluding fringe benefits) in training.[11]

- In 1989, Milliken, another Baldrige winner, spent $1,900 per employee for training.[12]
- In 1988, Hewlett-Packard's training investment was 5 percent *of its revenue.*[13]
- At Corning, a Baldrige finalist and frequently cited service/quality leader, employees spend about 4 to 5 percent of their time in training. David Luther, senior vice president and corporate director of quality, says, "In 1986, when we set that 5 percent goal, there was a great debate about the idea. Now, there is no discussion about training's importance." Corning's managers receive about 100 hours of training a year.[14]
- In the first year of its service/quality improvement effort, Wesley-Jessen trained all employees a minimum of 25 hours. Senior and middle management received 75 to 100 hours of skill development.
- At Nissan's plant in Smyrna, Tennessee, employees received from 16 to 360 hours of preemployment training. When they began the plant, 380 of the supervisors, managers, and technicians were sent to Japan for weeks of training and "hands-on" experience. Altogether, Nissan invested over $73 million in training at the truck plant.[15]

EDUCATION AND SKILLS: KNOWING ISN'T DOING

"The great end of life is not knowledge but action."

Aldous Huxley, *English novelist and essayist*

The differences among education and awareness, inspiration, and skill development can be confusing. Even training professionals, who ought to know better, often get these words and concepts mixed up. All three are needed to continually improve service/quality. A successful improvement effort can't get going until those involved understand what it's all about and why it's important and are turned on to make the journey. But then everyone needs the tools or skills to participate or lead the improvement process. This is where a huge majority of organizations get bogged down, lost, or headed down dead-end roads. Because of the widespread confusion about education/knowledge/inspiration and skill development, many of those wayward organizations never figure out why their investments went astray.

We deliberately separated our education and awareness cylinder (Chapter 9) from the skill cylinders because they are two very different—but highly related—things. However, many executives, managers, and improvement specialists routinely interchange the words *education* and *skill development* as if they were the same thing. *They are not.* Education introduces, or keeps everyone on top of, *what* needs to be done to continually improve service/quality. Skill development equips all the players with the tools, techniques, and skills to show them *how* they can contribute to and support the process. In 1990, the Conference Board's U.S. Quality Council surveyed a number of its members. Companies such as American Express, Corning, Florida Light and Power, IBM, Johnson and Johnson, Milliken, Westinghouse, Ford, and Xerox reviewed their service/quality training and development practices. If they had it to do over again, what would these service/quality pioneers do differently? "Rather than exhorting employees to 'do it right the first time,' they would equip them upfront with the skills to improve their performance."[16]

Many trainers, managers, executives, and service/quality coordinators fail to realize that *knowing about* a topic, no matter how brilliant the flashes of insight or the urgency to improve, does not mean people know *how to* make the change. For example, we know the way to get higher profit is to increase sales while decreasing costs, or the way to increase employee commitment is through involvement in teams, or the best way to cure insomnia is to get more sleep. But none of those insights shows us *how* to do it or builds the habits necessary to sustain the change. Beer, Eisenstat, and Spector's research on "why change programs don't produce change" found a high need to balance education and awareness with skill development:

> New *competencies* such as knowledge of the business as a whole, analytical skills, and interpersonal skills are necessary if people are to identify and solve problems as a team. If any of these elements are missing, the change process will break down. The problem with most companywide programs is they address only one or, at best, two of these factors. Just because a company issues a philosophy statement about teamwork doesn't mean its employees necessarily know what teams to form or how to function within them to improve coordination.[17]

WHAT SKILLS ARE NEEDED?

"He who is not prepared today will be less so tomorrow."

Ovid, *Roman poet*

Three key skill areas need to be strong throughout the organization to continuously improve service/quality: (1) technical, (2) data-based tools and techniques to improve processes and reduce ricochets, and (3) interpersonal, human, or people skills.

We won't look at technical skills because they are specific to each organization and vary broadly according to the products or services you produce. But these skills are at the very center of your inner product ring. If your organization's core technical competencies are not strong and continuously improving to at least stay abreast of your field, the rest doesn't matter—you are spiraling downward.

However, the data-based tools and techniques and interpersonal or people skills are very generic and have proved highly relevant and applicable to every organization. Throughout the rest of this book, but especially in the next three chapters, we will look at these vital skill areas and the key role they play in the service/quality improvement process. However, reading about these skills won't develop them. We'll look at how to develop skills shortly.

Data-Based Tools and Techniques

"Facts, when combined with ideas, constitute the greatest force in the world. They are greater than armaments, greater than finance, greater than science, business, and law because they are the common denominators of all of them."

Carl Ackerman, *American editor and writer*

These skills are refinements and improvements of the quality control methods pioneered by Walter Shewhart at Bell Labs, used so successfully in America to control armament production during World War II, and introduced in Japan by statistician W. Edwards Deming in 1950. These tools are used to identify and then control causes of variability in any production, administrative, delivery, or support process. Only when the process is in a state of reliable "control" can it be improved to reduce ricochets and costs while enhancing service and providing better support. Various statistical methods are at the core of these quality improvement tools and techniques.

Japanese quality pioneer and guru Kaoru Ishikawa says these tools and techniques are at the heart of Japan's phenomenal success through continuous quality improvement:

It was through these (statistical methods) that (Japan's) quality level has risen, reliability has risen, and cost has fallen. The key has been the dogged use of process analysis and quality analysis without fanfare for a long period of time. This has brought about improvement in technology.[18]

Data-based tools and techniques are extensive and varied in their degree of difficulty and application. In Chapter 14, you will be introduced to a broad range of the basic tools needed by all types of teams to contribute to the improvement process. Quality improvement coordinators or specialists in your organization also will have to be trained in the more advanced statistical methods such as sampling and testing techniques, design of experiments, multivariate analysis, operation research, and various other process control and process management tools. Again, the watchwords are "simplicity, useability, and readiness." *Too many organizations train their people in complex statistical methods that are beyond the organization's ability to use or support effectively.*

Interpersonal or People Skills

"Most entanglements are caused by vocal cords."

Pauline Brady, who chaired the second Xerox Quality Forum, sums up the experiences of a growing number of organizations implementing service/quality improvement processes: "There are two aspects to total quality management—a hard analytical side and a softer behavioral side. In many respects, it is the latter which is the more critical and the more difficult to achieve."[19] One of the most extensive research efforts ever mounted on this critical issue has proved that observation. Zenger-Miller conducted a study that consisted of surveys of more than 1,000 managers and quality improvement professionals and focus group interviews with dozens of them. The results showed that 80 percent of outside training expenditures went for technical and data-based tools and techniques training. Less than 20 percent of the training dollars spent went to developing interpersonal and leadership skills up, down, and across the organization.

However, when participants in the study were asked to identify where most of the blocks to service/quality improvement were, the ratio was almost exactly reversed: *80 percent of the problems were related to frontline interpersonal, management leadership, support, and involvement skills, and 20 percent were related to technical skills or data-based tools and techniques.* Roland Dumas, one of the Zenger-Miller researchers at the time, summarizes:

> We have found repeatedly that there are foundation skills, general leadership and interpersonal, that consistently make or break a quality effort. Through the process of elimination, the problem eventually comes home as a leadership issue. *That systems need to be integrated and led emerges as the long-term lesson.* Introducing new systems and technologies when people don't have the fundamental skills is a prescription for disaster.[20]

Over the years, Zenger-Miller has found that interpersonal and data-based skills are best built on a foundation of basic principles. These core philosophies are woven through each of the skill sets described in the next three chapters. Many organizations post these basic principles, along with their core values, in every training session and in many common work and meeting areas:

1. Focus on the work process, issue, or behavior, not on the person.
2. Maintain the self-confidence and self-esteem of others.
3. Maintain strong partnerships with your internal and external customers and suppliers.
4. Take initiative to improve work processes and partnerships.
5. Lead by example.

HOW ARE SKILLS DEVELOPED?

"I hear and I forget, I see and I remember, I do and I understand."

Chinese proverb

The goal of skill training is to change behavior. While many executives, managers, and training professionals would agree with the objective, a large number take dead-end roads to that destination. Just as many managers have trouble seeing the new team-based organizational paradigm, despite the overwhelming evidence to its effectiveness, many training professionals are conveniently ignoring the mountain of evidence showing that behavior change precedes rather than follows attitude or style change:

"Behavior change induces attitude change. That's the chief social-psychological lesson I have learned (and then re-learned many times) in the last 25 years. . . . Stanford psychologist Albert Bandura with his analyses of modeling behavior (is) fundamentally right. If we can get people to do something—to experiment, to try it, to learn about their native competence, to increase their self-esteem and self-control—well, then, the desired attitude change will follow."

Tom Peters[21]

"It is because attitude has the power to affect behavior that people are tempted to focus on it in the first place . . . if managers want to change behavior, there is good news—it can and should be done, starting with behavior. It turns out that there is a two-way street between attitude and behavior, and behavior has the power to change attitude . . . a change in behavior leads to a change in attitude."

Thomas Krause, John Hidley, and Stanley Hodson[22]

*Managerial myth: To change people's behavior, it is first necessary to change their atti-
tudes. "There is some validity to this, but mostly it is the other way around; if we first
change people's behavior, that will change their attitudes."*

Joseph Juran[23]

Most organizations set out to develop interpersonal or process analysis skills but then use an attitude-, knowledge-, or style-based approach.
It simply doesn't work. No amount of traveling on the wrong road
will get you to the right destination. And knowledge- or attitude-based
approaches are clearly the wrong road to skill development. Participants
can learn *about* leadership skills. They can even get a good idea of what
strong personal, coaching, or team leadership looks like. But no matter
how exciting, stimulating, challenging, thought-provoking, insightful,
well-researched, or well-designed your development program may be,
it will do little to change behavior if it is knowledge-based. Participants
may learn which skills need developing and why. But they won't actually
develop the skills or learn how to put the concepts into action. How
comfortable would you be on a plane if the pilot had just graduated from
a theoretical course but this was his or her first time actually in a cockpit?

Behavior Modeling

A well-researched and proven approach to skill building is called behavior modeling. In an article titled, "28 Techniques for Transforming Training into Performance," *Training* magazine editors Ron Zemke and John
Gunkler write, "The data is overwhelming: Programs that use behavior
modeling technology in their design have a better success rate with
respect to transfer of skills to the workplace."

Behavior modeling was developed in 1969 by Melvin Sorcher, a General Electric industrial psychologist, based on some pioneering work in
clinical psychology. He designed a training program for supervisors and
newly hired minority workers to reduce the horrendous turnover rate
GE was experiencing with these workers. Six months after the new
training, turnover rates had dropped from 70 percent to 30 percent and
productivity had increased. Based on such positive results, GE quickly
expanded the supervisory training.

Hearing of Mel Sorcher's success, Jack Zenger and Dale Miller invited
him to help them design a similar program for Syntex, the pharmaceutical firm where they were responsible for organization and human resource development. The training program achieved the same degree of
success—well beyond anything Zenger and Miller had experienced with

any other training approach. In their own consulting firm in 1977, Zenger and Miller received a number of requests to help clients develop their own version of this highly effective training. With Mel Sorcher's blessing, Zenger-Miller modified and refined the original behavior modeling concepts to develop "Supervision." Over the next few years, the success and popularity of this system, and its successor, "Frontline Leadership," led to a Zenger-Miller and Achieve growth rate unparalleled in the training system industry.

Behavior modeling is much more effective at building lasting skills and changing behavior than any other method. A typical session is three to four hours long and is given in a classroom setting with about 12 to 15 participants. The instructor is either a training professional, or increasingly, a senior line manager. Following are the typical behavior modeling steps used in a session:

1. *Understand why the skill is important.* Participants discuss their own or written examples. A short senior management "stump speech" can help underscore the skill area as well.

2. *Discuss the specific behaviors involved in the skill.* This always involves learning and discussing a set of generic "key actions" for that skill area. Uncomplicated, nontheoretical, and straightforward "how-to" skill steps are vital here.

3. *Watch a demonstration of the skill.* Carefully scripted, realistic videos allow participants to see and "get a feel" for the key actions being used in a variety of work settings.

4. *Practice the skill.* Participants move from "knowing to doing" with each one practicing their own use of the key actions in small groups using their own actual job situations.

5. *Receive constructive feedback.* All key action users get feedback from the small-group participants to reinforce their approach to that skill's key actions. They also receive coaching on ways to improve. This feedback and coaching build extremely valuable leadership, continuous learning, and team player skills that group members take back to their jobs.

6. *Identify opportunities for using the skill.* Each session concludes with all participants planning how they will use the skill in their job.

In 1991, Jack Zenger summarized the mounting research evidence of behavior modeling's effectiveness. Here are the findings that are especially important to organizations looking to maximize the service/quality skill training investment:

- Behavior modeling brings about behavioral change in the classroom and on the job by helping people to improve their methods and, in the process, their knowledge of and attitudes about their work.
- Over time, positive changes tend both to endure and increase.
- Behavior modeling succeeds with people in virtually every age group, culture, and learning style.
- Neither employees nor those who train them need to understand complex theories or vast amounts of information.
- With minimal preparation, line people often conduct behavior modeling sessions as effectively as professional trainers.[24]

Executives and Managers as Instructors

If your organization is serious about changing your culture to become a high-service/quality performer through customer-focused teams, then you need to have most of your skill development sessions delivered by line management. Delegating the building of your organization's core improvement competencies to outsiders or internal staff professionals launches your organization down the low road to "bits and pieces" improvement. When asked what companies can do to build a service/quality culture, Regis McKenna replied, "One answer is for management to do a lot of internal training. You don't want to bring in outside people, because you need to develop more of a mentoring process. And everyone must be involved."[25] Stay on the "outsiders training road" and eventually you will end up in the swamp.

This is not to suggest you exclude training professionals. On the contrary, *effective* human resource development managers can do much to ensure your training investments are sound. But they can't own the skill development process. When that happens, training becomes a series of classroom experiences unconnected to your organization's real world. *Unless and until you, your managers, and your supervisors practice what your training programs teach, you may as well not waste everyone's time and your organization's money.* In far too many organizations, leadership skills, well developed in the classroom, are contradicted by inconsistent executive and management behavior. That kind of futile effort only makes participants even more cynical about management's hypocrisy. Ray Stata, chairman and president of Analog Devices, says:

A manager must be a role model in learning. The manager must recognize that learning is part of the job, and must demonstrate by example that "learning" is as important as "doing." Managers must encourage and support learning, acting as facilitators and allocating time and resources to the process.[26]

The best way to keep training relevant is to have managers deliver it. A growing number of organizations are taking this approach, usually under the guidance of their training and development professionals. The manager as trainer has numerous advantages:

- Line managers are put on the spot to practice what they preach.
- A much larger number of participants can be included in a shorter time.
- Teaching pushes managers to master leadership skills. Kaoru Ishikawa says, "To teach is after all the best way to be trained."[27]
- The signals that skill development is important are loud and clear. At the world's largest Caterpillar dealer, Finning Ltd., President and CEO Jim Shepard and dozens of executives and managers deliver QUEST (quality enhancement through skills training). Quality improvement coordinator Bob Vaughan says, "We really notice a difference in employee attitude and morale, especially when employees see firsthand how motivated and committed their company president is toward quality improvement."
- Managers are in a much stronger position to provide follow-through and coaching on the job.
- The human resource development group stays close to, and better serves, its internal customers.
- Any useless theory or "nice to know" concepts are quickly cut out by busy managers who have time only for what's relevant and useful tomorrow morning to improve service/quality. Without line managers involved to this degree, Joseph Juran says:

There is a real risk that the training will become technique-oriented rather than result-oriented. . . . Such emphasis then carries over into evaluation of progress, so that progress is measured by such things as how many persons have been trained, how many control charts are in use, or how many pledge cards have been signed.[28]

Just-in-Time Training

"Practice is the best of all instructors."

Publilius Syrus, *Latin writer*

Providing teams with training just as the tools and techniques are about to be used or the interpersonal skills will be most needed is clearly the best way to change behavior. This follows management training that has just been implemented so that executives, managers, and supervisors are beginning to coach, support, and lead their teams, cross-functional colleagues, and individuals reporting to them.

The Conference Board's report on its survey of Quality Council members' training practices suggests, "Stress timely application of training." The report goes on to state the participants recommend cutting "the time lag between training and application . . . training and on-the-job application should be 'virtually simultaneous.' "[29] Skills, like muscles, atrophy when they're not used. Effective skill development processes are timed, supported, and followed through to maximize application and use. Massive across-the-board training efforts that have some people waiting to use their skills until other groups have also been trained are proving to be much less effective.

Use Your Training Effort to Communicate Your Vision and Values

Here is yet another reason to have senior-level managers involved in planning and delivering your training. William Cone, manager of professional development for Hughes Aircraft, points out, "Through training your employees you can have a greater degree of confidence that the work will progress through a pattern you designed."[30] In his book, *Managing an Organization*, Theodore Caplan adds another view of the strategic role training can play in the hands of an astute executive: "Because the importance of training is so commonly underestimated, the manager who wants to make a dramatic improvement in organizational effectiveness without challenging the status quo will find a training program a good way to start."[31]

Chapter Twelve

Cylinder Five: Personal Skills

"The greatest ability in business is to get along with others and influence their actions."

John Hancock,
American statesman

A chain is no stronger than its weakest link, and a team is no stronger than its weakest member. The 85/15 rule shows that systems, structures, or processes, and not people, are the major source of ricochets. However, only people can improve those things. And the people in the best position to improve a system, process, or practice are those who work in it. Not only will they come up with a more relevant change, but they also will own the change and work all that much harder to ensure its success—or keep changing it to continually make it better.

Getting anyone to embrace involvement in, or ownership of, a system, process, or practice can be done only through empowerment and voluntarism. Service/quality improvement depends on people who want to make things better and have been given the latitude to do so. As we've seen already, and will continue to explore, involvement, empowerment, and voluntarism come from a number of factors. Two of the most basic, which form the cornerstone for an involved, team-based organization, are confidence and competence. Whether you are a frontline contributor or a vice president, if you don't feel capable of and comfortable in working with others, the best tools, techniques, infrastructure, systems, and so on will be badly underutilized.

Empowering and enabling frontline contributors to become more involved in the improvement process calls for new skills. Even before using data-based tools and techniques to improve service/quality, team members need to strengthen their personal leadership skills. With these skills, team members will have the confidence and competence to use the tools, techniques, infrastructure, and other support to their full advantage to continually improve service/quality.

If your organization plunges your people straight into using data-based tools and techniques within team settings, they will likely get bogged down in all the "people problems" fairly quickly. Conflicts, emotion, misunderstandings, unfulfilled expectations, communication breakdowns, and poor teamwork block progress. Intact or cross-functional teams are most effective when their individual members know how to work well with each other. Another of Zenger-Miller's studies of the skill requirements for service/quality improvement showed that hundreds of quality coordinators ranked "giving feedback," "participating in group meetings," "listening," and "defining customer requirements" within the top five employee skills needed for continuous improvement.[1] This is consistent with the Z-M study cited in the last chapter showing that most companies had their ratio of people to technical and data-based improvement skills backward.

Too many organizations assume "if they knew better they'd do better." In other words, once we show everybody what's needed, how they should get along, what teamwork looks like, and the importance of feedback and communications, they will start behaving that way. But this deadly assumption is built on the shaky foundation of trying to change attitudes in order to change behavior. Behavior change needs to come first. And behavior is changed through skill development.

Personal skills are aimed especially at frontline employees because they have generally not received this type of training. And because they are now at the center of the improvement effort, they need a lot of help in building unfamiliar competencies. This leads to higher levels of confidence. As Time magazine noted in a cover story on the cause of poor service, "Businesses in general spend too little time training and motivating their frontline employees, whom they treat as the lowest workers on the ladder."[2] However, the fundamental skills found in this cylinder are not just for frontline employees. They are even more critical at the supervisor, manager, and executive levels because management establishes the tone and model for the organization. Putting well-trained employees into an unreceptive, unsupportive, or inconsistent environment wastes everyone's time. Even worse, it demotivates and frustrates employees more than if no training had occurred. Employees newly sensitized to the Basic Principles (see page 165) and more effective ways of dealing with each other will be more attuned to management's behavior.

Managers who send employees off "to be fixed" but aren't themselves vigorously practicing the same principles and skills will reduce voluntarism, decrease employee ownership, and kill commitment to higher service/quality. That is why the greatest success in building personal skills comes when this is done after supervisors, managers, and executives have been well trained in and are actively practicing these same skills as part of their own coaching and team leadership skill development. It's also why personal skills are best developed by line managers leading the improvement sessions. This not only visibly signals skill development as a top management priority, but it also puts managers on the spot to practice what they preach.

THE ROLE OF PERSONAL SKILLS

"Ninety percent of the friction of daily life is caused by the wrong tone of voice."

Personal leadership skills include the ability to communicate effectively, to plan, to negotiate, to resolve issues, to build strong relationships, and to be part of a team. Traditionally, responsibility for managing these functions has rested with management. Employees were paid to do what they were told. In other words, "You're a pair of hired hands. Check your brains at the door in the morning."

But today's complex technologies have transformed even the simplest jobs into more demanding positions. A growing number of employees are becoming (or should become) their organization's experts in those jobs. That dramatically changes their role. For one thing, employees must deal with broader organizational and interdepartmental issues because managers are no longer experts in every process and function. Increasingly, managers must rely on their people for expertise.

Industry Week Executive Editor Perry Pascarella devoted extensive sections of his book *The New Achievers* to the topic of management-employee participation. He builds a strong case for the role of skill development in making these new approaches work: "Many people are not in the right frame of mind for participation and involvement. In fact, the prospect can be downright frightening, especially if you lack the skills for dealing with others, for prioritizing problems, and solving problems in new ways." Perry says more than 90 percent of employees say they want to try more participative approaches. But "all this is new for many workers and will amount to nothing if the company does not provide training in problem solving, information gathering and analysis, and functioning effectively within a group."[3]

Although a team's effectiveness is most heavily dependent on the skills of its leader, building a strong team out of weak individuals is like pushing a large rock up a steep hill. It can be done, but it's very hard work. Developing strong personal service/quality skills within each team member not only teaches everyone how to contribute to the team's effectiveness, but it also gives team members the confidence to contribute effectively. When strong team members are led by an equally skilled team leader, the gains are breathtaking.

A component of personal skills is what John Kotter calls "relational." As chairman of the Organizational Behavior and Human Resources Management Area at the Harvard Business School, Kotter has spent years studying how managers, professionals, and frontline performers get things done through working with others. His sixth book, *Power and Influence*, devotes a chapter to "overcoming resistance and gaining cooperation without formal authority." As Kotter explains, these skills are often overlooked:

> Over the years, I have encountered literally hundreds of examples of capable people underestimating, to their detriment and the detriment of their organizations, how much others they depended on in lateral relationships would resist cooperating with them on something or how able they would be to resist.[4]

UNDERSTANDING PERSONAL SKILLS

"There is nothing but wind in a tire, but it makes riding in a car very smooth and pleasant."

Ferdinand Foch, *French Marshal*

A series of skill areas makes up this cylinder. These skills are often thought of as the lubrication that makes your technology and data-based improvement machinery run smoothly, efficiently, and friction-free. They typically form the basis of training given to team members (team leaders and management develop these same sets of skills in the coaching and team cylinders). For an easier overview, they are shown here in clusters. However, the points listed in each skill cluster may be more or less important in your own organization. For that reason, some of the subpoints may be separated and given expanded training sessions, followed by on-the-job coaching. As with all the skills cylinders, those listed throughout this chapter are grounded in the Basic Principles (page 165).

Works effectively

- Uses all available resources to get the job done.
- Knows the expected results of each new task.

- Assembles necessary materials before starting a task or task segment.
- Accepts change and helps new procedures work smoothly.

Communicates clearly; helps others do the same

- Helps others—especially the quiet ones—speak up at meetings.
- Provides facts and ideas at meetings.
- Helps keep meetings focused on the topic and purpose.
- Asks others for their reactions to the information given.

Provides positive mutual support

- Lets others know when they've done a good job.
- Makes people feel good about their work.
- Shows interest in the ideas and opinions of others.
- Shares ideas with others.

Seeks and accepts help when needed

- Asks for help as soon as he or she needs it.
- Allows others to help get the job done better.
- Keeps others informed of what's going on.
- Lets others know about problems and conflicts early.

Constructively channels emotion

- Keeps control of own anger and disappointment.
- Avoids letting own emotion get in the way of reaching results on the job.
- Deals with negative situations in a positive way.

THE CUSTOMER-SUPPLIER CHAIN

A beginning point for service/quality improvement is to have everyone in the organization identify where they fit within the service/quality customer-supplier chain. It soon becomes clear that everyone in the organization has internal suppliers, and many employees serve internal people as their next immediate customer as well. As you'll see in Chapter 17, this exercise is best done within the context of the larger organizationwide processes that senior management identified as making up the core of the organization's work activities.

Focusing on the customer-supplier chain helps all teams and individuals trace how what they do affects the organization's ultimate purpose—continuously more satisfied customers at continuously lower cost. Quality function deployment, process management, and other broad organizationwide approaches lay down a clear blueprint to bring the voice of the customer deep into all nooks and crannies of the organization. External customer needs become the unifying focus of all objectives, priorities, and measurements. At the other end of the chain, supplier management becomes a key part of ensuring that the information, materials, expertise, funding, or whatever is brought into the organization to help produce, deliver, or support the organization's core products and services contributes to ever higher service/quality at ever lower cost. Increasingly, the cost picture is expanded to look at the rework, errors, or "hassle factor" the supposedly less expensive suppliers may be creating.

However, this is all at the broad strategic or macro level. To ultimately make this strategy work, all teams and individuals need to learn how to deal more effectively with their immediate customer and suppliers (often internal). That brings us to another set of important personal skills everyone in the organization needs to push service/quality levels ever higher:

Customer and supplier skills

- Identifies key customers and suppliers for each major product or service being provided.
- Clarifies, weighs, and quantifies customer expectations for each major product or service.
- Works with customers to resolve areas of dissatisfaction and set a plan to better meet their expectations.
- Works with key suppliers to clarify his, her, or the team's needs and expectations of that supplier.

The internal customer-supplier chain as part of the upside-down organization rests on managers effectively serving the needs of those within the chain. As the American Society for Quality Control says, "The job of management is to make sure that the links between customers and suppliers—links that make up the service process—are given top priority."[5] Without that kind of management support, the internal customer-supplier chain pulls apart.

PERSONAL SKILLS IN ACTION

"Half the world is composed of people who have something to say and can't, and the other half who have nothing to say and keep on saying it."

Robert Frost, *American poet*

Following are a few examples of personal skills in use. As we discussed in the last chapter, however, skill development is more than just knowing what the skill looks like. Skills are developed primarily through practice and feedback.

- A division of Northern Telecom, a major telecommunications equipment manufacturer, found that frontline employees who received training in personal leadership skills acted more independently and took up far less of their supervisors' time. For example, by learning how to give each other direct feedback, employees resolved issues and differences between themselves, rather than gossiping, bickering, or tattling to management. Observed a delighted manager, "They do a better job, feel better about themselves, and communications have opened up considerably."

- A large hospital used personal leadership skills development to get employees more involved in problem solving and decision making. The effort improved service/quality in two ways: first, it sent a tangible signal on the expanding role and responsibilities employees were to have; second, it gave employees the interpersonal skills they needed to work together more effectively.

- A medical school uses local actors to fake symptoms so that medical students can practice and be rated on their bedside manner.[6] This training is part of a growing trend in medical schools to teach doctors how to treat patients as human beings, not just organisms to be repaired.

- By building her personal leadership skills, an order analyst at NCR Comten was better able to help coordinate the entire ordering process. With her newly found confidence, she organized a meeting with her peers from seven departments. Among other things, they decided to circulate information about the availability of parts before the shortages showed up. As a result of this and other initiatives, there is a new willingness to work together as a team.

- As a result of a personal leadership skills program delivered by managers to telephone operators of Bell Canada, service levels improved and so did morale. Pilot results were so encouraging the program was rapidly expanded. "We find the operators now feel more valuable as employees," explains the operations manager. "And the managers leading the training sessions have also learned a great deal about communicating with their staff."

- As part of a long-term drive to increase teamwork for higher service and productivity, a telecommunications company boosted the personal leadership skills of project clerks, coordinators, and clerical staff. As a result, these "nonleaders" began taking leadership action. They took the initiative to improve what they could in their jobs and with those on their team. The impact on team effectiveness was summed up by a manager: "Team efficiency increases greatly if members have the right kind of skills to be team players."
- A municipality found that employees who had participated in a personal leadership skills program were more willing to take on new work. They also organized their work more effectively, had better listening skills, and were eager to discuss suggestions for improvement.
- The transport and work equipment department of a major electrical utility met sharply increased demands for its internal service by developing all employees' personal leadership skills. Understanding, communication, and cooperation among various functions in the department improved significantly. Comments the department manager, "Our mechanics, accountants, and engineers can now talk to one another. We couldn't have handled our increased workload without increasing staff if we hadn't developed those skills."
- The Canadian division of the Japanese multinational company Matsushita Electric (Panasonic) used personal leadership skills development to strengthen its total quality control process. It found that employees were better able to participate in meetings, resolve issues with others, get their points across, give feedback, and work as team players.

COMMON TRAPS TO DEVELOPING PERSONAL SKILLS

Knowing versus Doing

Don't assume employees have the operational and interpersonal skills needed to enhance service/quality once they understand what needs to be done. Many solid improvement efforts have been badly weakened by a skills foundation that was not firm. Inspiration, education, and knowledge are vital, but they are not the whole equation.

One-Day-Workshop Wonders

A firm, lasting skill-development foundation is not built in a day or two. Sustained behavioral change comes from repetition, practice, and feedback, all supported by strong management follow-through. This is not the stuff of quick fixes and miracle cures. It takes at least six to eight two- to four-hour skill-building sessions before behavior begins to shift. And then the support trainees receive back on the job determines whether these skills will be permanent.

Misguided Mentoring

Be very careful about turning training and orientation of new employees over to the veterans in those jobs. Your new employees may not be learning the habits and practices you want to see developed.

Management Duplicity

You can't put training in place to "fix the front line" without having first strengthened management's coaching and team leadership skills. Not only is this dishonest, but it's wasteful. People aren't that stupid. If they see that supervisors, managers, and executives are not practicing the skills and techniques the employees are being taught, they'll get the message: "Be a good little student, jump through the hoops, get your nice diploma, put the books back on the shelf . . . and get back to the real world."

Delegating Development

Management's job is to coach, develop, and lead people, particularly in a team-based, upside-down organization. Personal skills training is much more short term when delivered by anybody else, no matter how good they are in the classroom. When management gives frontline teams the skills, tools, information, systems, and many of the other areas in the alignment section, they will run daily operations better than management ever did. This further frees management to provide proactive, strategic leadership, including more training and development. In turn, this enables and empowers teams to take over more of their own management tasks. This further frees management to provide. . . .

Chapter Thirteen

Cylinder Six: Coaching Skills

"A leader has to be an energizer and motivator, someone who inspires and guides others, who energizes the system and generates the magic that makes everyone want to do something extra."

Peter Drucker

The very notion of coaching employees to higher performance levels is heretical to some managers. Raised in the command-and-control days, many of these "two-by-four managers" believe that getting employees to do a better job means using rules, directives, power, manipulation, and, when "they just won't do as they're told," heavy amounts of discipline and punishment—as if they were dealing with spoiled three-year-olds.

Thankfully, that archaic view is falling out of favor. As we saw in Chapter 5, a team-based organization with broad involvement in the continuous improvement process has to be managed in a manner that *veers sharply away* from the way our traditional organizations have been managed. In a team-based organization, effective supervisors, managers, and executives nurture and develop teams and their individual members to continually higher performance levels. To shift process ownership and improvement activities to those closest to the action, management moves from being cops to coaches. A team-based organization demands that your *entire management group* must move toward the column C skills described on page 88.

In *A Passion for Excellence*, Nancy Austin and Tom Peters provide a good definition of management's new coaching role:

Coaching is the process of enabling others to act, of building on their strengths. . . . To coach is to facilitate, which literally means "to make easy"—not less demanding, less exciting or less intense, but less discouraging, less bound up with excessive controls. . . . Coaching is face-to-face leadership that pulls together people, . . . encourages them to step up to responsibility and continued achievement, and treats them as full-scale partners and contributors. . . . Every coach, at every level, is above all a value-shaper. . . . Perhaps surprisingly, the more elbow room a company grants to its people, the more important on-the-job coaching becomes.[1]

Nurturing and developing others is at the heart of coaching. Patricia Carrigan, a GM plant manager, sounds the alarm: "We have to get people excited about using their talents or we'll end up going down the tube together."[2] Part of that effort involves helping people to take more initiative and responsibility to improve service/quality; in effect, to make them leaders, regardless of their formal position. One of Deming's famous 14 points for quality improvement is "adopt and institute leadership." He goes on to explain, "The job of management is not supervision, but leadership."[3] A team-based organization must have an army of committed, turned-on "employee-leaders." There is no way for management to manage it alone.

WHY COACHING SKILLS ARE SO CRITICAL

"Good management consists of showing average people how to do the work of superior people."

John D. Rockefeller, *American capitalist and philanthropist*

How critical are coaching skills? *If the majority of your organization's managers aren't good to outstanding coaches, your entire improvement effort is doomed.* You will become one of those 70 percent of organizations that do not significantly improve service/quality despite big investments of time and money. Coaching skills are as fundamental to service/quality improvement as breathing is to living. You can't do one without the other.

You and your management staff need to begin strengthening your coaching skills very early. Here are some of the key reasons:

• The central focus and aim of the entire implementation architecture is on service/quality improvement activities driven by a variety of teams. *Those teams will barely get off the ground if they are not well coached and supported.*

• The first three points of the new organizational paradigm (page 84) will happen only through strong coaching skills.

• One of the impediments to cohesive and effective improvement teams is turnover and absenteeism. Advanced, strong teams often experience much lower turnover and absenteeism—another benefit of effective teamwork. Especially in the early team-forming stages, daily coaching or supervisory practices play a big role in motivating individual team members. Study after study shows that weak coaching or supervisory practices increase absenteeism and turnover. When team members are missing, or novices keep having to be brought up to speed, teams take longer to get going.

• Poorly treated employees pass on the treatment they get to others. Robert Desatnick found:

> How do you suppose the employee who is not given respect is going to treat the customer? With a lack of respect, of course. If a customer is feeling belligerent or grouchy, it will not be overlooked by the employee who feels "beaten on" most of the time. But the employee who is given respect is more tolerant of customers who complain—rightfully or wrongly.[4]

• Pride and commitment to continuous improvement will be stunted if employees don't believe they are treated fairly and supported in their improvement efforts. W. Edwards Deming warns, "Barriers against realization of pride of workmanship may in fact be one of the most important obstacles to reduction of cost and improvement of quality in the United States."[5]

• A result—and too often a goal—of traditional command-and-control management is employee fear. Managers "cracked the whip" and used heavy-handed discipline to force employees into compliance with what management deemed needed to be done. For over three decades, Arnold "Red" Auerbach has been the coach and general manager of "the most successful sports franchise in America," the Boston Celtics. He's found:

> If you have employees who work through fear, you're not going to get any ingenuity out of them. You're not going to get any employees who will take a gamble or come up with ideas. All you'll have are robots who are going to do their jobs, have a low-key approach, stay out of trouble. They'll put in their hours and go home.[6]

• Empowerment means giving power to the front line. But this could be as dangerous as giving a chain saw to someone who doesn't know which end to hold. Effectively empowering teams and individuals involves guiding and supporting their actions and decisions.

• Voluntarism and ownership for improvements are drawn out only in a supportive, encouraging atmosphere. Traditional "find the guilty party" management discourages "sticking your neck out," creates blaming and "buck passing," and dampens initiative.

• Performance evaluations and appraisals destroy continuous improvement because they focus on the 15 percent of the time the problem is people related rather than the 85 percent or more of the time poor service/quality is caused by the system, process, or structure. What's worse, most supervisors, managers, or executives' poor coaching skills throw buckets of salt into the wounds opened by performance management, pay for performance, and rating systems. Morale plummets, performance falls, and the root cause of the service/quality breakdown still isn't fixed.

- Only when management learns how to coach effectively can it *make the critical shift from solving problems to making sure problems are getting solved.*

WHY AREN'T SUPERVISORS, MANAGERS, AND EXECUTIVES BETTER COACHES?

Supervisors, managers, and executives are not better coaches because they don't know *how*. You may know "what" coaching is or even "why" it is important, but you probably don't know *how* to really do it. It's a new, unfamiliar skill—even though you may have been talking about it for some time. You also likely didn't get good coaching from most of the bosses you've had over the years, so you have not repeatedly seen the skill in action and felt its powerful effect on motivation and performance. And, you probably haven't received *skill-based* training on coaching. Rather, what you got, if anything, was education, awareness, style training, or inspiration. All of which has repeatedly proved to be *much less* effective than the behavior modeling "how-to" training we outlined in Chapter 11.

AN OVERVIEW OF KEY COACHING SKILLS

"Here lies a man who knew how to bring into his service men better than he was himself."
Andrew Carnegie's epitaph

Following is a brief overview of the key coaching tasks that require skill development and some basic skills that underpin their successful application.

Recognition

"I have never seen anyone who could do real work except under the stimulus of encouragement and enthusiasm and the approval of the people for whom they are working."
Charles Schwab, *American industrialist and steel executive*

Recognition is such a key element in every top service/quality organization that it has its own cylinder (see Chapter 16). Tom Peters says simply,

"Celebrate what you want more of." The use of recognition, encouragement, and positive feedback is so fundamental to effective coaching that *without it there is no coaching.* Period.

Ken Blanchard devoted a large section of *The One-Minute Manager* to "catching people doing things right." He believes recognition is at the heart of leading others effectively. But once again we run into the knowing-isn't-doing trap. It's a rare manager who won't agree that recognition and encouragement are critical elements of his or her job. But few of those good intentions are translated into daily actions. As Blanchard says, "Good thoughts in your head not delivered don't mean squat."

Managers at all levels do such an abysmal job of recognizing and encouraging their people for a number of reasons. The biggest reason of all is *they're not sure how.* It is, yet again, a skill issue.

Managers' lack of comfort with "catching people doing things right" is masked in a variety of ways. Charles Garfield's more than 20 years of research into the characteristics of over 400 peak performers identifies recognition as a crucial element of how those at the top of every field work with others to support their efforts. Garfield explodes a popular excuse made by managers who give little recognition:

> Want to ruin a team? Want to ruin an organization? Set up this kind of value system: the mature professional doesn't need positive feedback. That's why we're paying you. We don't have to tell you you're doing well, we expect it. However, if you make an error, 18 copies of an essential reprimand memo go to all levels of management. Your mother gets a copy, your first grade teacher gets a copy. In fact, we drop them from a blimp over your neighborhood. . . . You can't destroy an organization better than that.

Without lots of recognition, celebration, and encouragement, energy will fade, and your improvement journey will grind to a halt. You and your managers need *skill* development to increase your recognition-giving confidence, competence, and habit. *Are you developing those skills?*

Feedback

"The wise leader knows there are natural consequences for every act. The task is to shed light on these natural consequences, not to attack the behavior itself."

John Heider, *The Tao of Leadership*

A man walked into a drugstore to use the pay phone: "Hello, ABC Company, some time ago you had an opening for an operations manager. Is the position still available?'' After a slight pause, he continued: ''Oh, you have. Six months ago, huh? How's he working out?'' A somewhat longer pause. ''I see. Well, thank you. Bye.'' The druggist, having overhead the conversation, said in sympathy, ''I am sorry you couldn't go after that job.'' The man, surprised, turned and said, ''Oh, I'm not looking for a job. That was my own organization. I was calling to see how I was doing!''

We all want to know where we stand. In *The New Achievers*, Perry Pascarella writes:

> Numerous studies in recent years have shown that workers want recognition for their skills and accomplishments, feedback that tells them when they have accomplished something that someone else values, some ''say'' in the decisions that affect their work, and the opportunity to develop new skills or acquire new knowledge.[7]

One of the outstanding characteristics of an effective coach is the frequency and quality of the feedback he or she provides to reinforce, support, and help others continue to improve. Feedback is absolutely critical across the organization. Service/quality improvement can't happen without it. Operating without feedback loops is like blindly shooting at targets in the mist. You can't improve when you don't know how you're doing.

An organization with effective feedback loops has a culture that sees continuous feedback as continuous learning opportunities. Effective feedback loops generally start with how data, observations, suggestions, ideas, or support are passed on. These cultural feedback patterns are set by management. If most teams and their members are well coached, they will view feedback as a positive and much-needed step in the continuous improvement process. However, weak coaches often use feedback sessions as a time to beat up people (the ''gotcha'' variety), ''get it off their chest,'' or dump their laundry list of pet peeves. The predictable response is defensiveness, fear, and an aversion to more of this ''constructive criticism.''

Poor coaches generally add to their own personal feedback skill weakness by failing to provide feedback coaching and development (not to mention signals) to team members. This inevitably leads to ever weaker inter- and intrateam feedback loops. And so the pattern for a culture of feedback fighting and data denial is set as everyone shuts their eyes and clamps their hands over their ears. Another perfect example of how the human element, when skills are weak, so often overshadows technical ability and data-based tools and techniques.

Performance Management

"A good coach knows how to step on someone's toes without messing up their shoeshine."

In a team-based organization that has progressed to self-directed work teams, the work team establishes performance expectations, coaches along the way toward reaching those objectives, provides feedback, and takes corrective action including discipline or termination. Few organizations are that advanced. Most still rely heavily on supervisors and managers to manage the individual performance of the people in their part of the organization.

Building a team-based organization with ever higher levels of employee involvement and empowerment requires a very different approach to performance management. In his classic article, "From Control to Commitment in the Workplace," Harvard Business School Professor Richard Walton writes:

> Success depends on a superior level of (organizational) performance, a level that, in turn, requires the deep commitment, not merely the obedience—if you could obtain it—of workers. And as painful experience shows, this commitment cannot flourish in a workplace dominated by the familiar model of control.

Walton touches on some of the elements necessary for success at the supervisory level: "The commitment model requires first-line supervisors to facilitate rather than direct the work force, to impart rather than merely practice their technical and administrative expertise, and to help workers develop the ability to manage themselves."[8] But these skills have to start with executives and managers who model and teach them to the rest of the management staff. *Coaching is not something the top can order the middle to do for the bottom.*

In taking corrective action, many traditional managers see the world as black and white. On the one hand, they think they can be tough and hard-nosed and maintain high levels of platoon-sergeant discipline. Public ridicule, harsh punishment, and take-no-guff approaches characterize this world. The alternative, traditional managers believe, is the "country club" style of management. This approach is more concerned with relationships and "hand holding" than with getting the job done. It's a soft, easy-going environment where customers and employees are treated like kings, and where performance slips; where seldom is heard a negative word, and things fall through the cracks.

Country-club management is unproductive and will eventually kill any organization, argue traditional managers. And they're right. Those kinds of unbalanced organizations do struggle. "See," retorts the traditional manager, "that's why I have to use my trusty two-by-four. It may not be pretty, but it gets the job done. After all, business is business. Management is not a popularity contest."

That either/or view of correcting behavior or performance problems is a cop-out. The most effective organizations are filled with managers who have mastered the skill of holding people accountable to tough, uncompromising standards or goals while maintaining their self-esteem. They can use the Basic Principles (page 165) and still get the job done.

Effective service/quality coaches make clear what's expected and follow up. They emphasize the positive and look for ways to recognize and reward effective behavior. Good coaches draw out and act on other people's improvement ideas. And when things get off track, as they inevitably will, strong coaches know how to step on toes without messing up anybody's shoeshine.

All this requires skills, skills that don't seem to be present naturally. *How are your performance coaching skills? How do you know—where's your data?*

Fostering Continuous Improvement and Innovation

"Businesses that grow by development and improvement do not die. But when a business ceases to be creative, when it believes it has reached perfection and needs to do nothing but produce—no improvement, no development—it is done."

Henry Ford, *industrialist and automotive manufacturer*

Improvement and innovation, like profits, are a result, not an objective. There are no specific formulas or steps to innovation and improvement. It's like gardening. We can't grow anything—that is not a power mere mortals have. But we can establish the right conditions that will encourage and support vigorous growth.

The vigor of your organization's rate of innovation and continuous improvement is highly dependent on the atmosphere established by management. While that atmosphere can, and must, be established for the whole organization at a broad strategic level, local conditions needed for each plant species or work teams to flourish will vary. The recognition, feedback, training, performance management, and other coaching skills exercised locally by supervisors and managers play a *major* role in establishing the right "growing conditions" for team-based continuous improvement and innovation.

Managing Change

"I do not believe you can do today's job with yesterday's methods and be in business tomorrow."

Nelson Jackson

In your transition from a traditional organization to a customer-focused, team-based one, a multitude of changes will happen at many different levels. Most of this book is devoted to the broad strategic, macro changes needed across your organization. But, as with improvement and innovation, the success of your entire change process will be greatly determined by how those changes are managed at the local, day-to-day level.

Once again, supervisors and managers, who have the majority of contact with your teams, are in a prime position to help or hinder the overall change effort. *But they need coaching skills development. And they need these skills very early in your improvement effort.* Otherwise, employees and newly forming teams will be placed in a weed-infested, drought-stricken garden and left to fend for themselves—often not intentionally, but because their managers don't know *how* to help them grow.

Focusing Individuals and Teams on Service/Quality

This skill set is one of the first and most important steps in the change process. The messages first given to supervisors and managers, and then to employees, in the introductory education and awareness sessions (see Chapter 9) need to be followed through at the local level by local management. Here's how this vital bridging is described in a module of Zenger-Miller's QUEST (Quality Enhancement through Skills Training) development system:

> As a manager, you need to bridge the gulf between the long-range corporate strategy and the day-to-day reality of continuous improvement. By clarifying the part employees play in the big picture, you can help them translate concepts, directives, and slogans into on-the-job action. You are, in fact, a critical link between the executive vision for quality and the concrete daily behaviors that bring that vision to life.

Core Coaching Skills

The above coaching tasks need to be built on a few core coaching skills that underlie all these efforts. The most fundamental of the core skills are the Basic Principles (see page 165). This philosophical base underpins all the skill cylinders in Achieve's Service/Quality System.™ Other core skills include basic communication skills such as effective listening and information gathering as well as how to get your point across. Dealing with emotional behavior is another fundamental skill that needs to be woven throughout the development of all coaching skills.

Training and Development

"The intellect, character, and skill possessed by anyone are the product of certain original tendencies and the training which they have received."

Edward Lee Thorndike

There are two levels to the coaching skills found in this entire cylinder. The first level is where you and your managers actively build and use these coaching skills in supporting the work of your teams and their members. The second, and highest level, is developing these skills among team members so that they begin to coach each other. This level of coaching is needed if you are trying to build a strong team-based organization that is continuously improving service/quality.

That makes continuous training and development one of the key things a supervisor, manager, or executive can do to build a strong team-based organization. It's why we often find that top service/quality providers rely on their management staff to deliver education, awareness, and skill training throughout the organization. This generally starts at the top (or the bottom in an inverted organization) and cascades down (or up) with one management level training the next.

To reach this higher order of coaching and development, managers need training in how to train others. The trainers need to be trained. The most successful approach to training trainers is behavior modeling. Getting constructive, detailed feedback following a real practice with real situations after being shown various models or examples builds "take home" skills.

COACHING SKILLS IN ACTION

"You can buy a man's time; you can buy his physical presence at a given place; you can even buy his skilled muscular motions per hour. But you cannot buy enthusiasm . . . you cannot buy loyalty . . . you cannot buy the devotion of hearts, minds, or souls. You must earn these."

Clarence Francis

Following are examples of coaching skills in use:
- Through vastly improved coaching skills, a large urban transit organization reduced grievances by 40 percent and arbitration cases from 17

to zero over two years. As a result of a dramatically improved internal environment, customer service measurements also improved.

• A large university found that its managers were either jumping too hard on employees' performance problems or letting situations drag on until it was too late to resolve them. Both extremes damaged service/quality levels. By improving coaching skills, managers learned how to deal more effectively with their employees' performance problems. Managers' own performance expectations are now linked to the skills they've developed.

• After an oil company's managers developed their coaching skills, they started working out problems with employees earlier. They also offered reinforcement more effectively to employees and to each other.

• At Johnsville Foods, CEO Ralph Stayer used the promotion system to de-emphasize technical experience and "stress the need for coaching skills." He explains:

> Whenever someone became a coordinator, I made sure word got around that the promotion was for demonstrated abilities as a teacher, coach, and facilitator. This new promotion standard sent a new message: to get ahead at Johnsville, you need a talent for cultivating and encouraging problem solvers and responsibility takers.[9]

• When a nurse manager developed her coaching skills, patient satisfaction ratings increased. Also, staff turnover decreased, resulting in a more fully staffed and stable group. "Before I improved these skills, I'd become upset, lose my cool, and jump on people," reflected the manager. "I have now learned how to better convey my points and concerns to the staff."

• A large health center found that improving management's coaching skills reduced absenteeism, which in turn improved patient care by ensuring more consistent availability of qualified staff.

• An international packaging and printing company trains middle and senior managers to deliver their coaching skills development program to first-level supervisors. "We look for high-potential fast-track managers, regarding this as an important developmental tool for them," says the program's coordinator. Results have been better teamwork among supervisors and with their managers. The culture is now shifting from orders, rules, and regulations to participation, reinforcement, and commitment.

• Many top service/quality providers are strengthening their coaching by adding sections to performance reviews such as: "Was this person involved in the service/quality improvement effort? Did he or she foster and promote it? Did he or she set objectives? Were these objectives accomplished?''

COMMON PITFALLS AND TRAPS TO DEVELOPING COACHING SKILLS

Confusing "What" and "How"

Because this trap snares so many organizations, it bears repeating: Don't confuse inspiration and education with skills. Even if your supervisors, managers, and executives want to provide better coaching and know what it looks like, that doesn't mean they can deliver it. Skill building demands a development process that provides how-to steps and relevant models or examples with plenty of practice and feedback.

The Experience Assumption

Too often it's assumed that supervisors and managers already have coaching skills simply because they have managerial experience. Using ineffective approaches many times doesn't lead to higher service/quality. As the legendary Green Bay Packers coach Vince Lombardi once said, "Practice does not make perfect. Only perfect practice makes perfect." Make sure you and your managers are practicing the right things.

Underdevelopment

Many organizations throw a few one-day-wonder workshops at their service/quality performance coaches. The effect is usually about as lasting as the investment made. Sometimes it's better to do nothing than to provide weak development experiences in small doses.

Cutting Out the Coaches

Don't fail to involve your frontline supervisors and managers in planning and delivering your service/quality improvement strategies. Because service/quality coaching is vital to harnessing the vast energy available for improvement, this group's involvement and commitment is critical to your success.

Lack of Alignment

Moving your organization's management from cops to coaches starts with training. However, it has to go much further than that. Your management systems and practices, reward and recognition programs and methods, team improvement activities, as well as your management standards and measurements have to reflect and support management's vital coaching role.

Failing to Coach the Coaches

Research overwhelmingly shows that not following through with on-the-job coaching after skill-development sessions can result in failure rates as high as *87 percent* in applying the new skills to the job. So who's coaching your frontline coaches? If you don't train, hold accountable, and reinforce your executives and managers who provide this crucial support, only a small amount of your development investments will take. Just as your moments of truth are only as strong as the weakest link in your internal customer-supplier chain, the quality of the coaching your employees receive is only as strong as your executive-to-supervisory coaching chain.

Executives Not Leading by Example

This is the single biggest reason coaching skills are not developed throughout an organization and the cause of middle-management mush. Ensure that your executives practice the coaching skills preached by your development program. Supervisors and managers will imitate their leaders. If merely paying lip service to coaching skills got an executive to the top, why would his or her management staff give it much more attention? If executives are too busy to participate in developing their coaching skills, don't waste everyone else's time. Drop the whole skill-development program and prepare to slow or even abandon your service/quality improvement journey.

Chapter Fourteen

Cylinder Seven: Team Skills

"It's easy to get the players. Gettin' em to play together, that's the hardest part."

Casey Stengel

O ur whole implementation architecture (see page 99) is geared toward establishing and sustaining continuous service/quality improvement activities through a wide variety of teams. Baldrige winners, Deming winners, and other highly rated service/quality performers use numerous types of improvement teams. The old, now dysfunctional, traditional organizational model with its command-and-control hierarchies and vertical chimneys is being replaced by the new, fluid, flexible, and much more responsive team-based organization. Kaoru Ishikawa says simply, "Total quality control is a group activity and cannot be done by individuals. It calls for teamwork."[1]

With a team-based organization comes the clear and obvious need for team *skills*. That means helping team members and team leaders move beyond knowing why teams and teamwork are important and what their roles are to doing—adopting the behaviors that will optimize the team's effectiveness. This calls for everyone learning *how to* use data-based tools and techniques to harness the team's service/quality improvement energy and knowledge. It means team members must learn *how to* contribute to the team's improvement activities. And it means team leaders must learn *how to* lead and build teams to maximize teamwork. Theory, education, awareness, inspiration, or just organizing people into groups are all needed, but they aren't enough. Team members and leaders need how-to *skills*.

Many executives and managers plunge into trying to build a team-based organization without ensuring that the skills exist to make the strategy work. That's a prescription for disaster. "Training and team building are vital," says Doug Fernandez, a customer quality manager for the AT&T production facilities of its Network Cable Systems company. "You can't just put 10 people in a room and call them a team; that can do more damage than good. Without training in the dynamics of team building, people will get frustrated and lose interest."[2]

The type and timing of team-skills training is proving to be vital to success. Joseph Juran, who heavily influenced Japan's extensive use of teams, maintains that this type of training "should be aimed at changing behavior."[3] As was outlined in Chapter 11, the best behavior-based training—by a long shot—is behavior modeling. In timing of training, we increasingly find that "just-in-time" training is most effective. That is, team members and leaders are trained for a specific application of their new skills in an immediate improvement activity. Training legions of people in the anticipation that they will eventually use the training means that by the time they do, the skills have begun to atrophy. This is an important training implementation issue that will be covered in more depth in the deployment chapters ahead.

TEAM SKILLS FOR BOTH MEMBERS AND LEADERS

"It ain't the guns or the armament, or the money they can pay, it's the close cooperation that makes them win the day. It ain't the individual, nor the army as a whole, but the everlasting teamwork of every bloomin' soul."

J. Mason Knox, *American humorist*

Following is an overview of the skills areas *everyone* in your organization needs to provide a skill base and common language set on which you can build a team-based organization.

Data-Based Tools and Techniques

The Malcolm Baldrige National Quality Award application says:

Meeting quality improvement goals of the company requires that actions in setting, controlling, and changing systems and processes be based upon reliable information, data, and analysis. . . . Facts, data, and analysis support a variety of company purposes, such as planning, reviewing company performance, improving operations, and comparing company quality performance with competitors.

This "fact-based" management approach is very new language and approach for everyone in the organization. It is at the heart of moving beyond the symptoms and people who are the symptom carriers to fixing the root cause, which is almost always in the larger system or process.

Data-based management starts with collecting relevant data on the service/quality problem or process that is thought to need improvement. This may include internal or external surveys, systematic observations, various performance measures or leading indicators, organized feedback such as focus groups, and so on. The raw data then have to be turned into usable information that can form the basis for improvement actions. This is done through various analytical techniques to examine the data and its implications from various angles.

Data gathering and analysis require training. The most widely used, and well proven, approaches used today are derivations and refinements of Shewhart and Deming's statistical methods. Ishikawa divides these into various groups depending on their levels of difficulty. His elementary statistical methods are often called the "seven tools": (1) Pareto chart, (2) cause-and-effect diagram (also called Ishikawa or Fishbone diagram), (3) stratification, (4) check sheet, (5) histogram, (6) scatter diagram, and (7) control chart.[4] You and all your team members and leaders need to learn these techniques if you are going to drive your processes and service/quality results to new levels of performance.

However, in the 1980s, numerous companies (particularly manufacturers) fell headlong into the trap of going too deeply into these methods, especially statistical process control (SPC). Many organizations scared and turned off their people by overdosing on SPC. Management and quality professionals turned into SPC zealots with their newfound cure-all. They proved Maslow's old adage, "When the only tool you have is a hammer, everything looks like a nail." According to Ishikawa, the same thing happened in Japan as its managers began down the service/quality road in the 50s:

> It is true that statistical methods are effective, but we overemphasized their importance. As a result, people either feared or disliked quality control as something difficult. We overeducated people by giving them sophisticated methods where, at that stage, simple methods would have sufficed.[5]

Every team and team leader in your organization needs to learn how to use statistical tools, starting with senior management. But there are two big caveats. First, make sure your teams can walk with the basics before you try to make them run with more complicated or sophisticated applications. Just using these basic tools and techniques will put them miles ahead of the old "search for the guilty" or "it's my guess against your guess" approaches. Second, be sure your training is skill based, not just conceptual or theoretical. And if you time your behavior training to be given just as the team has a specific project, process, or problem to work on, skills will grow that much faster.

Process Management

Process management is emerging as a powerful new method for improving the flow of information, materials, transactions, and so on that traditionally was tossed up one vertical chimney and down the next. Broad process mapping, organizational modeling, blueprinting, flowcharting, and work process analysis are all skills that teams need in varying degrees depending on whether they are given a wide-angle lens or their mandate is a narrower focus. As you'll see further in the improvement activities cylinder (Chapter 17), data-based tools and techniques, process management, and problem-solving skills are highly interconnected and integral to improving any type of teams' contribution to improving service/quality.

Problem Solving

The main function of improvement teams is to identify and solve problems that inhibit higher service/quality. Yet in many organizations, team members and their leaders get only little or useless training. With little training, teams may plunge boldly in to develop the right solutions to the wrong problems or vice versa. The approach they use is to jump in with both feet, fur flying, hoping to emerge with a solution. Hungarian mathematician George Polya noted, "Success in solving the problem depends on choosing the right aspect, on attacking the fortress from its accessible side."[6] Too many teams attack problems they don't fully understand from whatever angle they happen to be facing. That's often because the team either doesn't have good data or the problem-solving process they are using to analyze it is not effective. Both call for more skill development.

The "trained" team leaders are too often given a process that is long and cumbersome. It may work well with Lone Ranger engineers solving complex technological problems, but it can easily tie a group of frontline problem solvers in knots.

All problem-solving approaches need not be simple. But whatever process is used, it must be clearly understood by everyone involved and geared toward the dynamics of people working in groups. Most approaches are neither.

There are three primary reasons employees need to be heavily involved in problem solving all across your organization. First, they are the experts in the processes within their own work areas or departments, and they have firsthand knowledge of the effectiveness of your bigger cross-functional or organizationwide processes. Their insights and understanding of what does and doesn't work are far greater than those of most managers and outside experts. They can make your processes and procedures much more relevant. Second, employee involvement is the best way to foster commitment to your organization and its goals. Today, employees want much more out of their jobs than just a paycheck. They want to make a real contribution to a meaningful cause (such as service/quality improvement). In *The Plateauing Trap*, Judith Bardwick writes, "Nothing creates more self-respect among employees than being included in the process of making decisions."[7] Third, your employees will implement the solutions decided on. The higher their degree of ownership for those solutions, the better will be their implementation. If they help plan the battle, they won't battle the plan.

Team Member Skills

Data-based tools and techniques, process management, and problem solving make up the machinery that effective teams use to continually improve service/quality. However, without constant lubrication and periodic maintenance, the best machinery in the world will grind to a halt. That's why the people skills are proving so important. Many seasoned travelers on the road to higher service/quality have found that people skills are critical to making the entire improvement process run smoothly.

How to participate in team meetings is an important people skill for team members to develop. For many frontline people, being involved in intact, and especially cross-functional, team meetings is a new and strange experience. If the team is going to get the most from the experience and the practical expertise team members have to offer, they will need help learning *how to* contribute to, and benefit from, meetings. And they can also learn how to help their co-workers do the same.

Being a team player is another important people skill team members need to learn to build a highly effective team. Team members need to develop ever stronger coaching skills so they can help each other more effectively. Team player skills include passing on good ideas, looking for ways to help a team member, giving recognition for things done well, and letting others know when help, resources, or support are needed. Showing team members *how to* be more effective team players is a fundamental step in building an ever more autonomous team. Self-directed work teams don't come into being without strong team player skills.

Resolving issues with others is yet another of the important team skills needed. When team members learn *how to* talk to each other (or customers, suppliers, and management outside their team) directly, there is less need for management to direct and control things. Issues are resolved quicker and tend to be longer lasting if those involved have been shown how to use a fact-based, problem-solving approach. When nagging issues between team members are avoided or ignored, smoothed over, or confronted in a "win-lose" power struggle, the team is either wrenched apart or teamwork is slowly choked off. The powerful improvement machinery begins to seize up for lack of people skills lubrication.

THE NEED FOR TEAM LEADERSHIP SKILLS

"Coming together is a beginning; keeping together is progress; working together is success."
Henry Ford, *industrialist and automotive manufacturer*

One of the major ingredients in strong teams is the *strength of the leaders*. In the 60s, Norman Maier of the University of Michigan conducted ground-breaking research on the factors contributing to group performance. After dozens of experiments with ineffective and effective groups, with strong and weak teams, and with creative and less creative groups, he concluded *the primary determinant of the team's success was the skill of the person leading it.* Following is an example of one of his findings on the impact of trained team leaders:[8]

Amount of Training	% Creative Solutions	% Satisfied with Solution
Little or none	3.4	62.1
Moderate	63.6	72.7
Great deal	85.3	100.0

As employee involvement and empowerment have become more popular in recent years, some managers have decided they had better play the game to get in on "the team stuff" and all its benefits. That's been their undoing—playing the employee involvement game. These manipulative managers see employee involvement as one more lever to be pulled, another string to be yanked. They put on an involvement act, unsupported by personal development of team skills or habits. They might, for example, bring people together to "decide" on action they have already set. The transparency of this kind of involvement soon becomes evident to all. As the manager pretends involvement, his or her group members pretend commitment.

We continually find that *the extent to which supervisors and managers embrace the movement toward an involved, team-based organization is heavily influenced by the strength of their team skills*. When supervisors and managers can confidently use team leadership skills to rally people around a problem or process improvement opportunity, they do so much more often. Strong team leaders have experienced what Koichi Tsukamoto, president of Wascoal Corporation in Japan, means with his comment, "One step by 100 persons is better than 100 steps by one person."[9]

But when their team skills are weak, managers resist the team-based approaches. Meetings, which are frequent and well used in a highly effective team-based organization, are avoided. As one frustrated manager put it coming out of yet another marathon meeting, "Perhaps hell is nothing more than an enormous conference of those who, with little or nothing to say, take an eternity to say it."

In the traditional (generally struggling) organization, "heroic management" reigns supreme as employees stand by and watch the weak team leader fight the fires alone. (Ironically, many weak team leaders believe frequent meetings are a sign of weak management!) Solutions to problems are initiated by management, as are the rescue efforts, because employees, on whom implementation depends for success, never owned them in the first place.

The general manager of a midsized computer company we worked with was extremely frustrated because his many attempts to bring his senior management group and their management groups together into a solid team had failed. He recounted all that he had done: wilderness retreats, team-building exercises, restructuring the organization around intact, process improvement and project teams. "We even wrote a manual on the need for teamwork and how to make it happen," he lamented. But teamwork wasn't happening. Further investigation revealed the reason: the general manager and his managers knew the whys and wherefores of team leadership—they could almost wax poetic on the virtues of group dynamics—but they didn't have the *skills* to put their good intentions into action. And since they didn't see the need to go through the time-consuming process of developing those skills, they didn't. And the teams didn't come together any better over the next year—about the time the general manager was fired.

The coaching skills covered in Chapter 13 and team leadership skills are inextricably linked. You can't have one without the other. In *Managing for Excellence*, David Bradford and Allan Cohen explain one way the two skill areas merge: "At the same time that the manager works to develop management responsibility in (frontline contributors), he or she must develop the (frontline contributor's) ability to share management of the unit's performance." That happens most effectively by pulling individuals together into a cohesive team. But, they warn, "neither willingness to accept responsibility nor ability to do so are automatic and instant."[10] In other words, everyone can benefit from skill development. Because skill development lays such a firm foundation for the entire service/quality improvement effort, these three cylinders are often the journey's starting point.

EFFECTIVE TEAM LEADERSHIP REDEFINES MANAGEMENT ROLES

"You do not lead by hitting people over the head. That's assault, not leadership."
Dwight D. Eisenhower, *U.S. president*

As we saw in the coaching cylinder, building a highly skilled, team-based organization will happen only if supervisors, managers, and executives transform their traditional command-and-control role. It is so obvious, but managers seem to need constant reminding: *You can't manage (command, demand, structure, order, control) your way to teamwork. You can only lead a group of people to pull together as a team.*

Pulling a team together requires a leader who takes a less directing, more facilitative approach. The team leader must move out of the spotlight and empower and assist the group to take over. The words of Chinese philosopher Lao-tzu express the kind of leadership that makes top-performing teams effective: "When the best leader's work is done, the people say, 'We did this ourselves.' "

The idea of turning over power and credit to the team is threatening to many traditional managers. In *Peak Performers*, psychologist and performance researcher Charles Garfield writes:

The five most misunderstood letters in the center of that word—power—call for a clear understanding of what "empowerment" means. It does not mean giving away your strength to someone else like Samson to the

Philistines. On the contrary, peak performers discover time and again that releasing the power in others, whether in co-workers or customers, benefits them in the long run. In developing, rewarding, and recognizing those around them, they are simply allowing the human assets with which they work to appreciate in value. The more they empower, the more they can achieve, and the more successful the whole enterprise becomes.[11]

Team leadership resting with one individual diminishes as the team becomes more autonomous. In that case, the management staff left in the flattening hierarchy evolves into developers, coaches, and supporters to the teams. This frees management to be much more strategic and proactive. They can look at broad organizationwide issues and processes and watch the horizon for gathering storm clouds while searching for dead-end roads and swamps. However, during the very long transition to self-directed work teams, or in any other type of team-based organization, *strong, highly skilled team leaders are essential to successful service/quality improvement*. Little will change without them.

AN OVERVIEW OF TEAM LEADERSHIP SKILLS

Facilitating Successful Meetings

"The wise leader does not intervene unnecessarily. The leader's presence is felt, but often the group runs itself."

John Heider, *The Tao of Leadership*

The only explanation is ignorance. Managers just don't know any better or they would make sweeping changes. In a lot of ways, it's like bad cost of quality: when you don't know how much waste there really is, you blissfully carry on wasting.

Too many managers are blissfully ignorant of the unbelievable waste of time and energy that passes for meetings in their organizations. If managers were allowed to waste their capital assets the way they waste human ones, heads would roll. Andy Grove, president of the fast-growing high-tech firm Intel Corp., puts it into perspective:

It's estimated that the dollar cost of a manager's time, including overhead allotted to it, is around $100 per hour (1982 dollars). A meeting attended by 10 managers for two hours thus costs the company $2,000. . . . Yet a manager can call a meeting and commit $2,000 worth of managerial resources on a whim. If that meeting is unnecessary or so poorly run it achieves nothing, that's $2,000 wasted.[12]

Too many of those meetings are poorly run. A survey conducted by the New York recruiting firm Robert Half International found that executives considered nearly a third of meetings a waste of time.[13] When you look at how much time you spend in meetings, that is a lot of wasted time! A number of studies put the amount of time managers spend in meetings as high as 40 percent. In a team-based organization, managers' meeting time increases as well as the time of all team members. Once meetings were considered an interruption of our work. In team-based organizations, meetings (formal sessions with agendas, impromptu gatherings with agendas generated on the spot, one-on-one get-togethers, ''coffee conferences,'' and so on) are becoming the job itself. Meetings are as essential to team effectiveness as good data and problem solving are to process improvement. If a third of those meetings are ineffective, the waste of salaries, benefits, and other staff overhead is massive. Call it the cost of poor skills.

Far too many meetings of, say, six people are not meetings of six people. Rather, they are meetings of three people with three spectators. Why are they all there? If they all had something to contribute, the leader was responsible for drawing it from them but failed to do so. If not, why waste their time?

To practice effective meeting leadership is to be truly a facilitator. Once most managers master these skills, their view of what constitutes strong team leadership is altered forever.

A team leader who is also the participants' manager must perform a delicate balancing act between facilitating the group discussion and unwittingly issuing management directives. George Odiorne of the University of Massachusetts explains the dilemma: ''There's a law of administration which I'd suggest holds true in almost every situation. That is, if the boss presents his solution first and asks for opinions about it, a vote of approval will follow almost every time.''[14]

A key to getting everyone to contribute fully is to manage diversity. Harvard's John Kotter explains:

> People who have studied decision-making processes have often observed that diversity and interdependence are essential ingredients in fostering original ideas. If there is only one person involved in a decision-making situation (no interdependence), or if the group of individuals involved all think pretty much the same way (no diversity), the breadth of information brought to bear on a problem is almost always narrow in scope. When a number of people are involved, and when they have different perspectives, more information gets into the process often because more conflict develops. The conflict forces people to stop and think and look for ways to resolve it.[15]

If it's not well managed, conflict can quickly wrench a team apart. Whether conflict helps or hinders the team's effort to improve service/quality depends, to a large extent, on the team skills of the leader. Editor and publisher Dagobert Runes puts his finger on one of the keys to managing team diversity and conflict: "Handle people with gloves, but issues, bare-fisted."[16]

Getting a group of diverse people with conflicting interests and varied backgrounds to pull together is a big part of what team leadership skills are all about. Any manager can get a group of people to consent, especially if they report to him or her. But it takes a skilled *leader* to get a group to truly be *committed*. Winston Churchill put it this way: "Parliament can compel people to obey or to submit, but it cannot compel them to agree." Strong team leaders get teams to agree to work together to put the *group's* plans into action.

If the improvement journey is to succeed, the team leader must get everyone committed to *focusing the team on quality*. Team members need to know "What does quality mean to me?" and "How does it affect my job?" Everyone must be convinced improvement is worth the effort, especially if this direction is new or your organization has a history of changing directions or making bold but empty declarations.

Many team leaders leave their groups hanging at the end of a meeting. Consensus, commitment, and even action are left in a state of suspended animation. Team members wander out unclear what's to happen next. As each goes off to do his or her own thing, subsequent meetings and fire-fighting actions are needed. Chris Argyis of the Harvard Graduate School of Education describes this all-too-familiar situation and one of the main reasons for it:

> Because the executives (trying to avoid interpersonal problems) don't say what they really mean or test the assumptions they really hold, their skills inhibit a resolution of the important intellectual issues. . . . Thus the meetings end with only lists and no decisions. . . . People's tendency to avoid conflict, to duck tough issues, becomes institutionalized and leads to a culture that can't tolerate straight talk.[17]

Sounding familiar?

Meetings Are a Microcosm of Your Culture

The Spanish novelist and dramatist Cervantes wrote, "By a small sample we may judge of the whole piece." Meetings are but a small slice of the supervisor, manager, or executive's miniculture. Taken together, an organization's meetings paint a picture of the whole culture.

Look at your meetings. What do they say about your team skills and culture? Who attends them? How do you split the airtime within the group? How much diversity is encouraged? How is conflict handled? What process do you use for problem solving? Do you draw contributions from the whole group? *How do you know?*

Other Team Leadership Skills

Facilitating successful meetings is fundamental to team leadership skills because mastering how to prepare and focus a team, encouraging diversity, handling disruptive behavior and conflict, keeping the session on track and moving, and setting action plans and following up are basic leadership skills widely applicable outside the meeting room.

Successful team leaders have strong coaching skills, especially if teams are to become more self-directed and less dependent on the leader for their effectiveness. Also, they know how to clarify roles and responsibilities of everyone on the team. This is especially important in the team's formative stages. Otherwise, time and energy are lost, while the odds that the team will not be successful sharply increase. Conflict and issue resolution are other important team leadership skills.

If you are determined to take your organization to partially or totally self-directed work teams, then your team leaders need to have skill levels at the column C level (see page 88). They need to become trainers and developers of all the team skills found in this cylinder. Your supervisors, managers, and executives *need to be at the center* of training everyone in data-based tools and techniques, process management, problem solving, and the people skills of effective teams. Outsiders and internal staff professionals can help line management, but line management should do the bulk of the training. Usually, outside training experts and internal staff professionals train management and support their training delivery work. *In a team-based organization, training and developing teams and individuals is management's central responsibility.*

TEAM SKILLS IN ACTION

"Two people working as a team will produce more than three people working as individuals."
                                                                    Charles McCormick

- Team skills helped Dow Chemical manage its quality improvement effort more effectively. "Meetings start and finish on time. Everyone participates. Diversity is encouraged but managed in a constructive fashion so it's not disruptive. Specific assignments with clear completion dates are made and accepted.''

• A major manufacturer implemented team-leadership-skill training from the CEO down to supervisors. The results were improved meeting effectiveness, better teamwork, and improved levels of internal service. Comments the corporate controller: ''Our management style is now much more organized with more participation from our engineers.''

• CEO Will Barrett and his key executives at Avco Financial Services were trained as instructors in the Canadian company's service/quality team-skills-development program. As part of a multiyear effort that dramatically improved service/quality—and profit levels—every employee became part of a quality team led by a trained leader. Barrett reflects on the successful process: ''We took a group of managers who had been 'bosses' their entire career and turned them into facilitators. They discovered, through the use of these new skills, what a tremendous wealth of talent we have.''

• After developing their team skills, members of the systems group of a major bank changed their approach to serve their internal customers better. For years, they would spend a week at a time in a branch reviewing operations and then making recommendations to branch management for improvement. By learning how to organize and lead groups, systems professionals began helping branch staff identify and improve their own operations. Not only did better problem solving result, but also commitment to—and implementation of—solutions improved dramatically.

• GM's Oshawa Plastics Plant found that support staff and professionals significantly increased their contributions to improving quality when they developed better team skills. Equipment, tool, and process engineers; office staff; and hourly electrical technicians were shown how to organize and lead groups and to use a step-by-step group problem-solving process.

• In *Deming Management at Work,* Mary Walton reports on a lesson in team ownership and training learned at the U.S. Navy's Naval Aviation Depot at Cherry Point, North Carolina. A number of overzealous facilitators headed to the floor to form improvement teams and lead them in the use of data-based tools and techniques. Improvement results were fast and impressive. But once the facilitators pulled out, 70 percent of the teams stopped using the new approaches. Those teams that kept going were ones that ''pushed the facilitator aside and said, 'It's our statistical process control. Lesson learned? You don't do it for me.' ''[18]

• Wesley-Jessen attributes the rapid and substantial results of its improvement process to extensive training of all management levels and improvement team members. This included over 75 hours in data-based tools and techniques, process management, coaching and personal skills, and the other people-oriented team skills.

COMMON PITFALLS AND TRAPS TO DEVELOPING TEAM SKILLS

What the Top Orders the Middle to Do for the Bottom

One of the key factors determining the skills of all management staff is the team leadership skills of senior management. Accustomed to using their technical or management system skills, most senior managers' team skills are rusty. Numerous organizations have proved that developing the skills of executives in this vital area has a profound and lasting impact on how quickly and effectively the rest of the organization follows.

Confusing Structure and Skills

Don't assume that bringing groups of people together creates teams. Far too many groups are loose collections of individuals, not teams. Extensive and continuous team *skill* development is needed. Form follows function. Teach people *how to* make teams work, and your organization's shift to a team-based operation will be much quicker and smoother.

Dangerous Assumptions and Shaky Foundations

Far too many teams are built on shaky skills. Weak skills are a major cause of the failure of many corrective action teams, employee involvement groups, service/quality task forces, and quality circles.

Reverting under Pressure

The truest test of teamwork, involvement, and empowerment is when the crunch is on. If you and your management team revert to command-and-control management, your credibility may be shot. That doesn't mean you have to give up your responsibility to make the tough decisions that may go against popular opinion. People want you to show that leadership strength—when it's called for. But how you go about it makes all the difference in the world. As much as possible, gather broad input and give people a chance to have their say. Once you've made your decision, reiterate the reasons for it and solicit the support of others.

A Weak Top Management Team

Get your own house in order first. It's amazing how many executives run around spouting off about the need for teamwork when their own executive team doesn't pull together. In "Twelve Actions to Build Strong U.S. Factories," Ernesto Poza says, "Top management that works effectively as a team sends strong signals down the organization that there is a commitment to the team concept and a flatter structure."[19] Don't be hypocritical. Your people aren't blind.

Chapter Fifteen

Cylinder Eight: Systems

"So much of what we call management consists of making it difficult for people to work."

Peter Drucker

This cylinder covers enormous territory. It plays a *major* role in determining whether your service/quality improvement efforts will develop real momentum or slowly sputter out.

The basic issue is simple. For whose convenience is your organization designed? If you're like 90 percent of organizations, your employees and customers would shout in unison: "You're designed for the convenience of you and your management team." In other words, you're both hard to do business with and hard to work for.

Cylinders 8 to 12 are all part of the column we call "alignment." The theme you will hear again and again is whether your systems, rewards and recognition, improvement activities, standards and measures, and marketing strategies are aligned to serve your customers and support your people who are serving the customers or producing your products or services.

ALIGNING SYSTEMS AROUND YOUR CUSTOMERS

"Early decline and certain death are the fate of companies whose policies are geared totally and obsessively to their own convenience at the total expense of the customer."

Ted Levitt

Most North American organizational systems are holdovers from the days of plentiful customers and resources. We could dictate the terms on which customers would have the privilege of doing business with us or employees would have the honor of working for us! Systems were designed to maximize internal efficiency. We didn't have to look at things from the customer's point of view because we assumed either they would always be there or we could turn up the heat on our sales and marketing people to bring us more customers that could be jammed into our way of doing business. *Times have changed, but our approach to systems design hasn't.* Karl Albrecht writes:

> Customer handling systems, customer record keeping systems, data processing systems, accounting systems, and reporting systems usually grow from the desires of various departments to make their own work easier. Seldom do they look at the designs of these systems with a view toward maximizing customer convenience or customer satisfaction.[1]

The overarching purpose of far too many systems, just as with many organizations, has become lost. This results in inside-out systems that add excess staff support professionals, management layers, complexity, and miles of red tape. It all adds up to higher costs, lower service/ quality, and frustrated customers and employees. For years, we have defined a dysfunctional bureaucracy as "a group of people for whom the original purpose of being together has been forgotten." R. E. Heckert, chairman of Du Pont, states, "We're not in business to amuse ourselves. We're here to serve our customers."[2] To which the American Society for Quality Control adds this warning: "Never allow your systems to serve themselves rather than being focused on service to the customer. If you do, you will be left with only the illusion of satisfied customers."[3]

Systems run in, through, around, and under the service/quality chain. Even if you hire the most capable and motivated people, train them and their managers well, and provide plenty of rewards, your organizational systems could severely cripple their best efforts. You may be sending them out there handcuffed and shackled. As the well-proven 85/15 rule tells us, *put a good performer up against a poor service/quality support system and the system will win 8.5 out of 10 times.* In many organizations, the service/quality being provided is *in spite of*, not because of, its systems.

Understanding all the factors affecting the strength of the service/ quality chain requires a broad view of the cross-functional, horizontal flow of information, materials, interactions, and work activities. Kaoru Ishikawa explains the expanded view of total quality control that has occurred in Japan over the past few decades: "Initially total participation extended only to the company president, directors, middle management, staff, foremen, line workers, and salesmen. But in recent years, the definition has been expanded to include subcontractors, distribution systems, and affiliated companies."[4]

SYSTEMS AND PROCESSES ARE INTERTWINED

"The art of progress is to preserve order amid change and to preserve change amid order."
Alfred North Whitehead, *British philosopher and mathematician*

In Chapter 5, we began to explore how many service/quality breakdowns and ricochets come from the fact our traditional organizations are structured by functional group—vertical chimneys—while work processes flow horizontally across the service/quality chain. In the new team-based, customer-focused organization, cross-functional process management is at the center of smashing the vertical chimneys and flattening the organization to improve service/quality and reduce costs. A study of the total quality management field by the Center for Advanced Management Studies, Graduate School of Business at Fordham University, led the center's director, Marta Mooney, to conclude Japan's economic success is explained by "that nation's use of the new management paradigm that concentrates on managing processes."[5]

Process management is central to our improvement activities cylinder (Chapter 17). Because improvement activities are central to the whole service/quality improvement journey, process management plays a very key role. In practice, systems and processes are inseparable. They are like air and water—both are equally critical to sustaining life. However, to better understand and improve these two vital organizational elements, we have separated them. As you will see in this and the improvement activities cylinder, deciding whether systems or process improvement comes first is a chicken-and-egg dilemma. Both need to improve together. Systems support, limit, or define processes. At the same time, process improvement activities show which systems need to be realigned to make the process more effective. The two are mutually dependent on each other.

AN OVERVIEW OF KEY SYSTEMS

"Businesses exert the tightest controls over the easiest things to control, rather than the most critical."

Kenneth Collins, *CBS Publications*

The hundreds of subsystems found throughout your organization either mirror or are subcomponents of a much smaller core of key systems.

These key systems need to be re-examined and analyzed to see whether they are helping or hindering continuous service/quality improvement. The data and perceptions to be gathered for each major system need to be focused on *the central question: "Is this system aligned to maximize customer service and continually improve quality?"* That means examining systems from the outside in and the front line down throughout your organization. And just as service/quality is a destination you never reach, system improvement is an unending task.

The following overview of key systems contributing to, or inhibiting, service/quality improvement is an introduction to the profound and far-reaching issues your organization will continually be wrestling with in the coming years. These systems are all major fields of study in themselves. Volumes of new books, numerous conferences, and hundreds of studies are rapidly emerging in many of these areas. Here's the million dollar continuous learning question: *What is your organization doing to ensure you're keeping up with all the changes sweeping across these systems?*

Human Resource Systems

"Many ineffective systems are the scar tissue of past mistakes."

Many human resource systems are designed both to serve management and to meet management's paranoid command-and-control needs. *Traditional organizations must be drastically changed if their human resource systems and practices are to be realigned around a team-based, customer-focused organization.* An upside-down organization means the human resource system must be focused on serving the front line. As Bill Marriott Jr. says, "At every opportunity I tell managers in the Marriott Corporation, 'Take care of the employees and they'll take care of the customers.' "[6]

Reward and recognition, hiring and orienting, education and awareness, and training are all important human resource systems that have their own cylinders. Two other key systems that need to be realigned around your organization's service/quality effort are (1) promotions and job assignments and (2) performance management.

Promotions and job assignments. As mentioned in Chapter 10, who gets promoted, or the plum assignments, and for what, speaks volumes about your organization's values. It also reflects whether your organization is aligned around meeting customers', employees', or management's needs. If, for example, coaching and team skills are considered important to your organization, then you will promote only those people who exemplify these skills. One of the turning points in Xerox's

"Leadership through Quality" process was when the skills and behavior changes it was trying to build became the criteria for promotion. Then everyone began to take the process seriously. *Are your promotion criteria aligned around the new service/quality organization you're trying to build?*

Performance management.   Because of the pervasive and dysfunctional assumption that "our work force creates most of our service/quality problems," traditional organizations use performance appraisal, merit rating, and individual management-by-objectives systems that *seriously damage teamwork, reinforce functional chimneys, and undermine service/quality performance.* "It's a natural outcome of our North American culture of 'rugged individualism,' " explains Dennis Beecroft, director of the Institute for Improvement in Quality and Productivity at the University of Waterloo (Ontario). "From the time one begins school, if not earlier, we are encouraged to perform as individuals, with individual rankings and grades. Working together in groups or teams is normally considered 'cheating' and carries most severe penalties."[7]

The negative effects of individually focused performance management systems are becoming glaringly apparent in building a team-based organization striving for higher service/quality levels. Following are some common problems with performance management systems:

• Management's role in hiring the wrong person and not providing effective orientations, training, rules, service/quality signals and personal examples, support, tools, technology, rewards, recognition and encouragement, coaching, team leadership, customer-focused measurement and feedback, faulty materials or information, improvement infrastructure—to name just a few factors—is not addressed. Rather, *the individual is held accountable for outcomes heavily dependent on factors outside his or her personal control.*

• Performance reviews are subject to what Cypress Semiconductor CEO T. J. Rodgers calls "the proximity effect." An individual's performance of, say, the past two months colors the overall appraisal given for the entire 12 months.[8]

• "Lone Ranger" behavior that often means maximizing individual performance at the expense of others in the organization is encouraged and rewarded.

• The traditional hierarchy and top-down management are reinforced with "subordinates" serving their bosses rather than their customers. This causes people to "play politics," "kiss up" to the boss, and become a "yes man" or "yes woman."

• The rating process is rarely motivational. Because most people believe they are above-average performers, high ratings are not surprising or motivating. Average or low ratings cause people to become either discouraged or upset with their boss, especially if compensation is tied into the rating system. That's why managers in every pay-for-performance or performance appraisal system eventually skew the scores to the high end of the rating scales.

- Deming, who fingers traditional performance management systems as one of the biggest enemies of service/quality improvement, thunders:

> It leaves people bitter, crushed, bruised, battered, desolate, despondent, dejected, feeling inferior, some even depressed, unfit for work for weeks after receipt of rating. . . . It is unfair, as it ascribes to the people in a group differences that may be caused totally by the system that they work in.[9]

- Given the negative impact of traditional performance management systems, the cost of administering them is a huge and useless overhead—another cost of poor quality.

What's the alternative? In the short term, scrap your traditional top-down management scoring system. It's doing you more harm than good. Over the longer term, you need to establish a performance appraisal process that begins with the external customer and works its way back through the service/quality chain. Everyone is measured, and often rewarded and recognized, on the basis of the service/quality level he or she provides to the next immediate internal or external customers. Coupled with that you need control and feedback systems based on strong individual coaching and, if you're headed toward more autonomous work teams, peer or team reviews. All of this needs to be supported by good execution of the other cylinders such as signaling, listening, continuous education and awareness, hiring and orienting, training, and so on. These factors have the biggest influence on individual performance.

Supplier Management

"Business is a lot like rowing upstream—when you stop trying to advance, you automatically drop back."

Reflecting on the early days of total quality control, Kaoru Ishikawa said, "One of the main factors that has supported the quality of Japanese products is the high level of quality control maintained by the suppliers. They have worked together with the purchasers to make quality possible." Supplier partnerships were pivotal to quality improvement concludes Ishikawa: "The genesis of Japanese products' high quality, reliability, and price advantage was in this turn of events."[10]

In 1950, when Deming was teaching the Japanese how to improve product quality, he used a flow diagram to show how the production process began with suppliers. They learned, says Deming, "the best solution to improvement of incoming materials is to make a partner of every vendor, and to work together with him on a long-term relationship of loyalty and trust." Deming explains the approach with this question: "How can a supplier be innovative and develop economy in his production processes when he can only look forward to short-term business with a purchaser?"[11]

As the service/quality revolution began to sweep across North America during the 80s, many organizations using materials, key technology, and even information from outside suppliers began to work in partnership with them to improve quality and reduce *overall* cost. Brian McDermott, editor of *Total Quality* newsletter, explains how the new quality economics is refocusing the way top service/quality organizations look at supplier costs: "The goal is still to get the best product from suppliers, but price isn't calculated on a single line. . . . Cost is spread over the entire process of conceptualizing, developing, and delivering a product or service."[12] To do that, Deming says, "The purchasing department must change its focus from lowest initial cost of material purchased to lowest total cost."[13]

As with so much else in service/quality improvement, the pay-offs of supplier partnering come from taking your eyes off the narrow interaction or price itself and looking at the bigger picture of total cost. Here are some examples of the savings of this new approach:

• Wallace Co., Inc., reduced its supplier base from over 2,000 to 325 in two years. This reduced administrative costs, and by helping to train suppliers in total quality management, Wallace saw an 8 percent improvement in on-time delivery and shipping accuracy.[14]

• Xerox Canada decreased the number of defective parts reaching its production line by 73 percent through working with its supplier on service/quality improvement.[15] Worldwide, Xerox's supplier defect rate has gone from 8 percent to 0.3 percent. "We estimated," says Robert Fletcher, manager of material quality assurance, "that paying people to inspect all those incoming parts to catch the bad ones and redoing all that work was costing us somewhere in the neighborhood of $75 to $100 million a year."[16]

• An investment of $2,500 in training supplier's employees in statistical quality control and requiring control charts with every shipment saved Globe Metallurgical over $250,000 a year.[17]

• Baxter Healthcare Corp. once received over 1,000 purchase orders a month from Monsanto to which it then sent 1,000 invoices. Today, it summarizes all these transactions on one invoice a week by computer.[18]

To realize the significant benefits of supplier partnerships, many leading service/quality performers are encouraging and rewarding those suppliers that adopt continuous improvement processes in their operations. For example, Motorola, Hewlett Packard, Celanese Chemical, Xerox, the U.S. Department of Defense, Ford, 3M, and a rapidly growing list of such organizations are narrowing their suppliers to those implementing quality improvement processes. An increasing number of companies, such as Motorola, are dealing only with suppliers that have set a date for applying for the Malcolm Baldrige National Quality Award.

Accounting Systems

"The more time you spend in reporting on what you are doing, the less time you have to do anything. Stability is achieved when you spend all your time doing nothing but reporting on the nothing you are doing."

Cohn's Law, *The Official Rules*[19]

Ninety percent of companies have an invoicing system that is not user-friendly. In fact, it may as well be written in a foreign language as far as most customers are concerned. But it's convenient for the accounting department. Invoicing is one of many accounting systems where alignment around customer or frontline needs is the last thing on the minds of the system designers. Their main concern has been how to make the system serve management or accounting's needs. Another example is budgeting and financial planning. Too often profit, not service/quality, becomes the overriding goal. This is built on the dysfunctional profit assumption we discussed in Chapter 4. Paradoxically, top service/quality providers have aggressive profit targets and are very profitable. But executives have learned that *profits are a result* of highly satisfied customers served by organizations with decreasing costs through continuous quality improvement.

Our accounting systems are about to go through the biggest revolution they have seen in almost a century. Richard Schonberger's study of leading management practices around the world leads him to conclude:

Much of the old house of cost management has already caved in. More will go, and a new spartan structure is rising. Judging by my large file of 1987-dated references, this is the year when leading companies and the accounting community defined the new structure. Those references include a book with a telling title: *Relevance Lost: The Rise and Fall of Management Accounting*.[20]

Much of the irrelevance of our current cost accounting methods stems from their basis in tracking direct labor cost. Where that was once over 50 percent in manufacturing, today it is less than 15 percent. What's lost is the huge and hidden bad cost of quality. These costs are generally buried in general and administrative overheads.

Schonberger reports that a number of companies such as Texas Instruments are replacing their backward-looking and elaborate financial control systems with data-based service/quality tools and techniques. And "in the spirit of cutting valueless transactions," he says, they are closing their books quarterly instead of monthly. Schonberger sees the potential for financial reporting to become a yearly event, and he goes even further. "Why," he asks, "should (accounting) house accounts payable and accounts receivable? The two work side by side, but they have nothing in common. . . . Move payables to purchasing and receivables to sales. That puts each accounting subgroup right next to its customer—next process in the chain."[21]

Technology

"Right from the start, we wrote programs for the convenience of the customer, instead of the machine. WordStar was in there before us, and I think they could have had the whole market, if they'd paid more attention to customers."

Alan Ashton, *cofounder and CEO, WordPerfect Corp.*[22]

In our high-tech age, many companies turn to automation and the latest technology to try to develop a productivity, service, or quality edge. These technical systems range from production, design, and delivery, to telecommunications, information management, and numerous office automation systems. While some of this technology has been useful, for many North American organizations, these highly touted technical systems have been a disaster—service/quality and productivity levels fell while costs soared.

Office automation and various management technologies have proved particularly disappointing. Productivity in many offices has not improved in decades. Information technology consultant Michael Hammer puts his finger on the main reason for this poor performance:

Heavy investments in information technology have delivered disappointing results—largely because companies tend to use technology to mechanize old ways of doing business. They leave existing processes intact and use computers simply to speed them up. . . . It is time to stop paving the cow paths. Instead of embedding outdated processes in silicon and software, we should obliterate them and start over.

Hammer calls this "re-engineering" and tells us "don't automate, obliterate."[23]

Look at your use of technology. *Who's serving whom?* Are you using new technology to automate old meandering processes? How internal and external customer-friendly are your technology-based systems? In *Delivering Quality Service*, Valarie Zeithaml, A. Parasuraman, and Len Berry write:

> Taking a customer-oriented approach to technology means identifying the customers for each technological initiative, learning their service expectations and perceptions, and eliciting their feedback to new technology concepts and prototypes. A new technology should be viewed as a new product; and like any new product, technology should be market-based.[24]

The American Society for Quality Control says, "Automation can help improve quality—or it can be the source of errors, delay, and frustration. Your success will be in direct proportion to your emphasis on quality."[25]

Telephone systems are too often one of the most visible and neglected pieces of technology. If management's needs are met, upgrading the system or training people to better use the current system are often low priorities. Are you paying a high price for the frustration and chaos caused by telephone problems in your organization? *How do you know?*

Just as with all your other systems, technology must be aligned with customer needs and supportive of the service/quality chain of processes that produce and support your products or services that fill those needs. The cart comes after the horse.

Structure

"The pyramids are solidly built, have a nice view from the top, and serve as a resting place for the dead."

Gerald Michaelson

Do your customers need a copy of your organization chart to deal with you? Are they bounced from one department to another? Are you structured around your products and services, around your management system, or around your customers and key processes? Do your customers think you're easy to do business with? What would your employees say? How do you *know?*

If your organization has been traditionally structured along functional and hierarchical lines, you will be reorganizing and restructuring your operations at some point in your service/quality improvement effort. In

Chapter 17, we will look further at the shape of things to come in moving toward high service/quality—the team-based organization introduced in Chapter 5.

Customer Systems

"Those who enter to buy, support me. Those who come to flatter, please me. Those who complain, teach me how I may please others so that more will come."

Marshall Field

Closely related to how your organization is structured is the way you deal with customers. How easy is it for your customers to complain to you (rather than just to other potential customers)? What is your recovery system for dissatisfied customers? Is the first person your customers contact able to help them or quickly put them in touch with the right person or team? Or does your customer system pass your customers around like a hot potato? Many organizations don't even have a customer system because they have never looked at their customer processes from the outside in. They were too busy organizing themselves for their own convenience from the inside out.

Distribution Systems

"Of all the decisions an executive makes, none are as important as the decisions about people because they determine the performance capacity of the organization."

Peter Drucker

Many manufacturers, processors (such as food or chemical), and service companies (such as airlines and insurance firms) use dealers, agents, or distributors to sell and service their products and deal with end-user customers. Franchising is one such system that has been experiencing explosive growth in the 80s and 90s. If this characterizes your organization, you need to pay *very* close attention to the service/quality levels offered by your dealers, distributors, agents, or franchisees. Numerous studies by the Strategic Planning Institute and others show that product quality and service are inseparable in the perceptions of over 70 percent of customers. Your product may be world-class quality, but if it's poorly represented or serviced, end-use customers will consider your product inferior.

Lele and Sheth report that the top car, farm equipment, and appliance manufacturers they studied "chose their intermediaries with great care." Typical is a Maytag executive: "We look for a quality retailer just as we do in looking for quality people to work for our company. We want a dealer who runs a good business, who's well-organized, who has competent salespeople and who is financially capable of operating a successful business."[26] You can attract the cream of the crop to represent you only when your organization has a reputation for high service/quality and helping the dealer, distributor, or franchisee to be successful.

One of the key issues with a distribution system is ensuring consistency and ever higher levels of service/quality. That's why some companies, such as Kentucky Fried Chicken, are buying back their franchises and running the restaurants themselves. A growing number of other manufacturers, processors, airlines, hotels, insurance firms, franchisers, and the like are significantly boosting the service/quality training and other support provided to those selling their products and services. Just as with frontline teams, the service/quality provided by those representing you will be highly dependent on the service/quality they get from your organization. They can't make the entire service/quality chain any stronger than the links you provide. How's your service to your distributors? How do you *know?*

Information Systems

"The boss was injured in an avalanche—his in-basket collapsed on him."

Are your information systems aligned for management control or service/quality? In a customer-focused, team-based organization, information systems serve and support those who are actually producing, servicing, or supporting the organization's basic product. That's the upside-down organization in action. Are your information systems serving or driving your frontline teams? How do you *know?*

In a traditional command-and-control organization, fear, politics, and "cover your backside" create far too many reports and memos. Get out of your office and talk to people. If the paper being shoveled around your organization isn't helping to improve service/quality, get rid of it. Who's asking for all this stuff, anyway? It's probably *not* your customers or frontline people.

Control Systems

"Bureaucracy defends the status quo long past the time when the quo has lost its status."
Laurence J. Peter

The way rules, procedures, policies, and regulations are used to control and focus behavior in an organization reveals management's true values concerning customers and its people. Take a long hard look at this area for two critical points: (1) Are your rules wrapping your frontline people in red tape and inhibiting their performance? and (2) What messages are your policies sending about how much you trust your employees and how smart you think they are? How does that affect their "voluntarism"? Who is *perceived* to be serving whom? How do you *know*?

REALIGNING YOUR SYSTEMS

"The way to achieve success is first to have a definite, clear, practical ideal—a goal, an objective. Second, have the necessary means to achieve your ends—wisdom, money, materials, and methods. Third, adjust all your means to that end."

Aristotle, *Greek philosopher*

The job is massive and never-ending. The changes are so deep and far-reaching that many organizations have trouble knowing where to start.

You begin systems alignment at the beginning—with your vision. Go back to the implementation architecture diagram on page 99. The three strategic questions forming the vision are (1) What business are we in (our strategic niche)? (2) What do we believe in (the values that will guide everyone's behavior)? (3) Where are we going (the vision of our *preferred future*)? Only when your executive team has a *clear and consistent* focus on the answers to these questions will you be able effectively to align your systems (and all the other cylinders in this section). Once your future state has been set, surveys and other methods of data gathering and internal/external customer listening will help you establish your current state and the gap between the two. Systems alignment then follows or begins to run in tandem with the implementation of the values and skill cylinders.

You will encounter in the systems cylinder some of the worst cases of what futurist Joel Barker calls "paradigm paralysis." Many of your people who may have understood the big picture of the new team-based organization will have a mental block when it comes to overhauling some key systems. These people will almost always be in management or staff support positions. They are rarely on the front line. And the traditional systems they will be fighting hardest to preserve are the ones in which they have a personal stake.

Helping your managers and staff support people let go of well-established but dysfunctional systems requires skill, a grounding in core values, internal and external data, and time. Your executives need to have the skills of signaling, education and awareness, coaching and team leadership solidly in place and in practice to more effectively lead systems realignment. Your executive team needs clear core values to know how to deal with the people who will be displaced by systems realignment. Often whole departments are eliminated, dramatically downsized, or redeployed. What guidance will your values give you as to how you will deal with these people? You will need data from external and internal (intact, project, and process teams) customers to determine best what system changes are called for to support improvement activities. And you will need time. It can't all be done overnight. Systems realignment is an evolutionary, long-term process.

Although systems realignment is long term and evolutionary, you can take a series of small but significant steps early in your service/quality implementation. Getting executives and managers to ask simple questions such as "what's the dumbest system/thing we do/have around here" of external customers and frontline teams can be *very* revealing. And when you act to fix or seriously examine ineffective systems, people start to take the improvement effort much more seriously. Identifying frontline irritants through questions, surveys, focus groups, "defective tools days" (employees bring in the equipment or identify the systems that aren't working), and other listening approaches can energize the whole effort. Often simple, but symbolic, improvements like cleaning the washrooms, putting a light in the parking lot, or improving signage can mean a lot—if that's what's irritating employees most. The whole improvement process is suddenly real and tangible, rather than a bunch of speeches, videos, meetings, and training sessions.

Systems alignment, as with all service/quality improvements in a team-based organization, calls for heavy involvement of those whom the systems are to be serving and supporting. "Systems development should be bottom up," urges Tom Peters. "Participation is more than a part of the system-design process—participation in system design is the key to effective system building; and effective systems building, in turn, is critical to sustaining a strategic quality thrust."[27] Participation generally starts small and builds as momentum gathers and data illuminate the path to outside-in and upside-down system realignment.

You need to establish a process for identifying and prioritizing systems to be realigned. There is so much to do, so little time, and so few resources. This is often done in conjunction with improvement activities. And as is the case with process management, a primary goal of systems alignment is simplification. As the poet Henry Wadsworth Longfellow once said, "In character, in manner, in style, the supreme excellence is simplicity."

Some organizations, such as Canadian Airlines, Wesley-Jessen, Eco-labs, and Matsushita (Panasonic) Canada, use a "blue card" and "green card" system to document recoveries and identify dysfunctional systems. Everyone in the organization is invited to submit, on preprinted blue cards or by computer, a description of actions taken to recover from any type of ricochet, which system it seemed to come from, and suggestions on how to permanently fix this process or system. These cards or reports are logged at a central source to begin compiling a composite picture of improvement opportunities and then forwarded to the process owner. Green cards are used to focus on particular processes or systems. They ask questions such as "I could do my job more effectively if . . . ," "I could serve my customers better if . . . ," "the dumbest things we do around here are . . . ," and so on. These cards are also tabulated to analysis trends and forwarded to the manager or team heading the improvement effort.

Like so much about participative systems realignment, these approaches work only if management actively practices the Basic Principles (page 165). If this looks like a search for the guilty or so much finger pointing, participation and willingness to change the system will be short-lived. It's also another example of why the values and skills cylinders need to be well under way before tackling some of the tougher and touchier systems issues.

EXAMPLES OF SYSTEMS ALIGNMENT

"The less there is to justify a tradition the harder it is to get rid of it."

Mark Twain, *American humorist*

There are thousands of powerful examples of systems realignment. Each of the many fields found in this extensive cylinder is in the midst of a widespread revolution demanded by the new customer-focused team-based organization. Here are just a few examples of some of the systems being realigned:

• At University of Alberta Hospitals, the service/quality improvement process caused nursing and dietary team members to question the decades-old control system of dietary staff signing in and out for shift changes at the patient care pods. They were concerned that all the traffic flow was disruptive. At first, dietary team members wrestled with where to move the function. Finally, the question was asked, "Do we really need to continue this practice?" It then became clear that this control system didn't fit with the team-based, empowered organization they were trying to become. It was stopped.

• B. C. Tel set up "Dumb Rules" and "Dumb Forms" committees with a senior executive on each one. The committees' mandate is to seek and destroy all those bureaucratic rules and forms that are no longer useful but never fade away gracefully on their own.

• To avoid the telephone runaround all too common with government and large companies, the Georgia Office of Consumer Affairs introduced the Tie Line. Local and incoming 800-number phone lines have a call-bridging capability. When consumers' questions or complaints can't be answered by the Tie Line counselors, they are bridged directly to whoever can best help. The counselor stays on the line to ensure the consumer gets the help he or she needs.[28]

• Federal Express's customer information system tells customers the exact status of a particular package within 30 minutes of the inquiry, or their money is refunded. Fred Smith, chairman and CEO, says, "Most customers understand that problems can occur. What they won't forgive is a lack of information, or having a problem handled poorly."[29]

• Texaco's Bakersfield Producing Division hosted a luncheon and site tour for the clerical staff of several key contractors. The event was both to recognize their contributions to Texaco's service/quality improvement process and to bring them closer to Texaco's accounting and payables system. The suppliers were also shown how their work related to Texaco's oil-field operations.

• An airline found that separate staff facilities for pilots and in-flight service crew prohibited the team meetings that were proving important to better coordinated customer service on board. So it rebuilt a joint facility to provide a physical structure that put people together and encouraged teamwork.

• In *Deming Management at Work*, Mary Walton reports:

In Brighton, Michigan, three plants belonging to a General Motors Power Train Division threw out a six-tier rating system that determines raises, promotions, and staff reductions, and substituted a process requiring feedback from peers, subordinates, and customers.[30]

• Four Seasons keeps a computerized profile of guest's preferences such as nonallergenic pillows or particular brands of tea.

• Cummins Engine Company believes "the goal of a system should be to serve customers efficiently." When Cummins decided to empower its distributors and dealers to determine whether a failure should be covered by the warranty, many managers were concerned that unjustified claims would skyrocket. In fact, because of substantial improvements in product quality, warranty costs have fallen 50 percent since 1979. "No increases have been seen that could be attributed to dishonest claims filing."[31]

COMMON PITFALLS AND TRAPS TO ALIGNING SYSTEMS

"A bureaucracy once established turns away from whatever task it is supposed to do and instead works to administer itself."

Max Weber, *father of sociology*

Rank Has Its Privileges

Executive parking spaces, washrooms, dining rooms, and other perks send elitist messages. These little extras carry an enormous cost in lost corporate energy. They convey a traditional organizational structure with executives on top and employees and customers at the bottom. Are they really worth the millions in lost energy and teamwork that they cost?

Responsible but Not Accountable

Telling people that improving service/quality is a key part of their job and then not holding them accountable makes the whole effort superficial. Ensure that service/quality improvement goals are part of managers' annual objectives and hold them to it. When service/quality goals become formal objectives, they become real.

Bureaucratic Bramble Bushes

Unless you prune old, dysfunctional systems, they will choke the potential your newer ones might offer. *You must have a process for identifying and changing management systems that hinder rather than help improve service/quality.* The best people to streamline your systems are those using them—if you *really* believe in the upside-down organization.

Creating Turf Warfare

A sure prescription for bureaucratic backbiting and empire-defending is to delegate the task of pruning systems. Removing policies, changing procedures, eliminating reports, reducing requirements, or dropping duties can be extremely threatening. Only senior management can cut through the bafflegab, doublespeak, and "not this system, you don't" defensiveness.

Not Practicing What You Preach

Make sure you're part of the solution, not the problem. Take a long, hard look at your own habits. How many reports and memos do you generate or ask for? Get constant feedback on this to continuously improve your personal habits.

Management-Directed Systems

If it makes your life easier or satisfies your command-and-control urges but inhibits service/quality improvement, you are paying a high price for that convenience or comfort. The effect a system has on your customers and those producing or supporting your products and services should be your *first* consideration.

Chapter Sixteen

Cylinder Nine: Reward and Recognition

"The most neglected form of compensation is the six-letter word thanks.*"*
Robert Townsend,
author and corporate-turnaround specialist

It's just more common sense: *what gets rewarded and recognized gets repeated*. But common sense is not common practice. Executives too often declare they want continuous service/quality improvement, but they reward good techno-managers or those who make their numbers—even though customer satisfaction or process quality may be slipping. Or executives proclaim they want to build a team-based organization and then reward "rugged individualism" because "he got the job done."

There are two basic ways of rewarding and recognizing employees to encourage and reinforce the kind of behavior and improvement activities your organization needs to drive it to higher service/quality. The first is financial compensation—how contributions are financially recognized. The second is nonmonetary—how people are provided with those all-important psychological payoffs (their "thanks pay"). Both need to be aligned with your focus on serving customers with a team-based organization.

You will not sustain your attempt at an organizational transformation without realigning your reward system and recognition strategies. Joseph Juran has found:

> To institutionalize annual quality improvement is a profound change in culture, requiring a correspondingly profound change in the systems of recognition and rewards. Lacking such a responsive change, the priorities of the operating managers will not change. Such was the experience of the 1980s.[1]

A study by the National Science Foundation concludes:

> The key to having workers who are both satisfied and productive is motivation, that is, arousing and maintaining the will to work effec-

tively—having workers who are effective not because they are coerced but because they are committed. Of all the factors which help to create motivated/satisfied workers, the principal one appears to be that effective performance be recognized and rewarded—in whatever terms are meaningful to the individual, be it financial or psychological or both.[2]

FINANCIAL REWARDS

"The definition of a living wage depends on whether you are getting it or giving it."

Most compensation systems such as pay for performance, profit or merit bonuses, job category ratings, and salary classifications are unaligned with the service/quality improvement process. Conflicting messages are sent by executives who loudly declare their undying commitment to customer satisfaction, process improvement, or teamwork and then fail to build the compensation system around those core values. But the conflict is fairly easily settled; managers, supervisors, and individual contributors concentrate on what they are rewarded for. If that's profit bonuses, they'll take a short-term approach to squeezing customers or markets for sales growth and indiscriminately slash costs. Or it may mean making themselves or their department look good at the expense of someone else.

Top service/quality providers are pioneering new ways to align their compensation with their improvement process. It generally starts with top management. In a customer-focused, upside-down organization, senior executives have substantial portions of their bonuses based on customer satisfaction and employee morale. It can't be any other way. You can't declare that the main reason your organization exists is to provide service/quality and then not focus compensation on these results. Similarly, declaring management's primary role is to support the front line and then not putting executives' money where their mouth is makes the words ring hollow.

The debate over the role money plays in motivating people has raged for years and shows little sign of being settled. What is clear, though, is that the perceived lack of money or undercompensation for doing a job is a demotivator. Former McDonald's Vice President Bob Desatnick cites a Science Foundation study that shows the huge price being paid for the widespread problem of unaligned compensation systems.

A recent national poll of thousands of workers asked, "If you were to improve service quality and productivity, do you believe you would be rewarded accordingly?" Only 22 percent said yes. As a consequence, 75 percent of the workers reported they deliberately withhold extra effort on the job. *Imagine the potential impact on customer service!* (his emphasis).[3]

A study done by the Public Agenda Foundation found that almost two-thirds of employees would like to see a better connection between performance and pay. And more than 70 percent believed *work had deteriorated* because there was no connection between pay and performance.[4]

The move to process improvement through teams is a major driver of the massive changes occurring in North American compensation systems. Our traditional approaches are based on specialization, individual or narrow functional results, and management's evaluation of contributions and performance. All of this discourages cross-functional teamwork. Even traditional suggestion systems can poison teams, especially those that pay individuals for their suggestions. Globe Metallurgical Vice President Ken Leach paints an all too common scene:

> Invariably we found the employees thought management grossly underestimated the value of their share. So we give somebody a check for $1,000 and they're mad at us because they're expecting $1,500 or $2,000. . . . Also, the people that worked with this employee were mad at him for getting the $1,000, and they were mad at us for giving it to him. Then three or four days later somebody would come in to us and say, "You know, I talked about this to old Bob in the locker room a month or so ago and damned if he didn't turn my idea in." So what do you do then?[5]

Organizations using various teams to drive their improvement activities are turning to a number of new compensation systems. One of those, increasingly used with self-directed work teams, is pay for skills (or pay for knowledge). Under this compensation system, team members are paid according to the skills they master to help the team reach its performance goals. Richard Schonberger's study of quality improvement practices in North America and Japan leads him to conclude:

> I am confident about few things. . . . One is the soundness of pay for knowledge. Since employee involvement *requires* that operators become multiskilled, the pay system must conform . . . not just for frontline employees. For professional, managerial, and staff support people, it becomes *more pay for learning more parts of the business.* Far too few companies are getting this done, even though we have heard over and over how effective this policy is in top Japanese companies (his emphasis).[6]

Gain-sharing is another compensation system with a steep growth curve. In gain-sharing, increases over an established baseline of costs, service/quality levels, productivity, or overall business performance are shared among the team or the entire organization according to some formula. Emphasis is often on group productivity or service/quality levels.

Employee involvement means involving employees in bonuses and rewards for their efforts. As Sony Chairman Akio Morita explains, this is one of the reasons Japanese companies have become such formidable competitors:

> Sometimes American companies use employees to make money for the management. That's why management gets a great bonus. . . . In Japan we don't pay bonus (only) to the managers. We pay bonus to the employees because if we make a profit, we want to have them enjoy it together with us.[7]

However, aligning compensation to your service/quality process is only half of it. There are plenty of examples of well-paid employees and managers who are not well motivated. The public sector and large, wealthy companies have many such people. The problem is not necessarily with the individuals. Often it is a sign that management failed to provide critical nonmonetary incentives, that management systems and processes are weak. Making this point in *The Wall Street Journal*, Robert Kelley of Carnegie-Mellon University writes, "High pay does not equal good service, and, as McDonald's has shown, low pay need not result in poor service. . . . High-quality service depends on high-quality management."[8]

RECOGNITION

"The glow of one warm thought is worth more to me than money."

Thomas Jefferson, *U.S. president*

Recognition is the most inexpensive, easy-to-use motivational technique available to management. Yet the degree to which this essential service/quality improvement tool is underused by most otherwise intelligent managers is bewildering. As we work with top-performing organizations and those aspiring to be, the two groups might as well be on different planets in their approaches to recognition, celebration, hoopla, and sincere "thanks pay." Comparing the companies highlighted in *In Search of Excellence* to average organizations, Tom Peters and Robert Waterman report:

> The volume of contrived opportunities for showering pins, buttons, badges, and medals on people is staggering at McDonald's, Tupperware, IBM, and many of the other top performers. They actively seek out and pursue endless opportunities to give out rewards.[9]

"We're supposed to be perfect our first day on the job and then show constant improvement," complains Ed Vargo, a Major League Baseball umpire. That kind of pressure is felt by everyone on the journey to continuous service/quality improvement. No matter how good you are or how well you've done something, it can always be done better. That relentless strain to improve can be very draining.

Effective recognition recharges everyone's batteries. And recharging often and effectively makes more energy available to take the organization further along its improvement journey. Consultant and author Pat Townsend points out:

> Just as the accumulation of small improvements can make a dramatic, lasting change in the organization's products or services, the repeated, numerous small occasions of taking note of the contributions of individuals and teams of individuals can create a different company.[10]

Tom Peters has found, "Fun, joy, and sharing success go hand in glove with world-class quality."[11] And the American Society for Quality Control says, "Celebration reaffirms the worth of the effort, creates a personal and organizational memory of the triumph, and renews energy for the next segment of the continuing improvement journey."[12]

RECOGNITION STRATEGIES

"I now perceive one immense omission in my psychology—the deepest principle of human nature is the craving to be appreciated."

William James, *pioneer of modern psychology*

The thousands of ways effective managers recognize solid performance can be broken into three main categories: (1) team recognition and celebration, (2) personal one-on-one "thanks" or "way to gos," and (3) individual recognition programs.

Team Recognition and Celebration

In a team-based organization, team recognition is obviously vital. Team recognition is often more effective than individual recognition, which can reduce teamwork. Charles Garfield outlines how that can happen: "Want to destroy a team? A great way to do it is to reward only the leader. So, he's up there getting a plaque from the CEO and the troops are in the front row planning his assassination." The delicate balancing act is to reward both individual initiative and team efforts without having one overshadow the other. But to build teamwork, you need to continually lean toward recognizing teams, rather than individuals.

Following are a few ways teams can be recognized:

- Have senior management cook or serve a special meal to thank the team for achieving a goal, completing a project, improving a process, and so on.
- Bring in doughnuts to congratulate a team for passing a milestone.
- Serve special meals in the cafeteria with balloons and streamers, where senior managers pass out accolades, thanks, awards, bonuses, and so forth.
- Post charts or posters showing team progress.
- Post or publish pictures of successful teams in newsletters along with stories of their improvement accomplishments.
- Have successful teams present their accomplishments to senior management or to others at special team fairs.
- Feature teams at industry or technical conferences.
- Give teams trips to suppliers or customers.
- Hand out plaques, pins, trophies, certificates, hats, mugs, or coasters to top-performing teams.
- Distribute to team members exclusive T-shirts, pen sets, calculators, and so on with a "winning" slogan or team name.
- Have senior managers drop into team meetings to say thanks for a job well done.
- Hold team competitions for prizes or honors for their progress in the improvement process.

Personal Thanks or "Way to Go"

"I can live for two months on a good compliment."

Mark Twain

As we discussed in the coaching cylinder (Chapter 13), personal recognition and praise are essential. Though the fanfare of public recognition adds sparkle, sincere, well-expressed appreciation given personally by a manager or team member goes a long way as well. Richard Schonberger says, "As badly as employers have mishandled monetary rewards, they have done worse in providing the intrinsic rewards of feeling good about oneself."[13] Recognizing and thanking each other is a contagious habit that only a handful of organizations are afflicted with. Most operate on the "no news is good news" approach. And it becomes a reinforcing cycle. As recognition and thanks become more scarce, the cultural norms move downward to lower levels of recognition and thanks. This causes even more scarcity.

Reversing the cycle to build a culture of recognition and thanks starts with management. These habits cascade down from senior management. If executives don't recognize and thank each other, then a vice president will not be in the habit of doing so with her managers. If a manager doesn't get much appreciation from her vice president, then she won't pass much on to her supervisors. If a supervisor doesn't get much appreciation from his manager, then he won't give much to his teams. If team members don't get a lot of thanks for their efforts at the local, day-to-day level, then they won't pass much appreciation on to each other. In the end, everybody's poorer, and the improvement effort loses energy.

Following are some ways to practice the dying skill of personal recognition and thanks:

- Send personal thank-you notes.
- Provide a simple, sincere thanks for successful completion of a task. Electronic Data Systems founder H. Ross Perot advocates recognizing someone "while the sweat is still on their brow."[14]
- Follow your praise with a congratulatory letter in the employee's file.
- Send a note or special card to a colleague or team member's house.
- Return a memo or report with your handwritten notes complimenting the quality of the work.
- Include personal notes of appreciation with birthday, anniversary, or Christmas cards.
- Pass along complimentary comments made by others, especially senior managers.
- Make a special point to repeat the positive feedback given during coaching discussions or performance reviews.
- Send a note to the team member's significant other at home complimenting the employee's work and thanking the significant other for his or her support.

Individual Recognition Programs

"I'm just a plowhand from Arkansas, but I have learned how to hold a team together. How to lift some men up, how to calm down others, until finally they've got one heartbeat together, a team. There's just three things I'd ever say:

If anything goes bad, I did it.
If anything goes semi-good, then we did it.
If anything goes real good, then you did it.
That's all it takes to get people to win football games for you.''

Coach Paul ''Bear'' Bryant[15]

In top service/quality organizations, formal individual recognition programs are giving way to team recognition. However, individual recognition programs don't disappear. In fact, most of us want to be on a highly recognized winning team, but we also want to stand out for our personal contributions and achievements.

The big difference in individual recognition programs within a team-based organization is how personal achievements are chosen for recognition. Most individual recognition programs have two common and glaring problems. First, the program is too often established and run by managers. This is very paternalistic and often condescending. In all their infinite wisdom, managers decide what will turn on employees. It frequently comes off as a cynical attempt to manipulate frontline contributors. The whole thing stems from the same dysfunctional assumption as most performance management systems—that individuals can control service/quality levels if they would just try hard enough. *The Service Edge* newsletter reports that Maritz Inc. researched *Fortune* 500 companies with active service/quality programs to look at their employee recognition practices. Jerry McAdams, Moritz vice president and author of *People, Performance and Pay*, reports, ''The majority of employees look unfavorably on management-driven rewards. Award nomination by employee peer group is always a better approach in the eyes of employees.''[16]

The second problem with many individual recognition programs, especially those run by managers, is that winners are either chosen at random or recognized for the wrong things. Random selection (which Deming calls a recognition lottery) may be done on the basis of fewest complaints, a glowing customer letter, a well-handled incident, and so on. This nonsystematic approach can be a nice thank you for the person receiving it—if the recognition has any meaning for the receiver. But rarely does it inspire others to do anything differently. Many believe they have done things every bit as good—or better—but the boss didn't happen to be around, the customer was less vocal in his or her appreciation, or any number of random events just didn't happen when they were performing. In other words, there is no process that says, ''If you achieve this measurable level of achievement, you will be recognized in this way.'' It's a lottery where the odds of winning are either so high there's no use worrying about it, or everybody eventually has a turn at winning so there's nothing special about it.

The most common kind of recognition for the wrong thing is team or individual recognition for heroic recoveries from internally created ricochets. This is symptomatic of an organization trying to deliver service/quality the hard and expensive way—by adding it on rather than building it in. The focus needs to shift from managing the problems to managing the process.

Do more internal customer listening. What do your people want in a recognition program?

KEYS TO EFFECTIVE REWARD AND RECOGNITION

"A rose on time is far more valuable than a thousand dollar gift that's too late."
Jim Rohn, *personal development author and speaker*

Following are a few tips and techniques to use in aligning your reward systems and recognition strategies:

- Closely align rewards and recognition with your data-based management systems (Chapter 15). Make sure rewards and recognition are predictable and based on a solid outside-in feedback process. Individuals and teams should be assessed by the internal or external customers they serve.

- Give everyone lots of information and feedback and make it as visual and visible as possible. You want to run a very transparent organization where it's clear who is making the greatest contributions to continuous service/quality improvement.

- Involve those to be rewarded and recognized in deciding who should be rewarded and recognized for what activities and results and how this should be done.

- Ensure that senior executives are highly visible in the recognition process. They should be handing out the awards, giving the thank-you speeches, and shaking lots of hands. This is one of their most powerful culture shaping and commitment signaling activities.

- Join the growing list of companies finding alternatives to upward career ladders that reward high performers with promotions. This traditional process too often takes an outstanding individual contributor and makes him or her into a second-rate manager. The flatter, team-based organization has fewer opportunities for upward mobility. The higher income and prestige found in promotions need to be built into horizontal opportunities for continuous job expansion and contributions to the team.

- Make recognition as immediate as possible, otherwise the excitement or connection to why it was significant will be lost.

- Make sure your compensation system is *perceived* to be fair and is aligned with your corporate service/quality objectives by the majority of people it affects before you add a number of formal team and individual recognition programs. How do you *know* how your compensation system is perceived?

- Provide plenty of training, follow-up, encouragement, and personal examples for giving personal one-on-one recognition and thanks.

- Don't allow recognition to focus only on the big successes or breakthroughs. Find lots of opportunities to celebrate and recognize the many small wins along the way. Tom Peters finds, "Constantly celebrating the *little* tries—that don't feel little at all to previously unempowered, fear-stricken workers—is a major factor separating winners from losers in strategic change programs" (his emphasis).[17] This creates the encouragement and energy to maintain the relentless pace of continuous improvement.

EXAMPLES OF REWARD SYSTEMS AND RECOGNITION STRATEGIES

"Praise does wonders for our sense of caring."

Here are how some organizations energize and align their people for higher service/quality:

- The distribution division of the rapidly growing Domino's Pizza holds an annual olympics to recognize key service/quality skills. Local and regional competitions decide who will compete for $4,000 in cash prizes or lavish vacations. The 14 areas of competition include veggie slicing (emphasizing quality and quantity of vegetables, sanitation, and appearance), traffic management (routing and coordinating team members and their trucks), dough making and catching, store delivery, driving, loading, and maintenance. Accountants compete not only on their bookkeeping skills but also on their interpersonal and phone skills. The judges are the Domino franchisees who are the customers of this group.[18]

- B.C. Tel recognizes good internal customer service with the People's Choice Awards. These awards are given to the managers identified by employees as the most help to them in their delivery of service/quality (the upside-down organization in action). The company also holds "operator appreciation days" for frontline performers and their families.

• Paul Revere Insurance developed a program based on the number of ideas each of its quality teams implemented, or its annual financial worth. The awards are: bronze—10 certified ideas or $10,000 in annual savings; silver—25 certified ideas or $25,000 in annual savings; gold—50 certified ideas or $50,000 in annual savings. The awards consist of gift certificates for $10 to $40, presented by a senior executive. Winners are also highlighted in internal publications and receive bronze, silver, or gold lapel pins. Cash awards go to the most valuable team, the most valuable player, and other categories at a year-end gala celebration.

• Xerox, NYNEX (holding company for the New York and New England Telephone Companies), US West, GTE, and other companies now base management bonuses on customer satisfaction and employee morale measures.

• As a regional manager for Holiday Inns in Tennessee, Drew Diamond initiated a highly successful recognition program. Each guest was given a book of coupons to present to employees who provide outstanding service. As the coupons came in, the manager would seek out and praise the employee for his or her efforts. Within a few months, service ratings jumped while employee absenteeism and tardiness fell.[19]

• Toyota Motor Sales U.S.A. incorporates customer satisfaction criteria in its national dealer recognition awards. Performance bonuses are based on total customer satisfaction achievements.[20]

• Richard Schonberger reports that Milliken "stands out above other Western companies in its use of visual recognition." Every area, office, or plant has what Schonberger calls "an alcove of excellence." These are display areas with "graphs showing overall team accomplishments; processes brought under control; steady improvements in scrap, lead time, inventories, flow distances, setup times; and other 'vital signs.' " Milliken also has numerous "walls of fame" displaying plaques, photos, recognition letters, and awards. The company's newsletter, *The Torch: Pursuit of Excellence*, is loaded with team and individual photos and accompanying stories of achievement. The company hands out many types of awards to individuals, teams, and suppliers. Roger Milliken and other senior executives figure prominently in the many ceremonies and celebrations.[21]

However, Milliken's incentives are now focused strictly on teams. The company dropped individual incentives. The use of teams to drive improvement activities and a team-based compensation system increased plant efficiency from 84 to 92 percent. The company also reduced the number of job categories from 19 to 5. "It has been incredibly well received by workers," says Milliken.[22]

• Once a quarter at Federal Express, all 11 divisions go through an internal selection process to choose the best success story among their quality action teams. Fred Smith and other senior managers present awards to these teams during special award ceremonies. Winners are widely publicized through Federal Express's vast internal communications network.[23]

• At Xerox, an employee team plans and coordinates the annual, worldwide "Team Excellence" day. Teams nominate themselves for their improvement activities through an application process that documents work processes and results.

In Canada, "Teamwork Days" are held in every district in the country. This often involves a "Teamwork Fair" where customers, senior managers, suppliers, and other Xerox teams are invited to look at the displays of the teams' accomplishments. Chairman Dave McCamus and other executives speak with each team about the work and thank team members for their contributions.

COMMON REWARD AND RECOGNITION PITFALLS AND TRAPS

"Some managers give recognition as if they expect a receipt."

Random Recognition

Don't have recognition lotteries. Set up a formal, disciplined system for generating rewards, hoopla, and celebration at all levels and in all divisions. But make sure your managers' coaching skills are strong so they are confident and competent enough to give plenty of recognition and build a "thank-you culture."

To keep others from thinking that those who get recognition or special honors are management's favorites ("How did you suck up for that award?"), use peer review, customer feedback, and solid service/quality measures.

Thankless Executives

Many managers do such a poor job of showing appreciation and building a "thank-you culture" because their senior managers take them for granted and give them little to no appreciation. Recognition, celebration, and hoopla are contagious. Are you a carrier?

Senior executives who attend the first few reward/recognition events must not be allowed to get bored with it and stop coming or get too busy with other things. Recognition programs need constant attention and must emanate clearly from on high.

Phoney Flattery

Employees quickly catch on to "I'm doing my recognition thing now." Managers who will not practice and develop their thanks or catching-them-doing-things-right skills should not have people leadership responsibilities. Recognition is at the core of effective coaching.

Jelly Bean Motivation

This phrase was coined by motivational expert M. Scott Myers to describe the empty praise that congratulates and thanks people for something that hasn't been done. It's "keep up the good work" from a manager who has no idea what work was really done. Ken Blanchard advises, "Feel free to praise, but praise specifically. By continually flattering people for no good reason, they'll come to expect applause, even when they are doing slipshod work."[24] Tom Peters adds, "Too many random congratulations only serve to devalue the truly earned ones. What managers must do is give more thought to just what kind of performance *does* earn applause, and then applaud it—loudly, sincerely, frequently."[25]

Tinsel and Trinkets

Recognition can't make up for paying people peanuts (which, as the wag said, only attracts monkeys). Formalized recognition programs can also reveal those managers who see employees not as partners to be listened to and involved in running the organization but as chattels to be exploited and manipulated. What messages are you sending? How do you *know?*

Frontline Fixation

Don't focus just on frontline servers who have the heaviest customer contact. Employees who "serve the servers" are also vital links in the service/quality chain, and they too need to be energized by recognition and rewards.

Big Bangs

A few mega-rewards to your superstars will have far less payoff than a large number of smaller rewards distributed broadly. Top-performing organizations set up recognition and reward programs that create many winners and recharge as large a number of individuals and team members as possible.

Chapter Seventeen

Cylinder 10: Improvement Activities

"The one who goes alone can start today; but he who travels with another must wait till that other is ready, and it may be a long time before they get off."

Henry David Thoreau

This is the cylinder where the action is. Everything that has come before, and will come after, is essentially to support this cylinder. As we said in Chapter 5, continuous service/quality improvement is heavily dependent on employee involvement. And the best way to harness employees' vital improvement efforts is through team-based approaches. Tom Peters writes:

> Getting everyone involved on teams is imperative. I'm sick and tired of 50,000-person companies bragging, in their annual reports, about their 125 quality teams. Take the number of people in the firm, divide by 10—if that's not close to your number of teams, you've got a problem.[1]

In this chapter, we will look at process management, the most common types of improvement teams, how they operate, what elements are needed to support and sustain their efforts, and how to get started.

One of the core changes in moving from a traditional organization to a team-based one is bringing the planning and thinking back together with implementing and doing. To maximize the relevance of the improvement (or change) and ownership for making it work, the thinking and doing are brought as close as possible to customers and the people making, serving, or supporting the organization's basic products or services. University of Tsukuba Professor Shoji Shiba has been a total quality management advisor since 1960 in Japan and a visiting professor at MIT. He explains the revolutionary changes this way:

The key change at the work group level is the uniting of improvements in daily operations with innovative improvements. These two have traditionally been separated, with the worker responsible for improvement in daily work and management responsible for innovative improvement.[2]

Richard Schonberger relates Japanese and pioneering North American experiences with the shift to frontline teams taking more control of managing daily operations:

> When focused teams take charge of their own resources, quality, and problem solving, overhead as a percentage of total cost plunges. Another result is sharp reductions in delays, wastes, customer returns, storages, and other hard-to-cost negative events—which are responsible for much of the cost transactions and costing apparatus.[3]

This shifts responsibility from management to frontline teams. And that has profound implications for how the improvement process is managed.

One of the biggest implications is how improvement suggestions are handled. Under the traditional approach, management devises various ways to encourage improvement ideas, including paying for those that prove to be effective. Management evaluates the ideas and decides which to pursue (this is a perfect example of separating improvement planning from its implementation). In its introductory stages, this type of suggestion system often produces a flood of ideas. Managers must now wade through these and pick the best ones to implement in processes they don't work with every day. On top of that, many supervisors aren't interested and already feel overworked. The predictable results are delays in responding to the suggestions, selection of weak as well as good ideas, and lack of ownership of those implementing the idea if they weren't involved in developing it. All of this leads to the kind of frustration expressed by someone who put a sign on a suggestion box that read, "Please do not put any more ideas in here because the handle is broken and it won't flush."

Deming shows the sharp contrast when teams are involved in both idea generation and implementation:

> Suggestions are considered by the group and the (person) that makes the suggestion is present. The decision does not fall on one person, but the group. The group comes to a conclusion for the good of the company. Once the decision is unanimous, everyone works together to deliver his best for the group. Any dissenter, or anyone that does not deliver his best, will find his way into another group or into other work.[4]

In a team-based organization, the ratio of idea pitchers to idea catchers is evened out. Employees go through the maturing process of solving the companies' problems with each other over coffee to taking on the tough management task of how to allocate diminishing resources to meet increasing service/quality demands.

PROCESS MANAGEMENT

"We had to change just about everything we do and align all our processes so that they drive quality."

David Kearns, *CEO, Xerox*[5]

If we are going to get at the true root causes of service/quality breakdowns and reduce their horrendously high costs, then we need to better manage the way work is done. That calls for new management methods. Our traditional methods of planning, organizing, and controlling what goes on in organizations have failed us. Doing more of the same—no matter how well it's done—won't help. New approaches are needed. These approaches must harness and direct the energy and power of teams at all levels of the organization.

Process management is fast proving to be that kind of approach. In one of its many reports on the rapidly emerging use of total quality management practices, the Conference Board offers this useful definition of process management: "Techniques used to define, document, measure, and continuously improve a series of cross-functional actions or operations. Effective 'management' requires the establishment of ownership and accountability for each process."[6]

Just as the words *service* and *quality* go hand in hand and are often used interchangeably, the words *process* and *system* are used together so often they have become almost synonymous. Processes occur at all levels of the organization. A broad macro process is generally focused across the whole enterprise. It is made up of a series of smaller micro processes, narrower work activities and individual tasks. Taken together, these might sometimes be referred to as a system. Supporting all of this, however, is another layer of foundation support systems outlined in Chapter 15.

The interplay of micro and macro processes and systems can get confusing. That's why the true source of ricochets and actions that will best improve root causes gets so mixed up. When you don't know where you are going, any road will take you there. If you and your teams don't have a clear picture of how your multilayered systems, macro and micro processes, work activities, and individual tasks fit together, how can you improve? You stumble around without a map. You either take familiar routes that don't take you anywhere, or you try new ones and get lost. Everyone gets frustrated, and progress is agonizingly slow and painful.

The biggest problem in many organizations is that the work of too many people is not part of a managed process. Work activities and individual tasks, at all levels, have never been effectively planned and organized as part of a bigger, cross-functional picture. Work is done "because we've always done it that way." That same lack of clear focus often fuses departments or groups in haphazard ways. Materials, information, paperwork, and customers are tossed from one vertical chimney to the next.

The only way any degree of service/quality is delivered to customers in most organizations is through the heroics of frontline people and lots of expensive checking, catching, and correcting of the inevitable ricochets firing out of uncontrolled systems and processes.

Variations in the process cause most ricochets. Deming breaks these into "special causes" and "common causes." One of the first steps is to analyze (define) the process to understand which type of cause created the problem, act to correct the cause (if possible), and monitor the results of those actions. If this is successful, that process, work step, or activity will have been raised to a new standard or level of performance. This will have to be maintained in order to establish a new level of predictability and repeatability.

Once this new standard is maintained, further analysis will point the way to other causes of variability or errors. The continuous improvement cycle is repeated until the process is consistently maintained at a level of no variability (zero defects) or it is decided that devoting the organization's limited resources to further improvements in this process is less important than turning attention to other important processes.

The Process Management Process

Just as there is no one best route to implement a service/quality improvement process, there is no one best way to build a team-based organization around the principles of process management. The following points are embedded in most successful applications of process management:

• Senior management takes an outside-in view of the organization's few strategic processes by looking at those processes that are customer satisfaction drivers, revenue generators, or major cost centers. This is done by looking at those processes through the customer's "line of visibility."

- Having identified the three or four strategic processes of the organization, the executive team maps the key roles and responsibilities for each one. For example, at Brigham and Woman's Hospital in Boston, key processes were identified as the flow of patients, information, materials (such as medications, food, supplies, and so on), and combinations of these three.
- Each of the strategic processes is "blueprinted" to gain a big picture understanding of the impact of supporting systems, interconnected work activities, subprocesses, and the like. A common result is executive horror at the holes in understanding, information, coordination, and customer-focus of most processes, as well as their general inefficiency, error rate, and sky-high costs. Another shock is the incredible number of extra, unplanned, and unnecessary steps in the process.
- In the first year, two or three organizationwide process improvement efforts are initiated. These are often chosen on the basis of this type of criteria:

- Clear customer feedback reveals this process is a major problem.
- It is a chronic, ongoing process or system problem that would significantly increase customer and employee satisfaction if improved and would visibly signal the strong commitment of the executive team to the service/quality improvement effort.
- It would provide a good pilot and wide-scale opportunity for many people to learn how to better manage process management.
- Good data exist that will make process management more likely to succeed or be better focused.
- Improving this process would have a significant effect on the bottom line or free people to reinvest further in other improvement activities.

- Senior executives establish process owners and form and lead process improvement teams. These teams often cascade through the organization as the strategic processes are broken into functional or departmental processes that then focus frontline improvement activities on removing constraints to the process.
- Monitoring, refocusing, as well as establishing and leading new process improvement teams become even more effective as higher quantities and quality of customer and process data begin to pour in.
- Process improvements lead to special improvement projects. This is usually further subprocess improvement work as well as improvement and strengthening of key support systems (see Chapter 15).

TYPES OF TEAMS

"Bees accomplish nothing save as they work together, and neither do people."
                                    Elbert Hubbard, *American publisher and writer*

Teams come in many shapes, sizes, and types, and they operate under a variety of names, descriptions, and mandates. However, whether they're managing a macro or micro process or working to improve a system, the vast array of team-based improvement activities have at their core four basic types of team configurations.

Intact Teams

An intact team is a group of frontline contributors, managers, or executives who work together on a day-to-day basis. Their improvement activities are aimed at the part of the organization or "task level" processes for which that department or group is responsible. They are sometimes referred to as functional teams, departmental teams, local improvement teams, in-scope teams, performance teams, or work teams.

During the early 1980s, quality control (QC) circles were a popular way to bring intact teams into the improvement process. These are generally small groups of employees who meet voluntarily to solve problems within their department. Usually these problems directly affect the group's output. The QC circle meets regularly and frequently until the problem is solved. At that time, the circle is disbanded or defines a new problem to work on. QC circle meetings are often led by a facilitator from elsewhere in the organization rather than by the department supervisor or manager.

QC circles are rarely used in their original form today. A 1985 study by the consulting firm A. T. Kearney found that of the 80 percent of Fortune 500 firms that had started QC circles since 1980, some 83 percent had abandoned them within 18 months of kicking them off.[7] The main problems were lack of a systemwide focus on processes and an almost total absence of the conditions needed to support teams. The danger of launching QC circles or any other narrow improvement team within its own functional chimney in the absence of large-scale process improvement is suboptimization. Teams work furiously to improve and add no value to the ultimate product or service.

Work cells and self-directed work teams. A fundamental shortcoming of traditional segmented organizations with their vertical chimneys is that it is difficult to coordinate work involving many people and departments. No one is really accountable or responsible for the output of the entire cross-functional process. Also, ownership and commitment to the process are low. To counteract these problems, many organizations are restructuring work teams to be more autonomous in the production or delivery process. Team members are trained to build most or all of the product, or to take care of the customers inside their own unit, with minimal support from others in the organization. These are sometimes called "work cells," self-directed work teams, or self-managing work teams.

Work cells help decentralize and delayer the bureaucracy that inevitably blossoms when an organizational unit grows beyond a few dozen people. "Chunking" organizations and work processes into their smallest pieces as close to the front line as possible simplifies operations. The resulting simplification and visibility of the work process reduce the number of steps and people involved. That drops error rates and puts customers closer to people who can take immediate action to respond to their needs. As these teams evolve and move closer to becoming self-directed, the cumbersome and expensive structure of management and staff support groups is reduced and refocused.

Increasingly, manufacturers are finding that when they give a team full responsibility for building a complete component, or even an entire product, quality improves, morale soars, and productivity jumps. This approach means breaking the traditional assembly line into "minifactories" throughout the manufacturing plant and pulling teams together to manage their own work cell. Each cell then becomes a self-contained link in the customer-supplier chain that pulls work through the factory starting with the outside customer.

Service organizations are starting to take similar approaches. By moving order or claims processing, accounts receivable, customer inquiries, or account administration to local offices, employees and customers form closer relationships. And as local service providers control more of the administrative processes, they respond more quickly and correct process problems that would have become lost in the old centralized bureaucratic maze.

Process Improvement Teams

A process improvement team is a group of frontline, performers, management, or support specialists staff who generally represent their part of the organization involved in a strategic, functional, or task-level process.

Once an organization is well along the journey to higher service/quality, process improvement teams operate at all levels of the organization. They may become intertwined with intact teams as members on a cross-functional process improvement team become two-way bridges between the intact team they represent and the ongoing improvement activities of the process improvement team. In time, many organizations restructure their intact teams around key processes. In some cases, intact teams and functional or task-level process improvement teams merge.

With macro or system-level processes, senior management is often involved, as process improvement team champions or leaders. This cascades through the organization as process improvement teams are formed to look at functional or task-level processes. Intact teams are then established or directed by the work of these process improvement teams.

A process improvement team starts by preparing a description or profile of the process: its purpose, customers, scope and boundaries, current performance, suppliers, and who's involved in the process. A blueprint of the larger systems, other processes, intact-level subprocesses, work activities, and possibly individual activities composes a picture of potential causes of variation and error. Data-based tools and techniques, especially statistical methods, are used to zero in on, and plan, process improvements, monitor the effectiveness of action taken, maintain the new standards, and identify further opportunities for improvement.

Project Teams

"Light is the task when many share the toil."

Homer, *Greek poet*

Where intact teams and process improvement teams are ongoing or very long term, project teams are temporary. Often called task forces, project teams are disbanded once their mission or mandate is fulfilled. Sometimes a process improvement team creates a project team. Other times, it's the other way around. Project teams are often used to look at systems realignment such as restructuring, changing the accounting system, shifting human resource policies, establishing a supplier management program, or re-examining distribution channels. In other cases, project teams may be used to solve or set up a longer-term process to deal with major organizational problems. This might include customer complaints or loss rates, employee dissatisfaction or morale problems, production or delivery problems, or new products and services that fail to perform as expected.

Project teams are often made up of managerial or staff support specialists. With major strategic or organizationwide issues, top managers and the most experienced internal professionals make up the teams. Teams may also include outside experts as well as key suppliers, distributors, customers, politicians, board members, or whoever may have a large stake in the issue or be able to provide the most help, or whose support is needed. These senior project teams often provide the direction for other ongoing improvement activities and the other teams. Sometimes, senior project teams are struck as a result of major organizational changes or problems identified by process improvement teams.

At other levels of the organization, project teams look at specific issues, root causes, or problems identified by process improvement teams or a number of intact teams. Usually these are local or interdepartment systems issues that may cut through or underpin a number of processes.

Steering Committees and Councils

"We must indeed all hang together, or most assuredly, we shall all hang separately."
Benjamin Franklin *on signing the Declaration of Independence*

This fourth type of team is a critical part of the deployment infrastructure that will be discussed in Chapter 20. A team-based organization needs a lot of coordination and support. All these teams can't just go off and start making changes on their own. That results in duplication, narrow focus, poor preparation, conflict, teams tripping over each other, and a host of related problems. A team-based organization is unlike any organizational form used before. It calls for markedly different methods of leadership and management.

Some of the most effective early improvement activities are those taken by the senior management steering committees as they start to plan, organize, and prepare the organization for the service/quality improvement journey. Small, but visible and meaningful, improvement activities initiated by senior management can go a long way toward getting people on board and moving this whole effort from rhetoric to reality.

THE ELEMENTS OF SUCCESS

As happened with quality circles in North America, the rising popularity of service/quality teams is leading organizations to install them in environments that aren't ready to sustain them. *For the majority of organiza-*

tions embarking on the service/quality improvement journey, improvement activities are the wrong place to start.

Whenever we are called in to organizations struggling to get out of the "quality quagmire," we inevitably find they are stuck because they jumped into this cylinder far too soon. Because this is where the real improvement action occurs, many managers want to "cut to the quick" and show their "bias for action" by getting a number of improvement teams under way fast. This is often accompanied by a fixation with one or two systems, reward and recognition programs, or standards and measurements (like statistical methods). These "action-oriented" executives want service/quality improvement by next Tuesday.

You can throw people together in a group, call them any kind of team you want, and give them a mandate. However, if some core elements are missing, your teams may get off the ground, but they will never soar to the heights of success. Following are some of the elements needed for improvement teams to successfully initiate continuous, effective improvement activities.

Trust and Partnerships

"Confidence placed in another often compels confidence in return."

Livy, *Roman historian*

"Where trust is lacking, there is suspicion, latent hostility, tension and conflict," says Four Seasons' John Sharpe. "Employees don't pull together. They don't share information. They don't volunteer. They won't risk making mistakes. Unless we develop a culture that cultivates trust, employees don't have much concern for the company. They become self-concerned and self-protective." Many organizations latch onto the team-based organizational model as if it were the latest new appliance that can be easily purchased from some consultant and plugged into the organization. The road to higher service/quality is littered with the burned-out carcasses of teams—and even entire organizations—destroyed by this simplistic approach. *Improvement teams work only in an atmosphere of trust, partnerships, and mutual respect.*

How do you build that essential trust? John Sharpe says: "I know of only two ways to win trust. One is to give it, something many companies find hard to do." Fred Allan, the chairman of Pitney-Bowes, adds this insight: "It is probably not love that makes the world go round, but rather those mutually supportive alliances through which partners recognize their dependence on each other for the achievement of shared and private goals. Treat employees like partners, and they will act like partners."[8] John Sharpe's second way to win trust is "to earn it through credibility. Management has to be credible."[9]

What does your organization's "trust index" tell you about your readiness to form and sustain improvement teams? *How do you know?*

Senior Management Signaling

"The way to gain a reputation is to endeavor to be what you desire to appear."

Socrates, *Athenian philosopher*

Senior executives must *actively lead* the improvement effort. Only then will the dysfunctional organizational systems and processes be seriously studied and improved. And *visible* senior executive leadership goes far beyond any words to show true commitment to the team-based improvement effort. The organization's values are alive and real. Joseph Juran says senior executive involvement in the improvement process is important so they will better understand what kind of work is involved, how much time it demands, how long the process can take, and what resources and support are needed. He says, "Lack of upper-management understanding of such realities has contributed to the failure of some well-intentioned efforts to institute annual quality improvement."[10]

Internal/External Customer Listening

"The person with the closed mind is usually the one with the open mouth."

Team improvement activities need to be continually focused on their overarching goal—to provide ever higher levels of customer satisfaction at continually lower cost. That can happen only through constant and relentless external and internal customer feedback. All team improvement activities must start from a clear understanding of what the team's external or internal customers are looking for. And team members will be less than enthusiastic participants in the improvement effort if they think their own needs are not listened to and responded to.

Education and Awareness

"I am still learning."

Michelangelo's *motto*

How can a team be effective if team members don't have the big picture? Teams often are involved in improvement activities without a clear sense of how their contribution fits into organizationwide and local efforts. Or team members may not be sold on the urgency and importance of their work. Or they may believe management is taking only a halfhearted stab at improving service/quality. And if teamwork is to flourish, teams must have a steady diet of feedback, other teams' experiences, and lots of continuous learning opportunities.

Skills

"To lead an untrained people to war is to throw them away."

Confucius

In an article titled "Total Quality Management: Barriers, Strategies, and Successes," *The Quality Letter for Healthcare Leaders* reports, "What George Washington University Medical Center came to realize was that, in the past, it had never provided managers with the tools, abilities, or leadership skills needed to implement quality improvements."[11] It isn't alone. Zenger-Miller and many other researchers continually find that organizations are trying to move down the road to higher service/quality with supervisors, managers, and executives who have weak coaching and team leadership skills. Predictably, teams wander off, get lost, or fizzle out.

Extensive training in data-based tools and techniques such as statistical methods is also needed before improvement teams can do meaningful work. The University of Michigan Medical Center was one of the pioneers participating in the National Demonstration Project on Industrial Quality Control and Health Care Quality. Ellen Gaucher and Eric Kratchwill were involved in leading the effort. They write of their experiences with team-based improvement activities, "The search for the root cause of problems requires extensive training."[12] And to keep the improvement machinery well lubricated, people skills must be strengthened among team members; otherwise, the friction becomes too great and things begin to grind to a halt.

Alignment

"The only things that evolve by themselves in an organization are disorder, friction, and malperformance."

Peter Drucker

Systems, reward and recognition, and standards and measures are major cylinders that need to support improvement activities. However, a reasonably strong implementation of each of these areas takes years. While improvement teams can't wait that long to get started, key issues within these areas need to be realigned in conjunction with improvement activities. This might include removing key systems constraints (many of which are minor irritants), adjusting reward systems and especially recognition practices toward teamwork, and establishing customer-focused standards and measures that provide direction and feedback to improvement teams.

Deployment

"Quality is never an accident; it is always the result of high intention, sincere effort, intelligent direction and skillful execution; it represents the wise choice of many alternatives."

Willa A. Foster

Deming has found that many executives "take refuge in formation" of various teams because they don't know how to deal with "problems of people." He says the result is:

These groups predictably disintegrate within a few months from the frustration, finding themselves unwilling parties to a cruel hoax, unable to accomplish anything, for the simple reason that no one in management will take action on suggestions for improvement. These are devastatingly cruel devices to get rid of the problems of people.[13]

The common problem is a lack of support structure and management process to help improvement teams grow and succeed. Many are poorly formed at the wrong level and then charged with solving process or system problems that are much bigger than their scope. As this becomes frustratingly evident to the team members, they begin to realize they've been "empowered" to battle the traditional organization culture and powerful stakeholders on their own. At the University of Michigan Medical Center, Gaucher and Kratchwill report, "Although we vigorously encouraged total quality management initiatives, we failed to properly plan for their support, and chaos ensued." They found that planning for the support of the teams now involves better training, resource allocation, monitoring progress and needs, and preparing for future growth.[14]

Standardization

"Quality is not an act. It is a habit."

Aristotle, *Greek philosopher*

Standardization brings predictability. And we rely on it everyday. Because of standardization, we can buy appliances that will run on the electrical current found in our household outlets. Clothing will usually fit our size range. Software will run on the computer systems compatible with it. Telephones and fax machines can be plugged into any appropriate telephone outlet. And we can pull into traffic with some degree of confidence that other drivers will behave in predictable ways (sometimes a deadly assumption).

The same predictability that frees us from having to start from scratch with many mundane daily activities needs to be found in the multitude of processes throughout your organization. It's the only way teams can make improvements. Just like it's much harder to hit a moving target, varying performance standards make service/quality improvement a haphazard task. You don't have to be a statistician to figure out that if the reliability and variability of the input to any process is inconsistent, then that process will be harder to control. Once you put a number of these varying processes together to form a macro process or bigger system, no one knows what is going to be delivered to the customer. Dealing with the ricochets and crises that inevitably result from an uncontrolled process or system wastes the team's time and energy. Creative new improvements become impossible.

Other times process management will show that a quantum leap is needed. Wholesale innovation or "reengineering" is called for, not just improvement. Once that structural, system, or major strategic change has been made, the new process needs to become standardized before it can be continuously improved.

GETTING IMPROVEMENT TEAMS STARTED

"Every noble work is at first impossible."

Thomas Carlyle, *Scottish historian and sociological writer*

Being at the heart of continuous improvement, improvement activities are a long-term, never-ending process. A number of elements and processes need to be in place to ensure success.

However, improvement activities can be started fairly quickly. You can't wait until all the teams are at the same point of readiness to get things under way. Some of your "vital few" systems and key processes needed urgent attention yesterday. Failing to deal with them quickly not only will make the long-term "trivial many" changes difficult, but it also will be harder to convince people in your organization that you're serious about improvement.

"Quick-start" implementation plans can be developed to immediately begin working on a few strategic processes or systems. These are usually senior-level process improvement or project teams that move through an accelerated training program and rapidly begin analyzing, planning, and implementing improvements. When these efforts are successful, resources are freed across the organization or in key areas to be redeployed in the longer-term improvement process. Once the first hurdle is jumped or milestone reached, the longer-term continuous improvement process is turned over to the growing number of process, project, and intact teams within the emerging team-based organization structure.

The "quick start" implementation plan should capitalize on opportunities for small quick fixes or power fixes that will make a significant personal difference to frontline contributors. This could be solving a persistent personal issue, buying badly needed equipment or tools, repainting the office, sprucing up the cafeteria, putting in a shower, or empowering frontline contributors and junior managers by increasing their signing authority, reducing approval stages, or giving them some discretionary "seed money" to make minor improvements in the workplace. *Never underestimate the signaling power found in these seemingly puny changes.* How do you know where to begin? *Ask!!*

Starting and sustaining improvement teams will be covered further in the upcoming deployment chapters.

EXAMPLES OF IMPROVEMENT ACTIVITIES

"Never one thing and seldom one person can make for a success. It takes a number of them merging into a perfect whole."

Marie Dressler

Here are some of the activities and results seen by a few of the organizations on the road to higher service/quality.

• A process improvement team at Becton Dickinson Canada saved $750,000 in material costs, increased yield rates by 7 percent, and substantially increased quality levels in the production of surgical gloves. Using the same data-based tools and techniques and people skills, another process improvement team reduced order entry errors by 25 percent.

• In the spirit of continuous improvement, intact teams at Texaco's Bakersfield Producing Division are producing a series of small improvements that, when taken together, are accumulating into big gains. One of the warehouse quality teams made $12,000 by converting 3,000 "dirty" junk brass valves to "clean" ones. When unusually cold weather damaged a large number of flow-line valves, the team analyzed salvage opportunities and hired a crew for $500 to remove the steel handles and increase the valves' salvage value by $12,500.

- Ecolabs' Canadian division used a number of project and process improvement teams to attain these results:

  - Backorders reduced by 85 percent.
  - Rework inventories—a result of mismixes and damaged goods—reduced 61 percent.
  - Inventories of raw materials and packaging dropped 33 percent.
  - Total investments in G. H. Wood Division inventories reduced over $2 million.
  - Distribution savings of $406,000 reached in the first year with a future potential of $900,000 more identified.
  - A purchase price variance task force achieved a $1.2 million saving.
  - A vendor rating system to bring suppliers into their service/quality improvement process cut materials on hold in half early in its implementation.

- A large utility cut its rotor change time in half at one of its generating stations. The process improvement team included supervisors, union leaders, and mechanics.
- Wesley-Jessen built its process improvement and project teams around the market research and other customer data coming from the customer listening cylinder. From this it identified its three strategic processes as volume forecasting, order processing, and business resource planning. Nine project teams have been formed to look at corresponding macro issues from each core process such as reject reduction, promotion planning, performance evaluation, and color variance (in contact lens production).
- Whenever a biomedical technician needed to order a part for servicing equipment at the University of Alberta Hospitals, he or she had to get the price three times—from the supplier, clinical engineering, and material management. It took nine days to place an order. A process improvement team formed by the two departments mapped out the process and simplified it. Now orders are filled out just once. The results

are faster turnaround, better relationships with suppliers, and fewer errors.

- On its way to bagging a Baldrige, Wallace Co., Inc. had a 600 percent increase in the participation of its frontline associates, a 37-fold increase in time allocated to service/quality improvement activities, and a 12-fold increase in innovative projects from its many improvement teams. The steering committees set up a tracking process to monitor who was involved in what improvement activities. In 1990, the goal of 100 percent companywide participation was reached.

In trying to determine where its largest potential quality waste was occurring, Wallace looked at which job functions involved the greatest number of people. Inside sales and order filling came out on top. In mapping out this key macro process, 72 discrete subprocesses such as telephone answering, invoicing, inventory control, and filing were uncovered. These were then put on a Pareto chart (one of the elementary seven statistical tools teams need to learn how to use) to discover which ones made the largest contributions. The top 10 percent were found to involve 81 percent of the company's associates and contribute 85 percent of the process variation. These were then targeted for improvement by various teams.[15]

- When Ford set out to design the Taurus, it assembled a team from all steps in the overall process—from design through assembly to marketing. The team spent years visiting assembly plants, major suppliers, the Service Managers Council, and insurance companies. It amassed thousands of ideas. But team members paid particular attention to the 1,400 suggestions from Ford employees, *especially those who would build the cars*. The result was an award-winning car with very low defect rates and production costs.[16]

- When Dow Jones, owner of *The Wall Street Journal* and other media companies, decided to install a printing press, it was told by the supplier that it would mean six weeks of repeated plant shutdowns. An operations team of employees developed a process that had the machinery operating within *six days*. The team has since improved the installation process so that it can be done over a weekend with *no* downtime.[17]

- At GM and Toyota's joint manufacturing venture, NUMMI, employees are extensively involved in running the plant through improvement teams. Despite below-average levels of automation, the plant quickly became top in productivity of all GM's plants. The absenteeism and grievance rates are also among GM's lowest. And the cars produced in NUMMI's plant are among the highest-quality cars built in North America.[18]

- "Workers who were once supposed to shut up and take orders are now encouraged to use their brains. A team of hourly and salaried employees figured out how to reduce from 52 to 30 the number of parts in the rear floor of Cadillacs and big Oldsmobiles. That squashed the number of stamping presses used from 93 to 10 . . . annual savings: a dazzling $52 million."[19]

COMMON IMPROVEMENT ACTIVITIES PITFALLS AND TRAPS

"Before you take aim, check your ammunition."

Jumping the Gun

Eager to begin enjoying the benefits of service/quality improvement teams, *too many organizations plunge ahead before they're ready.* A nurturing environment, supportive structure, all built on a solid skills foundation, must be in place before work on improvement activities can begin. While carefully selected quick-start activities should get under way immediately, the full implementation of this cylinder is phase two or even three of the long-term improvement process.

Underinvesting in Tools, Techniques, and Training

When the incredible results achieved by high-performing improvement teams are reported, the amount of investment made to equip those teams is often missed. *A direct and positive correlation exists between the results obtained and the amount of training and retraining given to the team members and their leaders.*

In Another World

Improvement teams can't function outside of the organization's systems. Team-based improvement activities are not separate "programs" to make a few changes around the fringes; they change the way work is done in the organization. Supervisors, managers, and executives must be held accountable for the success of the improvement teams within their area or under their guidance.

Baffling Boundaries

Improvement teams need clear mandates, parameters, and coordination; otherwise, they will just spin their wheels needlessly, overreach their mandate, or trip over each other. That's why steering committees and councils are so vital. And management needs to make it very clear that the partnership being built is a dynamic relationship that will give ever greater management responsibility to intact and process improvement teams as they strengthen and develop.

That's how top performing organizations are able to stay so lean—keeping managerial and professional overheads down while increasing flexibility and customer responsiveness.

Out of Focus

Improvement teams should always begin by focusing on external customers' expectations and tracing those back through the chain of service/quality to the process, functions, or activities the team is trying to improve. The best way to do that is to make frequent customer visits and do lots of customer listening. Another excellent way to stay customer-focused is to bring a constant stream of customers in to work with the improvement team. This step is especially important if the team's focus is on serving internal customers.

Rickety Rewards and Recognition

A key performance criterion for all managers, but especially senior executives, must be the amount of recognizing, celebrating, and hoopla they lavish on improvement teams making progress. The annual service/quality report, visible team measurements, and so on give managers the information they need to "catch people doing things right." If your organization is to sustain the momentum for the long improvement journey, this reinforcement *must stay at the top* of management's "to do" lists. It's a key source of team energy.

Team Mania

We constantly find organizations in trouble because they have launched too many improvement teams. The long and difficult transformation process to a team-based organization doesn't happen overnight. The first teams need a lot of training, nourishing, and support. As management learns how to lead, develop, and align a team-based organization and the success of improvement teams becomes clear, the number of teams can be rapidly increased.

Chapter Eighteen

Cylinder 11:
Standards and Measures

"Service quality can be measured. It is important to do so; because if you don't measure it, you won't improve it."
"The Strategic Management of Service Quality,"
PIMS Letter, the Strategic Planning Institute

*W*hat gets measured gets managed. Unless, and until, your organization aligns both the standards used to focus work activities and the measures used to provide feedback on everyone's progress with your overarching service/quality vision, you won't get far. Baldrige director Curt Reimann reports:

> The good companies adopt measures to assess where they're starting and to project where they're headed. Without measures, there's no sense of qualitative improvement. You're not going to improve your company's quality with a Monday morning meeting. There really is much more of a science to this than many people realize.[1]

Ron Zemke and Dick Schaaf found well-aligned standards and measures to be a key reason for the success of the companies they studied: "Far from leaving anything to chance, the Service 101 establish clear, customer-oriented performance standards throughout their organizations and then constantly and meticulously measure performance against those standards."[2]

THE BOTTOM LINE IS HISTORY

"Neither the quantity of output nor the 'bottom line' is by itself an adequate measure of the performance of management and enterprise."

Peter Drucker, *The New Realities*[3]

Traditional techno-managers have no trouble with the idea of performance standards and measures. Their organizations are brimming with them. But they are sophisticated (read, complex) measures of the wrong things. Proud of their bottom-line focus, techno-managers pay attention to end results instead of to the factors and processes that produce those results. And that, paradoxically, leads to lower results. Techno-managers spend more time counting and splitting the beans than figuring out how to grow more or keep them from spoiling.

The financial measures and systems that were so helpful in bringing order, control, and efficiency to the explosive economic growth of the 1950s, 60s, and 70s are now choking service/quality improvement. In *Relevance Lost: The Rise and Fall of Management Accounting,* Thomas Johnson and Robert Kaplan report that a growing number of experts are concluding, "Cost accounting is the number-one enemy of productivity." In his article titled, "The Performance Measurement Manifestor," Robert Eccles, Harvard Business School professor of business administration, writes:

> Many managers worry that income-based financial figures are better at measuring the consequences of yesterday's decisions than they are at indicating tomorrow's performance. Events of the past decade substantiate this concern. During the 1980s, many executives saw their companies' strong financial records deteriorate because of unnoticed declines in quality or customer satisfaction or because global competitors ate into their market share.[4]

Only through effectively measuring and managing the processes and factors that both increase your customers' perceptions of value and reduce your costs of poor quality will your financial results show winning scores. *By the time service/quality problems show up on your bottom line, you are way behind and in very serious trouble.* Solid service/quality measures act as an early warning system to whatever your bottom-line results are. Once you've isolated your key service/quality indicators and are closely monitoring them, they will help you see in advance what your organizational results will be—whether, for example, revenues are likely to move upward and costs head south, or the other way around.

TYPES OF MEASURES

"Just as a human being needs a diversity of measures to assess his or her health and performance, an organization needs a diversity of measures to assess its health and performance."
Peter Drucker[5]

As with the listening cylinder, measures can be broadly divided into those that are external and those that are internal. While the improvement process moves from the inside out, *good service/quality measures move from the outside in.* It all starts with external customer listening. Here's how the application for the Malcolm Baldrige National Quality Award puts it: ''. . . indicators should be selected to best represent the attributes that link customer requirements, customer satisfaction, and competitive performance as well as to operational effectiveness and efficiency.'' One rapidly growing approach that does this particularly well is quality function deployment (see page 121).

But the development of effective service/quality measures starts one step before customer listening. As our implementation architecture diagram shows (see page 99), it all starts with senior management's vision. The senior team must be able to answer these questions *in unison*: (1) What business are we in (our strategic niche)? (2) What do we believe in (the values that will guide everyone's behavior)? (3) Where are we going (the vision of our *preferred* future)? Standards and measures are then aligned with the data generated by customer listening that identify the gap between the vision, external and internal expectations in the areas defined by the vision, and current perceived performance levels. The Malcolm Baldrige application explains what this leads to at top service/quality organizations: ''A system of indicators thus represents a clear and objective basis for aligning all activities of the company toward well-defined goals and for tracking progress toward the goals.''

In reporting on the massive shift in performance measurement, Harvard Business School's Robert Eccles writes, ''At the heart of the revolution lies a radical decision: to shift from treating financial figures as the foundation for performance measurement to treating them as one among a broader set of measures.'' He adds, ''Quality measures represent the most positive step taken to date in broadening the basis of business performance measurement.''[6] In many high-performing organizations, senior executives in performance review meetings look at their key service/quality indicators and set action plans for the next steps in the continuous improvement journey. As one said, ''The financials—which provide historical scores—can be read on the plane after the meeting.''

Let's look at the service/quality measures helping organizations move ahead by looking out in front—not just in the rearview mirror.

Customer Satisfaction Measures

''The design and delivery of products and services begins with understanding stated and latent customer needs. Similarly, measurements of performance and improvement efforts should reflect the customer perspective.''

Pauline Brody, *chairperson, The Xerox Quality Forum II*[7]

As obvious as it may seem, many organizations speeding down the road to higher service/quality fall into the trap of rigorously measuring the service/quality results that are important to *them* or that they *think* their customers care about. This trap seems to ensnare many quality control and quality assurance professionals. Too often, they install data-based tools and techniques such as statistical methods or implement process management and do a great job of measuring the wrong things. The same is true for many of the standards set by service companies. Valarie Zeithaml, A. Parasuraman, and Len Berry conclude from their extensive studies:

> While some similarity may exist between customers' requirements and company standards, we find many instances where service companies are measuring and monitoring internal standards for features that customers do not care about while ignoring other features that customers do care about.[8]

What to measure and where to start is simple: *Start with those things your customers consider important.* In other words, your customers' (not your own) perceptions of what constitutes high service/quality must be at the center of your improvement strategies and measurements. For this reason, this cylinder is closely tied to customer listening (Chapter 8). You can't effectively measure your service/quality results unless you have been listening to your customers and developing a constant stream of *solid data* (not general impressions or hunches) on what's important to them. Otherwise, you could find yourself setting up measurements on product or service dimensions your customers don't care about. In *Managing Quality*, David Garvin warns, "An especially serious error of this sort is using long-standing quality metrics to set internal quality goals even though the external environment has changed."[9]

What do customers care most about?

"All versions of reality are in the nature of fiction. There is your story and my story, there's the journalist's story and the historian's story, there is the philosopher's and the scientist's story . . . reality is imagined."

Ronald Sukenick

Texas A&M Marketing Professor Len Berry has worked with Valarie Zeithaml, A. Parasuraman, and other market researchers to clarify which service dimensions customers are most concerned about. From focus groups and survey research in a variety of industries, they developed five statistically derived factors they call ServQual:

- *Tangibles*—appearance of physical facilities, equipment, personnel, and communications materials.
- *Reliability*—ability to perform the promised service dependably and accurately.
- *Responsiveness*—willingness to help customers and provide prompt service.
- *Assurance*—knowledge and courtesy of employees and their ability to convey trust and confidence.
- *Empathy*—caring, individualized attention the firm provides its customers.

Berry and his colleagues studied which of these are the most important to customers. They found:

> . . . reliability is the most critical dimension, *regardless of the service being studied* . . . an important message from customers to service providers: Appear neat and organized, be responsive, be reassuring, be empathic, and most of all, be reliable—*do what you say you are going to do* (their emphasis).[10]

However, as is too often the case, Berry and colleagues continually find that organizations are often performing most poorly on the dimensions customers care most about.

Whether these ServQual factors capture what is important to your organization's success is a question only your customers can answer. The big question is, *how do you know?*

Cues to customer satisfaction

"Sometimes the more measurable drives out the most important."

Rene Dubos

The customer listening cylinder uses a variety of methods to collect data on customer expectations, perceived value, and performance. Here are a few examples of the internal indicators most often monitored for early warning signs of customer dissatisfaction (as well as potential product, process, and cost problems). Negative trends in these indicators call for deeper analysis and more rigorous customer listening and measurement:

- Tracking and analyzing complaint patterns.
- Monitoring accounts receivable average days outstanding and identifying root causes of credit notes and other symptoms of quality problems.

- Regularly reviewing and analyzing customer feedback from surveys, 800 telephone numbers, suggestion systems, focus groups, advisory panels, user groups and conferences, as well as managing by wandering around among customers.
- Quantifying and analyzing the feedback and observations of frontline servers, salespeople, distributors or dealers, and improvement teams visiting customers.
- Tracking and studying trends in the "moments of truth" within the customer's line of visibility such as accuracy in delivery, invoicing, or reservations, response time, overbookings, product or service availability.

Process Measures

"The winning companies measure all of their processes. Motorola, for example, measures every one of its activities. They talk of defects per opportunity. Companies that aren't doing as well have limited measurements and limited access to comparative measurements."

Curt Reimann, *director of the Malcolm Baldrige National Quality Award*[11]

It's hard to improve what isn't defined. And it's hard to manage what isn't measured. As we saw in the last chapter, managing task-level, functional, and strategic processes is at the heart of service/quality improvement. *Significant and continuous process improvement can happen only with rigorous and continuous data-based process measurement.* Process measurement starts with customer listening and works its way back through the chain of service/quality. Each step in the multitude of processes and work activities, and each link in the chain, is a potential measurement point. The challenge, as with so much on the road to higher service/quality, is to keep things as useful and as simple as possible. *The key to effective measurement of service/quality is a small number of simple measures that channel the organization's energy and focus on the strategic areas with the highest potential return.*

Providing crisp and well-focused process measures typically means a massive change in the type, methods, and use of information systems. Many managers are, to use *Megatrends* author John Naisbitt's words, "drowning in information but starved for knowledge." In a report to a senior manager who asked for an assessment of the company's quality management process, Deming writes:

I find that in spite of the profusion of figures that you collect in your company, you are not discovering the main causes of poor quality. Costly computers turning out volumes of records will not improve quality. . . . An important step, as I see it, would be for you to take a hard look at your production of figures—your so-called information system. Fewer figures and better information about your processes and their capabilities would lead to improved uniformity (decreased variation—the prime cause of errors) and greater output, all at reduced cost.[12]

Data-based tools and techniques, particularly statistical methods, are vital to process measurement and continuous improvement. Every improvement team needs to know how to use basic control or run charts, causes-and-effect diagrams, check sheets, scatter diagrams, and the like. That's why building that skill foundation is so important. Just like everyone involved in business planning and budgeting had to learn financial language and tools, you and every team leader and member involved need to learn the language and tools of the service/quality improvement process. When a senior vice president doesn't know the difference between a Pareto chart, a flow chart, and a run chart, members of his or her improvement teams will be demoralized and unproductive.

In the search for process variability, auditing the process itself is critical. This involves asking questions like, Do standard operating procedures and checklists exist? Are they being followed? Are steps being performed the same way each time? The answers to these questions can spotlight sources of errors and inconsistencies. However, the reasons the process is weak or inconsistent often take you deeper into organizational systems, lack of good macro system management, low team member or leadership skill levels, unaligned reward and recognition, and so on.

Every process has quality indicators that, like a body's vital signs, reveal the process's basic health. *Continuous process improvement demands that these key indicators be identified and tracked*. In an organization that is well along the road to higher service/quality, every intact and process improvement team tracks its key process indicators. These are chosen in conjunction with the customers they are serving in the chain of service/quality and within the blueprint of organizationwide process maps. The indicators are generally posted for all to see and are widely published. A big part of the value of quality indicators is clear and broad visibility. When this is done in the spirit of the Basic Principles (page 165), vertical chimneys are smashed, the organization is flattened (you don't need staff checkers and management cops), and cross-functional coordination is enhanced.

Many organizations have hundreds, if not thousands, of quality indicators for all the macro and micro processes and work activities. But just as a weak pulse or erratic heartbeat doesn't automatically pinpoint the cause of the problem, quality indicators only show whether or not there is a problem. Further analysis is needed to get to the root cause of poor quality indicator results. And if your goal is continuous improvement, reliable process quality indicators are vital to measuring progress and assessing the effectiveness of improvement actions taken. Here are a few examples:

- Back-order rates.
- Accuracy rates in orders filled and shipped, invoicing, correspondence, computer codes, financial statements, claims processed, baggage handled, medication, lab tests, deliveries, and so on.
- Turnaround times.
- Response rates.
- Warranty claims.
- Rework or "redo" frequencies.
- Scrap and waste rates.
- Accidents.
- Mortality rates.
- Customer calls for help.
- Usage levels.
- Yields.
- System or production downtime rates.
- Phone call or personal wait times.
- Merchandise returned.
- Items out of stock.
- Inventory levels.
- Engineering changes.
- Completeness of files and records.
- Customer, employee, or management turnover rates.
- Energy usage.
- And so on.

Product Measures

"Order marches with weighty and measured strides; disorder is always in a hurry."
Napoleon Bonaparte

Product measures are usually quantifiable measures or indexes indicating the reliability, conformance to specifications, or effectiveness of a basic product or service. In manufacturing, visual inspections and sample testing (ideally statistical sampling) of the product have been done by quality control departments for decades. But these methods often don't test the "robustness" of a product's design under actual strenuous field operating conditions. In his study of manufacturers of room air conditioners, David Garvin reports on one method of tracking a product's reliability under actual operating conditions:

> The best and better plants generally had sophisticated computer systems that tracked field failures by individual models and components. To ensure rapid feedback, several plants had developed early warning systems that projected SCRs (service call rates) from limited data, sometimes using elaborate statistical methods.[13]

But because many companies don't have long lead times and don't want to risk their reputation testing various product designs in their customer's hands, "design of experiments" has become very popular among manufacturers. These are advanced statistical methods refined by Genichi Taguchi (so they are often called the Taguchi methods) to test combinations of various design and operating conditions. Computers are used to test possible combinations, which can run into the thousands with complex products.

Product testing can get very complicated or it can be fairly straightforward. More basic product measures might include electrical testing of components, test-driving new cars, final inspection of a new piece of machinery against a standard checklist, validation and pilot testing a new training system, or visual inspection and count of seminar binders before shipment.

Project Measures

"It's a funny thing about life, if you refuse to accept anything but the very best you very often get it."

William Somerset Maugham, *English novelist*

Successful project teams start with a clear mandate or goal. This could be a very broad macro process or organizationwide system improvement with a series of cascading teams, or it could be a fairly small, localized mission. However, as Yogi Berra once said, "If you don't know where you are going, chances are you'll end up someplace else." Project teams need clear goals either established by the project sponsors and agreed to by the team or set by the project team.

Project measures then are based on the project team's original mandate or goal. These measures monitor progress on the project, provide feedback, and once they are fulfilled, signal it is time to celebrate the team's success and either disband this temporary group or renew its mandate. No project team should ever be allowed to get started without first setting a clear and well-understood goal and corresponding measures. Typical project measures are money saved, cycle time reduced, time or effort saved, accuracy levels increased, errors reduced, customer satisfaction increased, downtime reduced, sales improved, decreased injuries, customer complaints diminished. . . .

Cost of Quality

"Measure twice and saw once."

As outlined in Chapter 3, cost of quality is the total cost to your organization of achieving its current level of service/quality performance. You may want to quickly review the bad COQ and good COQ that make up total cost of quality (page 48). Top service/quality providers have dramatically reduced their total COQ by investing in the good COQ to reduce bad COQ.

Cost of quality measures help organizations assess the return on investment of their service/quality efforts. Establishing your cost of poor quality, or bad COQ, can be an extremely useful way to rivet senior management's attention to the improvement effort. Elaborate COQ auditing procedures and methods are available. However, they often prove to be more expensive and time consuming than they are worth. Joseph Juran writes, "Experience shows that estimates are good enough. They provide information that is adequate for managerial decision making, and they do so with much less work and far less time."[14]

In the first stages of your improvement journey, you can get a sense of your worst areas of bad COQ by asking your people where they see the most waste. This can be done through the "blue/green card" process and other system assessment methods as outlined in Chapter 15. Pareto charts and other data-based tools and techniques can help you sort through the improvement opportunities and identify those that will provide the highest payoff for project, process improvement, and intact teams to tackle.

In beginning your improvement journey, you can chase your tail and get too detailed in COQ auditing. However, over the next few years, you will want to realign your cost accounting system to expose the huge and hidden bad cost of quality buried in your general and administrative overheads.

Measuring the Quality Improvement Process

"Hold yourself responsible for a higher standard than anybody else expects of you. Never excuse yourself."

Henry Ward Beecher, *American Congregational clergyman and writer*

To assess your progress in any long journey, you need to know how far you have come and how far you have to go to reach your next milestone. Assessing the quality of your service/quality improvement process is an invaluable way to ensure you're on the right track and your organization has its improvement priorities straight. World-class auditing processes like the Deming Application Prize, the Malcolm Baldrige National Quality Award, International Quality Standards (ISO 9000, Z299, Q90, Z8101), and the Canada Award for Business Excellence are based on the best practices of top service/quality providers. Measuring your improvement efforts against these audits and assessments allows you to learn from the experiences of others who have traveled this route before you. This saves your organization years of frustration and wasted effort heading down dead ends and taking big detours trying to find the route to higher performance. We will look at this useful measuring process further in Chapter 21.

Benchmarking

"Everyone takes the limits of his or her own field of vision for the limits of the world."

Arthur Schopenhauer, *German philosopher*

For years, runners, physicians, and various experts believed it was impossible to run a mile in less than four minutes. Then Roger Bannister did it. Within a short time, a number of others broke that barrier. Today, high school kids are running a mile in less than four minutes. Whether it's flying a machine through the air, landing on the moon, or sending a voice through wires, once an old paradigm has been shattered and replaced with a new one, people rapidly change perspectives and quickly move to building on the new possibilities. Time and time again, the limits to most systems, processes, methods, practices, or science turn out to be between our ears. Most barriers are psychological.

One of your biggest challenges will be getting your people to break their old we've-always-done-it-this-way paradigm and see new possibilities. Many of your processes and systems have become like oak trees planted in flowerpots; they have enormous growth potential but are severely constrained by artificially imposed limits. In the late 1970s, as Xerox was beginning to struggle for its life, benchmarking played a major role in turning things around. *Benchmarking* is a term taken from land surveying for a mark used as a reference point for elevation or direction comparisons.

One of the North American fathers of benchmarking is Robert Camp, who started the process in the logistics operations at Xerox. In his landmark book, *Benchmarking: The Search for Industry Best Practices That Lead to Superior Performance*, he writes:

> Benchmarking is the search for those best practices that will lead to superior performance of a company. . . . Traditional target-setting methods have failed U.S. managers and blindsided them to foreign competition. The Japanese term *dantotsu*, which means striving to be the "best of the best," incorporates the essence of the process they use to establish competitive advantage. We Americans have no such word, perhaps because we always assumed we were the best. We cannot assume that anymore.

Xerox CEO David Kearns says, "Benchmarking is the continuous process of measuring products, services, and practices against the toughest competitors or those companies recognized as industry leaders."[15]

Camp established four common types of benchmarking: (1) internal benchmarking—a comparison of internal operations, (2) competitive benchmarking—specific competitor-to-competitor comparisons for the product or function of interest, (3) functional benchmarking—comparisons to similar functions within the same broad industry or to industry leaders, and (4) generic benchmarking—comparison of business functions or processes that are the same regardless of industry.[16]

Benchmarking has a science to it, but it is really more of an art form. Getting information on other organizations, particularly competitors, can be a challenge. But as Camp says, "Sources of information are limited only by ones imagination."[17] This might include researching magazine articles or gathering industry or process statistics. Many top service/quality providers are very open about their best practices and will host visits, plant tours, and the like (that's how many Japanese firms set their first benchmarks against American companies in the 50s and 60s). In fact, Baldrige winners are required to provide this kind of guidance to advance American competitiveness through service/quality improvement.

Benchmarking is proving to be a very powerful antidote against paradigm paralysis. When management and improvement teams see that someone else is doing "what could never be done," traditional barriers and limits are destroyed and replaced by a new vision of what is possible. This often leads to establishment of much more aggressive improvement goals, higher service/quality standards, and major process and system breakthroughs. As the English poet and painter William Blake once observed, "What is now proved was once only imagined."

EXAMPLES OF STANDARDS AND MEASURES

"It is a capital mistake to theorize before one has data. Insensibly one begins to twist the facts to suit theories, instead of theories to suit facts."

The Adventures of Sherlock Holmes: Scandal in Bohemia

• During a three-year period, National Sea Products (High Liner is one of its brand names) reduced order-entry errors from 30 percent to 5 percent by identifying and tracking the 14 top problem areas in the entire process, initiating improvement activities in each area, and monitoring each area's key indicators. Visibility and wide publication of improvement progress and these indicators are fueling the drive to push the error rate even lower.

• One of the fundamental precepts Federal Express bases its successful service/quality improvement efforts on is "you can't manage what you can't measure." For many years, FedEx measured itself by percentage of on-time deliveries. In 1985, the company started an extensive series of customer satisfaction studies to see what yardsticks customers used to measure performance. The first thing the company realized was that what it thought was an outstanding delivery success rate of 99.1 percent translated into 2.5 million failures per year. That added up to a lot of negative "moments of truth" that turned off customers and created bad word of mouth.

Federal Express also learned that the customer's scorecard boiled down to 12 critical areas. But each one was not equal in severity in the customer's eyes. Through further research, FedEx developed a weighting scheme to assess its performance across the 12 dimensions. These "service quality indicators" are used to prioritize improvement activities; align reward, recognition, and other systems; and so on. Here are the categories and weights assigned to each failure:

Missed pickups	10 points
Lost packages	10 points
Damaged packages	10 points
Delivery on wrong day	5 points
Complaints rehandled	5 points
Overgoods	5 points
Delivery late on the right day	1 point
Invoice adjustments requested by customer	1 point
Calls abandoned by customers	1 point
Missing proof of delivery information	1 point
An international service quality indicator	1 point
Traces	1 point[18]

• A Pareto analysis of Wallace Co., Inc.'s, customer research data showed the three most important service/quality measures to its customers were on-time delivery performance, complete and accurate shipments, and error-free transactions. These criteria, along with product quality measures, were used to monitor the performance of suppliers.

These three customer criteria have also been used to establish every internal department's service/quality indicators. For example, order fillers track location errors, inventory availability errors, and percent of rush orders; receiving tracks vendor shipping errors; truck drivers track the number of scheduled deliveries not made, abnormal delays in unloading at customer locations, and improper loading of trucks; data entry monitors computer downtime at each branch and the number of documents processed versus the number that were complete when received; and accounts receivable tracks the reasons for credit memos and receivable days. Vice President and General Operations Manager Carl Anderson says, "For the first time in the history of this company we know exactly what's going on at every level. That kind of knowledge is power."

Over three years, Wallace's on-time delivery performance rose from 75 percent to 92 percent. Shipping accuracy and error-free transactions have remained very low during a 66 percent increase in the ratio of sales per employee. Many of Wallace's customers no longer find it necessary to check and verify the materials delivered to their locations.[19]

• Wesley-Jessen set up "service quality centers" throughout the company to help everyone "watch our progress on several service quality issues that affect the ultimate service we give to our external customers." Displays show back orders from the last day of each month, average daily sales, number of external customer phone calls connected in three rings, number of customer service and product complaints, examples of improvements from around the company, and complaint or compliment letters from customers.

Jim Moritz reports, "W-J has adopted six sigma (3.4 defects per million) as our standard measurement in those projects and processes where this measurement tool is applicable." It has also developed a ricochet tracking system software package that allows it to code, track, and measure every ricochet card received from an employee. Moritz says, "The end result is to correct every major ricochet with a written procedure that standardizes the process and permanently eliminates the error."

- Toyota Motor Sales U.S.A. conducts a new vehicle sales and delivery survey (NVSDS) of new car buyers. The Toyota service survey (TSS) goes to those customers who have had recent warranty work. The survey data are used to establish Toyota's three key indexes—the NVSDS index, TSS index, and OSI (owner satisfaction index). These indexes are the company's primary measurement tools and are used extensively to align systems, in reward and recognition, as well as in improvement activities throughout the company. Toyota also does competitive benchmarking by comparing its results to studies from Consumer Reports, Maritz data, and J. D. Power and Associates surveys.

Indexes and other feedback from the surveys is sent daily to dealers through the computer system. A monthly index report to each dealership gives the sales and service departments a snapshot of their customer satisfaction and provides comparative benchmark data for other Toyota dealers in their market area as well as nationwide. Dealer and executive bonuses and recognition programs are based on the indexes. Also, product quality reports and a product problem matrix report detailing problems for each model and component (air-conditioning, instrument panel, drivetrain, etc.) are sent monthly to worldwide headquarters in Japan. There the data are used to drive multifaceted, extensive design and manufacturing improvement efforts.

In 1990, Toyota's U.S. sales were up 12 percent compared to an overall industry decline of 6 percent.[20]

- Xerox's warehousing operation shattered its old paradigm and set dramatically higher performance standards and improvement goals after benchmarking with L. L. Bean's warehouse operation. In 1982, Robert Camp explains, Xerox learned L. L. Bean was "able to pick almost three times as many lines per man-day as the most efficient (Xerox) warehouse planned at the time." While the two operations were fairly different in the type of materials handled, "the L. L. Bean picking operation (was) substantially better than at Xerox." This provided the inspiration and example for Xerox's warehouse operations to make substantial improvements in the following years.[21]

- Based on extensive customer listening (focus groups, extensive surveys, customer visits, user groups, and so on), Hewlett-Packard separated its customer's definition of service/quality into two broad categories. The first category is the quality of the product. These standards and measures are:

- Functionality—the feature set, capabilities, compatibility, and security.
- Usability—the human factors, consistency, and documentation of the product.
- Reliability—the frequency and severity of failures, the predictability and accuracy of the product.
- Performance—the speed and efficiency of the product as well as the resource consumption.
- Supportability—maintainability and serviceability of the product along with its ability to be installed.

The second service/quality category refers to the quality of the relationship with the customer. These standards and measures are:

- Anticipation—the ability to identify, understand, and help solve customer needs before they become problems.
- Availability—the degree to which our products and services provide for uninterrupted usage at full functionality.
- Responsiveness—the ability to provide timely, accurate, and complete information and/or solutions to customer initiated requests for help.
- Transitions—the ease of initial startup and of ongoing changes as individual products and services evolve and conform to new needs and technologies.

These customer standards and measures drive a series of internal indicators such as response time, repair time, system downtime, turnaround time, installation times, customer-perceived quality of product education, and effectiveness of remote equipment diagnosis systems.[22]

- At Avco Financial Services' Canadian operation, a special task force was created to devise tools to measure quality. It took 12 people three months to develop the field quality index. The index has hundreds of components, including yardsticks such as customer retention, delinquency, and receivables. Among other monitoring techniques is an ongoing "Tell Us If You Love Us" customer poll run by branch offices and a periodic president's survey mailed directly to customers.
- Sewell Village Cadillac in Dallas, Texas, has built a thriving business and gained international renown for its obsessive attention to continual

service/quality improvement. Measurement has long been a cornerstone of its efforts. For example, a computerized system was installed to inform customer service representatives (called "lot lizards" at many dealerships) which cars to bring from the lot. The time it took to deliver the car to the customer was tracked and posted for all to see. Within a short time, average elapsed time dropped from four and a half minutes to two. Believing measurement is critical to improved service/quality, Carl Sewell says, "We measure everything we can think of in this dealership, and we share everything we measure."[23]

• Becton Dickinson Canada used classical process control techniques to further reduce the number of pinholes in its surgical gloves. Statistical measures were charted daily for all to see. An improvement team used fishbone diagrams and problem-solving techniques to narrow in on potential causes of pinholes. The manufacturing process was adjusted, quality trends charted, manufacturing adjusted, and so on, until quality exceeded the original goals.

• "The manufacturing people at both Motorola and Westinghouse have chosen lead-time reduction as a dominant measure; various divisions of Hewlett-Packard and General Electric have too," says Richard Schonberger in *World Class Manufacturing*. "Lead time is a sure and truthful measure, because a plant can reduce it only by solving problems that cause delays. . . . One by one, top companies are coming to the conclusion that reducing lead time is a simple and powerful measure of how well you're doing."[24]

COMMON STANDARDS AND MEASURES PITFALLS AND TRAPS

"The greatest of all faults I should say is to be conscious of none."

Thomas Carlyle, *British essayist and historian*

Inside-Out Measurement

Take a hard look at the assumptions on which your current performance standards and measures are based. Do your measures satisfy management's command-and-control paranoia ("snoopervision")? Are they inner-ring, product-focused? Where do your *customers'* needs and perceptions figure into your measurement and feedback systems? If they aren't shaping your *entire* measurement chain, you're destined to wander off track—and not even know it.

Managing Results

Results are the outcome: They can't be managed any more than you can turn back time. Like a score, they are a historical record of how you did. In competitive sports, you improve your score by improving your play in key strategic areas. To know what part of the game needs work, players need specific feedback. To improve service/quality, start by measuring key production processes and delivery steps.

The Measurement Stick

If measures are used as "gotchas" by management, not only will employees look for ways to "sweeten" the feedback making it less relevant, but they also will not own the improvement needed to ensure their success. Ron Zemke and Dick Schaaf write, "When the feedback system doesn't work, it's often because the information gathered is used incorrectly. It has stopped being feedback and become a chore, a threat, or something to be avoided."[25]

Moving Targets

Ensure that consistent measurement systems are used long enough to identify trends. Constant changes not only send inconsistent signals but also make progress tracking impossible.

Secret and Selective Feedback

Information on the standards and measures being used by intact, project, and process improvement teams should be highly visible and open to everyone. In top service/quality organizations, for example, there is a proliferation of charts and graphs showing trends in service/quality indicators within every functional department, process improvement team, and at many workstations. Tom Peters writes, "Access to virtually all information, by everyone at every level and on a continuous basis, is a vital part of quality-oriented change. It's at the core of the self-discipline, self-control, self-starting process."[26] Adds T. J. Rodgers, CEO of Cypress Semiconductor, "At Cypress, we collect information in such detail and share it so widely that the company is virtually transparent. This works against the political infighting and bureaucratic obfuscation that cripple so many organizations."[27]

Slow and Sluggish

Avoid acting too slowly or invisibly on feedback gathered. Completing surveys and providing "how are we doing" input leads people to expect signs of improvement. It's a major turnoff to think the whole activity was an exercise in futility.

Confusing Knowing and Doing

Deming says, "Measurement of productivity doesn't improve productivity."[28] Weighing yourself 10 times a day will not reduce your weight. No matter how sophisticated your standards and measures are, they are indicators only. Improvement happens through pulling teams together to analyze and improve activities, processes, and systems. Standards provide the improvement goals, and measures provide the feedback.

Set in Stone

Like the rest of the improvement process, standards and measures must be dynamic. They need to be continuously improving to keep up with your rapidly changing customer needs, the growing strength of your improvement teams, and evolving systems and measurement technology. Robert Eccles writes, "We are talking about a new philosophy of performance measurement that regards it as an ongoing, evolving process. And just as igniting the revolution will take special effort, so will maintaining its momentum and reaping the rewards in the years ahead."[29]

Chapter Nineteen

Cylinder 12:
Marketing Strategies

"The way to gain a reputation is to endeavor to be what you desire to appear."
Socrates,
Athenian philosopher

T he marketing strategies cylinder both precedes and follows the other 11 cylinders, so we will look at it in two parts. First, we'll look at the pivotal role your service/quality strategy plays in focusing the entire improvement effort before you can even get into any of the cylinders. This part of marketing strategies is a key element of the vision that heads our implementation architecture (page 99). When executed effectively, it answers the vital question, "What business are we in?" In the second part of this cylinder, we'll look at how effective marketing strategies build on, integrate with, and amplify the other improvement cylinders. We'll briefly see how marketing strategies help to build on and expand your customers' perceptions of value.

PART ONE: STRATEGY DETERMINES YOUR DESTINATION

"When a man does not know what harbor he is making for, no wind is the right wind."
Seneca, *Roman statesman and philosopher*

Harvard Business School Professor Michael Porter is a world-renowned expert on competitive strategy. He defines strategy as "a word that has many meanings and has been used in many ways. In business terms, strategy is fundamentally how to position a company in its competitive environment in a way which allows it to gain advantage against its competitors."[1] Positioning your organization (whether or not you have direct competitors) demands a clear focus on why you exist—what business you're in. In a *Fortune* article on the radical new approaches to long-term planning that have been emerging in the 1990s, Ronald Henkoff writes:

> Focus means figuring out, and building on, what the company does best. It means identifying the evolving needs of your customers, then developing the key skills—often called core competencies—critical to serving them. It means setting a clear, realistic mission and then working tirelessly to make sure everyone—from the chairman to the middle manager to the hourly employee—understands it.[2]

In the all too common absence of clear strategic focus, huge investments in customer listening, education and awareness, hiring and orienting, skill development, systems, reward and recognition, implementation activities, and standards and measures are either wasted, hit and miss, or badly underpowered. No matter how fast or well you travel down these roads, if they are not coming together to take you to your destination, you're wasting everybody's time. *Have you and your executive team agreed on your destination?*

A widespread and deadly trap many organizations fall into is failing to establish and lock in a key strategic focus. Many executive teams lack the clarity of vision or discipline to set their long-term core strategy and maintain their aim through the trial, error, and learning process that is part of every successful follow-through. Instead, they try to be everything to everybody or drift aimlessly from one short-term strategy to another searching for the magic formula that will catapult them to higher performance. In *The Customer Is Key: Gaining an Unbeatable Advantage through Customer Satisfaction*, Lele and Sheth report the haphazard use of generic strategies was one of the distinguishing characteristics of the lesser performers in their study. They write:

> Management will typically aim simultaneously to improve reliability, increase parts availability, reduce repair times, and, for good measure, cut product costs. Consequently, while a great deal of money may be spent, there is little tangible improvement in after-sales support or customer satisfaction.[3]

Like core values, your core strategy needs to be boiled down to something simple. This not only makes it more memorable, but it also forces management to zero in on the essence of the organization's being. That means a narrower focus. This makes alignment of organizational resources and activities much clearer. Not only does this more sharply define the road ahead for everyone in the organization, but it also allows your customers, suppliers, and other outsiders to get a better fix on who you are and what you do. As Karl Albrecht puts it, a strategy statement "explains the unique selling proposition that defines your positioning in your market."[4] Lele and Sheth illustrate how a clear, well-defined strategy statement can pull things together: "(John) Deere's entire strategy can be summarized in its slogan, 'Nothing runs like a Deere.' Everything and everyone—from design to testing to manufacturing to sales and right on through the dealer network—are oriented to keeping the customer's machine up and running."[5]

Developing a long-term strategy and boiling it down to a simple statement should be uncomplicated. Porter advises, "To have a strategy doesn't mean that you go through some formal process of developing one; it just means that through some mechanism, you've got a vision and you're implicitly following it." He reports his work shows "the odds of success are raised by going through the development of strategy in a conscious way." Porter does go on to argue for a formal planning process, although it should be done in a nonbureaucratic and informal way:

> A formal process may be nothing more than simply getting your management together one Saturday every year at your house and spending the morning thinking about the long term. . . . (This) gives you an excuse to sit down and say, okay, ladies and gentlemen, let's think about our future, let's think out the long term for at least a little while because the majority of our time we're going to spend fighting fires.[6]

As we discussed in Chapter 4, your strategy needs to be focused on what unique products or services you provide, not on profitability. Paradoxically, companies that set profit as their main goal are not generally profitable over the long term. Management loses sight of customers' and employees' goals in its myopic focus on its own financial goals. When North American organizations were the only game in town, or far ahead of everyone else, they could dictate terms to customers and employees. Those conditions are history. Today your strategy needs to focus on providing higher levels of customer-perceived value, while continuously improving levels of quality that are steadily lowering your operating costs. Service/quality is the overarching goal. The question is what dimensions of service/quality, for whom, and how far do you go?

SEGMENTATION AND STRATEGIC NICHES

"The mass market has split into ever multiplying, ever changing sets of mini-markets that demand a continually expanding range of options, models, types, sizes, colors, and customizations."

Alvin Toffler[7]

The "demassification of society" that futurist Alvin Toffler foretold in the 70s is here. Pick any industry, from cars to fast food to computers to entertainment to health care, and you will find that the number of choices available to customers today is exponentially greater than it was just a few years ago.

The proliferation of choices in an economy that is no longer growing at rates of the 1960s and 70s means more and more organizations are chasing fewer and fewer available dollars. That's just as true for companies competing in the marketplace to sell their products or services as it is for public-sector organizations competing against other public agencies to get support or funding for their services.

All of this makes it harder—in many cases impossible—to be all things to all people. Like an old Communist regime futilely trying to control the channels of communications, today's organizations are finding it impossible to control a market or public. And because no organization can be all things to all people, the successful ones are breaking their markets or customer groups into segments. Marketing guru Regis McKenna says, "From orange juice to jeans to beer, everything is becoming a niche market today . . . we're in a guerilla warfare environment." Segmentation has been a key to Toyota's phenomenal worldwide growth in the past two decades. Kazuo Morohoshi, head of its Tokyo Design Center, says, "We have learned that universal mass production is not enough. In the 21st century you personalize things to make them more reflective of individual needs."[8] McKenna reflects, "By finding a market segment and dominating it, you can create your reputation and identity. Then you expand. Today the way to get big is to think small."[9]

Choosing Your Customers

The Tennant Company defines what it calls "customer-focused quality" as, "Delivering full satisfaction *to those customers you choose to serve* that consistently meets and, over time, exceeds those customers' expectations" (emphasis added).[10] *Choosing to serve* one group of customers while letting go of business from others is sheer madness to many traditional executives. After all, they reason, "a buck is a buck. Who cares where it comes from as long as sales are growing."

But segmentation calls for defining and zeroing in on your ideal customers. Some customers carry more costs to service or are harder to reach. Others may provide sizable sales revenue, but they are using less profitable products and services. Once your executive team has decided what your strategic niche is, your sales and marketing strategies need to go after those customers that fit your ideal customer profile. And being more selective means letting go of customers that don't fit your strategy.

Defining your ideal customers can be done on the basis of their demographic and psychographic profiles including their service/quality expectations. Sales development consultants Bob Miller and Steve Heiman's book *Strategic Selling* outlines a sales system they designed to help organizations better match the customers salespeople are pursuing with the selling company's focus, strategy, and capabilities. In building the ideal customer profile, they define demographics as "the size and composition of selected human populations." Miller and Heiman define psychographics as "the values and attitudes shared by the individual buyers within a company, and held collectively by the company itself."[11]

Understanding the demographic and psychographic (including expectations) makeup of your target market helps you to more sharply target and deploy your organization's service/quality efforts. You want to build your customer base among those customers that fit your ideal customer profile. Over time, you will need to prune or let go those customers that don't fit the profile of your target market.

Has your organization defined its strategic niche? Are your marketing strategies focusing your service/quality efforts on your ideal customers? You can't be everything to everybody. What are you trying to be? Who do you want to perceive you as such?

DIFFERENTIATION

"One of the most important things an organization can do is determine exactly what business it is in."

Peter Drucker

What's your competitive edge? How does your organization add value? Is yours really just a "me-too" strategy? The answers to these questions are vital because they paint the picture of your destination. Before you put everyone in your organization on the road to higher service/quality, you need to be clear about where you're trying to go. How will you differentiate yourself from your competitors or other agencies competing for attention and dollars?

Segmentation and differentiation call for a narrower focus than most traditional companies have taken. Studies of top service/quality performers show they "stick to their knitting" and hone their strategic edge by focusing on core markets and service/quality attributes. In his study of the room air-conditioning industry, David Garvin found, "The best and better plants generally offered narrower product lines than their competitors."[12] A more precise focus allows top companies to build the organization around their core competencies or service/quality attributes. This allows a concentration of force that can further widen the differentiation gap with other companies in the same business. That's one of the main reasons quality function deployment is proving to be so successful. Diversification takes place around the organization's core competencies such as when Canon applied its lens technology from the camera business to move successfully into photocopiers.

But this is often not how North American businesses are structured. Often, organizational systems, especially structure, discourage segmentation and differentiation strategies around key customer groups or service/quality attributes. In his *Fortune* article on long-term planning, Ronald Henkoff writes:

> The traditional building block of American corporations, the semiautonomous strategic business unit, can actually impede a company's ability to focus on the future. . . . The division into strategic business units can also interfere with a company's ability to identify its core competencies—and key people.[13]

Market leaders often develop and hold their leads by going beyond customer listening. That is, they listen to the deeper need underlying the customer's service/quality expectation. In the 1960s, IBM developed a commanding market leadership in the growing computer business by going beyond selling "black boxes" to selling business solutions. IBM dug deep down to the business problems potential computer buyers were attempting to solve. That drove a different set of technical features and support services than if it had tried only to provide better "black boxes" than its competitors. It's been said that if Thomas Edison had uncovered only what people wanted and given it to them, today we would have bigger candles rather than light bulbs. Understanding what problems customers in your target markets are trying to solve at a deeper level can lead you to new innovative products or services that provide clear differentiation.

PART TWO: MARKETING TO EXPAND YOUR CUSTOMERS' PERCEPTION OF VALUE

"Fifty percent of Japanese companies do not have a marketing department, and 90 percent have no special section for marketing research. The reason is that everyone is considered to be a marketing specialist."

Hirotaka Takeuchi, *Harvard Business School*

The first part of marketing strategies is part of the vision that focuses and shapes the whole improvement effort. The second part of this cylinder puts it very deliberately at the end of all the cylinders for a reason: *you must first drive up your service/quality levels before you start broadcasting to the world how great you are.*

Dizzy Dean, former professional baseball player, reportedly said, ''If you've done it, it ain't bragging.'' Unfortunately, lots of companies do far too much empty bragging. In many companies, the service/quality program is directed by marketing and public relations specialists who lie to the organization's customers. Being astute observers of which way market preferences are blowing, marketers are aware that service/quality has become one of the issues in most purchasing decisions today. So they work with senior management to capitalize on that trend and design clever marketing campaigns to lure customers with promises of unsurpassed quality, fast and friendly service, and the like.

In a *Wall Street Journal* article titled ''Service with a Smile? Not by a Mile,'' Jim Mitchell writes, ''The message of the commercials is 'We want you!' The message of the service is 'We want you unless we have to be creative or courteous or better than barely adequate. In that case, get lost!' ''[14] In our consulting work, we see that service/quality is too often the first thing promised and the last thing delivered.

Outside-in Marketing: From Monologue to Dialogue

''In a world awash with forecasts, opinions, theories, seminars, consultants, and concepts, many companies have come to the conclusion that the only oracles worth listening to are their customers.''

Ronald Henkoff, ''How to Plan for 1995,'' *Fortune*[15]

One of the reasons so much marketing misses the mark or becomes empty bragging is because it is pushing features or services in one direction, from the inside out. Regis McKenna argues that today's effective advertising has evolved from a one-sided monologue to a two-way dialogue. He writes:

Marketing has shifted from tricking the customer to blaming the customer to satisfying the customer—and now to integrating the customer systematically. . . . It is a fundamental shift in the role and purpose of marketing; from manipulation of the customer to genuine customer involvement; from telling and selling to communications and sharing knowledge.[16]

This is a major change in marketing from pushing products or services to pulling them through your customer base.

Setting up a marketing dialogue with your customers calls for intensive customer listening. In *Managing in the Service Economy*, Harvard Business School's James Heskett writes, "Effective positioning requires marketing research, something foreign to nearly all but the best-managed service firms."[17] Strong customer listening will help you better set your original strategy. Michael Porter has found, "If you have a real dialogue with your customers, and a real perception of their needs, it's very difficult to remain for very long unaware of all the elements which ought to comprise your strategic thinking."[18]

Developing a dialogue through effective customer listening also helps you to avoid marketing those things your customers don't care about. This is a huge, common, and *very* expensive problem. Richard Schonberger writes, "My own rough guess is that half the time, money, and energy in sales and marketing goes for promoting what customers really don't want."[19] Valarie Zeithaml, A. Parasuraman, and Len Berry consistently found the same problem in their extensive research. Here's how they describe the end result:

> When senior executives with the authority and responsibility for setting priorities do not fully understand customers' service expectations, they may trigger a chain of bad decisions and suboptimal resource allocations that result in perceptions of poor service quality.[20]

When you are deciding what features, services, or achievements to tout in positioning your organization, the big question is whose service/quality criteria are you using? As Karl Albrecht puts it, "A final and very important test of your service strategy is to see whether it is congruent and compatible with the customer report card you developed as a result of your market research."[21]

TODAY'S MOST POWERFUL ADVERTISING

"Let advertisers spend the same amount of money improving their product that they do on advertising and they wouldn't need to advertise it."

Will Rogers

As we saw in Chapter 1, word-of-mouth advertising has become the most influential factor in purchasing decisions. In today's world, word of mouth is becoming increasingly diverse such as industry studies of top service/quality providers or consumer studies and reports. A nationwide 1990 survey of 250 quality managers sponsored by the American Society for Quality Control (Los Angeles section) found that 77 percent of the quality managers surveyed said "they rarely or never accept advertising claims of superior quality." The study also found that "75 percent of the survey respondents cited others' opinion as their most reliable predictor of quality."[22] Regis McKenna calls these kinds of findings "advertising's dirty little secret." He goes on to declare that advertising "serves no useful purpose."[23]

In typical hurry-up North American fashion, many executives try to "position" their company or buy a service/quality image through advertising and public relations. Although top performers are often heavy advertisers, that is not how they developed their service/quality images. Top performers did not get to the top with promotion and marketing leading the way.

INSIDE-OUT MARKETING

"Use what language you will, you can never say anything but what you are."
Ralph Waldo Emerson

A key marketing strategy to increase your customers' perception of value through higher service/quality is through your people. They manage the moments of truth. They raise or lower the perceptions of service/quality that your customers hold of you. Peter Drucker puts it this way, "Marketing . . . is the whole business seen from the point of view of its final result, that is, from the customer's point of view. Concern and responsibility for marketing must, therefore, permeate all areas of responsibility."[24] Permeation of customer orientation and service/quality marketing throughout your organization can happen only when those people who produce, serve, or support your products and services feel like partners.

It has been said that war is too important to be left to the generals. The same can be said of marketing. *Marketing service/quality cannot be left to marketing specialists.* The most effective service/quality marketing happens when frontline people are provided with the environment, tools, support, training, and confidence to act as ambassadors for your organization. In its fledgling years, IBM's motto was "Service Sells." The company spent an enormous amount of its limited time and what resources it had to get *everyone* to understand and act on the basic premise that if they weren't serving the customer directly, they had better be serving someone who is. At Disney, *every* employee in *all* parts of the organization is very clear about the value and primacy of Guests with a capital *G*.

The long-term effect of IBM, Disney, Four Seasons, Toyota, and other major-league performers' single-minded, relentless focus on top service/quality has been development of sterling reputations that no amount of marketing dollars could buy. And the companies' ability to increase, or even maintain, their market share is dependent to a large extent on how well they compete in a crowded service/quality-sensitive international marketplace. If they fail to continue briskly along in their service/quality improvement journey, they will surely be overtaken by changing customer expectations or by nimbler, more responsive competitors. Sure, marketing will help them build their business base. But ultimately the quality and desirability of their products and services will determine their fate.

So take another look in the mirror. Where has your marketing focus gone? How true are the service/quality claims you're making? What kind of ambassadors or marketers are your frontline people? How much more does it cost your organization to attract new customers than to keep the ones you have? What kind of "marketing" are your customers doing behind your back? (Review the research in Chapter 1 on customer turnover.) *How do you know?*

MANAGING CUSTOMER EXPECTATIONS

"The superior man is modest in his speech but exceeds in his actions."

Confucius

It's one thing to get customers in the door; meeting their expectations is another thing again. In fact, a growing number of exemplary service/quality providers are trapped by their own success or the success of their industry. Their customers expect ever higher levels of service/quality. Meeting basic requirements gets tougher, satisfying support needs grows increasingly harder, and providing delightful third-ring service becomes a gargantuan challenge.

In *Total Customer Service*, William Davidow and Bro Uttal write, "A winning position meets two criteria. It uniquely distinguishes a company from the competition, and it leads customers to expect slightly less service than a company can deliver."[25] The marketing dilemma is how to use service/quality as a competitive edge while ensuring customer expectations don't run ahead of the organization's ability to deliver to those levels. While competitive positioning strategies vary greatly from one industry and company to another, a number of similarities exist in the way leading organizations influence their customers' expectations so they can underpromise and overdeliver.

Here are some ways you can work to keep customer expectations within reach:

- *Be very careful of the promises you make or imply* in your advertising, brochures, marketing, and public relations activities.

- Ensure that your salespeople, schedulers, dispatchers, receptionists, order-desk staff, designers, or anyone in your organization who has contact with your customers are promising less than your organization can deliver.

- Continually research and test your customers' expectations and the factors that most influence them.

- Pay close attention to the expectations set for your products and services by their pricing levels.

- Make it a personal and ultimately an organizational habit to promise a little and deliver a lot.

- Make sure everyone inside your organization is working flat out to close the expectations-reality gap with their internal customers so the chain of service/quality isn't weakened.

- Choose your dealers, distributors, and other organizational representatives carefully and stay close to them to ensure they are not overpromising.

- Train your sales force and then make it a corporate strategy to go after only those market niches whose expectations match your delivery capabilities. All sales dollars are not equal. Some customers come with expectations that you can't meet or that will prove to be very expensive to your organization.

- Don't try to negotiate your customer's expectations downward. Not only will this become a lost improvement opportunity, but you also risk losing this customer to someone who can meet their expectations. Trying to lower expectations is too often done with internal or ''captive'' customers.

- Resist the temptation to pump up short-term sales or respond to a competitor's extravagant promises by inflating your sales and marketing claims. In time (and much quicker than it used to be), your customers will learn the truth and take revenge in painful monetary ways.

FROM STRATEGIC PLANNING TO STRATEGIC OPPORTUNISM

"The question that faces the strategic decision-maker is not what his organization should do tomorrow. It is: What do we have to do to be ready for an uncertain tomorrow."

Peter Drucker

In his investigation of long-term planning practices, *Fortune* writer Ronald Henkoff found, "At too many companies strategic planning has become overly bureaucratic, absurdly quantitative, and largely irrelevant."[26] Every organization must develop the habit of continuous learning, but there also must be some unlearning. Richard Schonberger writes, "One thing to unlearn is strategic planning. Rarely have so many highly paid people done so much of anything so earnestly with such poor results."[27] Henkoff reports, "GE was once the corporate citadel of quantitative forecasting. The 350-member planning staff churned out voluminous reports, meticulously detailed and exquisitely packaged. Now GE has but a score of full-time planners . . . they are there only to advise line managers."[28]

A continuously learning organization that is well tuned to the customers it is serving must be highly responsive to change. It has to be ready and able to "go with the flow" of its market, customer expectations, competitive environment, team needs, and the like. At the same time, the organization needs direction and an overall strategy to sort through its many options, alternatives, and conflicting demands. Increasingly, experts on organizational strategy recognize the delicate balance between purposeful planning and letting strategies evolve as a critical management issue. Building on the work of Barbara Hayes-Roth at Stanford University, Daniel Isenberg of Harvard Business School calls this balance "strategic opportunism," which he defines as "the ability to remain focused on long-term objectives while staying flexible enough to solve day-to-day problems and recognize new opportunities."[29]

McGill University Professor Henry Mintzberg sees this balance as part of management's job in "crafting strategy." He says, "A realized strategy can emerge in response to an evolving situation, or it can be brought about deliberately, through a process of formulation followed by implementation."[30] Strategic opportunism calls for the kind of service/quality organization we have been looking at throughout this book. Here's how Mintzberg explains it:

This strategist *finds* strategies no less than creates them, often in patterns that form inadvertently in its own behavior. . . . To manage in this context, then, is to create the climate within which a wide variety of strategies can grow. In more complex organizations, this may mean building flexible structures, hiring creative people, defining broad umbrella strategies, and watching for the patterns that emerge (his emphasis).[31]

Strategic opportunism is a major shift for many executives who are used to laying out long-term plans and rigid budgets. Becoming opportunistic in finding new paths to realize your organizational strategy calls for lots of experimentation, feedback, learning, and midcourse corrections. It also calls for the type of wide-scale employee involvement created by a team-based organization. As Michael Porter has found, "Strategy ultimately involves every member of the organization." Porter also says, "And the best companies are the ones where the strategy is well understood and well communicated at all levels; where everybody lives the strategy rather than it being some kind of artificial conception of the boss that he keeps secret and formulates in the back room."[32] In the deployment section, we'll see how to put the structure and process in place for organizationwide involvement in the implementation of your service/quality strategy.

EXAMPLES OF SEGMENTATION, NICHES, AND DIFFERENTIATION

"You can't be what you must be by being what you have been."

Here are a few ways companies have worked to implement the marketing strategies covered in part one of this cylinder:

• Credit card companies, hotels, banks, and airlines are just a few of the companies that have set up separate organizations and processes to deal with different segments of their market. Customers are segmented according to usage frequency, income levels, transaction size, willingness to pay premiums, and various other criteria. The expectations of each customer group are then researched and met in differing ways. This might include special phone lines, exclusive check-in counters, dedicated staff, newsletters, extended hours of availability, and so on.

• Network Equipment Technologies doesn't allow its salespeople to sell anything that isn't already in production. To leverage on its strength, NET also discourages the selling of its telecommunications switches in areas where it can't provide outstanding service. And to ensure that expectations are kept within reach, the last half of all sales commissions are paid only once the equipment is installed and the customer has verified that it is working as promised.[33]

- Frito-Lay found that using its 10,000 route drivers to sell cookies along with the company's well-known salty snacks didn't work. W. Leo Kiely III, senior vice president for sales and marketing, explains how this turned out to be a different market segment that Frito-Lay was not equipped to serve:

> On the surface it looked easy, but there were underlying problems. . . . Our other products turn in about seven days—that's very rapid. Cookies have a much slower turn, with 60- to 90-day shelf life. That is a different inventory problem for our drivers, so our regular visit two to three times a week turned out to be inefficient for cookies.[34]

- Members of the sales force at Genentech, a biotechnology firm, have become consultants to the pharmacists and physicians they call on. Using a laptop computer, a salesperson can access recent articles, research papers, or conference reports to provide an educational and research service to customers.[35]
- All local advertising done by agents for Northwestern Mutual must be cleared through home office. Descriptions of the company's insurance products and services are carefully monitored to ensure that expectations are not raised too high.[36]
- One of the keys to Domino's success in the pizza business has been specialization and simplicity. Its "fast, free, and friendly" strategy has been rapid home delivery of its only menu item—pizza. Domino's centralized preparation of pizza ingredients means the stores only have to assemble and cook the pizzas. Overhead has been minimized and focus narrowed by eliminating sit-down service.[37]

TOO MANY EXAMPLES OF MARKETING TO EXPAND CUSTOMER PERCEPTIONS ARE EMPTY PROMISES

"A vice president in an advertising agency is a 'molehill man' who has until 5 o'clock to make a molehill into a mountain. An accomplished molehill man will often have his mountain finished before lunch."

Fred Allen, *American comedian*

Look around you. There is no shortage of companies cleverly marketing service/quality. Probably 90 percent of all ads have the words *service* or *quality* in them somewhere. There is a shortage of organizations that actually deliver what they promise *as perceived by their customers*. Regis McKenna writes, "Companies that continue to see marketing as a bag of tricks will lose out in short order to companies that stress substance and real performance."[38] How's your organization doing? *A high score in service/quality advertising and marketing coupled with low scores in the other cylinders is a recipe for the long-term decline of your organization.*

Ultimately, service/quality marketing is an important piece in the entire improvement puzzle. But if you're like 95 percent of organizations, you need to work hard in part one of this cylinder as well as all the other cylinders before you worry about marketing and positioning yourself. *Total Quality* newsletter reports that a study done by Chicago-based *Business Marketing* magazine shows companies on the road to higher service/quality "tend to spread the message gradually." The study concluded, "The biggest mistake a company can make is to build a marketing effort around quality before it is reflected in the products and services."[39]

COMMON MARKETING STRATEGY PITFALLS AND TRAPS

Everything to Everybody

You can't do it all and be it all. Choose. What business are you in? What will differentiate your organization from everybody else? How will you add unique value for your customers?

Sloganeering

While you should work to boil your service/quality strategy down to a few words or a short phrase, don't let it become a trite, meaningless advertising slogan. The best way to avoid this is by advertising a slogan only when it reflects reality—*as perceived by your internal and external customers.* No matter how clever or expensive your advertising may be, calling yourself an outstanding service/quality provider doesn't make it so.

Big Acquisition, Little Retention

Many organizations spend big bucks and lots of resources getting customers in the door and then invest a few dollars in keeping them. As those neglected customers spread bad or mediocre word of mouth about your products and services, you need to invest even more in marketing to counteract this multiplying effect and continue attracting new customers to replace the ones you're losing. This is a very expensive, and ultimately, downward spiral. What's the investment ratio of your customer retention versus acquisition balance? According to whom?

Intentions and Capabilities

Execution is as important as planning. Both are needed together. However, many executives have personally developed or hired staff specialists to construct brilliant and elaborate strategic plans for segmentation or differentiation that limped along and eventually died. As James Heskett writes, ''An ingenious operating strategy intended to provide service aimed at a particular market segment is useless if the delivery system does not work.''[40] What are you doing to continuously improve your organization's strategy implementation and execution abilities?

Marketing Outside In

Although external service/quality marketing can help give your organization an image to live up to, it works only when employees think they are connected to the marketing effort and are partners in the improvement process. Any campaign to raise external customers' expectations *must* have its start with internal marketing if it is to be effectively followed through by employees and made real.

Raising Your Own Barriers

Don't fail to recognize how marketing service/quality to customers can make things tougher for your organization. Competitors or other agencies may respond with higher service/quality as well (or at least with similar claims). Customer expectations will also rise. All this underscores the need for *continuous service/quality improvement* that goes well beyond slick marketing campaigns.

In the long term, it is often more effective to sneak past your competitors with an intense service/quality improvement effort that keeps customers coming back and doing your marketing for you.

The Rhetoric-Reality Gap

Don't convince your customers that you care—show them. Don't just ''position'' service/quality—deliver it.

Chapter Twenty

Deployment: Infrastructure, Planning and Reporting, and Assigned Responsibilities

"For when the ancients said that a work well begun was half done, they meant that we ought to take the utmost pains in every undertaking to make a good beginning."

Polybius,
Greek historian

Imagine taking a caravan of hundreds or even thousands of untrained and inexperienced people on a long journey with no plan, no one in charge, no logistical support, no process to keep everyone informed, weak communication links to assess and update progress, no navigational instruments, and no map. Sheer madness? You bet!

But before you scoff at the stupidity of such an absurd scenario, look at your own service/quality improvement effort. How much of it is good intentions, dreamy destinations, and a "let's get at it" sort of enthusiasm? Does your executive team have a *unified* focus on what business you're in, what you believe in, and where you're going? Do you have a navigator for your journey? Are the roles and responsibilities of executives, managers, supervisors, and frontline performers clear? Is there a structure to support all the team improvement efforts? Are you getting regular reports of the progress made? Are your people well trained in traversing the unfamiliar terrain confronting them at every turn? Are the leadership skills in place to take you where you need to go? How effective are your information-gathering and communication processes? *Do you have a detailed plan providing a well-understood map for all travelers?*

As you've seen, continuous service/quality improvement is most effectively developed by building a powerful team-based organization. Successful transformation to a team-based organization depends on the culture from which the emerging teams grow and are supported. Only the "cultural change" road described in Chapter 6 will get you there. And that happens through an effective implementation of all the cylinders.

But you can't do it all at once. *The scope and magnitude of change is enormous.* It truly is a revolution, a whole new system of management. Many organizations fiercely declare they want to take the cultural change road, but instead drift over to the program road. The result is mediocre performance and more cynicism throughout the organization. To avoid this widespread problem, you need a management process and structure that will take your organization down the long hard road to cultural change. Ken Blanchard calls this "managing the journey." His experience meshes with our own as he goes on to declare that this is "a greater task than that of the manager of the past who was perhaps more focused on simply 'announcing the destination.' "[1]

THE NEED FOR A STRONG DEPLOYMENT PROCESS

"Most companies don't fail for lack of talent or strategic vision. They fail for lack of execution—the mundane blocking and tackling that the great companies consistently do well and strive to do better."

T. J. Rodgers, *CEO, Cypress Semiconductor*[2]

Deployment is increasingly used to describe the vital task of managing the many components of the journey to higher service/quality. The term comes from the military, where it means the strategic placement and call to action of troops at specific times and places to support the overall battle plan. The Oxford dictionary also says to deploy is to "bring (forces, arguments, etc.) into effective action." Deployment is an apt term to describe the task of training, planning, and coordinating the hundreds or thousands of people and improvement activities that need to be pulled together within the 12 cylinders to take your organization toward higher service/quality.

In this chapter, we will look at the three sections—infrastructure, planning and reporting, and assigned responsibilities—found under the deployment heading of our implementation architecture. In the next chapter, we'll pull these components together and look at the overall implementation process. These chapters (as with most of this book) are based on the service/quality consulting experiences we have had with dozens of major organizations over the past decade. During that time, we have conducted over 200 senior executive team retreats and have trained, supported, and consulted with hundreds of service/quality co-ordinators and senior managers leading or guiding the improvement process.

On the road to higher service/quality are three types of organizations: (1) green field—these organizations may have implemented a few improvement pieces in the past, but basically they're just starting; (2) mature-stuck—these organizations have been formally implementing a service/quality improvement process of some sort for a number of years and are now running into trouble or it has died; (3) mature-OK—this organization is a very rare, exemplary service/quality performer. The balance of this book is designed to show why green-field organizations most often become mature-stuck and what you can do to lead your organization toward mature-OK instead.

A strong deployment process, like a well-manufactured technical system, is robust. That is, it can withstand heavy use—sometimes even abuse—in very harsh operating conditions. A prime deployment goal of Charlie Stroupe, president, Wesley-Jessen, is to make the cultural transformation process so strong and deeply engrained that it goes well beyond any one individual. He stresses, "Quality must become a way of life and part of the job, and it can't be dependent on me being around to ride herd on it." *The strength and robustness of your entire improvement process depends on how well it is all deployed.*

Although there are clear success patterns, there is no one right way to implement the cylinders for all, or even any two, organizations. There are no "cookbook recipes" or "cookie-cutter solutions" that can be dropped into your organization. Each implementation effort is unique to that organization. And within an organization, each department, section, or division often calls for slightly different deployment strategies.

Even if there were a right way to improve the cylinders, "slam dunking" that plan on the organization would be the wrong way to proceed because this approach is likely to be less relevant and will certainly not be owned by the people who will make it or break it. The deployment process would be management's or, even worse, an outside consultant's.

While the details of deploying each service/quality improvement effort differ, the infrastructure, planning, roles, and steps that lead to success have a high degree of consistency and similarity. As Deming says, "The principles that will help to improve quality of product and of service are universal in nature."[3]

INFRASTRUCTURE

"Give me a lever long enough, and fulcrum strong enough, and single-handed I can move the world."

Archimedes, Syracusan geometrician

When we are asked to help a mature-stuck organization pull itself out of the quality quagmire, we often find either a weak infrastructure or none at all. A strong infrastructure, as the name implies, supports the whole deployment process by providing an organizationwide management structure for the improvement effort that ensures improvement teams have what they need to be effective. This generally works best when the service/quality infrastructure mirrors the organization's management structure.

Corporate Steering Committee/Quality Council

The corporate steering committee/quality council plays a pivotal role in establishing and managing all the other steps in the deployment process. *We have yet to see an organization that has a strong continuous improvement process in place that doesn't also have a strong and effective corporate steering committee.* Valarie Zeithaml, A. Parasuraman, and Len Berry report, "One constant in virtually all successful service-improvement case studies we have examined is a high-level, interdepartmental steering group to energize, manage, and coordinate the service-improvement effort."[4]

The role and mandate of the corporate steering committee vary from one organization to another. Here are some examples of the functions this group typically performs:

- Provide input to, modify/refine, and ultimately approve the implementation plan compiled by the corporate coordinator. This ensures that adequate financial and human resources are available to orient, train, and support all areas of the organization for the first two- to three-year implementation period.
- Develop the principles, policies, and guidelines that frame the improvement process effort (e.g., mandatory participation, improvement team parameters, amount and type of team involvement).
- Review and approve the role, mandate, and improvement plans of local service/quality councils and their implementation assistants.
- Become ambassadors, champions, and communicators of the continuous improvement process and its key messages.

- Coordinate cross-functional initiatives such as process improvement teams that cut across a number of departments or functions. The council may also act as a strategic process improvement team.
- Help managers, employees, and improvement teams establish priorities.
- Work with the senior executive and other executives or managers to resolve system and strategic process problems that hinder team improvement activities.
- Track and measure the effectiveness of the improvement and deployment process throughout the corporate and local efforts.
- Ensure that feedback loops are strong and effective in identifying successes and difficulties so all parts of the organization can continuously learn and readjust their efforts or establish benchmarks for higher performance.
- Publish an annual report that pulls together a comprehensive record of progress, best practices, and benchmarks.
- Develop and actively manage a reward and recognition program that celebrates successes, makes "heroes" of high-performing teams, and broadcasts their accomplishments inside and outside the organization.

Ideally, the corporate steering committee should have no more than 10 or 12 people. It *must* be chaired by the senior executive (president, chief administrator, division general manager, etc.) of that organization. This not only signals commitment, but it also helps bring service/quality improvement into the management process where it belongs. This makes perfect sense if you agree that the only reason any organization exists is to serve customers with the best possible quality processes that continually lower costs. A clear indication of whether this basic premise is rhetoric or reality is who chairs the corporate steering committee. Organizations that are on the less-effective service/quality program road have delegated this role to someone below the senior executive or, even worse, to a staff support person—if a corporate steering committee even exists.

With the senior executive as chair, the corporate coordinator acts as secretary to the corporate steering committee. This group often evolves as the organization's improvement process matures. In the beginning, the corporate steering committee's main responsibility is around the plan and startup of the improvement process. Because this involves a number of key strategic decisions, the corporate steering committee is often the senior operating team that normally reports to the senior executive. When that's the case, the group needs to make extraordinary efforts to avoid having operational issues overshadow and eventually crowd out the service/quality steering role. These steps include *always* putting corporate steering committee agenda items first at team meetings. The corporate steering committee needs to meet at least once a month. In the early stages, that may not be enough as a number of critical startup decisions often need to be made fairly quickly to maintain momentum.

As the improvement process gets rolling, the corporate steering committee may evolve and broaden. A number of senior executives might be replaced on the committee by perhaps union leaders or employees, key suppliers, dealer or distributor representatives, key or typical customers, managers and supervisors, human resources, or public relations/communications professionals. These replacements may be on a long-term, rotating, or onetime invitation basis. With plans in place and implementation well under way, the mature corporate steering committee strives to reflect or stay in regular touch with a cross-section of the organization's key stakeholders who help to coordinate and guide the improvement process.

At this stage, the corporate steering committee is looking broadly across the organization to align corporatewide systems, rewards and recognition, measurement, and marketing strategies to best support improvement activities coordinated by the senior special project and process improvement teams as well as the local steering committees that report to this group. Like a board of directors, the committee's focus is to provide high-level strategic direction and support. And because the senior executive is chairing the group, he or she will involve other senior executives or process owners as appropriate within the corporate steering committee or its subgroups.

Local Service/Quality Councils

Local service/quality councils (or functional service/quality councils) are similar in makeup and mandate to the corporate steering committee. However, these councils are much more concerned with their own implementation details than with the overall direction of the organization improvement effort. Local service/quality councils are generally formed along organizational lines. The head of each strategic business unit, department, division, or branch (functional units) who reports to the senior executive would chair his or her own local service/quality council. In that way, senior executives are both members of the corporate steering committee and head of a local service/quality council. In a large organization, this infrastructure might continue to cascade in this fashion to include most management levels (supervisors would be involved at the improvement team level). The role, structure, and mandate of local service/quality councils is usually first decided and then continually managed by the corporate steering committee (unless special pilots or other activities are under way).

A prime activity of the local service/quality council is coordinating and supporting the intact, project, and process improvement teams in its area. The council makes sure these teams have the training, tools, support, and understanding of their role to begin improving local service/ quality. Once the teams are off and running, the local service/quality council then works within its function or area, across functions, or at an organizationwide level through the corporate steering committee to remove management obstacles and align systems and processes to help improvement teams get the job done. One of the roles given to Avco Financial Services' quality councils in Canada is to "review ideas rejected by management to make sure that no potentially valuable suggestion is turned down because of someone's ingrained idea about how to do things." Local service/quality councils also look for ways to compile progress reports (which you'll see in the next section). These are used to recognize individuals and teams making service/quality improvements, to communicate and celebrate progress around the organization, and to merge with other local service/quality council reports to form the basis of feedback and continuous learning.

Another rich source of continuous learning comes from networking local service/quality councils. This is especially important in larger organizations where experiences may be lost, and councils or improvement teams end up reinventing the wheel. Networking is generally done through the corporate coordinator and the functional coordinator helping each local service/quality council. The most effective networks are those that meet at least once a quarter. The meetings should be designed to exchange experiences (best practices, "we'll never do that again," and so on), provide mutual support, explore opportunities to share resources, and give additional training (such as bringing in outside speakers). Midsized to smaller organizations (as well as larger ones) benefit from establishing an outside multiorganizational network. We began organizing these a few years ago for Achieve/Zenger-Miller clients and have seen their popularity and usefulness skyrocket. We all still have much to learn about the unfamiliar terrain we're traversing on the road to higher service/quality. Learning from other people's experience can substantially reduce both the learning curve and the high cost of finding out personally what doesn't work.

Infrastructure warning. During a recent CEO network meeting, it became clear that a dark side of the deployment process, especially infrastructure, was emerging. Many CEOs whose organizations have been using the structure described here found a tendency for the service/quality effort to drift toward becoming a separate program outside of day-to-day management. As we'll discuss later, this is compounded by weak or complacent line management and overcontrolling coordinators. The term *qualicrats* is being used to describe those staff people who, instead of supporting line management in the improvement effort, are carving out a new bureaucracy with themselves at the center.

PLANNING

"Few people plan to fail, they just fail to plan."

Lee Whistler

It is unbelievable how many otherwise sensible managers set out on their service/quality journey with a map that isn't much more than scratches on a napkin. Vague platitudes, generalities, a bit of training, and a lot of bravado constitute the "plans" of many organizations. From his perspective as a vice president at Baldrige-winning Globe Metallurgical and as a Baldrige examiner, Ken Leach has found, "Strategic quality planning is an area where companies are particularly weak. Very few companies have had a quality plan. If they did, it was usually done by the quality department, which had nothing to do with the people who were putting together the business plan for the company."[5] Setting out on your service/quality improvement journey without a solid plan is not only bad management, but it also virtually guarantees you won't get the organization where you're not sure it's going.

A robust deployment process always has a strong implementation plan at its center. We've yet to see an organization that meandered its way to high performance. Even if statistical process control, customer surveys or market research, training, recognition programs, or any other cylinders are well executed, they won't bring about cultural change unless they are pulled together within a strong strategic plan and supported by a solid infrastructure. Baldrige director Curt Reimann reports:

> You have to start with a plan and get the whole company rallied behind those goals in a deliberate way. We all do quality improvement; we promote a generalized good feeling that we're going to improve quality. But would people know what to do tomorrow if they're told today to improve quality?[6]

In developing their "Leadership Through Quality" program that saved the company, 25 top Xerox officers, steered by CEO David Kearns, spent three months hammering out their implementation plan.

Elements of the Service/Quality Plan

"The will to win is worth nothing unless you have the will to prepare."

Carl Carson

Early in the deployment process, the corporate coordinator prepares a discussion draft or skeletal plan for the corporate steering committee. This draft becomes the focal point for the committee as it begins the improvement effort. The coordinator and steering committee may take months of intensive work to make the final corporate plan. During that time, they gather input and work through the roles, responsibilities, structures, and other deployment details. But as top organizations have demonstrated so well, the time invested in the start of the voyage pays off with a blistering, relentless pace once the improvement journey begins.

A brief outline of the major components found in many corporate plans follows:

- *Background*—the reasons the organization is at this point, what has been done along these lines so far, and how this process will integrate with the past.
- *Theme* (if any is used)—such as, "Service Excellence," "Quality Has Value," "Caring Through Service Excellence," "Quality Is Job 1."
- *Definition of service/quality and improvement*—how you are going to get everyone talking the same language and defining "it" the same way; how broad is your definition and scope of service/quality improvement.
- *Vision*—a description of your preferred service/quality future concerning customers, employees, suppliers, systems and processes, shareholders, and industry leadership.
- *Values*—the three or four core organizational principles that provide the behavioral context for this plan and all organizational activities.
- *Service/quality policy statement*—this will be closely connected to your values. For example, "XYZ means quality. Our dedication to quality has served us well in the past and is essential to our success in the future. Quality is not an option or a luxury; it is not the exclusive domain of selected departments or functional groups. Quality is everyone's job."

- *Implementation schedule*—the heart of the plan. This section is often very detailed and specific. It lists activities, primary responsibilities, objectives, and target dates to improve performance in each of the 12 cylinders. This schedule is usually shown in two stages for each cylinder: the first 12 months and the following 12-month period.
- *Training subplan*—although this is part of the education and awareness, personal, coaching, and team cylinders within the above implementation schedule, it is often extensive (and certainly important) enough to warrant its own detailed plan.
- *Infrastructure*—how facilitators, trainers, functional coordinators, local service/quality councils, line managers, and improvement teams work together. And how they will link to the corporate steering committee and corporate plan.
- *Assigned responsibilities*—the responsibilities of the senior executive to frontline supervisors, individual contributors, coordinators, and improvement teams, and the way in which everyone will be held accountable for improvement activities.
- *Resources and budget*—the amount of money and time that will be devoted to the process, and the way it will be allocated.

Launch Strategies

"The beginning is the most important part of the work."

Plato

Most service/quality plans are built on combinations of three basic implementation strategies. In the next chapter, we will examine these further and see how they are commonly used as part of a larger rollout sequence. In the planning stages, your corporate steering committee will have to decide which type or combination of strategies will be used in what parts of your organization.

Do it, don't talk about it. This is often called the "whisper launch." We've seen it used successfully in those cynical organizations that have experienced a constant stream of BOHICAs ("bend over here it comes again"). A whisper launch generally follows the rollout sequence outlined in the next chapter. The big difference is that no announcements are made to employees about "the dawn of a new era." There are no posters, brass bands, flashy videos, or other promotions. Executives start with their own personal education and awareness, quietly form a corporate steering committee, and develop an implementation plan in conjunction with managers and perhaps supervisors. Executives, managers, and supervisors develop their data-based tools and techniques, coaching, and team leadership skills. These are immediately put to work blueprinting major processes and aligning underlying systems.

Any formal launch of the service/quality improvement process is delayed until management has rebuilt its credibility around its ability to *follow through and signal visible and lasting commitment to strategies*. Also, management waits for evidence that its newly articulated (or dusted off) values are perceived to be real and alive inside the organization.

A central strategy in a whisper launch is to fix chronic, outstanding system or process problems. The pleasant shock value of a few quiet power or quick fixes often snaps cynical managers, supervisors, and individual contributors into asking, "What's going on around here?" As a pattern of external-customer focus and executive support for those making, delivering, or supporting the organization's basic products or services becomes apparent, jaded organizational members become much more enthusiastic about joining in the continuous improvement journey.

Burn your bridges. This is the "go for it all" strategy. Bold announcements are made while education and awareness are rolled out across the whole organization. A full infrastructure is put in place with a very active corporate steering committee and a number of local service/quality councils, which immediately prepare detailed plans for rapid deployment of the full service/quality improvement process. Many improvement teams are formed, trained, and involved in improvement activities at all levels very quickly.

A burn-your-bridges strategy carries both huge risks and costs. But its payoffs can also be very high. With this approach, you risk turning off customers, employees, suppliers, and perhaps even shareholders when the effort encounters its first inevitable setbacks or doesn't produce big enough short-term success. This may eventually paint you into a corner and produce cynical stakeholders who hamper success, forcing you to turn this into a BOHICA as you grab the next "magic bullet" that comes along. When you go all out with a burn-your-bridges strategy, you often create your own obstacles by raising the expectations of your people and your customers too high. To meet those skyrocketing expectations, you're forced to use some cookie-cutter improvement process that hasn't been tailored to your organization, spend horrendous amounts for consultants, or make things up as you go without the benefit of pilots or experiments in your organization's culture. These conditions often lead organizations to become mature-stuck.

Burn your bridges is usually used when organizations are in deep trouble and have to dramatically and quickly raise service/quality levels or die. It can and has worked. But it is enormously stressful and has a fairly low success rate, especially where the sense of urgency is anything less then panic. The common cause of failure of this approach is a combination of strong education and awareness, lots of focus on team improvement activities and other alignment cylinders while providing poor skill training and a weak deployment process. Everyone gets excited, forms into teams, begins learning how bad their systems and processes are, and becomes equipped with sophisticated measurement weaponry. But because skills (especially human skills) and a supporting infrastructure are weak and there is no overall corporate plan assigning responsibilities throughout the organization, people eventually begin shooting each other.

Toe in the water. This is the opposite of burn your bridges. "Toe in the water" is much more tentative and experimental. It often involves pilots in selected parts of the organization with the corresponding limited infrastructure and plans. It has the advantages of limited risk and minimum commitment of resources. And it allows your organization to learn from your own experience as you go. You can then adjust and refocus your next pilots and eventually develop a highly customized deployment process that best fits your organization.

But this more tentative approach has the disadvantage of being very slow in changing your organizationwide culture. Also, you run the risk of the whole effort bogging down and slipping off senior management's agenda.

This pilot approach is used most often in combination with the other two. We'll look at that further in the next chapter.

A Tailored and Broadly Owned Plan

"Success depends on preparation, and without such preparation there is sure to be failure."
Confucius

In developing a service/quality improvement plan, the twin goals of relevance and ownership are again critical. Norman Rickard, vice president of quality for Xerox, says, "Each organization is unique and needs to develop its own implementation plans and processes based upon its unique culture."[7] There is no one best way or right plan for your organization. It needs to be tailored to your needs.

And that tailoring must happen from within. The best consultant in the world *might* be able—with enough expensive time and effort—to put together a relevant and workable plan for deployment of your service/quality improvement process. But the ownership within will be low. In mature-stuck organizations, we constantly see that low ownership leads to weak implementation. This is yet another example of how great plans often fizzle out because they aren't owned by those who must make them work.

Your corporate steering committee needs to work toward having as many people as possible feel ownership for the corporate plan, especially at the senior and middle-management levels. As much as possible, your local service/quality councils need to own the improvement activities occurring within the deployment process they are coordinating. Reflecting on his company's improvement journey, William Glavin, the former vice chairman of Xerox, said: "The most important challenge that we have globally is getting local ownership of ideas that are orchestrated and coordinated on a global basis. This has been very, very important to Xerox, and very, very, difficult."[8]

Here are some of our experiences at developing service/quality improvement plans with high relevance and ownership:

- Involve managers and supervisors as much as possible. They need to be the first (following the executive team) to get education and awareness and skill development. Their input to the corporate plan is sometimes gathered at these first sessions. They can—and need to—be involved in developing the local deployment strategies through their involvement on functional or local service/quality councils.

- A key responsibility of your corporate steering committee is to encourage local implementation plans that are unique and tailored but have a common planning format and terminology. Otherwise, you'll end up with a "tower of Babel" full of conflicting terms, definitions, models, training programs, and techniques. Networking and cross-functional improvement efforts will become next to impossible.

- Your planning format must be an "open system." That means it allows divisions or functions to fold in or build on successful cylinder improvements already under way before this new (or renewed) improvement process came along.

- Your corporate and local plans need to balance long-term goals for quantum leaps (Motorola's six sigma, Hewlett-Packard's factor of 10 improvement, Xerox's four times improvement in reliability) in performance with short-term "bite-sized" objectives that are doable. Benchmarking is a powerful process to use. It smashes the old paradigms that restrict possibility thinking and stymie innovation. Hewlett-Packard calls these SOWs—"same old way." Pictures of pigs hang everywhere as a reminder to find ways to break out of traditional approaches.

• Make sure local service/quality councils have the resources to support a robust deployment. If resources are limited, cut back and more narrowly focus the number and activities of councils.

• Don't bring your service/quality planning and business planning process together too soon. *They must eventually merge*, but the service/quality plans could be overshadowed by budgeting and other strategic planning if brought together too early. An indicator of when you're ready to merge the two is when your systems are fairly well aligned.

• Plans don't have to be elaborate or pretty (local ones can be just a few pages). The best ones—like any robust design—are simple, have few moving parts (not overly complicated), and can withstand the problems of a wobbly startup. But everyone involved in the improvement process should be part of a strategic service/quality plan and know where they fit in.

REPORTING

"In golf as in life, it's the follow-through that makes the difference."

Many managers can rouse excitement at the beginning. With fanfare, hoopla, and bold declarations of the new future ahead, or with convincing demonstrations of change to nagging systems, it's fairly easy to get all but the most cynical person eager to get going. But the truly determined travelers are separated from the dreamers and talkers as the journey wears on, the going gets tough, and the scenery becomes boringly repetitious. *Maintaining energy and commitment through the long term is critical.*

Momentum can be maintained in several ways. Strong execution of cylinder improvements, especially commitment (Chapter 7), education and awareness (Chapter 9), reward and recognition (Chapter 16), and effective skill development (Chapters 11 to 14), keeps improvement enthusiasm and activities high. And bringing the implementation assistants and facilitators together periodically to exchange ideas and experiences will help provide a forum for mutual support and encouragement, training and skills updating, and coordination of activities.

Measurement and Continuous Reporting

How senior executives follow through is also an important element in maintaining momentum. Reflecting on the successful transformation of B.C. Tel, past President Terry Heenan said:

> I think that much of our success was because we took a disciplined approach to follow-up. I started my executive meetings by having all of the vice presidents report on the leadership initiatives they were involved with, and the results they noticed as they lived our values. There is nothing that encourages people more to get things done than having to report on their accomplishments to their boss in front of their peer group.

Another critical element in maintaining the drive for service/quality improvement is measurement (Chapter 18). Remember, *what gets measured gets managed*. When results are visible for all to see and teams are held accountable for them as well as being rewarded for them, interest in keeping the improvement drive alive is very high. William Weisz, president of Motorola, discusses the impact of measurement on his company's award-winning improvement effort:

> There was a lot of frustration and concern by managers that with all this effort going on, they really were not able to measure the definitive results. Then we crossed that hurdle and began to definitely measure substantive improvement. It was like a snowball. The enthusiasm is higher today than it was in the beginning.[9]

To keep service/quality improvement high on everyone's agenda, your executive team needs to continually follow up and follow through on the results generated by the improvement process. At many top-performing organizations, service/quality reviews regularly comprise a half day or more of senior executives' time (led by the senior executive) once a month. These reviews are usually conducted by the corporate steering committee (which is chaired by the senior executive). As your improvement effort gets under way, each macro process owner and local service/quality council (chaired by functional executives)—in consultation with the corporate steering committee—would develop their key service/quality measures. Regular reports would then show the original goal or standard, current performance, and the gap between the two. This type of reporting also comes from the improvement teams back to their supporting service/quality council.

Annual Service/Quality Report

At the end of the first 12-month improvement period, and each year after that, every local service/quality council lists the accomplishments of the improvement teams. Depending on what measures are being used, this list may include a summary of the effects of those improvements on service/quality indicators, dollars saved, or reductions in cost of quality. The results found in these reports are then used as the basis for rewards, recognition, and celebrations.

The local reports are collected by the corporate coordinator on behalf of the corporate steering committee to form the annual report. A growing number of these reports resemble annual corporate reports to shareholders in terms of their professionalism, layout, and glossy, four-color printing. They look like high-quality documents! Also, annual corporate reports are now reporting on service/quality achievements.

In an intense, far-reaching improvement effort, pulling together all the progress made by the whole organization can be electrifying. Excitement, pride, and feelings of accomplishment run high as everyone sees just how far the organization has progressed. The annual service/quality report can be overwhelming in its show of how much is happening. During the highly vulnerable first 18 to 36 months, this report can protect the whole process from the executives, corporate parents, or shareholders who "pledge allegiance" to service/quality improvement, but get impatient because decades of deteriorating service/quality and rising costs aren't reversed overnight.

Often we find that in the interest of "getting on with it" and focusing on all that still has to be done, many organizations don't bother with the annual service/quality report. *This always proves to be a big mistake.* The annual service/quality report is every bit as critical as planning. It closes the planning loop by providing accountability and follow-through. And improvement teams, functional managers, and local service/quality councils are energized for the next year's plan by the recognition of their progress or the conspicuousness of their absence.

ASSIGNED RESPONSIBILITIES

"Action without a name, a 'who' attached to it, is meaningless."

Hannah Arendt

As we discussed in Chapter 4, a widely held and deadly assumption is that service/quality improvement can be delegated. Because the level of service/quality delivered by an organization is an outgrowth of its systems, processes, and procedures, there is no way to separate service/quality improvement from day-to-day management. Improvement is everybody's responsibility. But just as on any team, roles need to be clearly assigned and clarified. Otherwise, everybody may go out for a pass and nobody is left to block, tackle, and even coach.

Improvement responsibilities also need to be clearly assigned because the roles people are expected to play in an organization heavily influence their behavior. Michael Beer, Russell Eisenstat, and Bert Spector, organizational behavior and human resource management professors, found in their research on "why change programs don't produce change" that conventional wisdom that says once people "get religion" they will change their behavior is wrong. Rather, they found:

> Individual behavior is powerfully shaped by the organizational roles that people play. The most effective way to change behavior, therefore, is to put people into a new organizational context, which imposes new roles, responsibilities, and relationships on them. This creates a situation that, in a sense, "forces" new attitudes and behaviors on people.[10]

All service/quality improvement roles fall into either line operations or staff support functions. Service/quality improvement needs to be owned and implemented by line operations from CEO through to individual contributor. But staff professionals must play a number of vital support functions if the deployment process is to succeed. In the next few pages, we'll look at the most senior leadership and staff roles that support managers, supervisors, and frontline teams in their improvement activities (Chapter 17).

The Senior Executive

In our service/quality consulting work with dozens of organizations in many Western countries, we see a wide range of success, mediocrity, and failure in deploying improvement processes. *One variable that consistently tracks with an improvement effort's success is the behavior of the senior executive.* Assuming most of the other deployment factors are in place, chances of success rise exponentially when the CEO, division general manager, or strategic business unit president is actively leading the improvement process. When that senior executive has delegated or abdicated his or her active leadership role, the chances of the transformation process overcoming organizational resistance and inertia plummet sharply.

As was stressed repeatedly in signaling commitment (Chapter 7), *if the senior executive is not prepared to actively lead the journey, postpone it until he or she is ready to fulfill this critical role.* We've found that happens only when the senior executive believes service/quality is the organization's *only* overaching goal. Everything else is a supporting strategy to producing ever more satisfied customers at increasingly lower costs.

When the senior executive is prepared to lead the journey, he or she must:

- Approve and publish the corporate service/quality plan.
- Hold direct reports accountable for signal sending and implementing the plan.
- Practice the service/quality skills.
- Make service/quality improvement part of the executive's job.
- Seek behavioral coaching from the corporate coordinator.
- Originate and maintain a service/quality improvement budget.
- Chair the corporate steering committee.
- Shelter the process from assault.
- Personally attend celebrations and recognition events.
- Ensure that an annual service/quality report is written and published.
- Attend outside CEO networking or service/quality executive training events.

The Executive Team

Led by the senior executive, the executive team plays a pivotal role in deploying the improvement process throughout the organization. In our years of work with numerous executive teams, we were often asked for a checklist of key activities to support the service/quality implementation. While hardly a definitive list, we pooled our experience and produced this "coaching checklist" in response:

- Actively seeks opportunities to interpret, live, and defend core values.
- Holds others at *all levels* accountable for living the core values through discussion at regular meetings, corporate steering committee meetings, executive committee meetings, orientation sessions, any decision-making meetings, and so on.
- Actively solicits feedback on behaviors from the corporate coordinator and executive team and responds by changing behavior.
- Prepares and uses the service/quality stump speech at every opportunity.
- Holds regular local service/quality council meetings (at least once a month) to monitor progress of the service/quality plan.
- Thanks people for their feedback.
- Accepts "stage-managing" from the corporate coordinator.

- Manages by walking around (MBWA) at least once a week to reinforce core values, deliver stump speech, ask about service/quality improvements, and give reinforcement.
- Actively supports training by attending kick-offs and graduations, staying aware of skill training, linking training to service/quality goals, leading by example, and giving recognition and reinforcement.
- Identifies and participates in appropriate training for the executive team.
- Is actively involved in orientation sessions.
- Seeks out and acknowledges at least one good try per month at service/quality improvement (whether successful or not).
- Communicates with stakeholders as a standard calendar event (e.g., lunch with managers, breakfast with employees).
- Protects and defends the service/quality implementation from attack (budget cuts, board of directors, and so on).
- Instills calm and order when crises arise.

Corporate Coordinator

Almost without exception, top service/quality performers have someone devoted to this critical staff support role. *This is a full-time senior position reporting directly to the senior executive.*

Following are the duties of the corporate coordinator:

- Draft the corporate plan for the corporate steering committee to modify and implement.
- Compile and publish the annual service/quality report.
- Act as the secretary for the corporate steering committee.
- Chair the coordinators' network.
- Coach functional, tactical, and process improvement coordinators and ensure they are well trained.
- Keep the senior executive informed of the implementation progress.
- Represent the organization at national or international service/quality association meetings and conferences.
- Plan, design, and implement service/quality orientations.
- Assist in the selection of functional, tactical, and process improvement coordinators.

- Prepare education and awareness materials.
- Provide auditing, measurement, listening, and other feedback tools.
- Plan and organize celebration and recognition activities.
- Manage the implementation of service/quality training programs.
- Provide feedback, coaching, and "stage management" to maximize executive signaling.
- Provide or arrange consulting support on activities within each of the 12 cylinders.

Next to the senior executive, the corporate coordinator is one of the most significant variables in the entire deployment process. Many service/quality improvement efforts falter and get off track because of an ineffective corporate coordinator. Putting the right person in this position, given its pivotal role, is one of the most important decisions the executive team can make. As much care should go into selecting the corporate coordinator as for any key senior executive position. We have seen successful corporate coordinators with various backgrounds. Where coordinators come from in the organization is not as important to their success as their personal characteristics, skills, experience, and abilities.

Following are some of the most critical attributes for successful corporate coordinators. Because they describe an ideal candidate, it's rare that one person has them all. The executive team must decide which carry the most weight and then assess their candidates against their own weighted profile. The ideal corporate coordinator is:

- A true champion (whom Peter Drucker defines as "a monomaniac with a mission") of, and zealous believer in, service/quality improvement.
- A highly credible person among executives, managers, and front-line performers.
- A person with extensive experience in your organization or industry.
- An exceptional planner and manager of large-scale, strategic processes that require the coordination of many groups and people.
- A person able to stand firm with the executive team when giving difficult feedback or advocating new strategies.
- A high performer who quietly exemplifies the organization's values (this is not a soft resting place for old Fred to while away his time until retirement).

- A senior executive (who is freed of all other duties) or rising manager capable of becoming a senior executive within the next five to seven years (this is proving to be an outstanding position to develop future senior general managers with broad cross-functional vision, change management skills, and customer focus).
- A successful manager who is available full time and has no other duties or responsibilities.
- A good sideline coach or offstage director. In other words, she or he thrives on helping others become successful without personally needing public applause. However, senior line managers need to pay special attention to recognizing successful coordinators.
- A team player who knows how to build coalitions.
- A strong negotiator who is able to get the resources and support that is needed to keep the journey moving forward.
- An effective presenter and facilitator. While he or she most often stage-manages line executives and managers into the spotlight, the corporate coordinator needs to be able to manage groups and make clear, persuasive presentations.

Few coordinators are able to step into their new role without extensive and continuous education, skill training, and coaching. Those who have tried find they spend their first three to six months just educating themselves before they can even begin to provide any real support inside their organization. Coordinators can get themselves and their organization up and running much more quickly by participating in training that will help them steer their organizations around the many potholes that can seriously damage and even stop progress on the service/quality improvement journey.

Coordinators benefit most from training concentrated in these areas:

- The roles of tactical, process improvement, and functional and corporate coordinators, facilitators/trainers, and line management.
- Measurements of service/quality levels and processes.
- Preparation of comprehensive improvement plans (often an underrated and hastily done task).
- Ways to track and communicate successes and failures and to make recommendations.
- Techniques for conducting follow-up and networking activities.
- Examples from the experiences of other coordinators and the executives they report to and support.

- The strengths and weaknesses of the techniques and approaches of the most widely followed service/quality gurus.
- A long-term improvement framework and an inventory of skill-development sessions for employees and managers.
- A solid understanding of process management and benchmarking.
- The complex issues involved in cultural change and how managers can successfully manage the process.

Coordinators can fall into a number of traps, though we have found that three seem to be particularly alluring and are especially deadly. These are:

1. Usurping leadership from line management. Line managers and frontline performers *must* own and implement service/quality improvement as an integral part of their jobs. The coordinator is a staff support person, *not a manager.*
2. Putting the coordinator in the spotlight. Once the coordinator becomes the hero who takes credit for the effort's success, ownership of the program (no longer an operating process) is just around the corner.
3. Having the coordinator report too low in the organization. If this effort is not given a high profile and made the personal concern of the most senior executive in the division, department, ministry, or company, it will quickly move down everyone's list of priorities.

The use of coordinator teams is rapidly increasing. In the right circumstances and with the right people, this works very well. Typically, a coordinator team consists of the corporate coordinator and tactical coordinator who get trained together and work as a team developing the corporate plan and supporting its implementation.

Tactical Coordinator/Training Specialist

Where the corporate coordinator is concerned with the broad strategic deployment of the entire improvement effort, the tactical coordinator has a more specialized focus. He or she is responsible for the development and implementation of the training plan, which is a major component of the corporate plan. Working in tandem with the corporate coordinator, the tactical coordinator is often a human resource development or training professional. This role in deploying one of the most critical tactical components of the plan is often not a full-time, exclusive job.

Here are the primary duties of a tactical coordinator:

- Write the draft training plan, which is part of the overall corporate plan.
- Select, coach, train, and certify facilitators/trainers to implement the training curriculum.
- Provide quality assurance on the training implementation.
- Write the draft annual training report, which becomes part of the annual service/quality report.

Functional Coordinator

This position is the counterpart to the corporate coordinator at the functional level—usually a division, department, branch, plant, and so on. If the functional area is larger than a few hundred total employees, this position is also full time. As the corporate coordinator reports to the senior executive, the functional coordinator reports directly to the head of the area he or she is coordinating. If the function contains thousands of employees, the functional coordinator may have a few full-time or a number of part-time people who share some coordinating responsibilities.

The functional coordinator acts as secretary to the local service/quality council and drafts the local plan for the council's modification and implementation. He or she often plans and conducts the introductory education and awareness sessions and manages the ongoing communications process. The functional coordinator also administers customer and employee surveys, plans and organizes local recognition and celebration events, prepares the local annual report, and participates in the coordinator's network. Just as the corporate and tactical coordinators work together as a coordinator team, the functional coordinator usually works in tandem with local facilitators/trainers.

Facilitator/Trainer

This position is the local version of the tactical coordinator. We often see this role played by the tactical coordinator in smaller organizations. In larger organizations, or big functional areas, facilitators/trainers are often full time because of the heavy training component found in every successful service/quality improvement effort. In a growing number of cases, facilitators/trainers are line managers who do this on a part-time basis. As outlined in Chapter 11, there is a very strong argument to be made for this approach.

Facilitators/trainers are trained and certified to conduct education and awareness sessions as well as to deliver personal, coaching, and team skill development. Working with the tactical coordinator, they are often involved in assessing local training needs and modifying the training curriculum accordingly. In large organizations, there are often dozens, sometimes hundreds, of full-time and part-time facilitators/trainers.

Process Improvement Coordinator/Process Engineer

In those implementations that will involve a large number of process improvement teams, a full-time process engineer or process improvement specialist may be needed. This person is responsible for training, supporting, and documenting the progress of process improvement teams. He or she would also assist and coach the organization's executive process team owners and ensure that process standards and measurements are being used effectively throughout the organization. In smaller implementations, this role could be played by the corporate coordinator.

Having looked at the deployment infrastructure, planning and reporting, and assigned responsibilities, let's now look at how to pull the whole implementation process together for the long journey ahead.

Chapter Twenty-One

Getting It Together

"There is nothing more difficult to take in hand, more perilous to conduct, or more uncertain in its success, than to take the lead in the introduction of a new order of things."

Niccolo Machiavelli,
Florentine statesman and philosopher

A man took his son for entrance to Hiram College. "Can you arrange a shorter course for him to get through quicker?" asked the father. The college's president, James Garfield, replied, "Oh, yes. He can take a short course; it all depends on what you want to make of him. When God wants to make an oak, He takes a hundred years, but He takes only two months to make a squash."

There are no shortcuts on the service/quality journey. Some routes may be more direct and less difficult than others, but there's no avoiding the fact that the pathway to high service/quality is a long, unending, tough trip. That's why so many organizations start with great expectations and grand plans only to drift off the track and peter out. Identifying your destination is easy. Getting there is hard. Here's how John Fisher, senior vice president of Bank One Corporation, puts it:

> Getting a service quality improvement effort started in a big way and keeping it rolling is the major issue. Such a gigantic effort is required to overcome inertia that the size of the problem becomes its own roadblock. It is not just a matter of saying, "OK, people, let's smile and use the customer's name." Genuinely improving the quality of service is an everlasting effort. It's like switching from breathing air to breathing water.[1]

Our implementation architecture (page 99) is fairly simple and straightforward. The 12 cylinders (under the headings of Values, Skills, and Alignment) are "what" needs to be done. The deployment section outlined in the last chapter is "how" the cylinders are implemented. But knowing isn't doing and simple isn't easy. In the dozens of organizations we've worked with using our Service/Quality System™, we've seen the many traps, pitfalls, and problems on the road to higher service/quality ensnare many an unsuspecting organization. The roadway is filled with mature-stuck organizations struggling to make progress.

In this chapter, you'll get an overview of the common ways in which organizations inadvertently set themselves up for failure. We'll then look at a typical rollout sequence and explore the long-term time lines, investments, blocks, and implementation tips and techniques found in most successful improvement processes. That will be followed by a review of what we have found to be the most successful ways to get an organization off to a strong start (or restart) on the road to higher service/quality. The chapter ends with a look at the growing use of improvement process audits and quality awards as well as a summary of the ways you can "wire" your organization for a highly successful service/quality improvement effort.

FAILURE AND AVOIDANCE MODES

"He slept beneath the moon, He basked beneath the sun; He lived a life of going-to-do, And died with nothing done."

James Albery, *English dramatist*

In working with mature-stuck organizations, watching green-field organizations drift off track, or looking at the success of mature-OK organizations, we noticed a pattern of factors that caused the unsuccessful service/quality improvement efforts to fail. Some of the ineffective practices were because executive teams were avoiding the tough organizational issues and either fooling themselves or trying to fool others. Other defective implementations came from failure modes often built in to a weak deployment process. The underlying causes for many of these avoidance and failure modes can be found in executives' dysfunctional assumptions (see Chapter 4).

Here are the most common avoidance and failure modes:

"I think, therefore I am."   Just declaring yourself to be a quality or service organization doesn't make you one. Many executives have fallen into the abyss that separates good intentions and bold declarations from concrete *action*. Follow through, follow through, follow through!

"Let's pretend."   Speeches, memos, newsletters, videos, slogans, and advertising campaigns can make it look as though things are really happening—for a while. This is a particularly contemptuous way for leaders to avoid making any real changes. But it's one thing to fool yourself; it's another matter to try to fool customers and employees.

"Now I understand."   There's a world of difference between knowing and doing. Understanding the road to be traveled is not the journey, it is the preparation. The question on which the future of your organization depends is not what do you understand about service/quality improvement, but what are you *doing* about it?

"No one's home."   How many successful efforts do you know that had no one in charge? Unless and until you appoint navigators (coordinators and facilitators) to help managers, individuals, and teams make the service/quality journey, you won't get far.

And your strategic processes need ownership as well. There needs to be a senior executive who is managing the job of process improvement across your organization's vertical chimneys.

"Let's skip the hard stuff."   Clarifying values and developing skills are hard for many executive teams to come to grips with. Yet these form the base on which the easier improvement techniques are built. In the race to hurry up and get on with improvements, a weak skills and values base will inevitably throw you off track.

"Buddy, can you spare a dime?"   Service/quality isn't free, especially as you begin. You can't take a million-dollar trip on a hundred-dollar budget. However, the return on investments made in service/quality improvement is routinely measured in hundreds or thousands of percentage—a few years down the road.

"Snatching defeat from the jaws of victory."   Just as the results start to come in at the end of the initial launch phase, the old highly threatened culture will mount a formidable campaign to halt or reverse the process. This is a crucial time, because critical mass hasn't yet shifted organizational norms to embrace the new service/quality behaviors. Persistence and attention to the original plan are vital at this point, especially from senior management. Once you turn this corner, there is no going back. Your people will then begin climbing aboard. Those who don't will have to be left behind.

"Hurry up—and do it wrong." We live in an instant-gratification, hurry-up society. Once we set our sights on a destination or goal, we want it yesterday. Preparing for the service/quality journey is critical. And it takes time. But as the top performers continually show, the planning, training, and preparation pay huge improvement dividends.

"Hurry up—before I get bored." Far too many executives are looking for that service/quality silver bullet. They would like nothing better than to make a few bold strategic master strokes (reorganize, hire and fire a few key people, run a quick training program, put together a slick marketing campaign) and get on to other things. That's living in a fantasy world. *Service/quality improvement is tough, grinding work over a long time.* Just when you are getting bored with repeating the same old messages yet again, your frontline contributors are beginning to think maybe you really mean it this time. To move on to something "new" is to cause them to say, "Aha! They really were up to their old 'say one thing, do another' tricks again."

ROLLING OUT THE IMPROVEMENT PROCESS

While there is no one best way to implement a service/quality improvement process, many corporate steering committees and coordinators need a map of which routes have proved the most successful. *This becomes the basis for modifying, changing, and tailoring your own unique route to higher service/quality.*

The following diagram shows *roughly* the sequence of events and steps proving to work the best. In the interests of keeping this rollout diagram neat and readable, it presents a picture of an orderly, step-by-step implementation. If only real life were really so simple and straightforward! From "Select Key Processes" down, there are also a number of parallel tracks, overlaps, and events happening in a wide variety of sequences depending on particular organizationwide or local circumstances. The plan drafted by your corporate coordinator and modified by your corporate steering committee will determine the final rollout sequence in your organization.

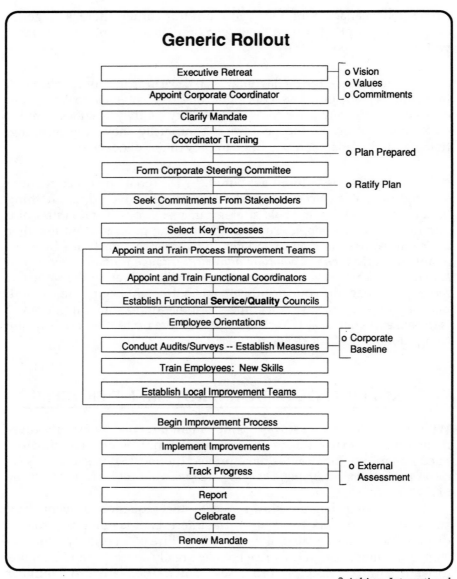

Generic Rollout

Executive Retreat	○ Vision
Appoint Corporate Coordinator	○ Values
	○ Commitments
Clarify Mandate	
Coordinator Training	
	○ Plan Prepared
Form Corporate Steering Committee	
	○ Ratify Plan
Seek Commitments From Stakeholders	
Select Key Processes	
Appoint and Train Process Improvement Teams	
Appoint and Train Functional Coordinators	
Establish Functional **Service/Quality** Councils	
Employee Orientations	
Conduct Audits/Surveys -- Establish Measures	○ Corporate Baseline
Train Employees: New Skills	
Establish Local Improvement Teams	
Begin Improvement Process	
Implement Improvements	
Track Progress	○ External Assessment
Report	
Celebrate	
Renew Mandate	

© Achieve International

Executive Retreat

"Every enterprise requires commitment to common goals and shared values. Without such commitment there is no enterprise, there is only a mob. . . . Management's first job is to

think through, set, and exemplify those objectives, values, and goals."

Peter Drucker[2]

In our earlier years of service/quality consulting, we trained client's coordinators, helped them write plans, supplied education and training modules, and provided consulting support. *But despite all the investment and effort, many of those implementations crashed, ground to a halt, or slowly sank in the mud.* It soon became clear the executive team was not focused on and strongly supporting the implementation effort. Many times it was simply because executives didn't know what to do or how to do it. In other cases, the executive team was not ready to support the deployment process and it should have never proceeded.

In the numerous implementations we have been involved in over the past few years, we have always insisted on starting the whole process with a two- to three-day retreat with the executive team. This has proved to be a critical step in the entire rollout process. It either results in the implementation process getting the resources, time, clarity, and support it needs or being abandoned (sometimes delayed) before wasting a lot of time and money as well as breeding better cynics in the organization ("there goes another one").

As has been stressed throughout this book, *the executive team, and especially the senior executive, is the most pivotal part of the whole service/quality improvement effort.* Failing to have this group well focused, trained, and actively leading the deployment process reduces the chances of a long-term transformation of your organization's culture to about nil. *The executive retreat is the single most important step in the whole rollout process.*

If executives are not willing or able to actively lead the rest of the rollout process, you need to find out immediately—not after you're under way. *The journey must be postponed or canceled if the executive team is not ready to fulfill its leadership role.* No matter how good all the training, coordinators, facilitators/trainers, or any other elements are, if the executive team doesn't actively lead the improvement effort and make it part of the management system, it will be a frustrating and ultimately unsuccessful trip.

The agenda for the executive retreat needs to be tailored to the team's needs. However, a number of steps are common to most retreats. The tailoring comes in the emphasis given to particular areas within the executive retreat agenda:

The service/quality revolution. The team assesses just how critical service/quality improvement is to the organization's future (Chapter 1) and begins to work on their stump speech.

What is service/quality?   Executives decide how their organization will define service/quality and the role customer perceptions play in that definition (Chapter 2).

Cost of quality (COQ).   The executive team looks at the huge cost of those "little errors" or ricochets that emanate from organizational systems and processes that are out of control. Team members also look at the investments and massive changes needed to build effective bridges that go beyond problem solving and crisis management (Chapter 3).

Dysfunctional assumptions.   This section has proved to be a key turning or turnoff point for executives. As the team explores the depths of the deep-rooted assumptions (Chapter 4) they hold about responsibility for service/quality levels, listening to customers, employees as sources of ricochets, and corporate goals such as profits, either the light bulbs go on and the group gets excited about the new vistas, or group members turn off and turn away from what causes great internal conflict or looks too farfetched.

The team-based organization.   Like dysfunctional assumptions, the discussion of the scope and depth of employee involvement needed through teams (Chapter 5) either turns on or turns off the executive team. In both these sections, it starts to become clear whether individual executives are in step with the philosophical bent or core values of their executive team. When the team is determined to charge toward building a team-based organization, those executives whose values don't mesh with these approaches will begin to stick out like skunks at a picnic.

Cylinder analysis.   To begin understanding the magnitude of the issues and changes required throughout the organization, executives familiarize themselves with the cylinders (Chapters 6 through 19) or whatever implementation framework (such as the Baldrige criteria) is being used. They move on to analyze what in their organization contributes to and inhibits higher performance in each cylinder or those considered highest priority. The team then brainstorms improvements they believe are needed in particular cylinders to begin providing input to the corporate plan, which will be prepared after the retreat.

Vision of the preferred future.   The executive team paints a picture of what it wants the organization to look like five years down the road ("where are we going?"). This is generally a key piece of the stump speech.

Clarifying core values.   Three or four unchanging, bedrock beliefs *shared by the team* are identified. These are designed to preserve the strengths of the past and determine the focus for the future. A service/quality policy may then be developed as an offshoot of the core values.

Walking the talk.   Executive team members set plans to signal the vision and values through their personal behavior (Chapter 7). They also establish how they will get feedback from customers, employees, and each other on how well they are perceived to be doing in leading the continuous improvement journey.

Deployment.   In this critical section (Chapters 20 and 21), executives are always sobered by the huge investments of their personal time and organizational resources to ensure implementation success. Once the team understands the infrastructure, planning and reporting, and assigned responsibilities needed, the "assessing commitment" questionnaire on page 341 has proved a useful catalyst to their vital "are we ready?" discussion. At this point, the decision will be to proceed with the whole rollout process, delay or abandon it, or get a corporate and tactical coordinator trained and have that person prepare a corporate plan for the executive team to consider. Once the team has the plan showing the full depth of investment needed, the group can truly decide just how ready it really is.

Executive skill building.   The series of skill-building sessions sometimes begins as day three of the executive retreat with the introduction of the Basic Principles (page 165) and an overview of the skills to be developed throughout the organization and how that can best be accomplished (Chapter 11). The executive team then continues through a series of tailored skill-building sessions to strengthen use of data-based tools and techniques as well as personal, coaching, and team skills (Chapters 12 to 14). Ideally, executives would follow this up with facilitator training that equips them *to develop these skills in their managers and supervisors.*

THE CONTINUOUS JOURNEY: A LONG-TERM IMPLEMENTATION

"When nothing seems to help, I go and look at a stonecutter hammering away at his rock perhaps a hundred times without as much as a crack showing in it. Yet at the hundred and first blow it will split in two, and I know it was not that blow that did it—but all that had gone before."

Jacob Riis

Because most of your organization's systems, processes, and management practices evolved over a long time, you can't transform them overnight. Yet we constantly run into organizations that get their improvement process badly stuck because they underestimated the time and effort involved. Our experience shows that for organizations of 100 to about 1,000 total employees, permanent and pervasive cultural change takes at least two to three years to really *start* taking hold. Organizations of thousands typically see the new culture *starting* to take root within three to five years. And major corporations with 50,000 to 100,000 and more employees can take closer to a decade.

Many of the midsized and larger organizations taking the less traveled and more difficult road to higher service/quality, and the improvement experts guiding them, use five to six years as a common time frame to get the changes fairly well under way. Joseph Juran says, "In all, a minimum of about six years will elapse before SQM (strategic quality management) is comfortably in place."[3] Reflecting on the experience of pulling Xerox back from the edge, CEO David Kearns said:

> It took Xerox almost five years of hard blocking and tackling, slugging it out in the trenches to get where we are. Our very best units are at least one year behind where we thought we would be when we put this program in place. It's tough work and we will never get there because quality improvement is an ongoing process.[4]

The exact time it will take your organization to get continuous improvement well in place depends on top management's strength of leadership, the quantity and quality of resources you invest, how well your deployment process is planned and executed, the speed of change in your industry, and how far you have to travel from where you are now to where you want to be.

In addition to long time frames, you and your executive team must be prepared for the enormous amount of extra work involved in implementing a comprehensive service/quality effort. While everyone, and especially management, is still trapped in a cycle of "fix-as-fail," a number of management staff and improvement teams need to find the time periodically to get off that expensive and exhausting treadmill and fix the underlying systems and processes. This is what's causing everybody to be so busy in the first place. Juran's decades of international consulting have led him to conclude:

> A lot of work is required. Whoever wants stunning results has to face the fact that the required effort adds substantially to the work loads of participating personnel, including upper managers. The estimates

vary, but none goes below 10 percent . . . failure to face this fact has doomed many well-intended efforts.[5]

The extra time and effort in a service/quality improvement process is devoted to education and awareness, skill development, and improvement activities. In the first 18 months, all of that work can add up to hundreds of hours for management staff and sometimes close to that for team members. It's not always extra time. Often, for example, service/quality skill-development sessions replace other training time already set aside. Or improvement team meetings might replace other staff or management meetings. As systems and processes are improved and ricochets reduced, time invested in learning and executing the improvement process (good COQ) is returned many times over by the time saved through reducing rework, recoveries, and crisis management (bad COQ).

Hitting the Wall: Managing Cultural Change

"The first thing you hear in the liftoff of a rocket is ignition. Then there is a lot of flame and fury, and for a while nothing moves. The most tenuous part of the liftoff is when the rocket first slowly starts to move. That's how change is in organizations. You have to generate a lot of energy at first, nothing will happen and you'll become very frustrated. Then when you do begin to see a few changes, you can't relax. That's when the guiding systems really need to be put in place."

Ben Schneider, *professor of business management and psychology,*
University of Maryland[6]

Depending on how fast your organization is launching your improvement process, sometime within your first one to two years you will likely hit a crisis point. What appears as a series of setbacks or a backlash against the whole effort occurs at a very vulnerable point; your old culture is cracking and crumbling before the new one gives anyone anything firm to grab hold of. We call this phenomenon "hitting the wall." And even though everybody knows that change occurs in fits and starts, many executive teams, coordinators, and service/quality champions are unprepared for hitting the wall. Because they have been working very hard for at least a year now, this crisis point is very discouraging and enervating. Hitting the wall is a time of great danger for your organization.

The source of the crisis and what looks like major setbacks are to be found in the lethal combination of change and expectations. As we've seen, the transformation process calls for huge and sweeping changes in every nook and cranny of the organization. In the early phases of the launch process, these changes are either relieving some major source of pain for many frontline performers or are fairly vague motherhood pronouncements of future intentions. So most frontline people assume change will affect others. *"They* will have to change" . . . "it's about time *they* changed that stupid system" . . . "I've been telling *them* for years that really ticks off our customers." Managers assume employees will have to change; supervisors assume managers will have to change; employees assume everyone but them will have to change. However, about the time an organization hits the wall, it's painfully evident that *everyone* in the organization will have to change.

This is often a huge and painful realization for employees and even management staff who have become great "coffee time problem solvers." Suddenly they find themselves empowered, enabled, and accountable for helping to solve the very problems they have complained about so bitterly in the past. Complaints are now responded to by appointment to an improvement team and involvement in helping to fix the underlying system or process. Everyone starts to yearn for the good old days when problems were "delegated up" to management or thrown down the vertical chimney of "them" in some other department or function. Taking responsibility to "put up or shut up" hurts. Realizing that problems are not as easy to solve as they first appear, or that "we" may be helping to create or amplify the problem doesn't feel great either.

Executives and senior managers also experience their share of change trauma. Most executives today love the idea of empowered and enabled teams hunting down and fixing ricochets at their source or taking bold action to delight customers. What they are unprepared for is the *deluge of demands for support and change that start flooding in from improvement teams*—once they decide this effort is not a BOHICA but is real. As one executive put it, "Empowered teams are a pain in the neck." Sacred systems and precious processes are ravaged and revamped. Management decisions are questioned and challenged. Worse, a few of these empowered teams have taken it on themselves to march boldly across traditional boundaries causing scattered turf wars to erupt. By month 18, corporate headquarters is beginning to look like West Beirut.

The second ingredient in the crisis is rising expectations. At the start of the quality process, expectations are usually low. Management and improvement teams map out their hopes and goals, but they are not really sure they are achievable—it is an exercise in faith. By month 18, some movement toward these goals is evident, but few breakthroughs have occurred. However, everyone in the organization is painfully aware of what a quality organization should look like and how it should behave. Everyone knows the difference between good and bad service/quality.

Unfortunately, this knowledge doesn't make people happy. Now they can see all the glaring deficiencies in the organization that have been there all along but were considered normal. Everyone can now recognize when the boss delivers a mixed service/quality signal or doesn't live up to the organization's stated values. *Everyone becomes keenly aware of poor internal service, and this puts considerable pressure on internal suppliers.* Most painful of all, everyone can now see the gaps in his or her own behavior and the output of the improvement team. All of this causes people to look back fondly on the "good old days" when things were predictable and ignorance was bliss.

There are no pat formulas to pull out when your organization hits the wall. The degree and severity of this crisis varies greatly from one organization to another. In a few cases, the "crisis" amounts to no more than a little bump in the road. In others, the improvement process is thrown off track and gets stuck. One way to reduce the severity of this critical old and new culture conflict point is to prepare everyone for it. In preparing coordinators to manage the change process in their organizations, we suggest they discuss the following "characteristics of organizations in transitions" as part of the education and awareness of management and improvement teams:

1. Feelings of high uncertainty, low stability, and poorly defined boundaries are rampant.
2. The quality of information is insufficient and conflicting.
3. Control becomes a major issue as inconsistencies are widely perceived.
4. People experience a great deal of stress.
5. There is plenty of high, but misdirected, energy.
6. Conflict, particularly between groups, increases.
7. The "good old days" are remembered and reverently longed for again.
8. Some waves of commitment toward "the new" begin to build.

The dangers of hitting the wall can be further minimized by a robust deployment process. Here are a few of the most critical elements we've found to reduce the crisis point or carry organizations successfully through it:

- Don't overpromise; keep expectations down.
- Build an expectation of setbacks into your rollout process. Tell everyone repeatedly that setbacks will occur and are normal.
- Make sure everyone has plenty of interpersonal skill training so they can manage the tough human issues associated with change.

- From the beginning, ensure that your reporting and feedback process is strong. It needs to provide a constant stream of all the improvements (no matter how small) and benefits flowing from the improvement process.
- Put a relaunch, including a follow-up executive retreat, at about month 12 in your corporate plan. Using your first annual service/quality report, review why the process was started and the goals and vision behind it and highlight progress to date.
- Make sure you have a few well-chosen and executed quick and power fixes as well as key process improvements led by senior executives under way within the first six months of your implementation.

GREAT BEGINNINGS: GETTING OFF TO A STRONG START

In planning and starting (or relaunching) your service/quality improvement journey, you have a number of important decisions to make and critical first steps to take. This section is designed to give you some of the "getting started" tips and techniques we've picked up as we've accompanied and guided organizations along the way. The advice found here will work only when used in conjunction with a strong infrastructure, solid planning and reporting, and clearly assigned roles.

Pilots and Startup Sites

"Companies are normally unable to move in a new direction across a broad front. Instead they move in single file: one division after another, one department after another, one new product after another. This tends to be true even if there has been an upper-management mandate requiring all to move."

Joseph Juran[7]

Few organizations are small enough, desperate enough, or willing to make the massive investments needed for an all out burn-your-bridges launch strategy (pages 304–305). Even for those that want to take this approach, we advise finding some way to start with a pilot in order to learn what works best in your organization.

Because most organizations are not implementing across the organization all at once, one of the first planning decisions is where to start. Consider this very carefully. It is a vital strategic decision that will either set you well along the improvement road or set your implementation back.

Pilot or startup sites are functional areas that would begin by setting up a local service/quality council, training a functional coordinator (and possibly their own tactical coordinator) and facilitators/trainers, and establishing a planning and reporting process.

Here are some factors to consider in picking those important first sites:

• The test or startup sites have a lot of autonomy in their key processes. If this is not the case, the key departments, executive process owners, or other significant players in the pilot sites' processes must also be deeply involved in this startup.

• Everyone from the senior executive to frontline contributor will be on some type of improvement team soon and receive just-in-time education and awareness, skill training, and alignment support from the organization. If this is not possible, it is probably because you've chosen too large a startup site. Narrow the focus until you can get everyone in your pilot site involved.

• Stay away from sites where there may be other major distractions or complications such as significant technological changes or structural changes like a reorganization.

• *Pick a site where the chances of success are very high.* This is critical to building support for the process and establishing a success record from the start. This is not the time to pick the toughest or most needy department or function in the belief that "if we can turn this one around, this process will work anywhere." There are already enough forces working against the far-reaching change service/quality improvement introduces. Don't compound things by taking your first tentative steps in hostile territory.

One of the key indicators of which sites will be successful is the senior management team—*especially the senior manager*—of that area.

As the pilot or test sites get under way, publicize their success and study what has and hasn't been effective about their implementation. This can then be applied to the next sites to get started.

Improvement Projects

Improvement projects are generally initiated and sponsored by the corporate steering committee, strategic process team, functional process team, or local service/quality council. The objective is to improve functional or corporate cross-functional processes or systems. During your startup phase, you will need to have improvement projects under way at both levels. Those projects are best selected as part of process management (improvement activities) and systems alignment. As we discussed in those cylinders, strategic processes are identified through blueprinting or mapping. System problems are generally identified through surveys and other internal listening approaches or by the corporate steering committee (looking for quick and power fixes) or local service/quality council deciding to work on a chronic problem that has been a major, long-standing sore spot for customers or employees. A large and far-reaching process or improvement project may need to be subdivided into multiple, smaller improvement projects that are more manageable. All of this activity is generally guided by the process management team with coaching from the process improvement coordinator.

As with site selection, your first improvement projects should both be selected with care and be well supported. Projects with a high probability of success must be chosen to begin the whole effort on a winning note. That doesn't necessarily mean they are problems that are easily solved. A high probability of success with tough problems can often come from senior management devoting key people and making substantial investments in fixing the root causes.

Small Wins

The Japanese call it "picking the low hanging fruit." Whether it's a site deciding what improvement projects to tackle or your corporate steering committee deciding which processes or systems to fix, there is nothing so motivating as success, no matter how small it may first be. Marjorie Placek, vice president of quality for Lancaster (Pennsylvania) Hospital, says, "People need to realize that even the smallest improvement is significant success because it generates the strength and confidence to tackle the bigger problems that lie ahead."[8] The wins that get the improvement process going may be as seemingly insignificant as moving the filing cabinet. But if you're a filing clerk who has spent three years cursing under your breath six times a day as you trekked over to wherever the cabinets inconveniently are, moving them to make your job easier may not be so small. In fact, it starts to take "that improvement stuff" beyond so many words to something that begins to look real, tangible, and rewarding.

Tom Peters calls small wins the "get on with it factor." And he puts it "at the head of my change-management list." He urges, "Start nudging people to rack up small wins. After a small win or two has been tallied, then explicitly urge forward the diffusion process."[9] The best way to diffuse your implementation process is to put together a string of small successes that begin to build a bigger sense of winning. Of course, wins are best assured by good site and project selection as you put together your corporate plan. And the flames of this success can be fanned by a strong reporting process.

Start with Data

"I may act on my intuition—but only if my hunches are supported by facts."

Lee Iacocca

A key internal and external data collection tool is surveys. In our implementation architecture, we place this just behind vision and ahead of any of the cylinders. Surveys are certainly not the only source of data; a number of others are outlined in the standards and measurement cylinder. However you do it, you can't plan your journey until you know where you are. As we show in our "Generic Rollout" diagram, data collection is needed to establish a baseline for your plan. The diagram shows a number of preparatory steps before you earnestly begin gathering data, but improvement can't get focused until you use data-based tools and techniques. Valarie Zeithaml, A. Parasuraman, and Len Berry are among the many improvement experts who find that the process can't get started until you have a strong base of data. Otherwise, they explain, "The likelihood of wrong decisions and wasted resources is very great. Individual biases, assumptions, and games playing are likely to rule service-improvement planning in the absence of data."[10]

Dealing with Resistance

Resistance to change isn't necessarily a negative sign. The worst response you can get in your transformation effort is apathy. Resistance often shows that people are taking the improvement process seriously. Apathy usually shows they are waiting "for this to pass." They don't believe it's real. Of course, these are generalizations. The causes and intensity of resistance need to be studied and understood. It may be a sign that your deployment process is not effective.

You also need to be prepared for resistance from your management staff—at all levels. If you do a reasonable to excellent job of introducing and executing your improvement effort, *you can expect anywhere from 10 to 20 percent of your supervisors, managers, and executives not to get on board.* The good news is that 80 to 90 percent of your management staff will get on board if they believe this is real, see clear signals of executive commitment, are given lots of skill development, and are involved in aligning management and support systems and processes.

How you deal with those supervisors, managers, and executives who don't embrace and execute the continuous improvement process will be *very* closely noted by everyone else in your organization. It will be a clear sign of whether you're determined to change the culture or just throw a few improvement programs and techniques around to see what sticks. In the pilot or startup phase, you are best to ignore these resisters and go with those managers ready, willing, and eager to get started. As success becomes evident and momentum builds, more and more "fence sitters" and skeptics (many have good reason—they have seen these "flavors-of-the-month" come and go before) will get on board.

Before you start blasting away at the hard-core resisters, make sure they have been given enough training and coaching. When you're sure they have been given a fair chance and plenty of good examples to follow, you may need to take stronger action. Many executives have found their improvement process takes hold when they remove or replace key management staff who are "dragging their feet" or blocking progress in their functional area, in their key process or system, or on their management team.

Getting Other Key Stakeholders on Board

Besides management and frontline contributors, you may need to get unions (if you have them) and the owners or overseers of your organization backing the improvement effort. You may not get enthusiastic endorsement for the organizational changes and long-term investments needed, but you want at least to neutralize resistance from these groups as much as possible.

If you have unions, involve them very early in your rollout sequence. This may be another reason for an experimental or pilot startup; unions are less likely to resist a trial, especially if they are invited to join in the implementation planning process. During this pilot, you hope to learn how to position the improvement process so that unions aren't threatened but would even partner with management. As with any group to which you're introducing this organizational transformation, you need to speak in terms of the benefits to union members. Job security, revenue and cost performance to support good wages and benefits, better morale, and increased safety (because systems and processes are under control) are some of the benefits you may want to point out.

If there are unresolved union issues, you may want to make this one of your first improvement projects to show union leadership and members not only that you're serious about working together with them, but also that this approach gets things done. However, as with choosing a site, pilot, or first project, if the chances of success with a particular union or location are very low (usually because of a long history of union-management problems), you may want to start somewhere else and come back here once you have more implementation experience and results to show.

Government agencies, public-sector organizations, and voluntary associations also need to get their politicians and boards of directors signed on early. The long-term investments and major systems and process alignments call for top-level support. You can't afford to get down the improvement road and have an arbitrary decision made by your board, council, politicians, and so on suddenly pull you backward or throw everything into the ditch. This is one of the major reasons public-sector organizations have an extra challenge maintaining the aim of their transformation effort. Arbitrary political decisions or new political administrations make long-term consistency especially tough to achieve.

To get and keep boards, politicians, and the like behind the improvement effort, you need to establish a continuous education and awareness process for them. If it's appropriate, get them in on the decision to proceed with the improvement effort in the first place. Give them the same introduction as you gave your management staff. If any of them are involved in systems or process improvement teams, make sure they are well trained. Include them in your service/quality reporting process to the same degree of operational detail they normally get into with your financial systems. Where possible, get them "out on a limb" giving stump speeches on service/quality improvement and its importance to your future.

Service/quality improvement can be a very unifying issue—when it's well managed. It often provides the common ground to pull all your unions, owners, politicians, suppliers, customers, employees together to work toward a common goal. But, *that's only if you have embraced and are clearly signaling that service/quality is your organization's only overarching goal*. Continuously expanding customers' perception of value, reducing costs by improving processes, and better supporting those making, selling, delivering, or supporting your basic products and services is easy for any of your stakeholders to believe in and get behind. In fact, as Japanese and leading North American organizations have shown, the positive ripple effects go well beyond your organization's walls. Improving people and organizations while using our precious resources more wisely enriches society. If you can't build and maintain a unifying and compelling case for service/quality improvement in your organization, step aside. You're not an effective leader.

QUALITY AWARDS AND AUDITS

"Thousands of organizations—businesses, government, health care, and education— whether or not they are currently eligible or plan to apply for awards, are using the examination for a variety of purposes. These purposes include training, self-assessment, quality system development, quality improvement, and strategic planning."

From Malcolm Baldrige National Quality Award application

On any long journey, every so often, you need to take stock. Are you still on course? Is a lot of time being wasted in covering unnecessary ground? How's everybody holding up? Could there be a better route to take or more effective mode of transportation? What can we learn from other travelers? Once every one to two years, your organization needs an objective audit or assessment of how well it's deploying the improvement process. Everyone working hard to improve service/quality needs feedback on how effective their efforts and the improvement process is. In other words, you need to benchmark your improvement efforts against world-class implementation frameworks or systems.

In Japan, just as it was originally intended, the Deming Application Prize has proved to be a very useful tool over the decades for Japanese organizations to compare their improvement efforts with "the best of the best." In the United States, the Baldrige Award is now being used very successfully the same way. In Canada, the Canadian Award for Business Excellence has been refined to reflect the rapid evolution of the quality field. In these countries, the hundreds of thousands of applications sent out each year go to organizations that have no immediate plans to apply for the prize or award. Rather, they are using the application's criteria to assess their progress. This is a very eye-opening and educational experience for many top managers who thought they were doing fairly well. When they benchmark against top performers that win these awards, some of the performance gaps can be canyon-sized. The examination then points to the areas needing the most work. And because the criteria for these quality awards are continuously updated and improved, they can keep companies on top of new techniques and areas of increasing importance. This is vitally important as definitions of service/ quality keep shifting and the emerging new field of total quality management keeps evolving at blinding speed.

The usefulness of objective outside evaluations of an organization's improvement process has spawned a major consulting boom. All kinds of human resource, efficiency, organization development, and other consultants have suddenly become service/quality experts. While some are exceptionally effective, many are not. As always, it is buyer beware. In the next chapter, you'll get some tips on choosing a consultant.

Some large organizations are developing independent internal improvement process audit and feedback techniques and services. Westinghouse has developed an internal analytical tool it calls "total quality fitness review." It has been used with over 200 of its business units to help those executives and managers assess their progress and readjust their improvement plans.[11] In a growing number of cases, large organizations are using their internal coordinator's network to find best practices, exchange experiences, and benchmark each other's deployment process. This is also being powerfully supplemented (or with midsized and smaller organizations fulfilled) by external coordinators' networks.

If you're already well along in your improvement process, how does it compare to the best of the best? *How do you know?*

WIRING FOR SUCCESS

". . . things are little different than when God told Noah to build an ark so that he, his family, and all the species of the earth could survive the flood he'd let loose in two weeks. Shocked, Noah said, 'Two weeks? God, do you know how long it takes to build an ark?' And God replied, 'Noah, how long can you tread water?' It got done in two weeks."

Ted Levitt, *Thinking About Management*[12]

A product using electrical components needs to be well designed and built to be robust enough to stand heavy use in harsh, demanding environments. So does a service/quality improvement process.

While this is by no means a definitive list, following is a summary of some key cylinder and deployment actions that we find best engineer an improvement process for success in the harsh world of cultural clashes and "hitting walls." If most of the elements or steps on this checklist are in place, the chances are very high that your organization will successfully get it together.

- Appoint a full-time corporate coordinator reporting directly to your organization's top senior executive.
- Put service/quality first on the agenda of every management group.
- Get customers and suppliers on your corporate steering committee.

- Write and publish an annual service/quality plan.
- Conduct regular visits to top service/quality organizations.
- Regularly invite speakers from top-performing organizations or others well along the path to speak to your people about their experiences.
- Get your executives out speaking on service/quality (but be careful of promises made or expectations raised).
- Put support, leadership, participation, and results for the service/quality improvement process into your performance management system (especially for senior and middle managers) very early in your rollout.
- Tie improvement process support, leadership, and results into management compensation.
- Get some early improvement wins. Ensure these are well publicized and celebrated.
- Conduct internal service/quality symposiums with broad participation within your organization. Broaden it further to include external suppliers, customers, and other organizations working to improve service/quality.
- Conduct regular external and internal customer surveys. Publish the results and begin tying (starting with senior then middle management) compensation to annual improvements in the service/quality ratings.
- Benchmark your key process and systems against similar ones found in other organizations (look inside and outside your own industry or sector). Benchmark your improvement process as well.
- Hire outside consultants or swap resources with other organizations to conduct annual third-party audits of your improvement process.
- Apply for an internationally recognized quality award or certification.
- Give your service/quality improvement effort a prominent place in your regular annual report (if your organization produces one).
- Publish and broadly distribute an annual service/quality report.
- Hold annual executive retreats to review progress and adjust next year's plans.
- Make sure everyone has the skills to initiate and manage improvements and the transition.

And remember to laugh and learn along the way.

Chapter Twenty-Two

Let's End with Your Beginning

"Either do not attempt at all, or go through with it."

Ovid,
Roman poet

Y ou've seen what's involved in improving service/quality. This journey is not for the faint of heart. It would be much easier to hire some professionals to delegate this to or throw a few programs around and see what sticks. It's even easier to do nothing . . . for now.

As you contemplate setting out on the service/quality journey, look hard at the level of commitment you and your management team have. If it's low, you won't go far before the potholes, detours, and obstacles bring the whole effort to a slow stall. Service/quality improvement calls for an assault on deeply rooted customs and procedures. It demands that resources be allocated in radically new ways with much heavier customer input. It requires staying power when it appears the organization's effectiveness is decreasing during the difficult transition from the old to the new culture. And the harder you try to turn things around, the louder will be the howls of pain and protest from your people.

Only a tiny fraction of executives are prepared to pay the price of improved performance—although many are interested. And that means the rich will continue to get richer, joined by only a few organizations making the grueling trek—and enjoying the rich rewards.

ASSESSING MANAGEMENT COMMITMENT

A woman rushed up to famed violinist Fritz Kreisler after a concert and cried, "I'd give my life to play as beautifully as you do." Kreisler replied, "I did."

There's commitment and then there's *commitment*. If you and your executive team say you're committed to taking your organization down the road to higher service/quality, how ready are you to be personally involved? Following is a scale of the wide range of executive commitment we often encounter:

1. *Permission.* This allows managers or staff support people to proceed as long as it doesn't cost too much and disrupt the "real business."

2. *Lip service.* This level of commitment gives speeches and writes memos exhorting everyone to improve service/quality. Some budgets and resources are allocated to a piecemeal series of improvement programs. There is no strategic service/quality improvement plan, the process is not part of operational management's responsibilities, and the executive is not personally involved in education or training.

3. *Passionate lip service.* The executive attends an abbreviated overview of the training being given to everyone else. Some elements of a deployment process are shakily in place. Passionate stump speeches urge everyone to "get going."

4. *Involved leadership.* The executive attends all training first in its entirety then gets trained to deliver the introductory education and awareness and skill-development sessions. Service/quality improvement is the first item on all meeting agendas and priority lists. Managers are held accountable and rewarded for their contributions to continuous improvement. The executive group leads the process management process. There is a strong and comprehensive deployment process—infrastructure, planning and reporting, and assigned responsibilities—in place.

5. *Strategic service/quality leadership.* Day-to-day operating decisions have been delegated to the myriad of increasingly autonomous improvement teams. The majority of the executive's time is spent with customers, suppliers, teams, and managers gathering input for long-term direction and "managing the organization's context" by providing meaning through the vision and values.

The degree of commitment builds and accumulates from the first level through the fifth. The effectiveness and lasting impact of your improvement effort is exponentially increased the closer you and your executive team are to level five.

Are you and your management team ready to embark on the service/quality journey? The following questionnaire will help you determine that. Circle the number that best describes the state of your executive team at the moment. Then add up your score.

To gauge your management team's commitment, have each member complete the questionnaire on her or his own and add up the scores to get a composite picture.

To what extent are you prepared to:

	Not at all	Somewhat		Absolutely	
1. Invest a substantial amount of personal and organizational time over a 3- to 5-year period in service/quality improvement?	1	2	3	4	5
2. Hold line managers accountable for service/quality improvement as much as for financial results?	1	2	3	4	5
3. Regularly review and reinforce service/quality improvement efforts?	1	2	3	4	5
4. Commit the financial and human resources needed for a full deployment?	1	2	3	4	5
5. Integrate improvement efforts with current strategic and financial planning?	1	2	3	4	5
6. Revise or replace personal habits or organizational systems and processes that hinder service/quality improvement?	1	2	3	4	5
7. Bring employee teams heavily into the improvement planning and implementation process?	1	2	3	4	5
8. Invest a *minimum* of 10 to 12 days per year in your own continuous education, learning, and skill development?	1	2	3	4	5
9. Seek continuous feedback on how well you are perceived to be signaling your service/quality vision and core values?	1	2	3	4	5
10. Ensure that coordinators and facilitators/trainers have plenty of training and highly visible support?	1	2	3	4	5
11. Personally lead steering committees, process and project improvement teams, become a trainer, and use data-based tools and techniques in decision making?	1	2	3	4	5
12. Maintain a steady and continuous stream of education and awareness across the whole organization?	1	2	3	4	5

Total score:

If your score was less than 45 points, don't bother packing yet—you're not going anywhere. If you set out now, you'll just strand everyone in the wilderness and build better cynics for the next time you announce a new destination. You and your management team need to take a

serious look at what is blocking your commitment and work to
strengthen it before you say anything to anyone about higher service/
quality.

If your score was between 46 and 55 points, you need to be cautious.
There may not be enough commitment to take your organization through
the long haul. A frank discussion of what is holding back full-scale
commitment is needed.

CHOOSING A GUIDE FOR THE JOURNEY

"People seldom improve when they have no model but themselves to copy after."

Oliver Goldsmith

Rarely have organizations been able to make substantial improvements
without outside help. We'll admit to some bias on this topic! But it's
clear a large majority of top performers relied on experienced, competent
guides to help them around the potholes, dead ends, and bogs on the
perilous road to higher service/quality. Professor and international total
quality management expert Shoji Shiba has found that outside consultants are needed "because a total quality revolution requires a change in
paradigms. This change is difficult to achieve by insiders."[1] W. Edwards
Deming agrees: "Competent men in every position, from top management to the humblest worker, know all there is to know about their work
except how to improve it. Help toward improvement can come only from
outside knowledge."[2]

Be very careful in selecting the consulting firm you will rely on to
guide your effort. It's a jungle out there! All kinds of "instant experts"
on service/quality improvement have miraculously appeared in the past
few years. Choosing your consulting help is every bit as important as
choosing your corporate coordinator; the wrong choice will become evident only once you're well down the wrong road or stuck in the "quality
quagmire." And as with any key external supplier, you will get the
most from your consulting investment if you build an open and strong
partnership.

Here are some suggestions for choosing a service/quality consulting
firm:

• Make sure the firm uses an "open system" approach. That means
it works with your existing improvement tools and techniques to incorporate them into whatever planning framework is being used rather
than being dogmatically tied to its "one and only way" or guru.

- Does the firm's improvement framework have a good balance of strategic (broad planning, deployment, and executive focus) and tactical tools (skill training, improvement team tools, process management techniques)?
- Will it make you consulting dependent or self-sufficient? Client self-sufficiency means the firm will train your coordinators and facilitators/trainers to become internal consultants and deliverers of both the strategic and tactical components of the improvement process. You will not have to constantly bring in expensive outside consultants to develop your corporate plan, design training, deliver seminars, and help to solve implementation issues.
- Ensure the consulting firm either has an array of skill modules, planning and analytical tools, survey and measurement systems, and team-based improvement processes or will work with you to find what's available and incorporate this into your deployment plan.
- Find out the extent and activeness of the consulting firm's coordinator and senior executive experience exchange, mutual support, and benchmarking network. Can you easily plug in to it to supplement the consulting help you're buying?
- Does the firm deliver the service and quality it preaches to everyone else?
- Is it using training and skill-development methods that are *well proven* to produce lasting behavior change when it's time to go beyond education and awareness?
- Does the consulting firm throw a series of its programs at you without a detailed, extensive, and internally owned service/quality plan? Do you have to pay it to write the plan for you, or will it train, guide, and support your coordinators and executives to prepare, introduce, and execute your own plan?
- How much of the firm's improvement process is conceptual, inspirational, and theoretical versus practical, immediately applicable, and concrete?

WHAT WE GET IS WHAT WE SEE

"If you don't know where you're going, any path will take you there."

Sioux proverb

If you and your management team are truly committed to journeying toward higher service/quality, you need to start with a vision of your destination. Visioning is a powerful tool that's underutilized and often misunderstood. The best leaders through the ages have (often uncon-sciously) used this powerful approach. Let's end this book where you need to begin your journey—visioning your preferred future.

Let's Get Personal

To appreciate the incredible power of organizational visioning, we need to start with a look at the evidence piling up from the world of personal performance and development. One of the most extensive studies in this field is the ongoing research of psychologist Charles Garfield. He has spent more than 20 years studying over 400 peak performers in various fields. Having been an Olympic weight lifter, Garfield's research began in the world of high-performing athletes. In his first book, *Peak Performance: Mental Training Techniques of the World's Greatest Athletes*, he writes, "All peak performers I have interviewed report that they use some form of mental rehearsal in both training and competition."[3]

   In the world of sports, visioning is a highly recognized success factor. James Hickman of the Washington Research Center in San Francisco says this technique is now the most widely applied mental tool in modern sports.[4] Visioning (often called imaging or visualization) provides such an important ingredient to successful athletic competition that almost every major team or competitor, especially at the Olympic level, now uses specially trained sports psychologists to supplement physical train-ing with mental conditioning.

   Lee Pulos, sports psychologist at the University of British Columbia, has worked with members of the Canadian National Women's Volleyball Team practicing visioning during their mental practice sessions. He ex-plains how the technique works: "What athletes have ideally executed in their minds' eye, they will be able to translate into action during practice or competition." He says they are "laying the proper neurologi-cal tracks" with this approach.[5] Olympic gold medalist Bruce Jenner says, "I always felt my greatest asset was not my physical ability; it was my mental ability."[6]

   Whether it's golf, baseball, or racket sports, you use visioning every time you play. It's the picture you have of the likely outcome as you step up to the tee, pick up a bat, or get ready to serve. In his book, *Golf My Way*, Jack Nicklaus describes how he has used visioning successfully throughout his career:

> First I "see" the ball where I want it to finish, nice and white and sitting up high on the bright green grass. Then the scene quickly changes, and

I "see" the ball going there: its trajectory and shape, even its behavior on landing. Then there is sort of a fade-out, and the next scene shows me making the kind of swing that will turn the previous images into reality.[7]

The Power of Negative Visioning

Our subconscious mind is neutral. Like a computer, it doesn't censure the commands we give it. It just follows instructions. Too often, when we step up to the ball, the images filling our head and sending instructions to our subconscious are negative. We see all the bad things that could happen. We expect the worst—and then get it!

Warren Bennis and Burt Nanus call this the Wallenda factor. In their five-year study of leadership, they found that visioning worked just as strongly in making our fears come true. The term came from discussions with the wife of Karl Wallenda, father of the famous Flying Wallendas, the high-wire performers. In 1978, Karl fell to his death while traversing a wire in downtown San Juan, Puerto Rico. His wife recalls Karl's deadly visioning: "All Karl thought about for three months prior to it was *falling*. It was the first time he'd ever thought about that, and it seemed to me he put all his energies into *not falling* rather than walking the tightrope."

From their study of more than 90 outstanding leaders in a number of fields, and many more less successful aspirants, Bennis and Nanus conclude: "From what we've learned from the interviews with successful leaders, it became increasingly clear that when Karl Wallenda poured his energies into *not falling* rather than walking the tightrope he was virtually destined to fall."[8]

We practice visioning every day. For most people, it entails running a series of things we don't want to happen into our subconscious, which, needing programming, eagerly accepts those as the day's instructions. Day by day, powerful images build up that limit our confidence and our accomplishments. Like the elephant that remains faithful to the tight circle around the stake, even when the chain is gone, we become prisoners of our own negative visions.

A fundamental difference that sets outstanding performers apart is their use of positive visioning to reprogram the flood of negative messages society has poured into their heads. Charles Garfield found:

> Peak performers, particularly in business, sports, and the arts, report a highly developed ability to imprint images of successful actions in the mind. They practice, mentally, specific skills and behaviors leading to those outcomes and achievements which they ultimately attain.[9]

ORGANIZATIONAL VISIONING

Just as every individual has a vision of the future, every organization does as well. Your organization's vision is simply a collection of everyone's individual vision.

Your organizational vision acts as a magnet. It attracts people, events, and circumstances to it. Another way of looking at visioning is as a self-fulfilling prophecy. What your people believe will happen, they will make happen, often unconsciously.

So the *big* question becomes, what is your organizational vision? Is it what you and your management team want to have happen, or is it a collection of everyone's fears and paranoia? What the majority of your people see, they will work to make reality.

Your Service/Quality Vision

As you get the organization ready to depart on your long and difficult improvement journey, a positive, compelling vision can go a long way toward providing the energy and enthusiasm your people need to make the trip successful. Many a weary traveler's footsteps have been lightened by thoughts of his or her destination. By keeping that exciting picture of what your destination will look and feel like in front of everyone, you'll be programming them to help take the organization there. The more powerful and well communicated your service/quality vision, the better it will lift everyone's sights from the many obstacles, dead ends, traps, and problems immediately in front of you. Any manager can point out all the reasons performance can't be improved. It takes a strong leader to move people's attention to the future that could be.

To establish your service/quality vision, imagine what your organization's preferred future looks like. As that picture takes shape, help your management team do the same. Put these images together to form a team vision. Now review signaling commitment (Chapter 7) and work with your team to change the collective vision of your organization as you begin the improvement journey outlined in this book.

To help you set your service/quality vision, relax, close your eyes, and picture yourself hovering in a balloon over your organization. It's five years from today and you have superman/woman eyes and ears. As you look down and listen, the universe is unfolding as it should for your organization—and it's wonderful! Record your observations as you hear interactions with frontline performers and customers, with managers and their teams, between people all over the organization. And bask in the warm glow of results beyond your wildest dreams. . . .

Bon voyage!

Notes

CHAPTER 1

1. Alvin Toffler, *Powershift* (New York: Bantam Books, 1990), p. 238.

2. *Pathways: New Thoughts on the Road to Quality Improvements* (Milwaukee, Wis.: American Society for Quality Control, 1989).

3. T. J. Rodgers, "No Excuses Management," *Harvard Business Review*, July–August 1990, p. 91.

4. Reprinted from *Out of the Crisis* by W. Edwards Deming by permission of MIT and W. Edwards Deming. Published by MIT, Center for Advanced Engineering Study, Cambridge, MA 02139. Copyright 1986 by W. Edwards Deming, p. 23.

5. Reprinted with permission of The Free Press, a Division of Macmillan, Inc., from *Management Quality: The Strategic and Competitive Edge* by David A. Garvin. Copyright © 1988 by David A. Garvin, p. 21.

6. "Total Quality Management," *The Xerox Quality Forum II*, July 31 to August 2, 1990, Leesburg, Va., p. 27.

7. *Behind the Eight Ball* (Milwaukee, Wis.: American Society for Quality Control, 1987), p. 20.

8. Ibid., p. 22.

9. From *TQC Wisdom of Japan: Managing for Total Quality Control*, Hajime Karatsu; English translation copyright © 1988 by Productivity, Inc., PO Box 3007, Cambridge, MA 02140. 1-617-497-546. Reprinted by permission, p. 2.

10. From the book *What is Total Quality Control? The Japanese Way*, by Kaoru Ishikawa, © 1985. Used by permission of the publisher, Prentice Hall/a Division of Simon & Schuster, Englewood Cliffs, NJ, p. 19.

11. Reprinted with permission of The Free Press, a Division of Macmillan, Inc., from *Juran on Leadership for Quality: An Executive Handbook* by Joseph M. Juran. Copyright © 1989 by Juran Institute, Inc., p. 9.

12. Bro Utall, "Companies That Serve You Best," *Fortune*, December 7, 1987, p. 98.

13. "Pul-eeze! Will Somebody Help Me?" *Time*, February 2, 1987, pp. 98–116.

14. Robert D. Buzzell and Bradley T. Gale, *The PIMS Principles: Linking Strategy to Performance* (New York: The Free Press, 1987).

15. "1987 ASQC/Gallup Survey," *Quality Progress*, December 1987, pp. 13–17.

16. John Humble, "Five Ways to Win the Service War," *The International Management Development Review*, 1989, p. 61.

17. From the book *What Is Total Quality Control? The Japanese Way*, by Kaoru Ishikawa, © 1985. Used by permission of the publisher, Prentice Hall/a Division of Simon & Schuster, Englewood Cliffs, NJ, p. 13.

18. Reprinted with permission of The Free Press, a Division of Macmillan, Inc., from *Building a Chain of Customers: Linking Business Functions to Create the World Class Company* by Richard J. Schonberger. Copyright © 1990 by Richard J. Schonberger, p. 1.

19. Marion Horton, "Wallace Goes for the Baldrige," *Supply House Times*, October 1990, p. 143.

20. Jay W. Spechler, *When America Does It Right: Case Studies in Service Quality* (Norcross, Ga.: Industrial Engineering and Management Press, 1988), pp. 23–24.

21. Ibid., pp. 109–10.

22. "Formulating a Quality Improvement Strategy," *PIMSLetter*, no. 31.

23. Milind M. Lele with Jagdish N. Sheth, *The Customer Is Key: Gaining an Unbeatable Advantage through Customer Satisfaction*, © 1987 By John Wiley & Sons, Inc. Reprinted by permission of John Wiley & Sons, Inc., p. 25.

24. "Formulating a Quality Improvement Strategy," *PIMSLetter*, pp. 1–2.

25. Christopher Hart, James Heskett, and W. Earl Sasser, Jr., "The Profitable Art of Service Recovery," *Harvard Business Review*, July–August 1990, p. 150.

26. Thomas Moore, "Would You Buy a Car from This Man?" *Fortune*, April 11, 1988, p. 72.

27. Excerpts from *Total Customer Service: The Ultimate Weapon* by William H. Davidow and Bro Uttal. Copyright © 1989 by William H. Davidow and Bro Uttal. Reprinted by permission of HarperCollins Publishers, pp. 32–33.

28. George R. Walther, "Reach Out to Accounts," *Success*, May 1990, p. 24.

29. *The Service Edge* newsletter, Lakewood Publications, Minneapolis, MN, January 1989, p. 5.

30. "Formulating a Quality Improvement Strategy," *PIMSLetter*, pp. 4–6.

31. *Consumer Complaint Handling in America: An Update Study Part II* (Washington, D.C.: Technical Assistance Research Program, March 31, 1986).

32. Regis McKenna, "Marketing in an Age of Diversity," *Harvard Business Review*, September–October 1988, p. 93.

33. *Consumer Complaint Handling in America*, pp. 49–50.

34. *Commitment Plus* 6, no. 2 (December 1990).

35. *The Hare and the Tortoise* (Milwaukee, Wis.: American Society for Quality Control, 1989), p. 14.

36. Ibid., p. 8.

37. Philip E. Atkinson, *Creating Culture Change: The Key to Successful Total Quality Management* (Bedford, U.K.: IFS Ltd, 1990), p. 3.

38. Alex Taylor III, "New Lessons from Japan's Carmakers," *Fortune*, October 22, 1990, pp. 165, 168.

39. Alex Taylor, III, "Why Toyota Keeps Getting Better and Better and Better," *Fortune*, November 19, 1990, p. 69.

40. *Behind the Eight Ball*, p. 22.

41. *The Hare and the Tortoise*, p. 6.

42. Jay W. Spechler, *When America Does It Right*, p. 23.

43. From a presentation made by Brian Kaznova, program manager, IBM Corp., *Closing the Service Gap* conference, April 1991, Orlando, Fla.

44. Lester Thurow, "Total Quality Management," *The Xerox Quality Forum II*, p. 16.

45. From *TQC Wisdom of Japan: Managing for Total Quality Control*, p. 35.

46. "Total Quality Management," *The Xerox Quality Forum II*, p. 23.

47. Reprinted by permission of the Putnam Publishing Group from *Deming Management at Work* by Mary Walton. Copyright © 1990 by Mary Walton, pp. 187–88.

48. From *Thriving on Chaos* by Tom Peters. Copyright © 1987 by Excel, a California Limited Partnership. Reprinted by permission of Alfred A. Knopf, Inc, p. 91.

49. Ibid., pp. 67–68.

50. "A New Way to Wake up a Giant," *Fortune*, October 22, 1990, p. 91.

51. Thomas R. Krause, John Hidley, and Stanley J. Hodson, *The Behavior-Based Safety Process: Managing Involvement for an Injury-Free Culture* (New York: Van Nostrand Reinhold, 1990), p. 38.

52. From *Commitment Plus*, December 1990, p. 3, and Patricia A. Galagan, "How Wallace Changed Its Mind," *Training and Development Journal*, June 1991.

53. From a presentation by Brian Kaznova, *Closing the Service Gap* conference.

54. From a condensation of Wallace's Malcolm Baldrige application.

55. Patrick L. Townsend and Joan E. Gebhardt, "The Quality Process: Little Things Mean a Lot," *Review of Business*, Winter 1990/91.

56. "Total Quality Management," *The Xerox Quality Forum II*, p. 15.

57. Reprinted with permission of The Free Press, a Division of Macmillan, Inc., from *Managing Quality: The Strategic and Competitive Edge* by David A. Garvin. Copyright © 1988 by David A. Garvin, pp. 184–85.

58. "Total Quality Management," *The Xerox Quality Forum II*, p. 4.

59. "1991 Application Guidelines," Malcolm Baldrige National Quality Award, p. 1.

60. Christopher W. L. Hart, Christopher Bogan, and Dan O'Brien, "Winning Isn't Everything," *Harvard Business Review*, January–February 1990, p. 208.

61. J. M. Juran, "Strategies for World-Class Quality," *Quality Progress*, March 1991, p. 85.

62. Excerpts from *The New Realities* by Peter F. Drucker. Copyright © 1989 by Peter F. Drucker. Reprinted by permission of HarperCollins Publishers, p. 221.

63. Reprinted from *Out of the Crisis* by W. Edwards Deming by permission of MIT and W. Edwards Deming. Published by MIT, Center for Advanced Engineering Study, Cambridge, MA 02139. Copyright 1986 by W. Edwards Deming, p. 6.

CHAPTER 2

1. Reprinted with permission of The Free Press, a Division of Macmillan, Inc., from *Managing Quality: The Strategic and Competitive Edge* by David A. Garvin. Copyright © 1988 by David A. Garvin. Introduction.

2. Reprinted with permission of The Free Press, a Division of Macmillan, Inc., from *Juran on Leadership for Quality: An Executive Handbook* by Joseph M. Juran. Copyright © 1989 by Juran Institute, Inc., pp. 14–15.

3. Speech delivered to *Closing the Service Gap* conference, June 1991, Toronto.

4. Reprinted with permission of The Free Press, a Division of Macmillan, Inc., from *Delivering Quality Service: Balancing Customer Perceptions and Expectations* by Valarie A. Zeithaml, A. Parasuraman, and Leonard L. Berry. Copyright © 1990 by The Free Press, p. 19.

5. Faye Rice, "How to Deal with Tougher Customers," *Fortune*, December 3, 1990, pp. 39–40.

6. Excerpts from *The New Realities* by Peter F. Drucker. Copyright © 1989 by Peter F. Drucker. Reprinted by permission of HarperCollins Publishers, p. 230.

7. Both quotes from *Total Quality*, Lakewood Publications, Minneapolis, Minn., September 1990, p. 6.

8. Reprinted with permission of The Free Press, a Division of Macmillan, Inc., from *Delivering Quality Service: Balancing Customer Perceptions and Expectations* by Valarie A. Zeithaml, A. Parasuraman, and Leonard L. Berry. Copyright © 1990 by The Free Press, p. 51.

9. From the book *What Is Total Quality Control? The Japanese Way*, by Kaoru Ishikawa, © 1985. Used by permission of the publisher, Prentice Hall/a Division of Simon & Schuster, Englewood Cliffs, NJ, p. 177.

10. Bernard Avishai and William Taylor, "Customers Drive a Technology-Driven Company," *Harvard Business Review*, November–December 1989, p. 113.

11. From a presentation by Brian Kaznova, *Closing the Service Gap* conference, April 1990, Orlando, Fla.

12. Theodore Levitt, *Thinking about Management* (New York: The Free Press, 1991), p. 134.

13. Excerpts from *Total Customer Service: The Ultimate Weapon* by William H. Davidow and Bro Uttal. Copyright © 1989 by William H. Davidow and Bro Uttal. Reprinted by permission of HarperCollins Publishers, p. 44.

14. James Brian Quinn, Thomas Doorley, and Penny Paquette, "Beyond Products: Services-Based Strategy," *Harvard Business Review*, March–April 1990, pp. 58, 59.

15. *WordPerfect Report* 5, no. 2 (May 1991), p. 1.

16. Excerpts from *Total Customer Service: The Ultimate Weapon* by William H. Davidow and Bro Uttal. Copyright © 1989 by William H. Davidow and Bro Uttal. Reprinted by permission of HarperCollins Publishers, p. 5.

17. *The Service Edge*, Lakewood Publications, Minneapolis, Minn., June 1991, p. 3.

18. George R. Walther, "Reach Out to Accounts," *Success*, May 1990, p. 24.

19. Regis McKenna, "Marketing Is Everything," *Harvard Business Review*, January–February 1991, p. 76.

20. From the book *What Is Total Quality Control? The Japanese Way*, by Kaoru Ishikawa, © 1985. Used by permission of the publisher, Prentice Hall/a Division of Simon & Schuster, Englewood Cliffs, NJ, p. 45.

21. Reprinted from *Out of the Crisis* by W. Edwards Deming by permission of MIT and W. Edwards Deming. Published by MIT, Center for Advanced Engineering Study, Cambridge, MA 02139. Copyright 1986 by W. Edwards Deming, p. 141.

22. Quotes and survey taken from *Now You See It* (Milwaukee, Wis.: American Society for Quality Control, 1988).

23. Jay W. Spechler, *When America Does It Right: Case Studies in Service Quality* (Norcross, Ga.: Industrial Engineering and Management Press, 1988), p. 109.

24. Richard T. Garfein, "Guiding Principles for Improving Customer Service," *Journal of Services Marketing*, Spring 1988.

25. From his speech to *Closing the Service Gap* conference, June 1991, Toronto.

26. Karl Albrecht, *At America's Service: How Corporations Can Revolutionize The Way They Treat Their Customers* (Homewood, Ill.: Dow Jones-Irwin, 1988), p. 36.

27. Toyota data and quotes taken from a speech delivered by Robert Schrandt to *Closing the Service Gap* conference, April 1991, Orlando, Fla.

CHAPTER 3

1. Excerpts from *Total Customer Service: The Ultimate Weapon* by William H. Davidow and Bro Uttal. Copyright © 1989 by William H. Davidow and Bro Uttal. Reprinted by permission of HarperCollins Publishers, pp. 20–22, 209.

2. *Consumer Complaint Handling in America: An Update Study—Part Two* (Washington, D.C.: Technical Assistance Research Program, March 31, 1986).

3. Christopher Hart, James Heskett, and W. Earl Sasser, Jr., "The Profitable Art of Service Recovery," *Harvard Business Review*, July–August 1990, p. 151.

4. *Consumer Complaint Handling in America.*

5. From Robert Schrandt's presentation to *Closing the Service Gap* conference, April 1991, Orlando, Fla.

6. Christopher Hart et al., "The Profitable Art of Service Recovery," p. 150.

7. Reprinted with permission of The Free Press, a Division of Macmillan, Inc., from *Delivering Quality Service: Balancing Customer Perceptions and Expectations* by Valarie A. Zeithaml, A. Parasuraman, and Leonard L. Berry. Copyright © 1990 by The Free Press, p. 31.

8. "The Case of the Complaining Customer," *Harvard Business Review*, May–June 1990, pp. 20–21.

9. *Total Quality*, Lakewood Publications, Minneapolis, Minn., May 1990, p. 5.

10. ASQC/Gallup poll and David Kearns' comments from "1987 ASQC/Gallup Survey," *Quality Progress*, December 1987, pp. 13–17.

11. *On a Silver Platter* (Milwaukee, Wis.: American Society for Quality Control, 1986).

12. Ibid., p. 11.

13. Reprinted with permission of The Free Press, a Division of Macmillan, Inc., from *Juran on Leadership for Quality: An Executive Handbook* by Joseph M. Juran. Copyright © 1989 by Juran Institute Inc., p. 199.

14. Frank Rose, "Now Quality Means Service Too," *Fortune*, April 22, 1991, pp. 100–2.

15. David Blumenthal and Glenn Laffel, "The Case for Using Industrial Management Science in Health Care Organizations," *Journal of the American Medical Association* 262, no. 20 (November 24, 1989), pp. 2871–72.

16. Reprinted by permission of The Putnam Publishing Group from *Deming Management at Work* by Mary Walton. Copyright © 1990 by Mary Walton, p. 80.

17. "How Good Is Your Service and, in the Utility Industry, Does It Really Matter?" working paper by John Goodman, president of TARP, May 1983.

18. Reprinted with permission of The Free Press, a Division of Macmillan, Inc., from *Managing Quality: The Strategic and Competitive Edge* by David A. Garvin. Copyright © 1988 by David A. Garvin, p. 80.

19. From the book *What Is Total Quality Control? The Japanese Way*, by Kaoru Ishikawa, © 1985. Used by permission of the publisher, Prentice Hall/a Division of Simon & Schuster, Englewood Cliffs, NJ, p. 45.

20. Ron Henkoff, "Cost Cutting: How to Do It Right," *Fortune*, April 9, 1990, pp. 40–41.

21. Reprinted with permission of The Free Press, a Division of Macmillan, Inc., from *Managing Quality: The Strategic and Competitive Edge* by David A. Garvin. Copyright © 1988 by David A. Garvin, p. 83.

22. D. Keith Denton, *Quality Service* (Houston: Gulf Publishing, 1989), p. 75.

23. Reprinted with permission of The Free Press, a Division of Macmillan, Inc., from *Juran on Leadership for Quality: An Executive Handbook* by Joseph M. Juran. Copyright © 1989 by Juran Institute Inc., pp. 39–40.

24. Harold Sirkin and George Stalk, Jr., "Fix the Process, Not the Problem," *Harvard Business Review*, July–August 1990, pp. 26–33.

25. From his speech at *Closing the Service Gap* conference, June 26, 1991, Toronto.

26. *Behind the Eight Ball* (Milwaukee, Wis.: American Society for Quality Control, 1987), p. 9.

27. From the book *What Is Total Quality Control? The Japanese Way*, by Kaoru Ishikawa, © 1985. Used by permission of the publisher, Prentice Hall/a Division of Simon & Schuster, Englewood Cliffs, NJ, pp. 55–56.

28. David Blumenthal and Glenn Laffel, "The Case for Using Industrial Management Science in Health Care Organizations," p. 2869.

29. Reprinted from *Out of the Crisis* by W. Edwards Deming by permission of MIT and W. Edwards Deming. Published by MIT, Center for Advanced Engineering Study, Cambridge, MA 02139. Copyright 1986 by W. Edwards Deming, p. 23.

30. Theodore Levitt, *Thinking about Management* (New York: The Free Press, 1991), p. 51.

31. Alex Taylor III, "Why Toyota Keeps Getting Better and Better and Better," *Fortune*, November 19, 1990, p. 66.

32. Reprinted with permission of The Free Press, a Division of Macmillan, Inc., from *Building a Chain of Customers: Linking Business Functions to Create the World Class Company* by Richard J. Schonberger. Copyright © 1990 by Richard J. Schonberger, p. 295.

33. Michael Beer, Russell Eisenstat, and Bert Spector, "Why Change Programs Don't Produce Change," *Harvard Business Review*, November–December 1990, p. 164.

34. From a presentation given by Len Schlesinger at the National Restaurant Association show in Chicago, May 1991.

35. John Bakke, "Special Qualities . . . How the Baldrige Winners Got Their Trophies," *Think*, no. 2 (1991), p. 12.

36. From a speech by Xerox Canada's Michel Desjardin at *Closing the Service Gap* conference, June 1991, Toronto.

37. *Commitment Plus*, December 1990, p. 4.

38. Alex Taylor III, "Why Toyota Keeps Getting Better and Better and Better," p. 67.

39. Peter Senge, *The Fifth Discipline: The Art and Practice of the Learning Organization* (New York: Doubleday, 1990), p. 139.

CHAPTER 4

1. Joel Dreyfuss, "Victories in the Quality Crusade," *Fortune*, October 10, 1988, p. 80.

2. From a presentation made by Carolyn Farquhar of the Conference Board of Canada, May 1991.

3. *Service Quality: Assessing the Economic Impact* (Cambridge, Mass.: Strategic Planning Institute, 1991).

4. *Inside* 5, no. 9 (November 1990).

5. Reprinted with permission of The Free Press, a Division of Macmillan, Inc. from *Delivering Quality Service: Balancing Customer Perceptions and Expectations* by Valarie A. Zeithaml, A. Parasuraman, and Leonard L. Berry. Copyright © 1990 by The Free Press, p. 135.

6. "Proclamations Won't Change Underlying Obstacles to Quality," *Total Quality*, Lakewood Publications, Minneapolis, Minn., April 1990, p. 6.

7. Ibid.

8. Ibid. Reprinted with David Nadler's permission.

9. "Total Quality Management," *The Xerox Quality Forum II*, July 31–August 2, 1990, Leesburg, Va., p. 18.

10. "Achieving Excellence in Service," *Training and Development Journal*, December 1985.

11. Karl Albrecht and Lawrence J. Bradford, *The Service Advantage: How to Identify and Fulfill Customer Needs* (Homewood, Ill.: Dow Jones-Irwin, 1990), p. 116.

12. From *The Service Edge* by Ron Zemke and Dick Schaaf. Copyright © 1989 by Ron Zemke and Dick Schaaf. Used by permission of New American Library, a division of Penguin Books USA Inc., p. 10.

13. Bro Uttal, "Companies That Serve You Best," *Fortune*, December 7, 1987, p. 108.

14. "The Race to Quality Improvement," excerpted from a paid advertising section prepared for the September 25, 1989, issue of *Fortune*.

15. From *The Service Edge* by Ron Zemke and Dick Schaaf. Copyright © 1989 by Ron Zemke and Dick Schaaf. Used by permission of New American Library, a division of Penguin Books USA Inc., p. 19.

16. Karl Albrecht and Lawrence J. Bradford, *The Service Advantage*, p. 9.

17. *Total Quality*, May 1990, p. 5.

18. Reprinted from *Out of the Crisis* by W. Edwards Deming by permission of MIT and W. Edwards Deming. Published by MIT, Center for Advanced Engineering Study, Cambridge, MA 02139. Copyright 1986 by W. Edwards Deming, p. 26.

19. Reprinted with permission of The Free Press, a Division of Macmillan, Inc., from *Building a Chain of Customers: Linking Business Functions to Create the World Class Company* by Richard J. Schonberger. Copyright © 1990 by Richard J. Schonberger.

20. Milind M. Lele with Jagdish N. Sheth, *The Customer Is Key: Gaining an Unbeatable Advantage through Customer Satisfaction*, © 1987 by John Wiley & Sons, Inc. Reprinted by permission of John Wiley & Sons, Inc., p. 119.

21. *Total Quality*, December 1990, p. 6.

22. *The Human Side of Quality: People, Pride, Performance* (Milwaukee, Wis.: American Society for Quality Control, 1990), p. 6.

23. Robert L. Desatnick, *Managing to Keep the Customer: How to Achieve and Sustain Superior Customer Service throughout the Organization* (San Francisco: Jossey-Bass, 1987), p. 20.

24. Reprinted from *Out of the Crisis* by W. Edwards Deming by permission of MIT and W. Edwards Deming. Published by MIT, Center for Advanced Engineering Study, Cambridge, MA 02139. Copyright 1986 by W. Edwards Deming, p. 134.

25. Karl Albrecht, *At America's Service: Corporations Can Revolutionize the Way They Treat Their Customers* (Homewood, Ill.: Dow Jones-Irwin, 1988), p. 4.

26. Thomas R. Krause, John Hidley, and Stanley J. Hodson, *The Behavior-Based Safety Process: Managing Involvement for an Injury-Free Culture* (New York: Van Nostrand Reinhold, 1990), p. 12.

27. Reprinted with permission of The Free Press, a Division of Macmillan, Inc., from *Juran on Leadership for Quality: An Executive Handbook* by Joseph M. Juran. Copyright © 1989 by Juran Institute Inc., p. 300.

28. Reprinted from *Out of the Crisis* by W. Edwards Deming by permission of MIT and W. Edwards Deming. Published by MIT, Center for Advanced Engineering Study, Cambridge, MA 02139. Copyright 1986 by W. Edwards Deming, p. 315.

29. Don Berwick, "Continuous Improvement as an Ideal in Health Care," *New England Journal of Medicine,* January 5, 1989, pp. 53–54, 56.

30. *The Service Edge* newsletter, Lakewood Publications, Minneapolis, Minn., November 1988, pp. 1–2.

31. Reprinted with permission of The Free Press, a Division of Macmillan, Inc., from *Delivering Quality Service: Balancing Customer Perceptions and Expectations* by Valarie A. Zeithaml, A. Parasuraman, and Leonard L. Berry. Copyright © 1990 by The Free Press, p. 142.

32. Karl Albrecht, *At America's Service,* p. 21.

33. Reprinted from *Out of the Crisis* by W. Edwards Deming by permission of MIT and W. Edwards Deming. Published by MIT, Center for Advanced Engineering Study, Cambridge, MA 02139. Copyright 1986 by W. Edwards Deming, p. 24.

34. From the book *What Is Total Quality Control? The Japanese Way,* by Kaoru Ishikawa, © 1985. Used by permission of the publisher, Prentice Hall/a Division of Simon & Schuster, Englewood Cliffs, NJ, p. 64.

35. *Pathways* (Milwaukee, Wis.: American Society for Quality Control, 1989).

36. Leonard L. Berry, David R. Bennett, and Carter W. Brown, *Service Quality: A Profit Strategy for Financial Institutions* (Homewood, Ill.: Dow Jones-Irwin, 1989), p. 106.

37. Ibid., p. 95.

38. Reprinted from *Out of the Crisis* by W. Edwards Deming by permission of MIT and W. Edwards Deming. Published by MIT, Center for Advanced Engineering Study, Cambridge, MA 02139. Copyright 1986 by W. Edwards Deming, p. 66.

39. Reprinted from *Out of the Crisis* by W. Edwards Deming by permission of MIT and W. Edwards Deming. Published by MIT, Center for Advanced Engineering

Study, Cambridge, MA 02139. Copyright 1986 by W. Edwards Deming, pp. 107, 109.

40. Reprinted with permission of The Free Press, a Division of Macmillan, Inc., from *Building a Chain of Customers: Linking Business Functions to Create the World Class Company* by Richard J. Schonberger. Copyright © 1990 by Richard J. Schonberger, p. 244.

41. From the book *What is Total Quality Control? The Japanese Way,* by Kaoru Ishikawa, © 1985. Use by permission of the publisher, Prentice Hall/a Division of Simon & Schuster, Englewood Cliffs, NJ, pp. 104–105.

42. From various pages of the employee booklet "Matsushita Management Philosophy," translation for Matsushita Electric Corporation of America, Secaucus, N.J.

43. Reprinted from *Out of the Crisis* by W. Edwards Deming by permission of MIT and W. Edwards Deming. Published by MIT, Center for Advanced Engineering Study, Cambridge, MA 02139. Copyright 1986 by W. Edwards Deming, p. 121.

44. D. Keith Denton, *Quality Service* (Houston: Gulf Publishing, 1989), p. 4.

45. Ibid., p. 7.

46. "Thriving on Crisis," *Success,* April 1990, p. 16.

47. *Total Quality,* November 1990, p. 8.

CHAPTER 5

1. Michael Hammer, "Reengineering Work: Don't Automate, Obliterate," *Harvard Business Review,* July–August 1990, p. 107.

2. Frank Rose, "A New Age for Business?" *Fortune,* October 8, 1990, p. 157.

3. From the book *What Is Total Quality Control? The Japanese Way,* by Kaoru Ishikawa, © 1985. Used by permission of the publisher, Prentice Hall/a Division of Simon & Schuster, Englewood Cliffs, NJ, p. 66.

4. Robert Kelley, "Poorly Served Employees Serve Customers Just As Poorly," *The Wall Street Journal,* October 13, 1987.

5. From *The Service Edge* by Ron Zemke and Dick Schaaf. Copyright © 1989 by Ron Zemke and Dick Schaaf. Reprinted by permission of New American Library, a division of Penguin Books USA Inc., pp. 68–69.

6. Robert L. Desatnick, "Service: A CEO's Perspective," *Management Review,* October 1987.

7. *Now You See It* (Milwaukee, Wis.: American Society for Quality Control, 1988), p. 9.

8. Excerpts from *Total Customer Service: The Ultimate Weapon* by William H. Davidow and Bro Uttal. Copyright © 1989 by William H. Davidow and Bro Uttal, pp. 101–102.

9. Philip Caldwell, "Cultivating Human Potential at Ford," *Journal of Business Strategy*, Spring 1984, p. 75.

10. John H. Zenger, Ed Musselwhite, Kathleen Hurson, and Craig Perrin, "Leadership in a Team Environment: The New American Manager," a white paper (San Jose, Calif.: Zenger-Miller, 1991).

11. *Employee Involvement Demands Management Involvement* (Scarsdale, N.Y.: Work in America Institute, March 7, 1990).

12. Waterman quote and "Mogie" Morgensen from Robert H. Waterman, Jr., *The Renewal Factor* (New York: Bantam, 1987).

13. John H. Zenger et al., "Leadership in a Team Environment."

14. Jack D. Orsburn, Linda Moran, Ed Musselwhite, and Jack Zenger, *Self-Directed Work Teams: The New American Challenge* (Homewood, Ill.: Business One Irwin, 1990), p. 8.

15. Ibid., p. vii.

16. From *Thriving on Chaos* by Tom Peters. Copyright © 1987 by Excel, a California Limited Partnership. Reprinted by permission of Alfred A. Knopf, Inc., p. 297.

17. "Made in USA: A Break in the Clouds," summary of an address given by J. M. Juran at *The Quest for Excellence* conference featuring the 1989 Baldrige winners, the Juran Institute, 1990, Wilton, Conn., p. 10.

18. From a summary of *Image at the Top: Crisis and Renaissance in Corporate Leadership* (Bristol, Vt.: Soundview Executive Book Summaries, September 1984).

19. Bernard Avishai and William Taylor, "Customers Drive a Technology-Driven Company: An Interview with George Fisher," *Harvard Business Review*, November–December 1989, pp. 107–8.

20. Karl Albrecht, *At America's Service: Corporations Can Revolutionize the Way They Treat Their Customers* (Homewood, Ill.: Dow Jones-Irwin, 1988), p. 135.

21. *The Service Edge* newsletter, Lakewood Publications, Minneapolis, Minn., March 1988, p. 8.

22. Alvin Toffler, *Powershift* (New York: Bantam Books, 1990), p. 222.

23. "Made in USA: A Break in the Clouds."

24. Excerpts from *The New Realities* by Peter F. Drucker. Copyright © 1989 by Peter F. Drucker. Reprinted by permission of HarperCollins Publishers, p. 207.

25. Alex Taylor III, "Why Toyota Keeps Getting Better and Better and Better," *Fortune*, November 1990, p. 68.

26. Alvin Toffler, *Powershift*, p. 185.

27. *Employee Involvement Demands Management Involvement*.

28. Jerome M. Rosow and Robert Zager, "New Roles for Managers" (New York: Work in America Institute, Inc., 1990).

29. Jack D. Orsburn et al., *Self-Directed Work Teams*, p. 208.

30. Reprinted with permission of The Free Press, a Division of Macmillan, Inc., from *Delivering Quality Service: Balancing Customer Perceptions and Expectations* by Valarie A. Zeithaml, A. Parasuraman, and Leonard L. Berry. Copyright © 1990 by The Free Press, p. 140.

31. Karl Albrecht, *At America's Service*, p. 230.

32. *Employee Involvement Demands Management Involvement.*

33. Quote and chart from John H. Zenger et al., "Leadership in a Team Environment."

34. Ibid.

35. Karl Albrecht, *At America's Service*, p. 89.

CHAPTER 6

1. Roger von Oech, *A Kick in the Seat of the Pants* (New York: Harper and Row, 1986), p. 117.

2. Frank Rose, "Now Quality Means Service Too," *Fortune*, April 22, 1991, p. 108.

3. Reprinted with permission of The Free Press, a Division of Macmillan, Inc., from *Juran on Leadership for Quality: An Executive Handbook* by Joseph M. Juran. Copyright © 1989 by Juran Institute Inc., p. 77.

4. Karl Albrecht, *At America's Service: How Corporations Can Revolutionize the Way They Treat Their Customers* (Homewood, Ill.: Dow Jones-Irwin, 1988), p. 56.

5. "Total Quality Management," *The Xerox Quality Forum II*, July 31 to August 2, 1990, Leesburg, Va., p. 35.

6. Reprinted with permission of The Free Press, a Division of Macmillan, Inc., from *Managing Quality: The Strategic and Competitive Edge* by David A. Garvin. Copyright © 1988 by David A. Garvin, pp. xii, 26.

7. Reprinted with permission of The Free Press, a Division of Macmillan, Inc., from *Juran on Leadership for Quality: An Executive Handbook* by Joseph M. Juran. Copyright © 1989 by Juran Institute Inc.

8. *Behind the Eight Ball* (Milwaukee, Wis.: American Society for Quality Control, 1987), p. 22.

9. "Total Quality Management," p. 28.

10. Frank Rose, "Now Quality Means Service Too," p. 100.

11. *Behind the Eight Ball.*

12. "Quality Improvement Can Be Demonstrated, Not Delegated from the Executive Suite," *Total Quality*, Lakewood Publications, Minneapolis, Minn., May 1990, p. 5.

13. From *TQC Wisdom of Japan: Managing for Total Quality Control*, Hajime Karatsu; English translation copyright © 1988 by Productivity, Inc., PO Box 3007, Cambridge, MA 02140. 1-617-497-5146. Reprinted by permission, p. 86.

14. *Quality First* (Milwaukee, Wis.: American Society for Quality Control, 1984).

15. *Total Quality*, May 1990, p. 5.

CHAPTER 7

1. J. M. Juran, "Strategies for World-Class Quality," *Quality Progress*, March 1991, p. 84.

2. Reprinted by permission of The Putnam Publishing Group from *Deming Management at Work* by Mary Walton. Copyright © 1990 by Mary Walton. P. 10.

3. Excerpts from *Total Customer Service: The Ultimate Weapon* by William H. Davidow and Bro Uttal. Copyright © 1989 by William H. Davidow and Bro Uttal. Reprinted by permission of HarperCollins Publishers, pp. xx, 94.

4. *A Survey of Employees' Attitudes Toward Their Jobs and Quality Improvement Programs* (Milwaukee, Wis.: American Society for Quality Control, 1990).

5. *Total Quality*, Lakewood Publications, Minneapolis, Minn., October 1990, p. 8.

6. Karl Albrecht, *At America's Service: How Corporations Can Revolutionize the Way They Treat Their Customers* (Homewood, Ill.: Dow Jones-Irwin, 1988), p. 229.

7. *Total Quality*, May 1990, p. 4.

8. "Total Quality Management," *The Xerox Quality Forum II*, July 31 to August 2, 1990, Leesburg, Va., p. 28.

9. Ibid., p. 22.

10. Michael Beer, Russell Eisenstat, and Bert Spector, "Why Change Programs Don't Produce Change," *Harvard Business Review*, November–December 1990, p. 166.

11. Reprinted from *Out of the Crisis* by W. Edwards Deming by permission of MIT and W. Edwards Deming. Published by MIT, Center for Advanced Engineering Study, Cambridge, MA 02139. Copyright 1986 by W. Edwards Deming, p. 20.

12. From *TQC Wisdom of Japan: Managing For Total Quality Control*, Hajime Karatsu; English translation copyright © 1988 by Productivity, Inc., PO Box 3007, Cambridge, MA 02140. 1-617-497-5146. Reprinted by permission, pp. 22–23, 86.

13. Tom Peters, "Making It Happen," *Journal for Quality and Participation*, March 1989.

14. Donald K. Clifford and Richard E. Cavanagh, *The Winning Performance: How America's High-Growth Companies Succeed* (New York: Bantam, 1985).

15. Karl Albrecht, *At America's Service*, p. 244.

16. Walter Kiechl III, "No Word from on High," *Fortune*, January 6, 1986.

17. *Pathways* (Milwaukee, Wis.: American Society for Quality Control, 1989), p. 17.

18. *Behind the Eight Ball* (Milwaukee, Wis.: American Society for Quality Control, 1987), p. 18.

19. *Total Quality*, March 1991, p. 6.

20. Karl Albrecht, *At America's Service*, p. 226.

21. "Customer Service You Can Taste," *Canadian Business*, June 1991, p. 21.

22. John Humble, "Five Ways to Win the Service War," *International Management Development Review*, 1989, p. 61.

23. Reprinted by permission of the Putnam Publishing Group from *Deming Management at Work* by Mary Walton. Copyright © 1990 by Mary Walton, p. 193.

24. "The Chairman Doesn't Blink," *Quality Progress*, March 1987, p. 23.

25. Patrick Townsend, "Paul Revere Group Forges New Approaches in Employee Involvement," *Personnel Journal*, September 1986.

26. Tom Peters, "More Effective Walking Around Management," *Boardroom Reports*, March 1, 1987.

CHAPTER 8

1. Reprinted with permission of The Free Press, a Division of Macmillan, Inc., from *Managing Quality: The Strategic and Competitive Edge* by David A. Garvin. Copyright © 1988 by David A. Garvin, p. 66.

2. Reprinted with permission of The Free Press, a Division of Macmillan, Inc., from *Building a Chain of Customers: Linking Business Functions to Create the World Class Company* by Richard J. Schonberger. Copyright © 1990 by Richard J. Schonberger, p. 34.

3. "The Strategic Management of Service Quality," *PIMSLetter*, no. 33.

4. Ibid., pp. 7–8.

5. Milind M. Lele with Jagdish N. Sheth, *The Customer Is Key: Gaining an Unbeatable Advantage through Customer Satisfaction*, © 1987 by John Wiley & Sons, Inc. Reprinted by permission of John Wiley & Sons, Inc., pp. 61, 63.

6. Patricia Sellers, "Getting Customers to Love You," *Fortune*, March 13, 1989, p. 38.

7. Leonard L. Berry, David R. Bennett, and Carter W. Brown, *Service Quality: A Profit Strategy for Financial Institutions* (Homewood, Ill.: Dow Jones-Irwin, 1989), p. 39.

8. Brian Quinn, "Managing Innovation: Controlled Chaos," *Harvard Business Review*, May–June 1985, p. 80.

9. Reprinted with permission of The Free Press, a Division of Macmillan, Inc., from *Delivering Quality Service: Balancing Customer Perceptions and Expectations* by

Valarie A. Zeithaml, A. Parasuraman, and Leonard L. Berry. Copyright © 1990 by The Free Press, p. 145.

10. Regis McKenna, "Marketing Is Everything," *Harvard Business Review*, January–February 1991, p. 76.

11. From *The Service Edge* by Ron Zemke and Dick Schaaf. Copyright © 1989 by Ron Zemke and Dick Schaaf. Used by permission of New American Library, a division of Penguin Books USA Inc., p. 31.

12. From *Thriving on Chaos* by Tom Peters. Copyright © 1987 by Excel, a California Limited Partnership. Reprinted by permission of Alfred A. Knopf, Inc., pp. 100–101.

13. Excerpts from *Total Customer Service: The Ultimate Weapon* by William H. Davidow and Bro Uttal. Copyright © 1989 by William H. Davidow and Bro Uttal. Reprinted by permission of HarperCollins Publishers, p. 75.

14. Karl Albrecht and Lawrence J. Bradford, *The Service Advantage: How to Identify and Fulfill Customer Needs* (Homewood, Ill.: Dow Jones-Irwin, 1990), p. 66.

15. Milind M. Lele with Jagdish N. Sheth, *The Customer Is Key: Gaining an Unbeatable Advantage through Customer Satisfaction,* © 1987 by John Wiley & Sons, Inc. Reprinted with permission of John Wiley & Sons, Inc., p. 212.

16. Bernard Avishai and William Taylor, "Customers Drive a Technology-Driven Company," *Harvard Business Review*, November–December 1989, p. 108.

17. Conway quote and Ford comments from "Product and Service Design Must Reflect the Voice of the Customer," *Total Quality*, Lakewood Publications, Minneapolis, Minn., September 1990, pp. 2–3.

18. Reprinted with permission of The Free Press, a Division of Macmillan, Inc., from *Delivering Quality Service: Balancing Customer Perceptions and Expectations* by Valarie A. Zeithaml, A. Parasuraman, and Leonard L. Berry. Copyright © 1990 by The Free Press, p. 146.

19. From John Sharpe's speech at *Closing the Service Gap* conference, June 1991, Toronto.

20. Faye Rice, "Champions of Communication," *Fortune*, June 3, 1991, p. 116.

21. Alan M. Kantrow, "Wide-Open Management at Chaparral Steel," *Harvard Business Review*, May–June 1986, pp. 100–101.

22. "Everybody Sells," *Success*, May 1990, p. 32.

23. "Journey Toward Quality: The Federal Express Story," paper presented by Martha Thomas at *Closing the Service Gap* conference, April 1991, Orlando, Fla.

24. Reprinted by permission of The Putnam Publishing Group from *Deming Management at Work* by Mary Walton. Copyright © 1990 by Mary Walton, p. 138.

25. Bro Uttal, "Companies That Serve You Best," *Fortune*, December 7, 1987, p. 108.

CHAPTER 9

1. Joseph F. Miraglia, "OEP: Motorola's Renewal Process," *Tapping the Network Journal*, Spring 1990.

2. *The Human Side of Quality* (Milwaukee, Wis.: American Society for Quality Control, 1990), p. 3.

3. Robert L. Desatnick, *Managing to Keep the Customer: How to Achieve and Sustain Superior Customer Service throughout the Organization* (San Francisco: Jossey-Bass, 1987), p. 58.

4. Reprinted by permission of The Putnam Publishing Group from *Deming Management at Work* by Mary Walton. Copyright © 1990 by Mary Walton, p. 122.

5. Karl Albrecht, *At America's Service: How Corporations Can Revolutionize the Way They Treat Their Customers* (Homewood, Ill.: Dow Jones-Irwin, 1988), p. 46.

6. Michael Beer, Russell Eisenstat, and Bert Spector, "Why Change Programs Don't Produce Change," *Harvard Business Review*, November–December 1990, p. 163.

7. Faye Rice, "Champions of Communication," *Fortune*, June 3, 1991, p. 111.

8. Robert L. Desatnick, *Managing to Keep the Customer*, pp. 22–23.

9. Alex Taylor III, "New Lessons from Japan's Carmakers," *Fortune*, October 22, 1990, p. 168.

10. Faye Rice, "Champions of Communication," p. 120.

11. Reprinted from *Out of the Crisis* by W. Edwards Deming by permission of MIT and W. Edwards Deming. Published by MIT, Center for Advanced Engineering Study, Cambridge, MA 02139. Copyright 1986 by W. Edwards Deming, p. 139.

12. Ralph Stayer, "How I learned to Let My Workers Lead," *Harvard Business Review*, November–December 1990.

13. Reprinted with permission of The Free Press, a Division of Macmillan, Inc., from *Managing Quality: The Strategic and Competitive Edge* by David A. Garvin. Copyright © 1988 by David A. Garvin, pp. 221–22.

14. Reprinted from *Out of the Crisis* by W. Edwards Deming by permission of MIT and W. Edwards Deming. Published by MIT, Center for Advanced Engineering Study, Cambridge, MA 02139. Copyright 1986 by W. Edwards Deming, p. 86.

15. *Reshaping the Enterprise for the 1990s: Issues, Initiatives, Risks* (Cambridge, Mass.: Strategic Planning Institute, October 1990).

16. Ralph Stayer, "How I Learned to Let My Workers Lead."

17. Donald Clifford and Richard Cavanagh, *The Winning Performance: How America's High-Growth Midsize Companies Succeed* (New York: Bantam, 1985), p. 78.

18. Jay W. Spechler, *When America Does It Right: Case Studies in Service Quality* (Norcross, Ga.: Industrial Engineering and Management Press, 1988), p. 103, 108–9.

19. Taken from a presentation by Nancy Burzon, director of quality education, GTE Corporation at *Closing the Service Gap* conference, April 1991, Orlando, Fla., and from Jay W. Spechler, *When America Does It Right*, p. 541.

20. Jay W. Spechler, *When America Does It Right*, p. 399.

21. Ibid., p. 570.

22. Milind M. Lele with Jagdish N. Sheth, *The Customer Is Key: Gaining an Unbeatable Advantage through Customer Satisfaction*, © 1987 by John Wiley & Sons, Inc. Reprinted by permission of John Wiley & Sons, Inc., pp. 124–25.

23. *Total Quality*, Lakewood Publications, Minneapolis, Minn., November 1990, pp. 1–3.

24. Faye Rice, "Champions of Communication," p. 116.

25. Alex Taylor III, "How Buick Is Bouncing Back," *Fortune*, May 6, 1991, p. 88.

CHAPTER 10

1. From a speech given by John Sharpe to *Closing the Service Gap* conference, June 1991, Toronto.

2. From *The Service Edge* by Ron Zemke and Dick Schaaf. Copyright © 1989 by Ron Zemke and Dick Schaaf. Used by permission of New American Library, a division of Penguin Books USA Inc., p. 58.

3. T. J. Rodgers, "No Excuses Management," *Harvard Business Review*, July–August 1990, p. 86.

4. From a presentation by Len Schlesinger of Harvard Business School made at the National Restaurant Association show, May 1991, Chicago.

5. Richard Pascale, "Fitting New Employees into the Company Culture," *Fortune*, May 28, 1984, p. 28.

6. From a presentation by Len Schlesinger at the National Restaurant Association show, May 1991, Chicago.

7. T. J. Rodgers, "No Excuses Management."

8. Excerpts from *Total Customer Service: The Ultimate Weapon* by William H. Davidow and Bro Uttal. Copyright © 1989 by William H. Davidow and Bro Uttal. Reprinted by permission of HarperCollins Publishers, p. 122.

9. T. J. Rodgers, "No Excuses Management."

10. From *Thriving on Chaos* by Tom Peters. Copyright © 1987 by Excel, a California Limited Partnership. Reprinted by permission of Alfred A. Knopf, Inc., p. 315.

11. Robert L. Desatnick, *Managing to Keep the Customer: How to Achieve and Sustain Superior Customer Service throughout the Organization* (San Francisco: Jossey-Bass, 1987), p. 36.

12. Ibid., pp. 38, 87.

13. *The Service Edge* newsletter, Lakewood Publications, Minneapolis, Minn., April 1989, pp. 6–7.

14. *The Service Edge* newsletter, March 1990, p. 3.

15. Terrence Deal and Allan Kennedy, *Corporate Cultures: The Rites and Rituals of Corporate Life* (Reading, Mass.: Addison Wesley, 1982), p. 49.

16. Ibid., p. 144.

17. Peter Drucker, *The Changing World of the Executive* (New York: Times Books, 1982), p. 12.

18. Terrence Deal and Allan Kennedy, *Corporate Cultures*, p. 144.

19. Reprinted by permission of The Putnam Publishing Group from *Deming Management at Work* by Mary Walton. Copyright © 1990 by Mary Walton, p. 199.

20. Excerpts from *Total Customer Service: The Ultimate Weapon* by William H. Davidow and Bro Uttal. Copyright © 1989 by William H. Davidow and Bro Uttal. Reprinted by permission of HarperCollins Publishers.

21. Bro Uttal, "Companies That Serve You Best," *Fortune*, December 7, 1987, pp. 100–101.

22. T. J. Rodgers, "No Excuses Management."

CHAPTER 11

1. Reprinted with permission of The Free Press, a Division of Macmillan, Inc., from *Building a Chain of Customers: Linking Business Functions to Create the World Class Company* by Richard J. Schonberger. Copyright © 1990 by Richard J. Schonberger, p. 125.

2. Reprinted with permission of The Free Press, a Division of Macmillan, Inc., from *Delivering Quality Service: Balancing Customer Perceptions and Expectations* by Valarie A. Zeithaml, A. Parasuraman, and Leonard L. Berry. Copyright © 1990 by The Free Press, p. 91.

3. John H. Zenger, "A Thousand Dancing Elephants: Organizational Transformation through Behavior Modeling," a white paper (San Jose, Calif.: Zenger-Miller, 1991).

4. Reprinted by permission of The Putnam Publishing Group from *Deming Management at Work* by Mary Walton. Copyright © 1990 by Mary Walton, p. 174.

5. From *Thriving on Chaos* by Tom Peters. Copyright © 1987 by Excel, a California Limited Partnership. Reprinted by permission of Alfred A. Knopf, Inc., p. 215.

6. Richard Schonberger, *World Class Manufacturing: The Lessons of Simplicity Applied* (New York: The Free Press, 1986), p. 215.

7. Tom Peters, *Thriving on Chaos*, pp. 75–76.

8. From a June 1991 presentation made by Susan Robinson, former Xerox Canada vice president of training.

9. Presentation by Martha Thomas, *Closing the Service Gap* conference, April 1991, Orlando, Fla.

10. Patricia A. Galagan, "How Wallace Changed Its Mind," *Training and Development*, June 1991, pp. 23–28.

11. *Total Quality*, Lakewood Publications, Minneapolis, Minn., October 1990, p. 6.

12. J. M. Juran, "Strategies for World-Class Quality," *Quality Progress*, March 1991, p. 82.

13. Reprinted with permission of The Free Press, a Division of Macmillan, Inc., from *Building a Chain of Customers: Linking Business Functions to Create the World Class Company* by Richard J. Schonberger. Copyright © 1990 by Richard J. Schonberger, p. 139.

14. *Total Quality*, June 1990, pp. 3–4.

15. D. Keith Denton, *Quality Service* (Houston: Gulf Publishing, 1989), p. 96.

16. Kathryn L. Troy, "Quality Training: What Top Companies Have Learned," Report Number 959 (New York: The Conference Board, 1991).

17. Michael Beer, Russell A. Eisenstat, and Bert Spector, "Why Change Programs Don't Produce Change," *Harvard Business Review*, November–December 1990, p. 160.

18. From the book *What Is Total Quality Control? The Japanese Way*, by Kaoru Ishikawa, © 1985. Used by permission of the publisher, Prentice Hall/a Division of Simon & Schuster, Englewood Cliffs, NJ, p. 204.

19. "Total Quality Management," *The Xerox Quality Forum II*, July 31 to August 2, 1990, Leesburg, Va., p. 5.

20. Roland Dumas, "Company-Wide Quality Programs: How to Avoid Common Pitfalls and Create Competitive Challenge," *Quality Progress*, May 1989, and "Join Forces for Total Quality Control," *Quality*, May 1989.

21. Tom Peters, "Making It Happen," *Journal for Quality and Participation*, March 1989.

22. Thomas R. Krause, John Hidley, and Stanley J. Hodson, *The Behavior-Based Safety Process: Managing Involvement for an Injury-Free Culture* (New York: Van Nostrand Reinhold, 1990), pp. 14, 15.

23. Reprinted with permission of The Free Press, a Division of Macmillan, Inc., from *Juran on Leadership for Quality: An Executive Handbook* by Joseph M. Juran. Copyright © 1989 by Juran Institute Inc., p. 300.

24. John H. Zenger, "A Thousand Dancing Elephants."

25. Anne R. Field, "First Strike," *Success*, October 1989, p. 48.

26. "Total Quality Management," *The Xerox Quality Forum II*, July 31 to August 2, 1990, Leesburg, Va., p. 26.

27. From the book *What Is Total Quality Control? The Japanese Way*, by Kaoru Ishikawa, © 1985. Used by permission of the publisher, Prentice Hall/a Division of Simon & Schuster, Englewood Cliffs, NJ, p. 38.

28. Reprinted with permission of The Free Press, a Division of Macmillan, Inc., from *Juran on Leadership for Quality: An Executive Handbook* by Joseph M. Juran. Copyright © 1989 by Juran Institute Inc., p. 342.

29. Kathryn L. Troy, "Quality Training: What Top Companies Have Learned."

30. Lewis D. Eigen and Jonathon P. Siegel, *Manager's Book of Quotations* (New York: Amacom, 1989), p. 489.

31. Ibid., p. 488.

CHAPTER 12

1. Nancy Cushing, Jennifer Cauble, and Craig Perrin, "Partners in Quality: The Human Resource Link to Organization-Wide Quality Initiatives," a white paper (San Jose, Calif.: Zenger-Miller, 1989).

2. Stephen Klopp, "Pul-eeze! Will Somebody Help Me?" *Time*, February 2, 1987, pp. 47–53.

3. Perry Pascarella, *The New Achievers* (New York: The Free Press, 1984), p. 123.

4. John Kotter, *Power and Influence: Beyond Formal Authority* (New York: The Free Press, 1985), p. 68.

5. *On a Silver Platter* (Milwaukee, Wis.: American Society for Quality Control, 1986), p. 21.

6. "Let's Make Good Service Part of the Job," *Toronto Star*, April 28, 1988, p. D5.

CHAPTER 13

1. Nancy Austin and Tom Peters, *A Passion for Excellence: The Leadership Difference* (New York: Random House, 1985), pp. 325–30.

2. *MTS Digest*, April/June 1987.

3. Reprinted from *Out of the Crisis* by W. Edwards Deming by permission of MIT and W. Edwards Deming. Published by MIT, Center for Advanced Engineering Study, Cambridge, MA 02139. Copyright 1986 by W. Edwards Deming, p. 54.

4. Robert L. Desatnick, *Managing to Keep the Customer: How to Achieve and Sustain Superior Customer Service throughout the Organization* (San Francisco: Jossey-Bass, 1987), pp. 24–25.

5. Reprinted from *Out of the Crisis* by W. Edwards Deming by permission of MIT and W. Edwards Deming. Published by MIT, Center for Advanced Engineering Study, Cambridge, MA 02139. Copyright 1986 by W. Edwards Deming, p. 83.

6. Alan M. Webber, "Red Auerbauch on Management," *Harvard Business Review*, March–April 1987, p. 86.

7. Perry Pascarella, *The New Achievers* (New York: The Free Press, 1984), p.23.

8. Richard Walton, "From Control to Commitment in the Workplace," *Harvard Business Review*, March–April 1985.

9. Ralph Stayer, "How I Learned to Let My Workers Lead," *Harvard Business Review*, November–December 1990, p. 80.

CHAPTER 14

1. From the book *What Is Total Quality Control? The Japanese Way*, by Kaoru Ishikawa, © 1985. Used by permission of the publisher, Prentice Hall/a Division of Simon & Schuster, Englewood Cliffs, NJ, p. 89.

2. *Total Quality*, Lakewood Publications, Minneapolis, Minn., September 1990, p. 5.

3. J. M. Juran, *Made in USA: A Break in the Clouds* (Wilton, Conn.: Juran Institute, 1990).

4. From the book *What Is Total Quality Control? The Japanese Way*, by Kaoru Ishikawa, © 1985. Used by permission of the publisher, Prentice Hall/a Division of Simon & Schuster, Englewood Cliffs, NJ, p. 198.

5. From the book *What Is Total Quality Control? The Japanese Way*, by Kaoru Ishikawa, © 1985. Used by permission of the publisher, Prentice Hall/a Division of Simon & Schuster, Englewood Cliffs, NJ, p. 18.

6. Lewis D. Eigen and Jonathon P. Siegel, *Manager's Book of Quotations* (New York: Amacom, 1989), p. 356.

7. Judith Bardwick, *The Plateauing Trap* (New York: Amacom, 1986).

8. Norman Maier, *Problem Solving Discussions and Conferences* (New York: McGraw-Hill, 1963).

9. Lewis D. Eigen and Jonathon P. Siegel, *Manager's Book of Quotations*, p. 473.

10. David Bradford and Allan Cohen, *Managing for Excellence* (New York: John Wiley & Sons, 1984).

11. Charles Garfield, *Peak Performers: The New Heroes of American Business* (New York: Morrow, 1986), p. 182.

12. Andy Grove, "How (and Why) to Run a Meeting," *Fortune*, July 11, 1983, p. 132.

13. "Meetings of the Mind," *Success*, December 1986.

14. George Odiorne, *How Managers Make Things Happen* (Englewood Cliffs, NJ: Prentice Hall, 1982).

15. John Kotter, *Power and Influence: Beyond Formal Authority* (New York: The Free Press, 1985), pp. 32–33.

16. Lewis D. Eigen and Jonathon P. Siegel, *Manager's Book of Quotations*, p. 80.

17. Chris Argyis, *Harvard Business Review*, September–October 1986.

18. Reprinted by permission of The Putnam Publishing Group from *Deming Management at Work* by Mary Walton. Copyright © 1990 by Mary Walton, p. 172.

19. Ernesto Poza, "Twelve Actions to Build Strong U.S. Factories," *Sloan Management Review*, Fall 1983.

CHAPTER 15

1. Karl Albrecht, *At America's Service: How Corporations Can Revolutionize the Way They Treat Their Customers* (Homewood, Ill.: Dow Jones-Irwin, 1988), p. 207.

2. *Now You See It* (Milwaukee, Wis.: American Society for Quality Control, 1988), p. 11.

3. Ibid.

4. From the book *What Is Total Quality Control? The Japanese Way*, by Kaoru Ishikawa, © 1985. Used by permission of the publisher, Prentice Hall/a Division of Simon & Schuster, Englewood Cliffs, NJ, p. 91.

5. "Total Quality Management," *The Xerox Quality Forum II*, July 31 to August 2, 1990, Leesburg, Va., p. 30.

6. Karl Albrecht, *At America's Service*, p. vi.

7. Dennis Beecroft, from a paper presented to the *World Class Quality Forum* sponsored by the American Society for Quality Control, March 1991, Toronto.

8. T. J. Rodgers, "No Excuses Management," *Harvard Business Review*, July–August 1990, p. 89.

9. Reprinted from *Out of the Crisis* by W. Edwards Deming by permission of MIT and W. Edwards Deming. Published by MIT, Center for Advanced Engineering Study, Cambridge, MA 02139. Copyright 1986 by W. Edwards Deming, p. 102.

10. From the book *What Is Total Quality Control? The Japanese Way*, by Kaoru Ishikawa, © 1985. Used by permission of the publisher, Prentice Hall/a Division of Simon & Schuster, Englewood Cliffs, NJ, p. 156.

11. Reprinted from *Out of the Crisis* by W. Edwards Deming by permission of MIT and W. Edwards Deming. Published by MIT, Center for Advanced Engineering Study, Cambridge, MA 02139. Copyright 1986 by W. Edwards Deming. Pp. 35, 43.

12. *Total Quality*, Lakewood Publications, Minneapolis, Minn., June 1991, p. 1.

13. Reprinted from *Out of the Crisis* by W. Edwards Deming by permission of MIT and W. Edwards Deming. Published by MIT, Center for Advanced Engineering Study, Cambridge, MA 02139. Copyright 1986 by W. Edwards Deming, p. 33.

14. From a condensation of the Wallace Co., Inc., Baldrige application, p. 9.

15. Presentation by Michel Desjardin to *Closing the Service Gap* conference, June 1991, Toronto.

16. *The Hare and the Tortoise* (Milwaukee, Wis.: American Society for Quality Control, 1989), pp. 6, 8.

17. Reprinted by permission of The Putnam Publishing Group from *Deming Management at Work* by Mary Walton. Copyright © 1990 by Mary Walton, p. 212.

18. *Total Quality*, June 1991, p. 3.

19. Paul Dickson, *The Official Rules* (New York: Dell, 1978), p. 53.

20. Reprinted with permission of The Free Press, a Division of Macmillan, Inc., from *Building a Chain of Customers: Linking Business Functions to Create the World Class Company* by Richard J. Schonberger. Copyright © 1990 by Richard J. Schonberger, p. 164.

21. Ibid., p. 185.

22. "Thriving on Crisis," *Success*, April 1990, p. 16.

23. Michael Hammer, "Reengineering Work: Don't Automate, Obliterate," *Harvard Business Review*, July–August 1990, p. 104.

24. Reprinted with permission of The Free Press, a Division of Macmillan, Inc., from *Delivering Quality Service: Balancing Customer Perceptions and Expectations* by Valarie A. Zeithaml, A. Parasuraman, and Leonard L. Berry. Copyright © 1990 by The Free Press, p. 163.

25. *On a Silver Platter* (Milwaukee, Wis.: American Society for Quality Control, 1986), p. 27.

26. Milind M. Lele with Jagdish N. Sheth, *The Customer Is Key: Gaining an Unbeatable Advantage through Customer Satisfaction,* © 1987 by John Wiley & Sons, Inc. Reprinted by permission of John Wiley & Sons, Inc., p. 170.

27. Tom Peters, "Making It Happen," *Journal for Quality and Participation*, March 1989.

28. *Consumer Complaint Handling in America: An Update Study Part II* (Washington, D.C.: Technical Assistance Research Program, March 31, 1986), p. 5.

29. From a letter Fred Smith sent to *Harvard Business Review*, September–October 1988, p. 174.

30. Reprinted by permission of The Putnam Publishing Group from *Deming Management at Work* by Mary Walton. Copyright © 1990 by Mary Walton.

31. Jay W. Spechler, *When America Does It Right: Case Studies in Service Quality* (Norcross, Ga.: Industrial Engineering and Management Press, 1988), p. 207–8.

CHAPTER 16

1. Reprinted with permission of The Free Press, a Division of Macmillan, Inc., from *Juran on Leadership for Quality: An Executive Handbook* by Joseph M. Juran. Copyright © 1989 by Juran Institute Inc., p. 77.

2. H. James Harrington, *The Improvement Process: How Leading American Companies Improve Quality* (New York: McGraw-Hill, 1987), p. 191.

3. Robert Desatnick, "Service: A CEO's Perspective," *Management Review*, October 1987.

4. H. James Harrington, *The Improvement Process*, p. 191.

5. Reprinted by permission of The Putnam Publishing Group from *Deming Management at Work* by Mary Walton. Copyright © 1990 by Mary Walton, p. 215.

6. Reprinted with permission of The Free Press, a Division of Macmillan, Inc., from *Building a Chain of Customers: Linking Business Functions to Create the World Class Company* by Richard J. Schonberger. Copyright © 1990 by Richard J. Schonberger, pp. 189-90.

7. Lewis D. Eigen and Jonathon P. Siegel, *Manager's Book of Quotations* (New York: Amacom, 1989), p. 401.

8. Robert Kelley, "Poorly Served Employees Serve Customers Just As Poorly," *The Wall Street Journal*, October 13, 1987, p. 15.

9. Tom Peters and Robert Waterman, *In Search of Excellence: Lessons from America's Best-Run Companies* (New York: Harper and Row, 1982), p. 269.

10. Patrick Townsend and Joan Gebhardt, "The Quality Process: Little Things Mean a Lot," *Review of Business*, Winter 1990/1991.

11. Tom Peters, "Making It Happen," *Journal for Quality and Participation*, March 1989.

12. *The Hare and the Tortoise* (Milwaukee, Wis.: American Society for Quality Control, 1989), p. 8.

13. Reprinted with permission of The Free Press, a Division of Macmillan, Inc., from *Building a Chain of Customers: Linking Business Functions to Create the World Class Company* by Richard J. Schonberger. Copyright © 1990 by Richard J. Schonberger, p. 192.

14. *Life*, February 1988.

15. Michael LeBoeuf, *GMP: The Greatest Management Principle in the World* (New York: Berkley Books, 1985), p. 88.

16. *The Service Edge* newsletter, Lakewood Publications, Minneapolis, Minn., December 1989, p. 8.

17. Tom Peters, "Making It Happen."

18. From *Thriving on Chaos* by Tom Peters. Copyright © 1987 by Excel, a California Limited Partnership. Reprinted by permission of Alfred A. Knopf, Inc.

19. Ken Blanchard, "Accentuate the Positive," *Success*, November 1986, p. 8.

20. From the presentation given by Bob Schrandt at *Closing the Service Gap* conference, April 1991, Orlando, Fla.

21. Reprinted with permission of The Free Press, a Division of Macmillan, Inc., from *Building a Chain of Customers: Linking Business Functions to Create the World Class*

Company by Richard J. Schonberger. Copyright © 1990 by Richard J. Schonberger, pp. 197–98.

22. *Total Quality*, Lakewood Publications, Minneapolis, Minn., November 1990, p. 8.

23. Speech given by Martha Thomas at *Closing the Service Gap* conference, April 1991, Orlando, Fla.

24. Ken Blanchard, ''Jelly Bean Motivation,'' *Success*, February 1986, p. 8.

25. Tom Peters, ''Is a Paycheck Enough?'' *Success*, November 1985, p. 14.

CHAPTER 17

1. Tom Peters, ''Making It Happen,'' *Journal for Quality and Participation*, March 1989.

2. ''Total Quality Management,'' *The Xerox Quality Forum II*, July 31 to August 2, 1990, Leesburg, Va., p. 18.

3. Reprinted with permission of The Free Press, a Division of Macmillan, Inc., from *Building a Chain of Customers: Linking Business Functions to Create the World Class Company* by Richard J. Schonberger. Copyright © 1990 by Richard J. Schonberger, p. 12.

4. Reprinted from *Out of the Crisis* by W. Edwards Deming by permission of MIT and W. Edwards Deming. Published by MIT, Center for Advanced Engineering Study, Cambridge, MA 02139. Copyright 1986 by W. Edwards Deming, p. 108.

5. ''Total Quality Management,'' *The Xerox Quality Forum II*, p. 12.

6. Kathryn L. Troy, ''Quality Training: What Top Companies Have Learned,'' Report Number 959 (New York: The Conference Board, 1991).

7. From *Thriving on Chaos* by Tom Peters. Copyright © 1987 by Excel, a California Limited Partnership. Reprinted by permission of Alfred A. Knopf, Inc., p. 282.

8. Lewis D. Eigen and Jonathon P. Siegel, *Manager's Book of Quotations* (New York: Amacom, 1989), p. 164.

9. All Sharpe's quotes are from a speech given to *Closing the Service Gap* conference, June 1991, Toronto.

10. Reprinted with permission of The Free Press, a Division of Macmillan, Inc., from *Juran on Leadership for Quality: An Executive Handbook* by Joseph M. Juran. Copyright © 1989 by Juran Institute Inc., p. 58.

11. ''Total Quality Management: Barriers, Strategies, and Successes,'' *The Quality Letter for Healthcare Leaders*, May 1991, p. 5.

12. Ibid., p. 9.

13. Reprinted from *Out of the Crisis* by W. Edwards Deming by permission of MIT and W. Edwards Deming. Published by MIT, Center for Advanced Engineering Study, Cambridge, MA 02139. Copyright 1986 by W. Edwards Deming, p. 85.

14. "Total Quality Management: Barriers, Strategies, and Successes," p. 9.

15. From Wallace's condensed Baldrige application.

16. Robert H. Waterman, Jr., *The Renewal Factor: How the Best Get and Keep the Competitive Edge* (New York: Bantam, 1987), pp. 81–83.

17. Ibid., pp. 72–73.

18. From *Thriving on Chaos* by Tom Peters. Copyright © 1987 by Excel, a California Limited Partnership. Reprinted by permission of Alfred A. Knopf, Inc., p. 290.

19. "The Task Facing General Motors," *Fortune*, March 13, 1989, p. 53.

CHAPTER 18

1. *Total Quality*, Lakewood Publications, Minneapolis, Minn., May 1990, p. 4.

2. From *The Service Edge* by Ron Zemke and Dick Schaaf. Copyright © 1989 by Ron Zemke and Dick Schaaf. Used by permission of New American Library, a division of Penguin Books USA Inc., p. 47.

3. Excerpts from *The New Realities* by Peter F. Drucker. Copyright © 1989 by Peter F. Drucker. Reprinted by permission of HarperCollins Publishers, p. 230.

4. Robert Eccles, "The Performance Measurement Manifesto," *Harvard Business Review*, January–February 1991, p. 132.

5. Excerpts from *The New Realities* by Peter F. Drucker. Copyright © 1989 by Peter F. Drucker. Reprinted by permission of HarperCollins Publishers, p. 230.

6. Robert Eccles, "The Performance Measurement Manifesto," pp. 131, 133.

7. "Total Quality Management," *The Xerox Quality Forum II*, July 31 to August 2, 1990, Leesburg, Va., p. 6.

8. Reprinted with permission of The Free Press, a Division of Macmillan, Inc., from *Delivering Quality Service: Balancing Customer Perceptions and Expectations* by Valarie A. Zeithaml, A. Parasuraman, and Leonard L. Berry. Copyright © 1990 by The Free Press, p. 83.

9. Reprinted with permission of The Free Press, a Division of Macmillan, Inc., from *Managing Quality: The Strategic and Competitive Edge* by David A. Garvin. Copyright © 1988 by David A. Garvin, p. 64.

10. Reprinted with permission of The Free Press, a Division of Macmillan, Inc., from *Delivering Quality Service: Balancing Customer Perceptions and Expectations* by Valarie A. Zeithaml, A. Parasuraman, and Leonard L. Berry. Copyright © 1990 by The Free Press, pp. 26–27.

11. *Total Quality*, May 1990, p. 4.

12. Reprinted from *Out of the Crisis* by W. Edwards Deming by permission of MIT and W. Edwards Deming. Published by MIT, Center for Advanced Engineering Study, Cambridge, MA 02139. Copyright 1986 by W. Edwards Deming, p. 405.

13. Reprinted with permission of The Free Press, a Division of Macmillan, Inc., from *Managing Quality: The Strategic and Competitive Edge* by David A. Garvin. Copyright © 1988 by David A. Garvin, p. 168.

14. Reprinted with permission of The Free Press, a Division of Macmillan, Inc., from *Juran on Leadership for Quality: An Executive Handbook* by Joseph M. Juran. Copyright © 1989 by Juran Institute Inc., p. 54.

15. Robert C. Camp, *Benchmarking: The Search for Industry Best Practices That Lead to Superior Performance* (Milwaukee, Wis.: ASQC Quality Press, 1989), pp. xi, 10.

16. Ibid., p. 254.

17. Ibid., p. 16.

18. From a paper delivered by Martha Thomas at *Closing the Service Gap* conference, April 1991, Orlando, Fla.

19. From a condensation of its Baldrige application and Marion Horton, "Wallace Goes for the Baldrige," *Supply House Times*, October 1990, p. 249.

20. From a presentation given by Robert Schrandt at *Closing the Service Gap* conference, April 1991, Orlando, Fla.

21. Robert C. Camp, *Benchmarking*, pp. 157–58.

22. Jay W. Spechler, *When America Does It Right: Case Studies in Service Quality* (Norcross, Ga.: Industrial Engineering and Management Press, 1988), pp. 326–28.

23. Leonard L. Berry, David R. Bennett, and Carter W. Brown, *Service Quality: A Profit Strategy for Financial Institutions* (Homewood, Ill.: Dow Jones-Irwin, 1989), p. 178.

24. Richard J. Schonberger, *World Class Manufacturing* (New York: The Free Press, 1986), p. 13.

25. From *The Service Edge* by Ron Zemke and Dick Schaaf. Copyright © 1989 by Ron Zemke and Dick Schaaf. Used by permission of New American Library, a division of Penguin Books USA Inc., p. 57.

26. Tom Peters, "Making It Happen," *Journal for Quality and Participation*, March 1989.

27. T. J. Rodgers, "No Excuses Management," *Harvard Business Review*, July–August 1990, p. 85.

28. Reprinted from *Out of the Crisis* by W. Edwards Deming by permission of MIT and W. Edwards Deming. Published by MIT, Center for Advanced Engineering Study, Cambridge, MA 02139. Copyright 1986 by W. Edwards Deming, p. 15.

29. Robert Eccles, "The Performance Measurement Manifesto," p. 137.

CHAPTER 19

1. Michael Porter, "Michael Porter on Competitive Strategy," *The International Management Development Review*, 1989, p. 69.

2. Ronald Henkoff, "How to Plan for 1995," *Fortune*, December 31, 1990, p. 70.

3. Milind M. Lele with Jagdish N. Sheth, *The Customer Is Key: Gaining an Unbeatable Advantage through Customer Satisfaction,* © 1987 by John Wiley & Sons, Inc. Reprinted by permission of John Wiley & Sons, Inc., p. 198.

4. Karl Albrecht, *At America's Service: How Corporations Can Revolutionize the Way They Treat Their Customers* (Homewood, Ill.: Dow Jones-Irwin, 1988), p. 180.

5. Milind M. Lele with Jagdish N. Sheth, *The Customer Is Key: Gaining an Unbeatable Advantage through Customer Satisfaction,* © 1987 by John Wiley & Sons, Inc. Reprinted by permission of John Wiley & Sons, Inc., p. 99.

6. Michael Porter, "Michael Porter on Competitive Strategy," p. 74.

7. Alvin Toffler, *The Third Wave* (New York: William Morrow and Company, 1980), p. 248.

8. Alex Taylor III, "Why Toyota Keeps Getting Better and Better and Better," *Fortune,* November 19, 1990, p. 72.

9. All McKenna quotes in this paragraph from Anne R. Field, "First Strike," *Success,* October 1989.

10. From a presentation made by Dick Applin at *Closing the Service Gap* conference, October 1990, Nashville.

11. Robert B. Miller and Stephen Heiman with Tad Tuleju, *Strategic Selling* (New York: William Morrow and Company, 1985), p. 271.

12. Reprinted with permission of The Free Press, a Division of Macmillan, Inc., from *Managing Quality: The Strategic and Competitive Edge* by David A. Garvin. Copyright © 1988 by David A. Garvin, p. 156.

13. Ronald Henkoff, "How to Plan for 1995," p. 74.

14. Quoted in Leonard L. Berry, David R. Bennett, and Carter W. Brown, *Service Quality: A Profit Strategy for Financial Institutions* (Homewood, Ill.: Dow Jones-Irwin, 1989), p. 38.

15. Ronald Henkoff, "How to Plan for 1995," p. 72.

16. Regis McKenna, "Marketing Is Everything," *Harvard Business Review,* January–February 1991, pp. 68, 70.

17. James L. Heskett, *Managing in the Service Economy* (Boston: Harvard Business School Press, 1986), p. 31.

18. Michael Porter, "Michael Porter on Competitive Strategy," p. 74.

19. Reprinted with permission of The Free Press, a Division of Macmillan, Inc., from *Building a Chain of Customers: Linking Business Functions to Create the World Class Company* by Richard J. Schonberger. Copyright © 1990 by Richard J. Schonberger. P. 142.

20. Reprinted with permission of The Free Press, a Division of Macmillan, Inc., from *Delivering Quality Service: Balancing Customer Perceptions and Expectations* by Valarie A. Zeithaml, A. Parasuraman, and Leonard L. Berry. Copyright © 1990 by The Free Press, p. 38.

21. Karl Albrecht, *At America's Service,* p. 178.

22. Dennis P. Hall, Robert Peak, and Christopher Van Buren, "Selling and Telling the Quality Story," *Quality Progress*, August 1991, p. 78.

23. Regis McKenna, "Marketing Is Everything," p. 75.

24. Peter Drucker, *People and Performance* (New York: Harper and Row, 1977).

25. Excerpts from *Total Customer Service: The Ultimate Weapon* by William H. Davidow and Bro Uttal. Copyright © 1989 by William H. Davidow and Bro Uttal. Reprinted by permission of HarperCollins Publishers, p. 81.

26. Ronald Henkoff, "How to Plan for 1995," p. 70.

27. Reprinted with permission of The Free Press, a Division of Macmillan, Inc., from *Building a Chain of Customers: Linking Business Functions to Create the World Class Company* by Richard J. Schonberger. Copyright © 1990 by Richard J. Schonberger, p. 295.

28. Ronald Henkoff, "How to Plan for 1995," p. 72.

29. Daniel J. Isenberg, "The Tactics of Strategic Opportunism," *Harvard Business Review*, March–April 1987, p. 92.

30. Henry Mintzberg, "Crafting Strategy," *Harvard Business Review*, July–August 1987, p. 68.

31. Ibid., pp. 73, 75.

32. Michael Porter, "Michael Porter on Competitive Strategy," p. 71.

33. Excerpts from *Total Customer Service: The Ultimate Weapon* by William H. Davidow and Bro Uttal. Copyright © 1989 by William H. Davidow and Bro Uttal. Reprinted by permission of HarperCollins Publishers, p. 161.

34. Ibid., p. 69.

35. Regis McKenna, "Marketing Is Everything," p. 78.

36. Milind M. Lele with Jagdish N. Sheth, *The Customer Is Key: Gaining an Unbeatable Advantage through Customer Satisfaction*, © 1987 by John Wiley & Sons, Inc. Reprinted by permission of John Wiley & Sons, Inc., p. 65.

37. D. Keith Denton, *Quality Service* (Houston: Gulf Publishing, 1989), pp. 55–56.

38. Regis McKenna, "Marketing Is Everything," p. 70.

39. *Total Quality*, July–August 1990, p. 3.

40. James L. Heskett, *Managing in the Service Economy*, p. 20.

CHAPTER 20

1. "Managing Change for Global Competitiveness; An OSTD (Ontario Institute of Training and Development) Interview with Dr. Kenneth Blanchard," *OSTD Update*, March 1990, p. 4.

2. T. J. Rodgers, "No Excuses Management," *Harvard Business Review*, July–August 1990, p. 84.

3. Reprinted from *Out of the Crisis* by W. Edwards Deming by permission of MIT and W. Edwards Deming. Published by MIT, Center for Advanced Engineering Study, Cambridge, MA 02139. Copyright 1986 by W. Edwards Deming, p. 130.

4. Reprinted with permission of The Free Press, a Division of Macmillan, Inc., from *Delivering Quality Service: Balancing Customer Perceptions and Expectations* by Valarie A. Zeithaml, A. Parasuraman, and Leonard L. Berry. Copyright © 1990 by The Free Press, p. 148.

5. "Total Quality Management," *The Xerox Quality Forum II*, July 31 to August 2, 1990, Leesburg, Va., p. 23.

6. *Total Quality*, May 1990, p. 4.

7. "Total Quality Management," *The Xerox Quality Forum II*, p. 4.

8. *Reshaping the Enterprise for the 1990s: Issues, Initiatives, Risks* (Cambridge, Mass.: Strategic Planning Institute, October 1990).

9. H. James Harrington, *The Improvement Process: How Leading American Companies Improve Quality* (New York: McGraw-Hill, 1987), p. 84.

10. Michael Beer, Russell A. Eisenstat, and Bert Spector, "Why Change Programs Don't Produce Change," *Harvard Business Review*, November–December 1990, p. 159.

CHAPTER 21

1. Leonard L. Berry, David R. Bennett, and Carter W. Brown, *Service Quality: A Profit Strategy for Financial Institutions* (Homewood, Ill.: Dow Jones-Irwin, 1989), p. 38.

2. *The New Realities* by Peter F. Drucker. Copyright © 1989 by Peter F. Drucker. Reprinted by permission of HarperCollins Publishers, p. 230.

3. Reprinted with permission of The Free Press, a Division of Macmillan, Inc., from *Juran on Leadership for Quality: An Executive Handbook* by Joseph M. Juran. Copyright © 1989 by Juran Institute Inc., p. 215.

4. *The Hare and the Tortoise* (Milwaukee, Wis.: American Society for Quality Control, 1989), p. 14.

5. J. M. Juran, "Strategies for World-Class Quality," *Quality Progress*, March 1991, p. 83.

6. *The Service Edge* newsletter, Lakewood Publications, Minneapolis, Minn., March 1990, p. 3.

7. Reprinted with permission of The Free Press, a Division of Macmillan, Inc., from *Juran on Leadership for Quality: An Executive Handbook* by Joseph M. Juran. Copyright © 1989 by Juran Institute Inc., pp. 184–85.

8. "Overcoming Organizational Barriers to Total Quality Management," *The Quality Letter for Healthcare Leaders*, May 1991, p. 4.

9. Tom Peters, "Making It Happen," *Journal for Quality and Participation*, March 1989.

10. Reprinted with permission of The Free Press, a Division of Macmillan, Inc., from *Delivering Quality Service: Balancing Customer Perceptions and Expectations* by Valarie A. Zeithaml, A. Parasuraman, and Leonard L. Berry. Copyright © 1990 by The Free Press, p. 144.

11. Jay W. Spechler, *When America Does It Right: Case Studies in Service Quality* (Norcross, Ga.: Industrial Engineering and Management Press, 1988), pp. 149–50.

12. Theodore Levitt, *Thinking About Management* (New York: The Free Press, 1991), p. 95.

CHAPTER 22

1. "Total Quality Management," *The Xerox Quality Forum II*, July 31 to August 2, 1990, Leesburg, Va., p. 19.

2. Reprinted from *Out of the Crisis* by W. Edwards Deming by permission of MIT and W. Edwards Deming. Published by MIT, Center for Advanced Engineering Study, Cambridge, MA 02139. Copyright 1986 by W. Edwards Deming, p. 405.

3. Charles Garfield, *Peak Performance: Mental Training Techniques of the World's Greatest Athletes* (Los Angeles: Tarcher, 1984), p. 132.

4. Alan James Mayer, "The Power of the Mind's Eye," *Enroute*.

5. Charles Garfield, *Peak Performance*, p. 131.

6. Ibid., p. 9.

7. Ibid., p. 145.

8. Warren Bennis and Burt Nanus, *Leaders: The Strategies for Taking Charge* (New York: Harper and Row, 1985), p. 70.

9. Charles Garfield, *Peak Performers: The New Heroes of American Business* (New York: William Morrow and Company, 1986), p. 146.

Index